Study Guide for Accounting 8e

Chapters 1–14

Helen Brubeck
San Jose State University

PRENTICE HALL

Upper Saddle River, New Jersey 07458

PRENTICE HALL

Upper Saddle River, New Jersey 07458

VP/Editorial Director: Natalie E. Anderson
AVP/Executive Editor: Jodi McPherson
Director, Product Development: Pamela Hersperger
Editorial Project Manager: Rebecca Knauer
Editorial Assistant: Rosalinda Simone
Development Editor: Karen Misler
AVP/Executive Editor, Media: Richard Keaveny
AVP/Executive Producer: Lisa Strite
Editorial Media Project Manager: Ashley Lulling
Production Media Project Manager: Lorena Cerisano
Marketing Manager: Maggie Moylan
Marketing Assistant: Justin Jacob
Senior Managing Editor: Cynthia Zonneveld
Associate Managing Editor: Camille Trentacoste
Production Project Manager: Rhonda Aversa
Permissions Coordinator: Charles Morris
Senior Operations Specialist: Nick Sklitsis
Senior Art Director: Jonathan Boylan
Cover Design: Integra Software Services, Ltd
Director, Image Resource Center: Melinda Patelli
Manager, Rights and Permissions: Zina Arabia
Manager: Visual Research: Beth Brenzel
Manager, Cover Visual Research & Permissions: Karen Sanatar
Image Permission Coordinator: Jan Marc Quisuming
Photo Researcher: Teri Stratford
Composition: GEX Publishing Services

Full-Service Project Management: GEX Publishing Services
Printer/Binder: Courier/Kendallville
Typeface: 8/10 Sabon

Credits and acknowledgments borrowed from other sources and reproduced, with permission, in this textbook appear on appropriate page within text.

Copyright © 2009, 2007, 2005, 2002, 1999 by Pearson Education, Inc., Upper Saddle River, New Jersey, 07458. Pearson Prentice Hall. All rights reserved. Printed in the United States of America. This publication is protected by Copyright and permission should be obtained from the publisher prior to any prohibited reproduction, storage in a retrieval system, or transmission in any form or by any means, electronic, mechanical, photocopying, recording, or likewise. For information regarding permission(s), write to: Rights and Permissions Department.

Pearson Prentice Hall™ is a trademark of Pearson Education, Inc.
Pearson® is a registered trademark of Pearson plc
Prentice Hall® is a registered trademark of Pearson Education, Inc.
Pearson Education Ltd., London
Pearson Education North Asia Ltd., Hong Kong
Pearson Education Singapore, Pte. Ltd

Pearson Educación de Mexico, S.A. de C.V.
Pearson Education, Canada, Inc.
Pearson Education Malaysia, Pte. Ltd.
Pearson Education–Japan
Pearson Education, Upper Saddle River, New Jersey
Pearson Education Australia PTY, Limited

Prentice Hall
is an imprint of

PEARSON

www.pearsonhighered.com

10 9 8 7 6 5 4 3 2
ISBN-13: 978-0-13-606481-7

Contents for Study Guide

1 Accounting and the Business Environment 1
▶ *Demo Doc/Demo Doc Solutions* *4*
■ Quick Practice Questions 12   Quick Practice Solutions 20
The Power of Practice 27

2 Recording Business Transactions 29
▶ *Demo Doc/Demo Doc Solutions* *31*
■ Quick Practice Questions 39   Quick Practice Solutions 51
The Power of Practice 61

3 The Adjusting Process 63
▶ *Demo Doc/Demo Doc Solutions* *65*
■ Quick Practice Questions 74   Quick Practice Solutions 86
The Power of Practice 97

4 Completing the Accounting Cycle 99
▶ *Demo Doc/Demo Doc Solutions* *101*
■ Quick Practice Questions 110   Quick Practice Solutions 118
The Power of Practice 126

5 Merchandising Operations 127
▶ *Demo Doc/Demo Doc Solutions* *129*
■ Quick Practice Questions 137   Quick Practice Solutions 145
The Power of Practice 153

6 Merchandise Inventory 155
▶ *Demo Docs/Demo Docs Solutions* *158*
■ Quick Practice Questions 169   Quick Practice Solutions 175
The Power of Practice 185

7 Internal Control and Cash 187
▶ *Demo Docs/Demo Docs Solutions* *190*
■ Quick Practice Questions 201   Quick Practice Solutions 211
The Power of Practice 221

8 Receivables 223
▶ *Demo Docs/Demo Docs Solutions* *226*
■ Quick Practice Questions 243   Quick Practice Solutions 255
The Power of Practice 268

9 Plant Assets and Intangibles 269
▶ **Demo Docs/Demo Docs Solutions** *271*
■ Quick Practice Questions 289 Quick Practice Solutions 299
The Power of Practice 310

10 Current Liabilities, Payroll, and Long-Term Liabilities 311
▶ **Demo Docs/Demo Docs Solutions** *314*
■ Quick Practice Questions 329 Quick Practice Solutions 344
The Power of Practice 358

11 Corporations: Paid-In Capital and the Balance Sheet 359
▶ **Demo Docs/Demo Docs Solutions** *362*
■ Quick Practice Questions 373 Quick Practice Solutions 381
The Power of Practice 389

12 Corporations: Effects on Retained Earnings and the Income Statement 391
▶ **Demo Docs/Demo Docs Solutions** *394*
■ Quick Practice Questions 407 Quick Practice Solutions 418
The Power of Practice 428

13 Statement of Cash Flows 429
▶ **Demo Docs/Demo Docs Solutions** *431*
■ Quick Practice Questions 446 Quick Practice Solutions 456
The Power of Practice 465

14 Financial Statement Analysis 467
▶ **Demo Docs/Demo Docs Solutions** *469*
■ Quick Practice Questions 477 Quick Practice Solutions 486
The Power of Practice 496

Glindex   G–1

Contents for Student Edition

1 Accounting and the Business Environment   1

Accounting Vocabulary: The Language of Business   2

Decision Makers: The Users of Accounting Information   2
- Individuals   2
- Businesses   2
- Investors   3
- Creditors   3
- Taxing Authorities   3
- Financial Accounting and Management Accounting   3

The Accounting Profession and the Organizations that Govern it   3
- Governing Organizations   4
- Ethics in Accounting and Business   5
- Standards of Professional Conduct   5

Types of Business Organizations   5
- Four Types of Business Organizations   5

Distinguishing Characteristics and Organization of a Corporation   7
- Separate Legal Entity   7
- Continuous Life and Transferability of Ownership   7
- No Mutual Agency   8
- Limited Liability of Stockholders   8
- Separation of Ownership and Management   8
- Corporate Taxation   8
- Government Regulation   8
- Organization of a Corporation   9

Accounting Concepts and Principles   9
- The Entity Concept   10
- The Reliability (Objectivity) Principle   10
- The Cost Principle   10
- The Going-Concern Concept   10
- The Stable Monetary Unit Concept   11

The Accounting Equation   11
- Assets and Liabilities   11
- Owners' Equity   12

Accounting for Business Transactions   13
- Transactions Analysis for Smart Touch Learning   14

Preparing the Financial Statements—the User Perspective of Accounting   18
- The Financial Statements   20
- Headings   20

Using Financial Statements to Evaluate Business Performance   23
- Relationships Among the Financial Statements   23

▶ *Decision Guidelines*   25

▶ *Summary Problem*   26

Review and Assignment Material   28

▶ *Chapter 1 Demo Doc: Transaction Analysis Using Accounting Equation/Financial Statement Preparation*   54

Contents   v

2 Recording Business Transactions 63

The Account, the Journal, and the Ledger 64
  Assets 64
  Liabilities 65
  Stockholders' Equity 66
  Chart of Accounts 66

Debits, Credits, and Double-Entry Accounting 68
  The T-Account 68
  Increases and Decreases in the Accounts 69

List the Steps of the Transaction Recording Process 70
  Posting (Copying Information) from the Journal to the Ledger 71
  Expanding the Rules of Debit and Credit: Revenues and Expenses 72
  The Normal Balance of An Account 73
  Source Documents—The Origin of the Steps 74

Journalizing Transactions and Posting to the Ledger 74
  Practice Journalizing with Specific Examples 74
  The Ledger Accounts After Posting 80

Preparing the Trial Balance from the T-Accounts 81
  Correcting Trial Balance Errors 82
  Details of Journals and Ledgers 83
  The Four-Column Account: An Alternative to the T-Account 84

▶ *Decision Guidelines* 85

▶ *Summary Problem* 86

Review and Assignment Material 90

▶ *Chapter 2 Demo Doc: Debit/Credit Transaction Analysis* 123

3 The Adjusting Process 133

Accrual Accounting Versus Cash-Basis Accounting 134

Other Accounting Principles 135
  The Accounting Period 135
  The Revenue Principle 136
  The Matching Principle 137
  The Time-Period Concept 137

Why We Adjust the Accounts 138

Two Categories of Adjusting Entries 139
  Prepaid Expenses 139
  Depreciation 142
  Accrued Expenses 144
  Accrued Revenues 146
  Unearned Revenues 146
  Summary of the Adjusting Process 149

The Adjusted Trial Balance 152

The Financial Statements 153
  Preparing the Statements 153
  Relationships Among the Financial Statements 153

Ethical Issues in Accrual Accounting 155

▶ *Decision Guidelines* 156

▶ *Summary Problem* 157

Review and Assignment Material 162

Chapter Appendix 3A: Alternative Treatment of Prepaid Expenses and Unearned Revenues   190

▶ **Chapter 3 Demo Doc: Preparation of Adjusting Entries, Adjusted Trial Balance, and Financial Statements   194**

4 Completing the Accounting Cycle   206

The Work Sheet   207
Net Income   210
Net Loss   210

▶ **Summary Problem 1   211**

Completing the Accounting Cycle   213
Preparing the Financial Statements from a Work Sheet   213
Recording the Adjusting Entries from a Work Sheet   213

Closing the Accounts   216
Closing Temporary Accounts   217

Postclosing Trial Balance   219

Classifying Assets and Liabilities   219
Assets   220
Liabilities   220
The Classified Balance Sheet   221
Balance Sheet Forms   221

Accounting Ratios   222
Current Ratio   223
Debt Ratio   223

▶ **Decision Guidelines   224**

▶ **Summary Problem 2   225**

Review and Assignment Material   229

Chapter Appendix 4A: Reversing Entries: An Optional Step   256

Comprehensive Problem for Chapters 1–4: Journalizing, Posting, Work Sheet, Adjusting, Closing the Financial Statements   260

▶ **Chapter 4 Demo Doc: Accounting Work Sheets and Closing Entries   262**

5 Merchandising Operations   270

What Are Merchandising Operations?   272
The Operating Cycle of a Merchandising Business   272
Inventory Systems: Perpetual and Periodic   273
Perpetual Inventory Systems   273

Accounting for Inventory in the Perpetual System   274
Purchase of Inventory   274

Sale of Inventory   279

▶ **Summary Problem 1   284**

Adjusting and Closing the Accounts of a Merchandiser   286
Adjusting Inventory Based on a Physical Count   286
Closing the Accounts of a Merchandiser   287

Preparing a Merchandiser's Financial Statements   288
Income Statement Formats: Multi-Step and Single-Step   290

Two Ratios for Decision Making   290
The Gross Profit Percentage   290
The Rate of Inventory Turnover   291

▶ **Decision Guidelines   292**

▶ **Summary Problem 2   294**

Review and Assignment Material 297

Chapter Appendix 5A: Work Sheet for a Merchandising Business 319

Chapter Appendix 5B: Accounting for Merchandise in a Periodic Inventory System 323

Comprehensive Problem for Chapters 1–5: Completing a Merchandiser's Accounting Cycle 329

6 Merchandise Inventory 331

Accounting Principles and Inventories 332

Inventory Costing Methods 333

Inventory Accounting in a Perpetual System 336
First-In, First-Out (FIFO) Method 336
Last-In, First-Out (LIFO) Method 338
Average Cost Method 340

Comparing FIFO, LIFO, and Average Cost 341

▶ **Summary Problem 1** 343

Lower-of-Cost-or-Market Rule 346

Effects of Inventory Errors 347
Estimating Ending Inventory 348
Ethical Issues 349

▶ **Decision Guidelines** 350

▶ **Summary Problem 2** 351

Review and Assignment Material 352

Chapter Appendix 6A: Accounting for Inventory in a Periodic System 371

7 Internal Control and Cash 378

Internal Control 379

The Sarbanes-Oxley Act (SOX) 380

The Components of Internal Control 380
Internal Control Procedures 381

Internal Controls for E-Commerce 384
The Limitations of Internal Control—Costs and Benefits 385

The Bank Account as a Control Device 386

The Bank Reconciliation 388
Preparing the Bank Reconciliation 389
Online Banking 392

▶ **Summary Problem 1** 394

Internal Control over Cash Receipts 396

Internal Control over Cash Payments 397
Controls over Payment by Check 397
Controlling Small Cash Payments 399

The Petty Cash Fund 399

Ethics and Accounting 402
Corporate and Professional Codes of Ethics 402
Ethical Issues in Accounting 402

▶ **Decision Guidelines** 404

▶ **Summary Problem 2** 405

Review and Assignment Material 406

8 Receivables 429

Receivables: An Introduction 430
  Types of Receivables 430

Internal Control over Collection of Receivables 431

▶ *Decision Guidelines* 432

Accounting for Uncollectibles (Bad Debts) 433
  The Allowance Method 433
    Estimating Uncollectibles 434
    Identifying and Writing Off Uncollectible Accounts 437
    Recovery of Accounts Previously Written Off—Allowance Method 437
  The Direct Write-Off Method 439
    Recovery of Accounts Previously Written Off—Direct Write-Off Method 439

Reporting Receivables on the Balance Sheet 440

Credit-Card, Bankcard, and Debit-Card Sales 441
  Credit-Card Sales 441
  Bankcard Sales 442
  Debit-Card Sales 442

▶ *Summary Problem 1* 443

Notes Receivable 445
  Identifying Maturity Date 445
  Computing Interest on a Note 446
  Accruing Interest Revenue 447
  Dishonored Notes Receivable 449
  Computers and Receivables 450

Using Accounting Information for Decision Making 450
  Acid-Test (or Quick) Ratio 451
  Days' Sales in Receivables 451

▶ *Decision Guidelines* 453

▶ *Summary Problem 2* 454

Review and Assignment Material 455

Chapter Appendix 8A: Discounting a Note Receivable 477

9 Plant Assets and Intangibles 480

Measuring the Cost of a Plant Asset 482
  Land and Land Improvements 482
  Buildings 484
  Machinery and Equipment 484
  Furniture and Fixtures 484
  A Lump-Sum (Basket) Purchase of Assets 484
  Capital Expenditures 486

Depreciation 487
  Causes of Depreciation 487
  Measuring Depreciation 487
  Depreciation Methods 488
  Comparing Depreciation Methods 491
  Other Issues in Accounting for Plant Assets 493

▶ *Summary Problem 1* 495

Disposing of a Plant Asset 497
  Situation A – Scrap the Truck 499

Accounting for Natural Resources 502

Accounting for Intangible Assets 502
   Specific Intangibles 503
   Accounting for Research and Development Costs 505

Ethical Issues 505

▶ *Decision Guidelines* 506

▶ *Summary Problem 2* 507

Review and Assignment Material 508

10 Current Liabilities, Payroll, and Long-Term Liabilities 524

Current Liabilities of Known Amount 525
   Accounts Payable 525
   Short-Term Notes Payable 526
   Sales Tax Payable 526
   Current Portion of Long-Term Notes Payable 527
   Accrued Expenses (Accrued Liabilities) 527
   Unearned Revenues 528

Current Liabilities that must be Estimated 528
   Estimated Warranty Payable 528
   Contingent Liabilities 529

▶ *Decision Guidelines* 531

▶ *Summary Problem 1* 532

Accounting for Payroll 533
   Gross Pay and Net (Take-Home) Pay 533
   Payroll Withholding Deductions 534
   Employer Payroll Taxes 536

Journalizing Payroll Transactions 537
   Internal Control over Payroll 538

▶ *Decision Guidelines* 539

▶ *Summary Problem 2* 540

Bonds: An Introduction 542
   Types of Bonds 542
   Bond Prices 542
   Present Value 544
   Bond Interest Rates 544

Accounting for Bonds Payable - Straight Line Method 545
   Issuing Bonds Payable at Maturity (Par) Value 545
   Issuing Bonds Payable at a Discount 546

▶ *Decision Guidelines* 548

   Issuing Bonds Payable at a Premium 549
   Adjusting Entries for Bonds Payable 550
   Issuing Bonds Payable Between Interest Dates 551

Reporting Liabilities on the Balance Sheet 552

Issuing Bonds Versus Stock 552

Ethical Issues in Reporting Liabilities 553
▶ *Decision Guidelines 554*
▶ *Summary Problem 3 555*
Review and Assignment Material 556

Chapter Appendix 10A: The Time Value of Money: Present Value of a Bond and Effective-Interest Amortization 576

Chapter Appendix 10B: Retiring and Converting Bonds Payable 589

Comprehensive Problem for Chapters 7–10: Comparing Two Businesses 593

11 Corporations: Paid-In Capital and the Balance Sheet 595

Corporations: An Overview 596
  Capital Stock 596

Stockholders' Equity Basics 597
  Stockholders' Rights 598
  Classes of Stock 598

Issuing Stock 599
  Issuing Common Stock 600
  Issuing Preferred Stock 603
  Ethical Considerations 603
  Review of Accounting for Paid-In Capital 604

▶ *Decision Guidelines 605*
▶ *Summary Problem 1 606*

Retained Earnings 608

Accounting for Cash Dividends 609
  Dividend Dates 609
  Declaring and Paying Dividends 610
  Dividing Dividends Between Preferred and Common 611
  Dividends on Cumulative and Noncumulative Preferred 611

Different Values of Stock 612
  Market Value 612
  Liquidation Value 613
  Book Value 613

Evaluating Operations 614
  Rate of Return on Total Assets 614
  Rate of Return on Common Stockholders' Equity 615

Accounting for Income Taxes by Corporations 616

▶ *Decision Guidelines 617*
▶ *Summary Problem 2 618*

Review and Assignment Material 620

12 Corporations: Effects on Retained Earnings and the Income Statement 641

Stock Dividends 642

Stock Splits 645
Stock Dividends and Stock Splits Compared 647

Treasury Stock 647
Treasury Stock Basics 647
Purchase of Treasury Stock 648
Sale of Treasury Stock 648
Retirement of Stock 650

Restrictions on Retained Earnings 650
Variations in Reporting Stockholders' Equity 651

▶ *Decision Guidelines* 652

▶ *Summary Problem 1* 654

The Corporate Income Statement 656
Continuing Operations 656
Special Items 657
Earnings per Share 658
Statement of Retained Earnings 659
Combined Statement of Income and Retained Earnings 660
Prior-Period Adjustments 660
Reporting Comprehensive Income 661

▶ *Decision Guidelines* 662

▶ *Summary Problem 2* 663

Review and Assignment Material 665

13 The Statement of Cash Flows 681

Introduction: The Statement of Cash Flows 682
Cash Equivalents 682

Operating, Investing, and Financing Activities 683
Two Formats for Operating Activities 684

Preparing the Statement of Cash Flows by the Indirect Method 684
Cash Flows from Operating Activities 686
Cash Flows from Investing Activities 689
Cash Flows from Financing Activities 691
Net Change in Cash and Cash Balances 693
Noncash Investing and Financing Activities 694

Measuring Cash Adequacy: Free Cash Flow 696

▶ *Decision Guidelines* 697

▶ *Summary Problem* 698

Review and Assignment Material 701

Chapter Appendix 13A: Preparing The Statement Of Cash Flows By The Direct Method 721

Chapter Appendix 13B: Preparing the Indirect Statement of Cash Flows Using a Spreadsheet 739

14 Financial Statement Analysis 745

Horizontal Analysis 746
    Illustration: Smart Touch Learning, Inc. 747
    Horizontal Analysis of the Income Statement 748
    Horizontal Analysis of the Balance Sheet 748
    Trend Percentages 748

Vertical Analysis 749

How Do We Compare One Company with Another? 751
    Benchmarking 752
    Benchmarking Against a Key Competitor 752
    Benchmarking Against the Industry Average 752

▶ *Summary Problem 1* 753

Using Ratios to Make Decisions 755
    Measuring Ability to Pay Current Liabilities 755
    Measuring Ability to Sell Inventory and Collect Receivables 757
    Measuring Ability to Pay Long-Term Debt 759
    Measuring Profitability 760
    Analyzing Stock Investments 762

Red Flags in Financial Statement Analysis 764

▶ *Decision Guidelines* 765

▶ *Summary Problem 2* 767

Review and Assignment Material 769

Comprehensive Problem for Chapters 13 and 14: Analyzing a Company for its Investment Potential 790

STUDENTS WILL "GET IT" ANYTIME, ANYWHERE WITH HORNGREN/HARRISON/OLIVER'S STUDENT LEARNING SYSTEM!

Overview of Student Learning System

Students understand (or "get it") right after you do a problem in class. However, as soon as they leave class, their ability to do the problems and complete their homework diminishes with each passing hour. Often, this results in students struggling to complete their homework on their own. Even worse, the frustration can lead to students quitting on the material altogether and falling behind in the course. As a result, an entire class can fall behind as instructors attempt to keep everyone on the same page.

With the *Accounting 8e* Student Learning System, all features of the **student textbook, study resources and online homework system** are designed to work together to provide students with more "I Get It!" moments. The consistency, repetition and strong details throughout the entire student learning system allow students to achieve success both inside and outside the classroom while keeping both instructors and students on track.

- **Replication of the Classroom Experience with Demo Doc Examples:** The Demo Doc Examples consist of entire problems, worked through step-by-step and from start to finish, narrated with the kind of comments that INSTRUCTORS would say in class. These Demo Doc Examples exist in the first four chapters of this text to support the critical accounting cycle chapters, as well as in the Study Guide as a Flash animation and in print. The Flash versions are also on MyAccountingLab's online homework and as a part of the instructor package for both traditional and online courses.

- **Consistency, Repetition and Details Throughout The Learning Process:** Consistency is stressed across all mediums: text, student, and instructor supplements. Students will experience consistency, repetition and strong details throughout the chapter, the end of chapter examples and in MyAccountingLab in both look and feel, and language. This minimizes confusion, ensures clarity, and allows students to focus on what's important—the accounting topics. As a result, students will develop a solid understanding throughout each step of the learning process.

- **Experiencing the Power of Practice with MyAccountingLab:** The online homework system combines "I get it!" moments with the power of practice. Students can work on book-match and algorithmic problems assigned by the instructor or use the Study Plan for self-assessment and customized study outlines.

Components of the Student Learning System

▸ Duplicating the Classroom Experience

DEMO DOCS – Introductory accounting students consistently tell us "When doing homework, I get stuck trying to solve problems the way they were demonstrated in class." Likewise, instructors consistently tell us, "I have so much to cover in so little time; I can't afford to go back and review homework in class." These challenges inspired us to develop Demo Docs. Demo Docs are comprehensive, worked-through problems that are available for every chapter of our introductory accounting text. Demo Docs will aid students when they are trying to solve exercises and problems on their own with the goal being to help students duplicate the classroom experience outside of class. Entire problems, mirroring end-of-chapter material, are presented and then solved along with annotated explanations written in a conversational style; essentially imitating what an instructor might say if standing over a student's shoulder. All Demo Docs are in the textbook in print, in the study guide in print version as well as on CD in Flash, and online in MyAccountingLab so that students can easily refer to them as needed.

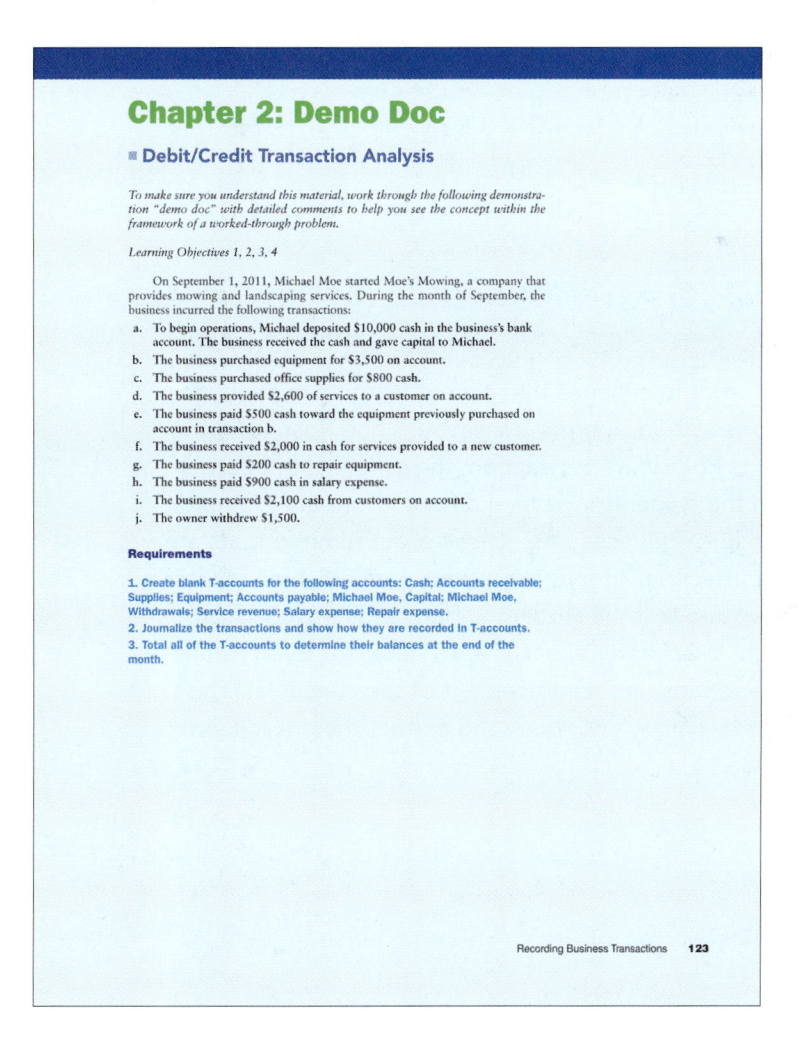

Chapter 2: Demo Doc

Debit/Credit Transaction Analysis

To make sure you understand this material, work through the following demonstration "demo doc" with detailed comments to help you see the concept within the framework of a worked-through problem.

Learning Objectives 1, 2, 3, 4

On September 1, 2011, Michael Moe started Moe's Mowing, a company that provides mowing and landscaping services. During the month of September, the business incurred the following transactions:

a. To begin operations, Michael deposited $10,000 cash in the business's bank account. The business received the cash and gave capital to Michael.
b. The business purchased equipment for $3,500 on account.
c. The business purchased office supplies for $800 cash.
d. The business provided $2,600 of services to a customer on account.
e. The business paid $500 cash toward the equipment previously purchased on account in transaction b.
f. The business received $2,000 in cash for services provided to a new customer.
g. The business paid $200 cash to repair equipment.
h. The business paid $900 cash in salary expense.
i. The business received $2,100 cash from customers on account.
j. The owner withdrew $1,500.

Requirements

1. Create blank T-accounts for the following accounts: Cash; Accounts receivable; Supplies; Equipment; Accounts payable; Michael Moe, Capital; Michael Moe, Withdrawals; Service revenue; Salary expense; Repair expense.
2. Journalize the transactions and show how they are recorded in T-accounts.
3. Total all of the T-accounts to determine their balances at the end of the month.

Recording Business Transactions   123

▶ Consistency, Repetition and Details in the Learning Process

The entire package matters. Consistency in terminology and problem set-ups from one medium to another—test bank to study guide to MyAccountingLab—is critical to success in the classroom. So when students ask "Where do the numbers come from?," they can go to our text or go online and see what to do. If the material is worded one way in the text, you can count on it being worded the same way in the supplements for instructors and students.

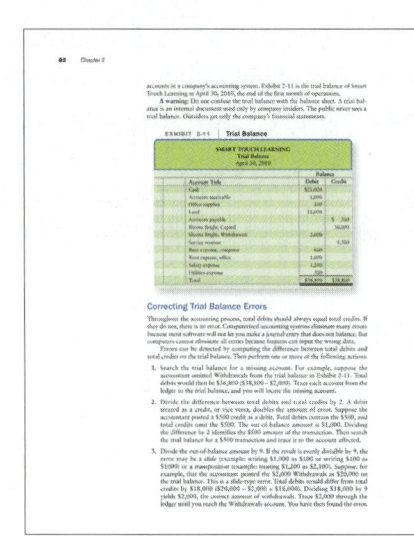

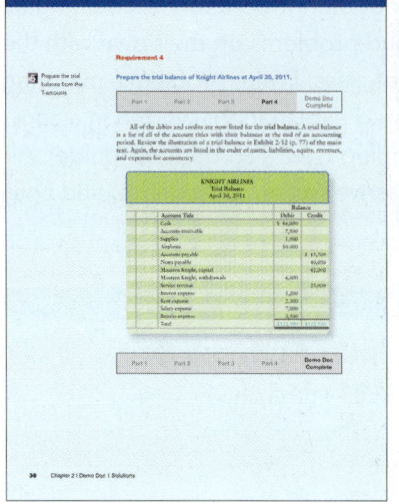

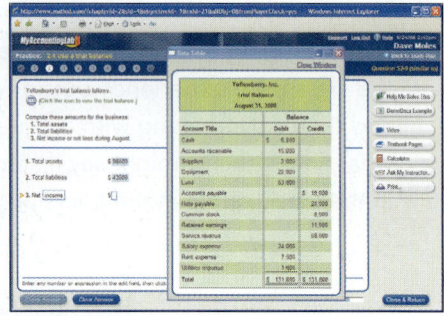

The entire student learning system reinforces consistency, repetition and clear details in order to enhance the student learning experience. For example, on pages 80-86, Journal Transactions and Posting to the Ledger is addressed. For EVERY transaction, the same set of information is presented to the students in several different formats – in text, in journal entry, and in ledger accounts. These exact same formats are shown for EVERY transaction. In repeating these formats, the authors eliminate the assumption that the student understands the concept completely. As such, the chapter explains each detail for EVERY transaction to provide repetition and reinforcement of the concepts. This also allows students to quickly find, track and correct their mistakes in the learning process.

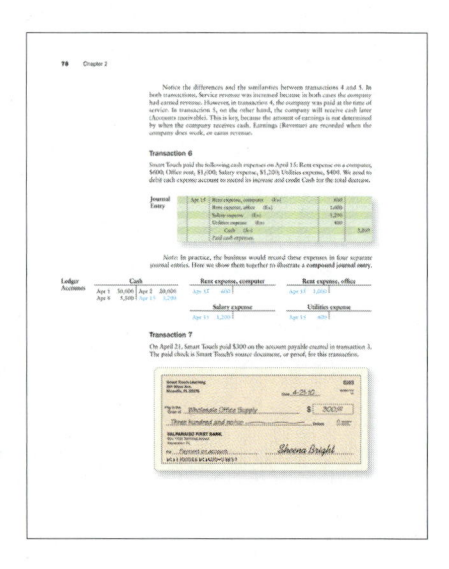

▶ *NEW* **CONSISTENT EXAMPLES** – Three different sets of 'Company Facts' carry through all "in chapter examples." As a result, students gain a sense of familiarity with the context of these examples throughout the text. This consistency provides a level of comfort with the examples and allows students to focus on learning the accounting principles as they are presented.

▶ *NEW* **CONTINUING EXERCISE** – The unique 'Continuing Exercise' takes a single company and adds transactions or questions in each chapter to the existing fact pattern. As students move throughout the text, they complete additional "steps" in this comprehensive exercise. Students are able to see the 'big picture' and learn how the accounting topics build off one another. Accounting is a process and the continuing exercise allows students to put it all together.

▶ *NEW* **CONTINUING PROBLEM** – For more detailed and in-depth practice, a 'Continuing Problem' is also available. Like the Continuing Exercise, the Continuing Problems takes a single company and adds transactions or questions in each chapter to the existing fact pattern. As students move throughout the text, they complete additional "steps" in completing this comprehensive problem. Again, students are able to see the 'big picture' and learn how the accounting topics build off one another.

▶ *NEW* **UNIQUE PRACTICE SET WITHIN CHAPTERS 1-8** – An in-text "Practice Set" is built into Chapters 1–8 of the student text. Students do not have to purchase any additional material for their practice sets and instructors no longer have to create their own. Since the Practice Set is written by the same authors that write the student textbook, students will once again have consistency. Students will also be able to complete the Practice Set within MyAccountingLab, for automatic grading and immediate feedback.

*Additional separate practice sets are also available.

- Runners Corporation Lab Manual   Containing numerous simulated real-world examples, the Runners Corporation practice set is available complete with data files for Peachtree, QuickBooks, and PH General Ledger. Each practice set also includes business stationery for manual entry work.

- A-1 Photography-Manual Lab Manual   Containing numerous simulated real-world examples, the A-1 Photography practice set is available complete with data files for Peachtree, QuickBooks, and PH General Ledger. Each set includes business stationery for manual entry work.

CLUTTER-FREE DESIGN – The reviewer-inspired design is built on the premise that "Less is More." Extraneous boxes and features, as well as non-essential bells and whistles, removed. The authors know that excess crowds out what really matters—the concepts, the problems, and the learning objectives. In addition, the equations are called out in a blue box so students can quickly locate them when studying.

▶ Additional Features to Create More "I Get It" Moments

DECISION GUIDELINES – Decision Guidelines explain why the accounting concepts addressed in the chapter are important in business. The left hand side of the table explains the decision or action being asked of the student in the simplest terms. The right hand side of the table shows the accounting topics that will help them facilitate those decisions. In accounting, good numbers equate to good decisions while inaccurate numbers can lead to poor decisions. The Decision Guidelines help illustrate this concept for students.

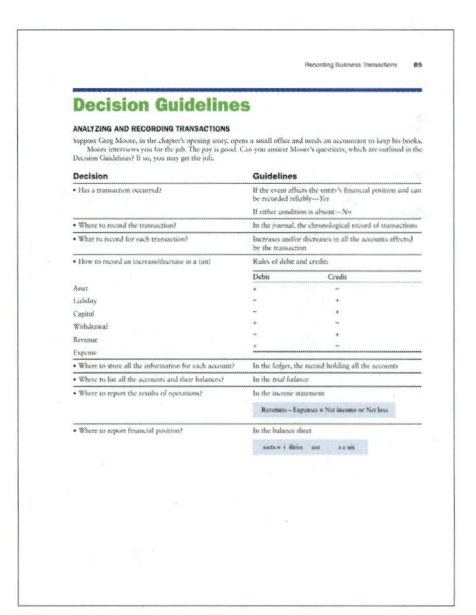

▶ *NEW* **SUCCESS KEYS/ LEARNING OBJECTIVES** – To build cohesiveness, clearly defined learning objectives are labeled throughout the chapter sections, end-of-chapter questions and also in MyAccountingLab. After a student finishes reading a section within a chapter, they can turn to the back of the chapter and complete the labeled questions in order to self-assess their understanding. If the student doesn't "get it," they can sign on to MyAccountingLab for interactive learning resources to answer their questions and also to complete additional practice.

Every learning Objective has at least one Starter, Exercise or Problem to teach and assess the students.

▶ *NEW* **STOP AND THINK** – The 'Stop and Think' sections relate accounting concepts to students everyday lives by using examples that make sense to students.

▶ *NEW* **COMPLETION TIME FOR END-OF-CHAPTER MATERIAL** – All Starters, Exercises and Problems in the textbook list the average completion time for students.

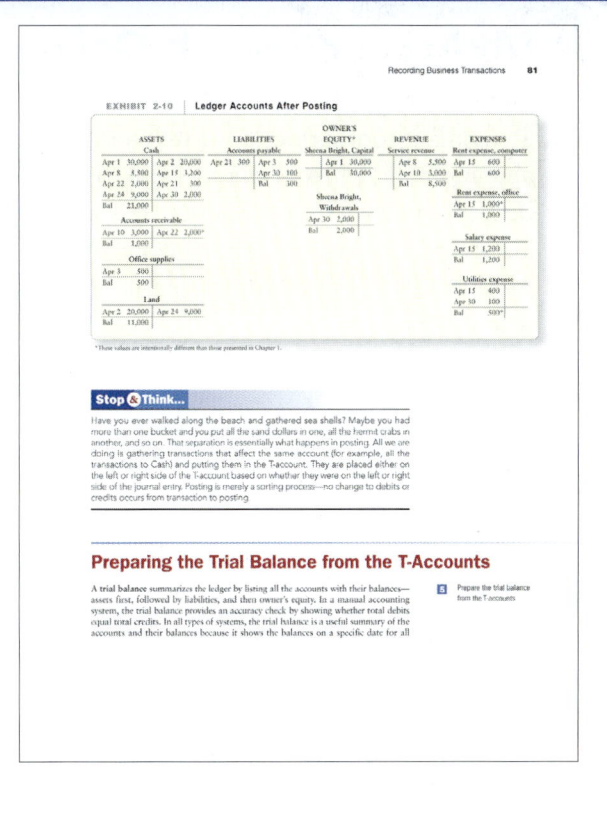

▶ *NEW* **TABLE OF CONTENTS** – The authors slightly restructured the table of contents to respond to customers' current level of coverage in the Principles of Accounting course. Financial coverage is consolidated into 14 chapters so it can be effectively covered in one semester. The Financial chapters are also arranged to reflect the order of working through a balance sheet. In addition, the managerial chapters represent a more logical flow, including all costing chapters grouped together.

The Power of Practice – Student Resources

▶ *NEW* **FIVE BOOK-MATCH SETS OF PROBLEMS AND EXERCISES (A, B, C, D, E)**

- **Problems**: Students will have access to A and B Problems within the text. Static Problem Sets C, D and E can be assigned by the instructor and completed by students through MyAccountingLab.

- **Exercises**: Students will have access to exercise set A within the text. Static exercise sets B, C, D, E can be assigned by the instructor and completed by the student through MyAccountingLab.

▸ MyAccountingLab Online Homework and Assessment

MyAccountingLab is where "I get it!" moments meet the power of practice. This online homework and assessment tool supports the text and resources by providing students "I get it!" moments at their teachable moment, whether that is 1 P.M. or 1 A.M. MyAccountingLab is packed with algorithmic problems because practice makes perfect. It is also includes the exact same end-of-chapter material in the text that instructors can assign for homework. MyAccountingLab features the same look and feel for exercises and problems with journal entries and financial statements so that students are familiar and comfortable working with the material.

▸ Study Guide including Flash Demo Doc CD and Working Papers

Demo Docs are available in the Study Guide— both in print and on CD in Flash, so students can easily refer to them when needed. The Study Guide also includes a summary of key topics and multiple-choice and short-answer questions that students can use to test their knowledge.

Free electronic working papers are included on the accompanying CD.

▸ Companion Web Site— www.pearsonhighered.com/horngren

The book's Web site at www.pearsonhighered.com/horngren—contains the following:

- Self-study quizzes for each chapter
- Microsoft Excel templates that students can use to complete homework assignments for each chapter (e-working papers)
- Samples of the Flash Demo Docs for students to work through the accounting cycle

Study Guide for Accounting

Chapters 1–14

8e

1 Accounting and the Business Environment

WHAT YOU PROBABLY ALREADY KNOW

You want to purchase a cell phone and service plan. It would be easy to visit the closest store and buy the phone and company service plan the salesperson recommends. But would that necessarily be the selection that best services your needs with the least cost? Perhaps not. Before making this decision, it might make sense to:

1. gather information from reliable sources;
2. identify the various options and relevant costs;
3. evaluate the cost/benefit relationship of the different plans; and
4. make the decision.

Financial decisions require thoughtful analysis utilizing accurate, reliable, and relevant information. The choice may be finding the best investment for your savings, deciding to purchase or lease a car, or choosing the optimal cell phone service plan. The process that is undertaken to manage our personal financial lives is the same as that employed by managers and owners of businesses. This chapter will explain the importance of accounting to the many users of financial information and how such data are accumulated and reported.

Learning Objectives/Success Keys

1 Define accounting vocabulary.

Accounting is an information system that measures business activities, processes that information into reports, and communicates the results to decision makers. It is often referred to as the language of business. It's important as you begin your study of accounting to understand the basic accounting vocabulary. Make sure you review the first three sections in Chapter 1 of the textbook carefully, as well as the list of interchangeable terms commonly used in accounting. *Review Exhibit 1-3 (p. 4) in the main text to observe the flow of information between accounting and related organizations and users. Compare the three forms of business organization in Exhibit 1-4 (p. 7).*

2 Define the users of financial information.

Financial accounting information is used by individuals, businesses, investors, creditors, and taxing authorities. These users are known as decision makers. In other words, these people are reading the financial accounting information because they are hoping that it will assist them in coming to a decision about the accounting entity to which the statements relate.

3 Describe the accounting profession and the organizations that govern it.

All businesses need accountants. Accountants must deal with everything in a company in order to record all of its activities and therefore accountants often have the broadest view of what's going on in that company.

The Financial Accounting Standards Board (FASB) formulates accounting standards in the United States, while Certified public accountants, or CPAs, are licensed professional accountants who serve the general public.

4 Indentify the different types of business organizations.

Businesses can be organized as proprietorships, partnerships, or corporations. To allow for more liability protection, the Limited-Liability Partnership (LLP) and Limited-Liability Company (LLC) business organizations can also be used. *Review Exhibit 1-4 (p. 7) in the text to see the differences among these types of organizations.*

5 Delineate the distinguishing characteristics and organization of a proprietorship.

Sole proprietorships are businesses owned by a single person, who is usually also the main managed of the business. Proprietorships are distinct from their owners, and have separate accounting.

6 Apply accounting concepts and principles.

The basic accounting concepts and principles include the entity concept, the reliability (objectivity) principle, the cost principle, the going-concern principle, and the stable-monetary-unit concept. Make sure you understand these concepts and principles and how they are applied in the business world.

7 Define and use the accounting equation.

It is critical to understand each of the basic components of the **accounting equation:**

$$Assets = Liabilities + Owner's\ Equity$$

Review carefully "The Accounting Equation" section of the main text to understand these important components. Owner's equity can be confusing. Pay special attention to Exhibit 1-6 (p. 11), which summarizes the four types of transactions that affect owner's equity.

8 Depict accounting for business transactions.

A business **transaction** is an event that can be measured and affects any of the components of the accounting equation: assets, liabilities, or owner's equity. Use the accounting equation to record the effects of each business transaction. **Make sure that the amount of the increase or decrease on the left side of the equation (assets) is the same as that on the right side (liabilities and owner's equity.)** *This is a simple but crucial concept to understand. Review the analysis of transactions in Exhibit 1-7 (p. 13).*

9 Explain and prepare the financial statements.

Business transactions are analyzed, recorded, classified, and reported in the financial statements. Financial statements are commonly prepared on a monthly, quarterly, or annual basis and include the income statement, statement of owner's equity, balance sheet, and statement of cash flows. *Refer to Exhibit 1-8 (p. 19) for examples of the four financial statements.*

10 Use financial statements to evaluate business performance.

Financial statements communicate important information necessary for users to make business decisions. Together the financial statements provide useful information to evaluate business performance.

Demo Doc 1

Basic Transactions

Learning Objectives 1–10

Rick Baldwin opened Rick's Delivery Service on August 1, 2011. He is the sole proprietor of the business. During the month of August, Rick had the following transactions:

a. Rick invested $6,000 of his personal funds in the business.
b. The business paid $650 cash for supplies.
c. The business purchased bicycles, paying $1,000 in cash and putting $2,000 on account.
d. The business paid $700 on the accounts to the bicycle store.
e. The business performed delivery services for customers totaling $1,200. These customers paid in cash.
f. The business performed delivery services for customers on account, totaling $2,400.
g. The business collected $550 on account.
h. The business paid rent (for the month of August) of $850.
i. The business paid employees $1,800 for the month of August.
j. Rick purchased groceries for his own use, paying $100 cash from his personal bank account.
k. The business received a telephone bill for $175. As of August 31, 2011, it had not been paid.
l. Rick withdrew $900 cash from the business for personal use.

Requirements

1. What type of business organization is Rick's Delivery Service? Describe this type of organization. Does this business need accountants?

2. Analyze the preceding transactions in terms of their effects on the accounting equation of Rick's Delivery Service.

3. Prepare the income statement, statement of owner's equity, and balance sheet of the business as of August 31, 2011.

4. Was the delivery service profitable for the month of August? Given this level of profit or loss, do you think the withdrawal of $900 was appropriate?

5. Who will likely be the primary user of the financial statements for Rick's Delivery Service?

Demo Doc 1 Solutions

3 Describe the accounting profession and the organizations that govern it

Requirement 1

What type of business organization is Rick's Delivery Service? Describe of this type of organization. Does this business need accountants?

| **Part 1** | Part 2 | Part 3 | Part 4 | Part 5 | Part 6 | Part 7 | Demo Doc Complete |

4 Identify the different types of business organizations

5 Delineate the distinguishing characteristics and organization of a proprietorship

Rick's Delivery Service is a sole proprietorship. The accounting records of a sole proprietorship do *not* include the proprietor's (owner's) personal records. However, from a *legal* perspective, the business is the proprietor.

All businesses need accountants, including Rick's Delivery Service.

Requirement 2

Analyze the preceding transactions in terms of their effects on the accounting equation of Rick's Delivery Service.

| Part 1 | **Part 2** | Part 3 | Part 4 | Part 5 | Part 6 | Part 7 | Demo Doc Complete |

1 Use accounting vocabulary

6 Apply accounting concepts and principles

7 Define and use the accounting equation

8 Depict accounting for business transactions

The accounting equation is:

$$\text{Assets} = \text{Liabilities} + \text{Owner's Equity}$$

It is critical to understand each of these basic components:

Assets are economic resources that should benefit the business in the future. Common examples of these would be cash, inventory, equipment, and furniture.

Liabilities are debts or obligations to outsiders. The most common liability is an account payable, an amount owed to a supplier for goods or services. A note payable is a written promise of future payment and usually requires the payment of interest in addition to the repayment of the debt, unlike accounts payable.

Owner's equity represents the owner's interest in the business. It is the amount remaining after subtracting liabilities from assets.

Transaction analysis is a critical first step in understanding how individual transactions are treated in accounting.

a. Rick invested $6,000 of his personal funds in the business.

Rick is using his own money, but he is giving it *to the business*. This means that the business is involved and it is a recordable transaction.

From the business's perspective, this increases Cash (an asset) by $6,000 and increases Rick Baldwin, Capital (owner's equity) by $6,000.

Demo Doc 1 Solutions | Chapter 1   5

b. The business paid $650 cash for supplies.

The supplies are an asset that increased by $650. Because they were paid for with cash, the Cash account (an asset) is decreased by $650.

c. The business purchased bicycles, paying $1,000 in cash and putting $2,000 on account.

The Bicycles account (an asset) is increasing. But by how much? What is the cost of the bicycles? If $1,000 is paid in cash and $2,000 is bought on account, the *total cost* is $1,000 + $2,000 = $3,000. Why? This is the total amount that the business will (eventually) end up paying in order to acquire the bicycles. This is consistent with the cost principle.

So the Bicycles account (an asset) is increased by $3,000, whereas the Cash account (an asset) is decreased by $1,000.

The $2,000 on account relates to accounts *pay*able (because it will have to be *paid* later). Because we now have *more* money that has to be paid later, it is an increase in Accounts Payable (a liability) of $2,000.

The end result is that Bicycles (an asset) is increased by $3,000, Cash (an asset) is decreased by $1,000, and Accounts Payable (a liability) is increased by $2,000.

d. The business paid $700 on the payable to the bicycle store.

Think of Accounts Payable (a liability) as a list of companies to which the business owes money. In other words, it is a list of companies to which the business will *pay* money at some future time. In this particular problem, the business owes money to the company from which it purchased bicycles on account (see transaction c). When the business *pays* the money in full, it can cross this company off the list of companies to which it owes money. Right now, the business is paying only part of the money owed to the bicycle store. This decreases Accounts Payable (a liability) by $700 and decreases Cash (an asset) by $700.

e. The business performed delivery services for customers totaling $1,200. These customers paid in cash.

When the business *performs services*, it means that it is doing work for customers. Doing work for customers is the way that the business makes money. By performing services, the business is earning revenues.

This means that Service Revenues is increased (which increases owner's equity) by $1,200. Because the business receives the cash the customers paid, Cash is also increased (an asset) by $1,200.

f. The business performed delivery services for customers on account, totaling $2,400.

Again, the delivery service is performing services for customers, which means that it is earning revenues. This results in an increase in Service Revenues (owner's equity) of $2,400.

However, this time the customers charged the services on account. This is money that the business will *receive* in the future (when the customers eventually pay) so it is called accounts *receiv*able. Accounts Receivable (an asset) is increased by $2,400.

g. The business collected $550 on account.

Think of Accounts Receivable (an asset) as a list of customers from whom the business will collect money. In other words, it is a list of customers from whom the business will *receive* money at some future time. In this particular situation, these customers received services but did not pay at that time (see transaction f). Later, when the business collects (*receives*) the cash in full from any particular customer, it can cross that customer off the list. This is a decrease to Accounts Receivable (an asset) of $550.

Because the cash is received, Cash (an asset) is increased by $550.

h. The business paid rent (for the month of August) of $850.

The rent has *already been used*. By the end of August, the service has been operating and using the space for the entire month. This means that the *benefit* of the rent has already been received or used up. This means that this is a rent *expense*. [Note that if the rent was paid for *September*, it would not yet be used up and would still be a *future* benefit (an asset) and *not* an expense. This issue will be discussed in Chapter 3.]

So Rent Expense is increased by $850, which is a decrease to owner's equity. The question states that the rent was *paid*. This means it was *paid in cash*. Therefore, Cash (an asset) is decreased by $850.

i. The business paid employees $1,800 for the month of August.

Again, the transaction states that the business *paid* the employees, meaning that it *paid in cash*. Therefore, Cash (an asset) is decreased by $1,800.

The work the employees have given to the business has *already been used*. By the end of August, the delivery service has had the employees working and delivering for customers for the entire month. This means that the *benefit* of the work has already been received, so it is a salary *expense*. Salary Expense is increased by $1,800, which is a decrease to owner's equity.

j. Rick purchased groceries for his own use, paying $100 cash from his personal bank account.

These groceries were purchased with Rick's *personal* money for Rick's *personal* use. Therefore, this purchase does not relate to the business and is not a recordable transaction for the delivery service.

k. The business received a telephone bill for $175. As of August 31, 2011, it had not been paid.

Utilities (such as water, gas, electricity, phone, and Internet service) are generally not billed until *after* they have been used. If these utilities have already been used, then they are utilities *expenses*. So, Utility Expense is increased by $175, which is a decrease to owner's equity.

Because the bill has not yet been *paid* as of August 31, it is an account *pay*able. This increases Accounts Payable (a liability) by $175.

l. Rick withdrew $900 cash from the business for personal use.

Although Rick is taking the money, the cash is coming from the *business*, so this is a recordable transaction for the business. There is a decrease of $900 to Cash (an asset). Because Rick is the owner, this results in an increase of $900 to Owner Withdrawals, which is a decrease to owner's equity.

Requirement 3

Prepare the income statement, statement of owners equity, and balance sheet of the business as of August 31, 2011.

| Part 1 | Part 2 | **Part 3** | Part 4 | Part 5 | Part 6 | Part 7 | Demo Doc Complete |

7 Define and use the accounting equation

Here's how the transactions from Requirement 1 look in the accounting equation:

	ASSETS				=	LIABILITIES	+	OWNER'S EQUITY	TYPE OF OWNER'S EQUITY TRANSACTION
	Cash	+ Accounts receivable	+ Supplies	+ Bicycles		Accounts payable		Rick Baldwin, Capital	
a.	+$6,000							+6,000	*Owner investment*
b.	−650		+$650						
c.	−1,000			+$3,000		+$2,000			
d.	−700					−700			
e.	+1,200							+1,200	*Service revenue*
f.		+2,400						−2,400	*Service revenue*
g.	+550	−550							
h.	−850							−850	*Rent expense*
i.	−1,800							−1,800	*Salary expense*
j.	Not a transaction of the business.								
k.						+175		−175	*Utilities expense*
l.	−900							−900	*Owner withdrawal*
	$1,850	$1,850	$650	$3,000		$1,475		$5,875	
		$7,350					$7,350		

9 Explain and prepare the financial statements

Remember that financial statements communicate important information necessary for users to make business decisions. An overview of the financial statements is as follows:

- **Income Statement**—Lists the revenues and expenses to determine net income or net loss for a period. Net income results if revenues exceed expenses; the reverse results in a net loss.

- **Statement of Owner's Equity**—Shows the changes in owner's equity during the period. Investments from owners and net income increase equity; owner withdrawals and net losses decrease equity.
- **Balance Sheet**—Lists the assets, liabilities, and owner's equity at a point in time, usually at the end of a month.
- **Statement of Cash Flows**—Report of cash receipts (inflows) and cash payments (outflows) for a period of time. (The statement of cash flow is covered in Chapter 17.)

The income statement is the first statement that should be prepared because the other financial statements rely on the net income number calculated on the income statement.

The income statement lists all revenues and expenses. It uses the following formula to calculate net income:

$$\text{Revenues} - \text{Expenses} = \text{Net income}$$

So, to create an income statement, we only need to list the revenue accounts and then subtract the list of expense accounts to calculate net income.

We can read these amounts from the accounting equation work sheet.

There are two transactions impacting service revenue: **e** and **f**. Transaction **e** increases service revenue by $1,200 and transaction **f** increases service revenue by $2,400. This means that total service revenue for the month was:

$$\$1,200 + \$2,400 = \$3,600$$

Rent expense of $850, salary expense of $1,800, and utilities expense of $175 were recorded in transactions **h**, **i**, and **k** (respectively).

RICK'S DELIVERY SERVICE
Income Statement
Month Ended August 31, 2011

Revenue:		
Service revenue		$3,600*
Expenses:		
Rent expense	$ 850	
Salary expense	1,800	
Utilities expense	175	
Total expenses		2,825
Net income		$ 775

*(= $1,200 + $2,400)

| Part 1 | Part 2 | Part 3 | **Part 4** | Part 5 | Part 6 | Part 7 | Demo Doc Complete |

Net income is used on the statement of owner's equity to calculate the new balance in the Capital account. This calculation uses the following formula:

> Beginning capital amount
> + Owner investments
> + Net income
> – Owner withdrawals
> = Ending capital amount

Again, we just have to recreate this formula on the statement:

RICK'S DELIVERY SERVICE
Statement of Owner's Equity
Month Ended August 31, 2011

Rick Baldwin, capital, August 1, 2011		$ 0
Add: Investment by owner		6,000
Net income for month		775
		6,775
Less: Withdrawals by owner		(900)
Rick Baldwin, capital, August 31, 2011		$5,875

| Part 1 | Part 2 | Part 3 | Part 4 | **Part 5** | Part 6 | Part 7 | Demo Doc Complete |

The ending capital amount is used on the balance sheet. The balance sheet is just a listing of all assets, liabilities, and equity, with the accounting equation verified at the bottom:

RICK'S DELIVERY SERVICE
Balance Sheet
August 31, 2011

Assets		Liabilities	
Cash	$1,850	Accounts payable	$1,475
Accounts receivable	1,850		
Supplies	650	Equity	
Bicycles	3,000	Rick Baldwin, capital	5,875
Total assets	$7,350	Total liabilities and equity	$7,350

10 Chapter 1 | Demo Doc 1 Solutions

Requirement 4

Was the delivery service profitable for the month of August? Given this level of profit or loss, do you think the withdrawal of $900 was appropriate?

| Part 1 | Part 2 | Part 3 | Part 4 | Part 5 | **Part 6** | Part 7 | Demo Doc Complete |

10 Use the financial statements to evaluate business performance

Evaluating business performance is critical to making sound business decisions. For example, reviewing the income statement shows the results of operations, how much the business generated in net income, or if it incurred a net loss. The statement of owner's equity indicates what caused the change in owner's equity for the period. The balance sheet is a statement of financial condition or financial position, which includes the ending owner's equity. The statement of cash flows would identify the cash receipts and cash payments from operating, investing, and financing activities.

From the income statement prepared in Requirement 2, we can see that the delivery service earned $775 of profit during the month of August. The level of withdrawals ($900) seems high given that it is more than the amount of profit earned during the month.

Requirement 5

Who will likely be the primary user of the financial statements for Rick's Delivery Service?

| Part 1 | Part 2 | Part 3 | Part 4 | Part 5 | Part 6 | **Part 7** | Demo Doc Complete |

2 Define the users of financial information

As the sole owner and manager, Rick Baldwin will likely be the primary user of the financial statements for Rick's Delivery Service.

| Part 1 | Part 2 | Part 3 | Part 4 | Part 5 | Part 6 | Part 7 | **Demo Doc Complete** |

Quick Practice Questions

True/False

_____ 1. Financial accounting produces financial information and reports to be used by managers inside a business.

_____ 2. An audit is a financial examination performed by independent accountants.

_____ 3. The top financial position in private accounting is the rank of partner.

_____ 4. Professional accounting organizations and most companies have standards of ethical behavior.

_____ 5. A proprietorship's owners are called shareholders.

_____ 6. An advantage of the partnership form of business is that the life of the entity is indefinite.

_____ 7. The life of a sole proprietorship is limited to the owner's choice or death.

_____ 8. The entity concept separates business transactions from personal transactions.

_____ 9. A business has a net loss when total revenues are greater than total expenses.

_____ 10. The statement of owner's equity reports the cash coming in and going out.

Multiple Choice

1. What is the private organization that is primarily responsible for formulating accounting standards?
   a. The Internal Revenue Service
   b. The Securities and Exchange Commission
   c. The American Institute of Certified Public Accountants
   d. The Financial Accounting Standards Board

2. What is the watchdog agency created by the Sarbanes-Oxley Act?
   a. The American Institute of Certified Public Accountants
   b. The Public Companies Accounting Oversight Board
   c. The Internal Revenue Service
   d. The Financial Accounting Standards Board

3. Financial accounting provides financial statements and financial information that are intended to be used by whom?
   a. Management of the company
   b. Potential investors
   c. Employees of the company
   d. The board of directors

4. What is the purpose of financial accounting information?
   a. Help managers plan and control business operations
   b. Comply with the IRS rules
   c. Help investors, creditors, and others make decisions
   d. Provide information to employees

5. What characteristic is necessary for information to be useful?
   a. Relevance
   b. Reliability
   c. Comparability
   d. All of the above

6. Sue Mason owns a bagel shop as a sole proprietorship. Sue includes her personal home, car, and boat on the books of her business. Which of the following is violated?
   a. Entity concept
   b. Going-concern concept
   c. Cost principle
   d. Reliability principle

7. Which of the following is the accounting equation?
   a. Assets – Liabilities = Owner's Equity
   b. Assets + Liabilities = Owner's Equity
   c. Assets = Liabilities + Owner's Equity
   d. Assets + Liabilities = Net income

8. If the assets of a business are $410,000 and the liabilities total $200,000, how much is the owner's equity?
   a. $150,000
   b. $160,000
   c. $210,000
   d. $610,000

9. Which financial statement contains a listing of assets, liabilities, and owner's equity?
   a. Balance sheet
   b. Statement of owner's equity
   c. Income statement
   d. Statement of cash flows

10. What is the claim of a business owner to the assets of the business called?
    a. Liabilities
    b. Owner's equity
    c. Revenue
    d. Withdrawals

Quick Exercises

1-1. Fill in the statements that follow with the correct type of business organization.
   a. A _____ is a separate legal entity approved by the state.
   b. A _____ is an entity with one owner where the business and not the owner is liable for the company's debts.
   c. A _____ is an entity with two or more owners who are personally liable for the company's debts.

1-2. Match the following terms with the best description.

   Terms
   a. Entity concept
   b. Reliability principle
   c. Cost principle
   d. Going-concern concept
   e. Stable-monetary-unit concept

   Description
   ___ An organization or part of an organization is separate from other organizations and individuals.
   ___ An item should be recorded at the actual amount paid.
   ___ An entity is expected to remain in business in the future.
   ___ Assumption that the dollar's purchasing power is constant.
   ___ Accounting data should be neutral, unbiased information that can be confirmed by others.

1-3. Determine the missing amounts:
   a. Assets = $50,000; Liabilities = $30,000; Owner's Equity = _____?
   b. Liabilities = $35,000; Owner's Equity = $75,000; Assets = _____?
   c. Assets = $105,000; Owner's Equity = $50,000; Liabilities = _____?

1-4. Write a brief explanation for the following transactions:

	ASSETS				LIABILITIES	+	OWNER'S EQUITY
	Cash	+ Accounts receivable	+ Supplies		Accounts payable		Capital
a.	20,000			=			20,000
b.			1,000	=	1,000		
c.	−2,500			=			−2,500
d.		5,200		=			5,200
e.	3,000	−3,000		=			

a. _____
b. _____
c. _____
d. _____
e. _____

1-5. On which of the following three financial statements would you expect to find the items (a)–(f)?

Income Statement (IS)
Balance Sheet (BS)
Statement of Cash Flows (CF)

a. _____ Accounts Payable
b. _____ Service Revenue
c. _____ Collections from Customer
d. _____ Utilities Expense
e. _____ Office Supplies
f. _____ Payments to Suppliers

Do It Yourself! Question 1

Jennifer Hill opened a Laundromat business on October 1, 2011. She is the sole proprietor of the business.

Requirement

1 Use accounting vocabulary

6 Apply accounting concepts and principles

7 Define and use the accounting equation

8 Depict accounting for business transactions

1. For each transaction of the business during the month of October, analyze the transaction in terms of its effect on the accounting equation of Jennifer's Laundromat.

a. Jennifer invested $10,000 of her personal funds in the business.

b. The Laundromat purchased washing machines, paying $4,000 in cash and putting another $5,000 on account.

c. Jennifer purchased a washing machine for use in her home costing $2,100 on her personal account.

d. The business paid $500 cash for supplies.

e. The Laundromat performed cleaning services for customers totaling $2,500. These customers paid in cash.

f. The Laundromat also performed cleaning services for customers on account totaling $3,700.

g. The Laundromat paid rent (for the month of October) of $1,000.

h. The business paid employees $1,500 for the month of October.

i. The Laundromat received a utility bill for $750. As of October 31, 2011, it had not been paid.

j. Jennifer withdrew $2,000 cash from the business for personal use.

k. The Laundromat collected $2,250 on account.

l. The amount of $2,400 was paid on the account to the washing machine store.

7 Define and use the accounting equation

9 Explained the financial statements

2. Prepare the income statement, statement of owner's equity, and balance sheet of the business as of October 31, 2011.

Assets	Liabilities	Equity	Type of Owner's Equity Transaction

18 Chapter 1 | Do It Yourself! Question 1

Do It Yourself! Question 1 | Chapter 1   **19**

Quick Practice Solutions

True/False

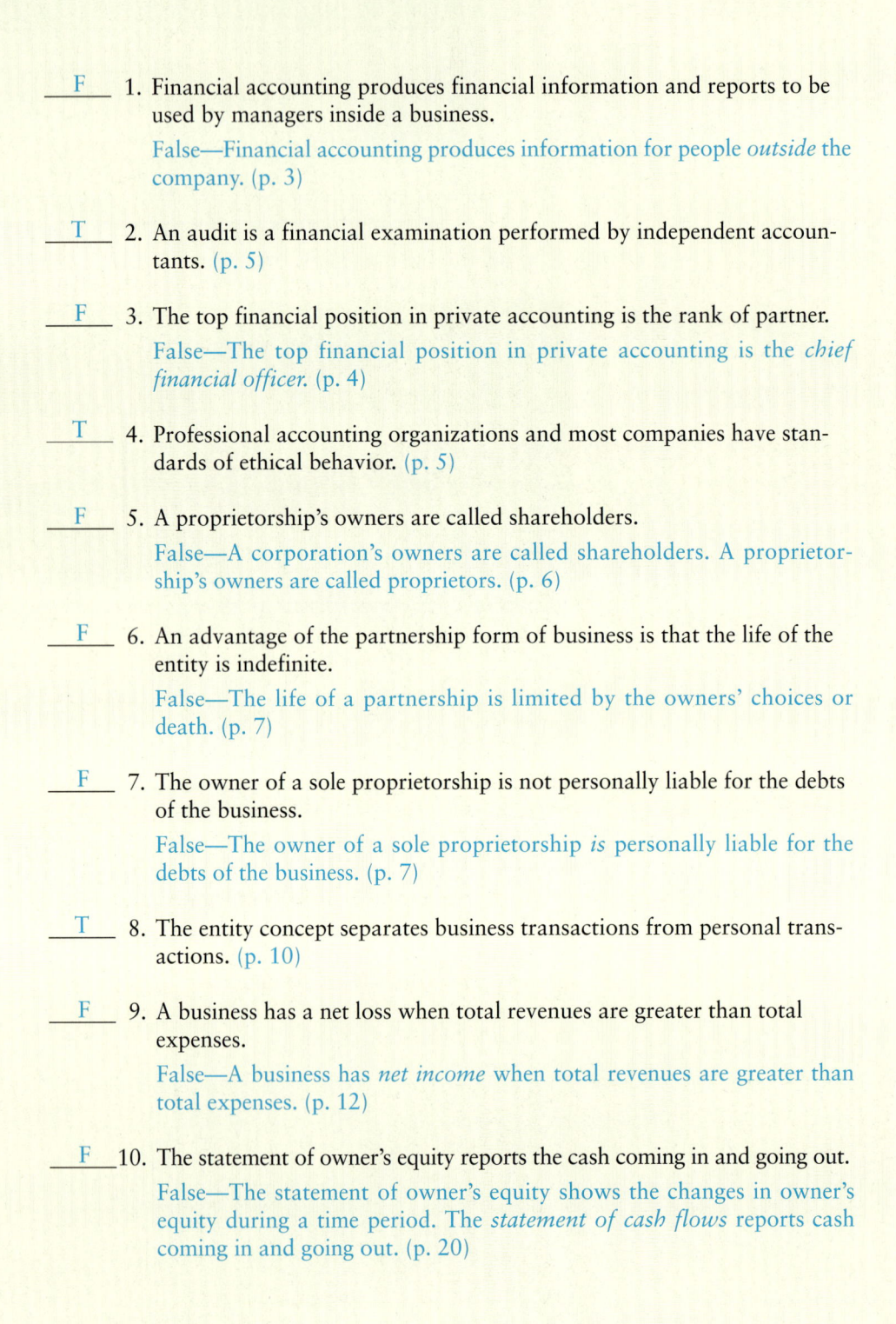

__F__ 1. Financial accounting produces financial information and reports to be used by managers inside a business.

False—Financial accounting produces information for people *outside* the company. (p. 3)

__T__ 2. An audit is a financial examination performed by independent accountants. (p. 5)

__F__ 3. The top financial position in private accounting is the rank of partner.

False—The top financial position in private accounting is the *chief financial officer*. (p. 4)

__T__ 4. Professional accounting organizations and most companies have standards of ethical behavior. (p. 5)

__F__ 5. A proprietorship's owners are called shareholders.

False—A corporation's owners are called shareholders. A proprietorship's owners are called proprietors. (p. 6)

__F__ 6. An advantage of the partnership form of business is that the life of the entity is indefinite.

False—The life of a partnership is limited by the owners' choices or death. (p. 7)

__F__ 7. The owner of a sole proprietorship is not personally liable for the debts of the business.

False—The owner of a sole proprietorship *is* personally liable for the debts of the business. (p. 7)

__T__ 8. The entity concept separates business transactions from personal transactions. (p. 10)

__F__ 9. A business has a net loss when total revenues are greater than total expenses.

False—A business has *net income* when total revenues are greater than total expenses. (p. 12)

__F__ 10. The statement of owner's equity reports the cash coming in and going out.

False—The statement of owner's equity shows the changes in owner's equity during a time period. The *statement of cash flows* reports cash coming in and going out. (p. 20)

Multiple Choice

1. What is the private organization that is primarily responsible for formulating accounting standards? (p. 4)
   a. The Internal Revenue Service
   b. The Securities and Exchange Commission
   c. The American Institute of Certified Public Accountants
   d. The Financial Accounting Standards Board

2. What is the watchdog agency created by the Sarbanes-Oxley Act? (p. 5)
   a. The American Institute of Certified Public Accountants
   b. The Public Companies Accounting Oversight Board
   c. The Internal Revenue Service
   d. The Financial Accounting Standards Board

3. Financial accounting provides financial statements and financial information that are intended to be used by whom? (p. 3)
   a. Management of the company
   b. Potential investors
   c. Employees of the company
   d. The board of directors

4. What is the purpose of financial accounting information? (p. 3)
   a. To help managers plan and control business operations
   b. To comply with the IRS rules
   c. To help investors, creditors, and others make decisions
   d. To provide information to employees

5. What characteristic is necessary for information to be useful? (p. 5)
   a. Relevance
   b. Reliability
   c. Comparability
   d. All of the above

6. Sue Mason owns a bagel shop as a sole proprietorship. Sue includes her personal home, car, and boat on the books of her business. Which of the following is violated? (p. 10)
   a. Entity concept
   b. Going-concern concept
   c. Cost principle
   d. Reliability principle

7. Which is the accounting equation? (p. 11)

   a. Assets − Liabilities = Owner's Equity
   b. Assets + Liabilities = Owner's Equity
   c. Assets = Liabilities + Owner's Equity
   d. Assets + Liabilities = Net income

8. If the assets of a business are $410,000 and the liabilities total $200,000, how much is the owner's equity? (p. 11)
   a. $150,000
   b. $160,000
   c. $210,000
   d. $610,000

9. Which financial statement contains a listing of assets, liabilities, and owner's equity? (p. 20)
   a. Balance sheet
   b. Statement of owner's equity
   c. Income statement
   d. Statement of cash flows

10. What is the claim of a business owner to the assets of the business called? (p. 12)
    a. Liabilities
    b. Owner's equity
    c. Revenue
    d. Withdrawals

Quick Exercises

1-1. Fill in the statements that follow with the correct type of business organization. (p. 7)

   a. A corporation is a separate legal entity approved by the state.
   b. A limited-liability corporation is an entity with one owner where the business and not the owner is liable for the company's debts.
   c. A partnership is an entity with two or more owners who are personally liable for the company's debts.

1-2. Match the following terms with the best description. (p. 10)

Terms

   a. Entity concept
   b. Reliability principle
   c. Cost principle
   d. Going-concern concept
   e. Stable-monetary-unit concept

Description

   __a__ An organization or part of an organization is separate from other organizations and individuals.
   __c__ An item should be recorded at the actual amount paid.
   __d__ An entity is expected to remain in business in the future.
   __e__ Assumption that the dollar's purchasing power is constant.
   __b__ Accounting data should be neutral, unbiased information that can be confirmed by others.

1-3. Determine the missing amounts: (p. 11)

a. Assets = $50,000; Liabilities = $30,000; Owner's Equity = $20,000   ($50,000 − $30,000)

b. Liabilities = $35,000; Owner's Equity = $75,000; Assets = $110,000   ($35,000 + $75,000)

c. Assets = $105,000; Owner's Equity = $50,000; Liabilities = $55,000   ($105,000 − $50,000)

1-4. Write a brief explanation for the following transactions: (p. 14)

	ASSETS			=	LIABILITIES	+	OWNER'S EQUITY
	Cash	+ Accounts receivable	+ Supplies		Accounts payable		Capital
a.	20,000						20,000
b.			1,000		1,000		
c.	−2,500						−2,500
d.		5,200					5,200
e.	3,000	−3,000					

a. The owner invested $20,000 cash in the business.
b. Purchased $1,000 of supplies on account.
c. Paid $2,500 for an expense *or* the owner withdrew $2,500 for personal use.
d. Performed services for customer on account, $5,200.
e. Received $3,000 cash from customers on account.

1-5. On which of the following three financial statements would you expect to find the items (a)–(f)? (p. 20)

Income Statement (IS)
Balance Sheet (BS)
Statement of Cash Flows (CF)

a. __BS__ Accounts Payable
b. __IS__ Service Revenue
c. __CF__ Collections from Customer
d. __IS__ Utilities Expense
e. __BS__ Office Supplies
f. __CF__ Payments to Suppliers

Do It Yourself! Question 1 Solutions

Requirement

1. For each transaction of the business during the month of October, analyze and describe the transaction in terms of its effect on the accounting equation of Jennifer's Laundromat.

a. Jennifer invested $10,000 of her personal funds in the business.

Cash (an asset) is increased by $10,000 and Jennifer Hill, Capital (owner's equity) is increased by $10,000.

b. The Laundromat purchased washing machines, paying $4,000 in cash and putting another $5,000 on account.

Washing Machines (an asset) is increased by $9,000, whereas Cash (an asset) is decreased by $4,000. Accounts Payable (a liability) is increased by $5,000.

c. Jennifer purchased a washing machine for use in her home costing $2,100 on her personal account.

This does not relate to the business and is not a recordable transaction for the Laundromat.

d. The business paid $500 cash for supplies.

Supplies (an asset) is increased by $500 and Cash (an asset) is decreased by $500.

e. The Laundromat performed cleaning services for customers totaling $2,500. These customers paid in cash.

Service Revenues (owner's equity) is increased by $2,500. Cash (an asset) is increased by $2,500.

f. The Laundromat also performed cleaning services for customers on account totaling $3,700.

Service Revenues (owner's equity) is increased by $3,700. Accounts Receivable (an asset) is increased by $3,700.

g. The Laundromat paid rent (for the month of October) of $1,000.

Rent Expense is increased by $1,000, which is a decrease to owner's equity. Cash (an asset) is decreased by $1,000.

h. The business paid employees $1,500 for the month of October.

Salary Expense is increased by $1,500, which is a decrease to owner's equity. Cash (an asset) is decreased by $1,500.

i. The Laundromat received a utility bill for $750. As of October 31, 2011, it had not been paid.

Utility Expense is increased by $750, which is a decrease to owner's equity. Accounts Payable (a liability) is increased by $750.

j. Jennifer withdrew $2,000 cash from the business for personal use.

This is a recordable transaction for the business. Cash (an asset) is decreased by $2,000. This results in an increase of $2,000 to Owner Withdrawals, which is a decrease to owner's equity.

k. The Laundromat collected $2,250 of accounts receivable.

Accounts Receivable (an asset) is decreased by $2,250. Because the cash is received, Cash is increased (an asset) by $2,250.

l. The amount of $2,400 was paid on the accounts payable to the washing machine store.

Accounts Payable (a liability) is decreased by $2,400 and Cash (an asset) is decreased by $2,400.

2. Prepare the income statement, balance sheet, and statement of owner's equity of the business as of October 31, 2011.

	Cash	+	Accounts receivable	+	Supplies	+	Washing Machines	=	Accounts payable	+	Jennifer Hill, Capital	Type of Owner's Equity Transaction
	+$10,000										+$10,000	Owner investment
a.	−4,000						+$9,000		+$5,000			
b.	Not a transaction of the business.											
c.	−$500				+$500							
d.	+2,500										+2,500	Service revenue
e.			+$3,700								+3,700	Service revenue
f.	−1,000										−1,000	Rent expense
g.	−1,500										−1,500	Salary expense
h.									+750		−750	Utilities expense
i.	−2,000											
j.	+2,250		−2,250								−2,000	Owner withdrawal
k.												
l.	−2,400								−2,400			
	$3,350		$1,450		$500		$9,000		$3,350		$10,950	
			$14,300								$14,300	

Assets total: $14,300 = Liabilities + Owner's Equity total: $14,300

JENNIFER'S LAUNDROMAT
Income Statement
Month Ended October 31, 2011

Revenue:		
Service revenue		$6,200*
Expenses:		
Salary expense	$1,500	
Rent expense	1,000	
Utilities expense	750	
Total expenses		3,250
Net income		$2,950

*(= $2,500 + $3,700)

JENNIFER'S LAUNDROMAT
Statement of Owner's Equity
Month Ended October 31, 2011

Jennifer Hill, capital, October 1, 2011	$ 0
Add: Investment by owner	10,000
Net income for month	2,950
	12,950
Less: Withdrawals by owner	(2,000)
Jennifer Hill, capital, October 31, 2011	$10,950

JENNIFER'S LAUNDROMAT
Balance Sheet
October 31, 2011

Assets		Liabilities	
Cash	$3,350	Accounts payable	$3,350
Accounts receivable	1,450		
Supplies	500	Equity	
Washing machines	9,000	Jennifer Hill, capital	10,950
Total assets	$14,300	Total liabilities and equity	$14,300

The Power of Practice

For more practice using the skills learned in this chapter, visit MyAccountingLab. There you will find algorithmically generated questions that are based on these Demo Docs and your main textbook's Review and Assess Your Progress sections.

Go to MyAccountingLab and follow these steps:

1. Direct your URL to www.myaccountinglab.com.
2. Log in using your name and password.
3. Click the MyAccountingLab link.
4. Click Study Plan in the left navigation bar.
5. From the table of contents, select Chapter 1, Accounting and the Business Environment.
6. Click a link to work tutorial exercises.

2 Recording Business Transactions

WHAT YOU PROBABLY ALREADY KNOW

If you have a checking account, you know that once a month you receive a statement from the bank. The statement shows the beginning cash balance, increases, decreases, and the ending cash balance. The account balance is the amount that the bank *owes* you, their customer. Your balance represents a *liability* to the bank. The deposits you make *increase* the bank's liability to you. The withdrawals or checks you write *decrease* that liability. Instead of using the terms increase and decrease, businesses have used a system of accounting for over 500 years with debits and credits. Either a debit *or* a credit may signify an increase to the account, *depending upon the type of account:* **asset**, **liability**, or **owner's equity**. Your checking account balance is a **liability** to your bank; does a debit or credit indicate an increase? When you take money out of the bank, it *decreases* the bank's liability to you because you've received back a portion of your account balance and is shown as a *debit* on the bank statement. When you deposit money into your account, it *increases* the banks' liability to you and is reflected as a *credit* on the bank statement. So, you can see that you probably already know that the rule for a liability account is that increases are shown as credits and decreases as debits.

Learning Objectives/Success Keys

1 Explain accounts, journals, and ledgers as they relate to recording transactions, and describe common accounts.

You learned in Chapter 1 that accounting is known as the language of business. The first several chapters contain many new terms that are used in the remaining chapters and are important for you to understand. These terms include the journal, account, ledger, trial balance, and chart of accounts. It is crucial that you understand these terms now before you proceed with your study of accounting. Also, carefully review the detailed description of the various specific asset, liability, and owner's equity accounts in Chapter 1 of the main text.

2 Define debits, credits, and normal account balances. Use double-entry accounting and T-accounts.

A business transaction affects two or more specific accounts. There are two sides to an account, the left (debit) side, and the right (credit) side. Remember that *debit only means left* and *credit only means right*. Increases are recorded on one side and decreases on the other. Depending on the type of account, a debit may indicate an increase **or** a decrease. Assets are on the left side of the equation; they increase on the left (debit) side. Liabilities and owner's equity are on the right side of the equation; they increase on the right (credit) side. *This is a basic concept, but crucial to understand. Review Exhibit 2-8 (p. 68) for the debit and credit rules.*

3 List the steps of the transaction recording process.

Remember the five steps in transaction analysis. You will practice this in Demo Doc 1. The more you practice this, the easier it will be to understand.

4 Journalize and post sample transactions to the ledger.

The journal shows the accounts that are debited and credited to record business transactions in chronological order. Debits and credits *only* reflect increases and decreases to the accounts. To obtain a specific account balance, it is helpful to collect the debit and credit information recorded in the journal in one place. Posting, copying the debits and credits from the journal into the account ledger, provides this information. The difference between the total debits and total credits in each account is the balance. The balance is shown on the larger side, normally the side to record the increase. *Review the posting process in Exhibits 2-6 (p. 68) and 2-10 (p. 70). Observe in Exhibit 2-11 (p. 77) that the entries on the increase side of each account balance exceed those on the decrease side. Note that the account balances are on the side where the increases are recorded.*

5 Prepare the trial balance from the T-accounts.

After transactions are recorded in the journal and posted to the ledger, a trial balance is prepared. The trial balance is a listing of all of the accounts with their balances. In a manual accounting system, it is useful as a check to determine that the total debits equal the total credits. If they are unequal, an error has been made and must be investigated before proceeding. *Review the trial balance in Exhibit 2-12 (p. 77).*

Demo Doc 1

Debit/Credit Transaction Analysis

Learning Objectives 1–5

Knight Airlines provides private plane transportation for businesspeople. Knight had the following trial balance on April 1, 2011:

KNIGHT AIRLINES
Trial Balance
April 1, 2011

Account Title	Balance Debit	Balance Credit
Cash	$50,000	
Accounts receivable	8,000	
Accounts payable		$16,000
Maureen Knight, capital		42,000
Total	$58,000	$58,000

During April, the business had the following transactions:

a. Purchased a new airplane for $50,000. Knight paid $10,000 down and signed a note payable for the remainder.

b. Purchased supplies worth $1,000 on account.

c. Paid $5,000 on account.

d. Transported customers on its planes for fees totaling $25,000. The amount of $7,500 was received in cash with the remainder on account.

e. Received $18,000 on account.

f. Paid the following in cash: interest, $1,200; rent, $2,300; salaries, $7,000.

g. Received a bill for airplane repair costs of $3,500 that will be paid next month.

h. Maureen Knight withdrew $6,000 for personal use.

Requirements

1. Open the following accounts, with the balances indicated, in the ledger of Knight Airlines. Use the T-account format.

- **Assets**—Cash, $50,000; Accounts Receivable, $8,000; Supplies, no balance; Airplanes, no balance
- **Liabilities**—Accounts Payable, $16,000; Notes Payable, no balance
- *Owner's Equity*—Maureen Knight, Capital, $42,000; Maureen Knight, Withdrawals, no balance
- **Revenues**—Service Revenue, no balance
- **Expenses**—(none have balances) Interest Expense, Rent Expense, Salary Expense, Repairs Expense

2. Journalize each transaction. Key journal entries by transaction letter.

3. Post to the ledger.

4. Prepare the trial balance of Knight Airlines at April 30, 2011.

Demo Doc 1 Solutions

Requirement 1

Open the following accounts, with the balances indicated, in the ledger of Knight Airlines. Use the T-account format.

- **Assets**—Cash, $50,000; Accounts Receivable, $8,000; Supplies, no balance; Airplanes, no balance
- **Liabilities**—Accounts Payable, $16,000; Notes Payable, no balance
- **Owner's Equity**—Maureen Knight, Capital, $42,000; Maureen Knight, Withdrawals, no balance
- **Revenues**—Service Revenue, no balance
- **Expenses**—(none have balances) Interest Expense, Rent Expense, Salary Expense, Repairs Expense

Part 1	Part 2	Part 3	Part 4	Demo Doc Complete

Remember, an **account** is a record showing increases, decreases, and the balance of a particular asset, liability, or owner's equity. A T-account is a visual diagram of the additions and subtractions made to the accounts. A **chart of accounts** is a list of all of the business's account titles and account numbers assigned to those titles. A chart of accounts does not include account balances. Review the sample chart of accounts in Exhibit 2-2 (p. 63) of the main text.

Opening a T-account simply means drawing a blank account (the "T") and putting the account title on top. To help find the accounts later, they are usually organized into assets, liabilities, owner's equity, revenue, and expenses (in that order). If the account has a starting balance, it *must* be put in on the correct side.

Remember that debits are always on the left side of the T-account and credits are always on the right side. This is true for *every* account.

The correct side is the side of *increase* in the account (unless you are specifically told differently in the question). This is because we expect all accounts to have a *positive* balance (that is, more increases than decreases).

For assets, an increase is a debit, so we would expect all assets to have a debit balance. For liabilities and owner's equity, an increase is a credit, so we would expect all of these accounts to have a credit balance. By the same reasoning, we expect revenues to have a credit balance and expenses and withdrawals to have a debit balance.

The balances listed in Requirement 1 are simply the amounts from the starting trial balance. We actually did not need to be told how much to put in each account because we could have read the numbers directly from the April 1 trial balance.

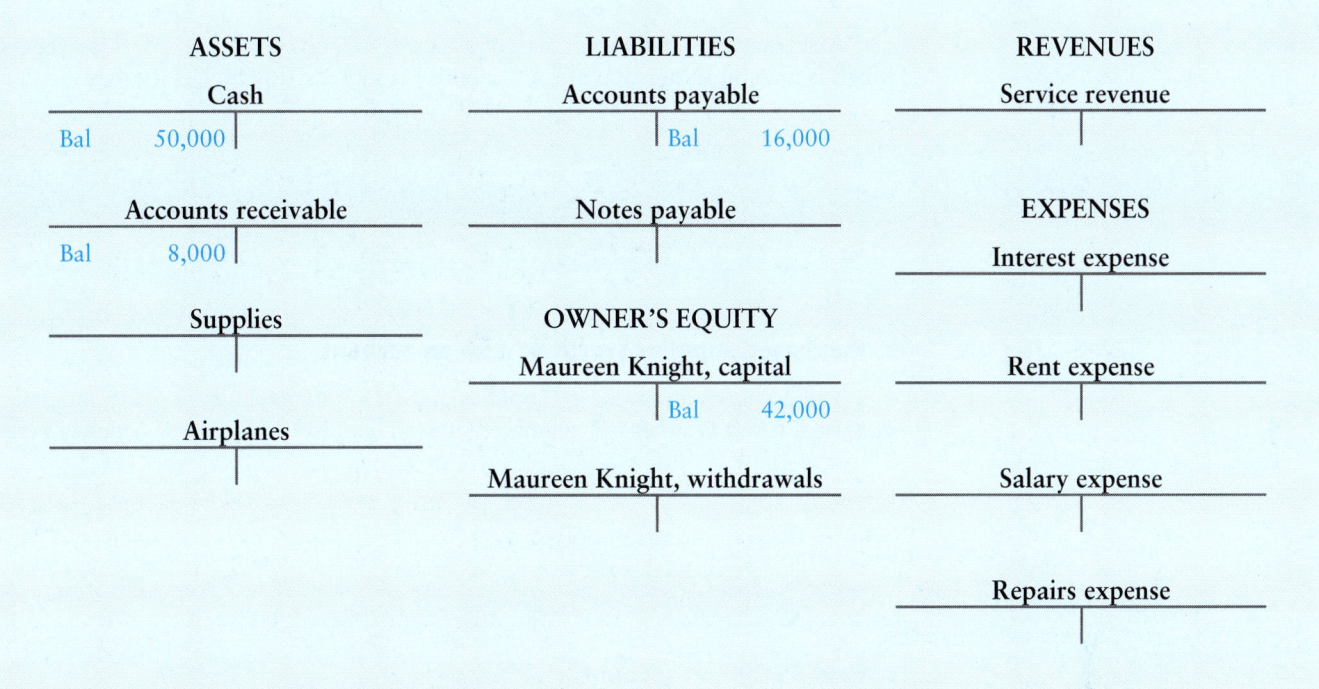

ASSETS	LIABILITIES	REVENUES
Cash	Accounts payable	Service revenue
Bal 50,000	Bal 16,000	
Accounts receivable	Notes payable	EXPENSES
Bal 8,000		Interest expense
Supplies	OWNER'S EQUITY	
	Maureen Knight, capital	Rent expense
Airplanes	Bal 42,000	
	Maureen Knight, withdrawals	Salary expense
		Repairs expense

Requirement 2

1 Explain accounts, journals, and ledgers as they relate to recording transactions, and describe common accounts

2 Define debits, credits, and normal account balances. Use double-entry accounting and T-accounts

3 List the steps of the transaction recording process

Journalize each transaction. Key journal entries by transaction letter.

| Part 1 | **Part 2** | Part 3 | Part 4 | Demo Doc Complete |

Feel free to reference Exhibit 2-2 (p. 63 in text) for help in completing this exercise.

The business transactions discussed in Chapter 1 are recorded in chronological order in a **journal**. Similar to journaling that you may do for a class or at home, it provides a history of events that have taken place over a period of time. The recorded data in the journal are copied into the two or more specific accounts affected by the business transaction.

Remember, the steps to analyzing a transaction are (1) identify the accounts affected and the type of account, and (2) determine whether the account is increased or decreased and apply the rules for debits and credits.

After you've done this analysis, the third and final step to record transactions in the journal is to (3) enter the debit account followed by indenting the credit account in the journal. Include a brief explanation of the transaction below the journal entry.

a. Purchased a new airplane for $50,000. Knight paid $10,000 down and signed a note payable for the remainder.

The accounts involved are Airplanes, Cash, and Notes Payable. The airplane cost $50,000 and $10,000 was paid in cash, so that means that the note payable was for $50,000 − $10,000 = $40,000.

Airplanes (an asset) is increased, which is a debit. Cash (an asset) is decreased, which is a credit. Notes Payable (a liability) is increased, which is a credit.

a.	Airplanes	50,000	
	Cash		10,000
	Notes payable ($50,000 − $10,000)		40,000
	Purchased airplane.		

b. Purchased supplies worth $1,000 on account.

The accounts involved are Supplies and Accounts Payable. Supplies (an asset) is increased, which is a debit. Accounts Payable (a liability) is increased, which is a credit.

b.	Supplies	1,000	
	Accounts payable		1,000
	Purchased supplies.		

c. Paid $5,000 on account.

The accounts involved are Accounts Payable and Cash. Accounts Payable (a liability) is decreased, which is a debit. Cash (an asset) is decreased, which is a credit.

c.	Accounts payable	5,000	
	Cash		5,000
	Paid on account.		

d. Transported customers on its planes for fees totaling $25,000. Cash of $7,500 was received with the remainder on account.

Knight's business is flying customers to where they want to go. This means that transporting customers is "performing services" and the business earned service revenue. The other accounts involved are Cash (because cash was received) and Accounts Receivable (because some customers charged to their accounts). The total revenue was $25,000 and $7,500 was paid in cash. This means that $25,000 − $7,500 = $17,500 was charged to the customers' accounts.

Service Revenue (revenues) is increased, which is a credit. Cash (an asset) is increased, which is a debit. Accounts Receivable (an asset) is increased, which is a debit.

d.	Cash	7,500	
	Accounts receivable ($25,000 − $7,500)	17,500	
	Service revenue		25,000
	Performed services on account and for cash.		

e. Received $18,000 on account.

The accounts involved are Cash and Accounts Receivable. Cash (an asset) is increased, which is a debit. Accounts Receivable (an asset) is decreased, which is a credit.

e.	Cash	18,000	
	Accounts receivable		18,000
	Received cash on account.		

f. Paid the following in cash: interest, $1,200; rent, $2,300; salaries, $7,000.

The accounts involved are Interest Expense, Rent Expense, Salary Expense, and Cash.

Interest Expense, Rent Expense, and Salary Expense (all expenses) are all increased, which are debits. Cash (an asset) is decreased, which is a credit.

f.	Interest expense	1,200	
	Rent expense	2,300	
	Salary expense	7,000	
	Cash		10,500
	Paid expenses.		

g. Received a bill for airplane repair costs of $3,500 that will be paid next month.

Repairs are not billed until *after* they have been performed. So the bill received was for repairs made *in the past*. This means that it is a *past* benefit and should be recorded as an expense. So the accounts involved are Repairs Expense and Accounts Payable.

Repairs Expense (an expense) is increased, which is a debit. Accounts Payable (a liability) is increased, which is a credit.

g.	Repairs expense	3,500	
	Accounts payable		3,500
	Received repair bill.		

h. Maureen Knight withdrew $6,000 for personal use.

The accounts involved are Maureen Knight, Withdrawals and Cash. Maureen Knight, Withdrawals is increased, which is a debit. This results in a *decrease to owner's equity*, which is a debit. Cash (an asset) is decreased, which is a credit.

h.	Maureen Knight, withdrawals	6,000	
	Cash		6,000
	Owner withdrawal.		

4 Journalize and post sample transactions to the ledger

Requirement 3

Post to the ledger.

| Part 1 | Part 2 | **Part 3** | Part 4 | Demo Doc Complete |

The entire group of accounts is called the **ledger**. A manual system would have a book of account pages and a computerized system would have a printout of all of the accounts. Review Exhibit 2-1 (p. 63) in the main text to follow the flow of accounts into the ledger.

All amounts in the journal entries are put into the individual ledger T-accounts. Debits go on the left side and credits go on the right side.

To add up a T-account, total the debit/left side and total the credit/right side. Subtract the smaller number from the bigger number and put the difference on the side of the bigger number. This gives the *balance* in the T-account (the *net* total of both sides combined).

For example, with Accounts Receivable, the two numbers on the left side total $8,000 + $17,500 = $25,500. The credit/right side totals $18,000. The difference is $25,500 − $18,000 = $7,500. We put the $7,500 on the debit side because that was the side of the bigger number of $25,500.

Another way to think of computing the balance of T-accounts is:

> Beginning balance in T-account
> + Increases to T-account
> – Decreases to T-account
> T-account balance (total)

ASSETS

Cash

Bal	50,000			
		a.	10,000	
		c.	5,000	
d.	7,500			
e.	18,000			
		f.	10,500	
		h.	6,000	
Bal	44,000			

Accounts receivable

Bal	8,000			
d.	17,500			
		e.	18,000	
Bal	7,500			

Supplies

b.	1,000	
Bal	1,000	

Airplanes

a.	50,000	
Bal	50,000	

LIABILITIES

Accounts payable

		Bal	16,000	
		b.	1,000	
c.	5,000			
		g.	3,500	
		Bal	15,500	

Notes payable

	a.	40,000
	Bal	40,000

OWNER'S EQUITY

Maureen Knight, capital

	Bal	42,000
	Bal	42,000

Maureen Knight, withdrawals

h.	6,000	
Bal	6,000	

REVENUES

Service revenue

	d.	25,000	
	Bal	25,000	

EXPENSES

Interest expense

f.	1,200	
Bal	1,200	

Rent expense

f.	2,300	
Bal	2,300	

Salary expense

f.	7,000	
Bal	7,000	

Repairs expense

g.	3,500	
Bal	3,500	

Requirement 4

5 Prepare the trial balance from the T-accounts

Prepare the trial balance of Knight Airlines at April 30, 2011.

| Part 1 | Part 2 | Part 3 | **Part 4** | Demo Doc Complete |

All of the debits and credits are now listed for the **trial balance**. A trial balance is a list of all of the account titles with their balances at the end of an accounting period. Review the illustration of a trial balance in Exhibit 2-12 (p. 77) of the main text. Again, the accounts are listed in the order of assets, liabilities, equity, revenues, and expenses for consistency.

KNIGHT AIRLINES
Trial Balance
April 30, 2011

Account Title	Balance Debit	Balance Credit
Cash	$ 44,000	
Accounts receivable	7,500	
Supplies	1,000	
Airplanes	50,000	
Accounts payable		$ 15,500
Notes payable		40,000
Maureen Knight, capital		42,000
Maureen Knight, withdrawals	6,000	
Service revenue		25,000
Interest expense	1,200	
Rent expense	2,300	
Salary expense	7,000	
Repairs expense	3,500	
Total	$122,500	$122,500

| Part 1 | Part 2 | Part 3 | Part 4 | Demo Doc Complete |

Quick Practice Questions

True/False

_____ 1. A ledger is a chronological record of transactions.

_____ 2. A chart of accounts lists all of the accounts and their balances.

_____ 3. An asset is an economic resource that will benefit the business in the future.

_____ 4. A note receivable is a written pledge that the customer will pay a fixed amount of money by a certain date.

_____ 5. Posting is the process of transferring information from the trial balance to the financial statements.

_____ 6. Prepaid expenses are listed as expenses on the income statement.

_____ 7. When an owner withdraws cash from the business, assets and owner's equity decrease.

_____ 8. When a business makes a payment on account, assets decrease and liabilities increase.

_____ 9. Every transaction affects only two accounts.

_____ 10. T-accounts help to summarize transactions.

Multiple Choice

1. A business transaction is first recorded in which of the following?
   a. Chart of accounts
   b. Journal
   c. Ledger
   d. Trial balance

2. A trial balance is which of the following?
   a. A record holding all the accounts
   b. A detailed record of the changes in a particular asset, liability, or owner's equity account
   c. A chronological record of transactions
   d. A list of all the accounts with their balances

3. Which sequence of actions correctly summarizes the accounting process?
   a. Prepare a trial balance, journalize transactions, post to the accounts
   b. Post to the accounts, journalize the transactions, prepare a trial balance
   c. Journalize transactions, post to the accounts, prepare a trial balance
   d. Journalize transactions, prepare a trial balance, post to the accounts

4. Which of the following accounts increase with a credit?
   a. Cash
   b. Owner's Capital
   c. Accounts Payable
   d. Both (b) and (c) increase when credited

5. A business makes a cash payment of $12,000 to a creditor. Which of the following occurs?
   a. Cash is credited for $12,000.
   b. Cash is debited for $12,000.
   c. Accounts Payable is credited for $12,000.
   d. Both (a) and (c).

6. Liabilities are which of the following?
   a. Debts or obligations owed to creditors
   b. Economic resources that will benefit the entity in the future
   c. Owner's claim to the assets of the business
   d. Amounts earned by providing products or services

7. Which account would normally have a debit balance?
   a. Accrued Liabilities
   b. Notes Payable
   c. Owner's Capital
   d. Accounts Receivable

8. Which of the following is the correct journal entry for a purchase of equipment for $50,000 cash?

	Accounts	Dr	Cr
a.	Equipment	50,000	
	Cash		50,000
b.	Equipment	50,000	
	Owner's capital		50,000
c.	Accounts receivable	50,000	
	Equipment		50,000
d.	Cash	50,000	
	Equipment		50,000

9. Which of the following is the correct journal entry for purchasing $5,000 worth of supplies on account?

	Accounts	Dr	Cr
a.	Supplies	5,000	
	Cash		5,000
b.	Accounts payable	5,000	
	Supplies		5,000
c.	Supplies	5,000	
	Accounts payable		5,000
d.	Cash	5,000	
	Supplies		5,000

10. Which of the following is the correct journal entry for providing $20,000 worth of consulting services for cash?

	Accounts	Dr	Cr
a.	Service revenue	20,000	
	Cash		20,000
b.	Accounts receivable	20,000	
	Service revenue		20,000
c.	Accounts receivable	20,000	
	Cash		20,000
d.	Cash	20,000	
	Service revenue		20,000

Quick Exercises

2-1. Indicate whether a debit or credit is required to record an increase for each of these accounts.

_____ Cash   _____ Prepaid Rent
_____ Owner, Withdrawals   _____ Notes Payable
_____ Salaries Expense   _____ Land
_____ Service Revenue   _____ Utilities Expense

2-2. Write a brief explanation for the following transactions:

	Accounts	Debit	Credit
a.	Cash	10,000	
	Owner, capital		10,000

	Accounts	Debit	Credit
b.	Supplies	500	
	Accounts payable		500

	Accounts	Debit	Credit
c.	Cash	3,000	
	Service revenue		3,000

	Accounts	Debit	Credit
d.	Accounts receivable	2,000	
	Service revenue		2,000

	Accounts	Debit	Credit
e.	Accounts payable	300	
	Cash		300

2-3. Identify the following as an asset, liability, owner's equity, revenue, or expense account. Also indicate the normal balance as a debit or credit.

	Account	Normal Balance
a. Building	_____	_____
b. Accounts Payable	_____	_____
c. Cash	_____	_____
d. Accounts Receivable	_____	_____
e. Prepaid Insurance	_____	_____
f. Supplies	_____	_____
g. Utilities Expense	_____	_____
h. Owner, Capital	_____	_____
i. Owner, Withdrawals	_____	_____

2-4. Journalize the following transactions for the Reid Public Relations Company using these accounts: Cash, Accounts Receivable, Notes Receivable, Supplies, Prepaid Insurance, Accounts Payable, Notes Payable, Reid Capital, Reid Withdrawals, Service Revenue, Salaries Expense, Rent Expense, Insurance Expense.

March 1   J. Reid invested $25,000 cash to begin her public relations company.

Date	Accounts	Debit	Credit

March 2 Paid $3,000 for March rent.

Date	Accounts	Debit	Credit

March 4 Purchased $825 of supplies on account.

Date	Accounts	Debit	Credit

March 5 Performed $10,000 of services for a client on account.

Date	Accounts	Debit	Credit

March 8 Paid salaries of $2,500.

Date	Accounts	Debit	Credit

March 15 Paid the semiannual insurance premium of $1,800 for the period March 15 to September 15.

Date	Accounts	Debit	Credit

March 20   Signed a bank note and borrowed $20,000 cash.

Date	Accounts	Debit	Credit

March 25   Received $10,000 from customers on account. (See March 5.)

Date	Accounts	Debit	Credit

2-5. Find the errors in the trial balance shown here and prepare a corrected trial balance using the form on the next page.

COLEMAN COPY CENTER
Trial Balance
March 31, 2011

Account Title	Debit	Credit
Cash	$30,000	
Accounts receivable		$ 2,000
Supplies	600	
Land	50,000	
Accounts payable	2,600	
Note payable		35,000
Jo Coleman, capital		42,550
Jo Coleman, withdrawals		2,400
Service revenue		9,300
Salary expense		2,500
Rent expense		1,200
Interest expense		500
Utilities expense		250
Total	$83,200	$95,700

COLEMAN COPY CENTER
Trial Balance
March 31, 2011

	Account Title	Balance Debit	Credit
	Cash		
	Accounts receivable		
	Supplies		
	Land		
	Accounts payable		
	Note payable		
	Jo Coleman, capital		
	Jo Coleman, withdrawals		
	Service revenue		
	Salary expense		
	Rent expense		
	Interest expense		
	Utilities expense		
	Total		

Do It Yourself! Question 1

Debit/Credit Transaction Analysis

Ted's Repair Shop had the following trial balance on September 1, 2011:

TED'S REPAIR SHOP
Trial Balance
September 1, 2011

Account Title	Balance Debit	Balance Credit
Cash	$6,000	
Accounts receivable	1,200	
Accounts payable		$ 700
Ted Johnson, capital		6,500
Total	$7,200	$7,200

Requirements

1 Explain accounts, journals, and ledgers as they relate to recording transactions, and describe common accounts

2 Define debits, credits, and normal account balances. Use double-entry accounting and T-accounts

3 List the steps of the transaction recording process

1. Journalize each of the following transactions. Key journal entries by transaction letter.

a. Performed repairs for customers and earned $800 in cash and $1,500 of revenue on account.

Date	Accounts	Debit	Credit

b. Paid $200 cash for supplies.

Date	Accounts	Debit	Credit

c. Took out a loan of $2,000 cash from City Bank.

Date	Accounts	Debit	Credit

d. Paid $3,000 cash to purchase repair tools.

Date	Accounts	Debit	Credit

e. Paid the following in cash: interest, $75; rent, $825; salaries, $1,000.

Date	Accounts	Debit	Credit

f. Received a telephone bill of $100 that will be paid next month.

Date	Accounts	Debit	Credit

g. Paid $500 on account.

Date	Accounts	Debit	Credit

h. Received $1,100 on account.

Date	Accounts	Debit	Credit

i. Ted withdrew $1,300 for personal use.

Date	Accounts	Debit	Credit

2. Open the following accounts, with the balances indicated, in the ledger of Ted's Repair Shop. Use the T-account format.

- **Assets**—Cash, $6,000; Accounts Receivable, $1,200; Supplies, no balance; Repair Tools, no balance
- **Liabilities**—Accounts Payable, $700; Loans Payable, no balance
- **Owner's Equity**—Ted Johnson, Capital, $6,500; Ted Johnson, Withdrawals, no balance
- **Revenues**—Service Revenue, no balance
- **Expenses**—(none have balances) Interest Expense, Rent Expense, Salary Expense, Utilities Expense

4 Journalize and post sample transactions to the ledger

3. Post all transactions in Requirement 1 to the ledger.

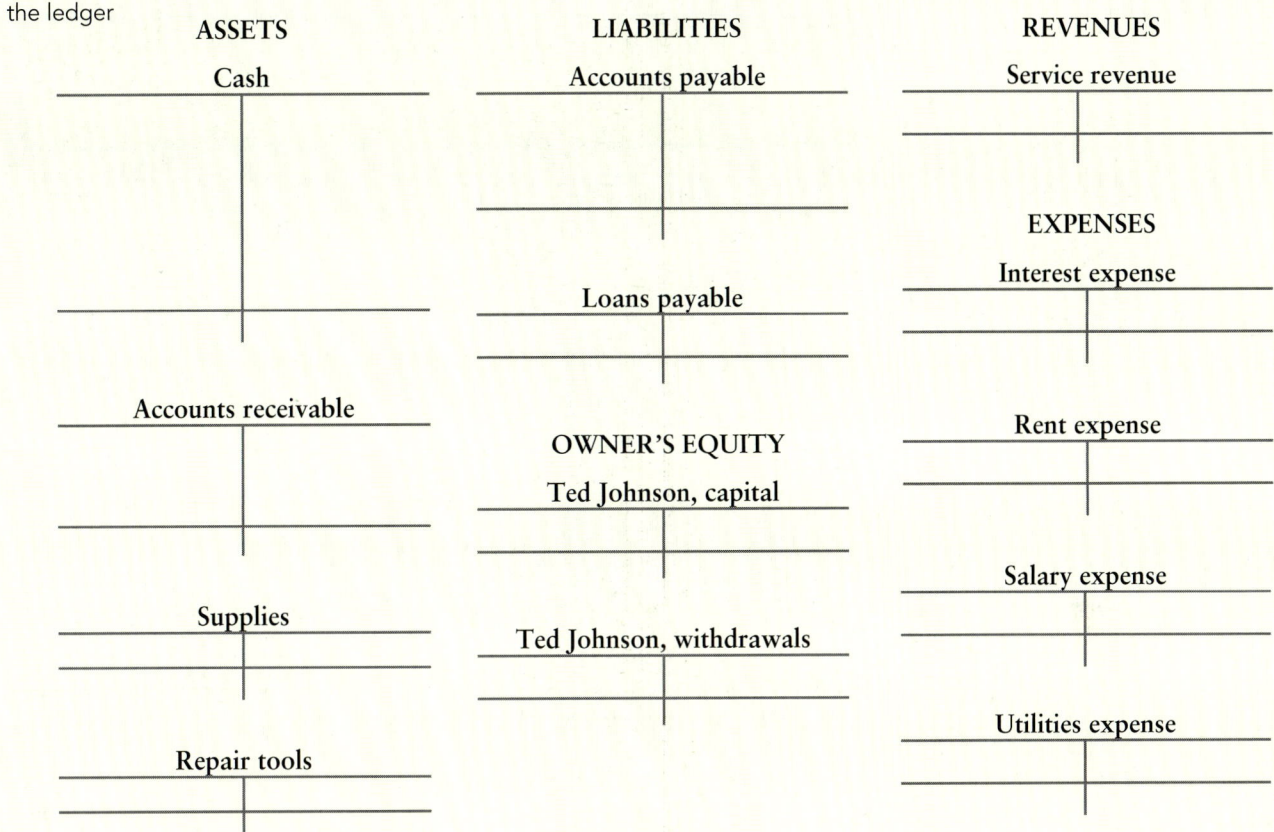

ASSETS	LIABILITIES	REVENUES
Cash	Accounts payable	Service revenue
	Loans payable	**EXPENSES**
		Interest expense
Accounts receivable	**OWNER'S EQUITY**	Rent expense
	Ted Johnson, capital	
Supplies	Ted Johnson, withdrawals	Salary expense
Repair tools		Utilities expense

Do It Yourself! Question 1 | Chapter 2

5 Prepare the trial balance from the T-accounts

4. Prepare the trial balance of Ted's Repair Shop at September 30, 2011.

TED'S REPAIR SHOP
Trial Balance
September 30, 2011

Account Title	Balance Debit	Credit

Quick Practice Solutions

True/False

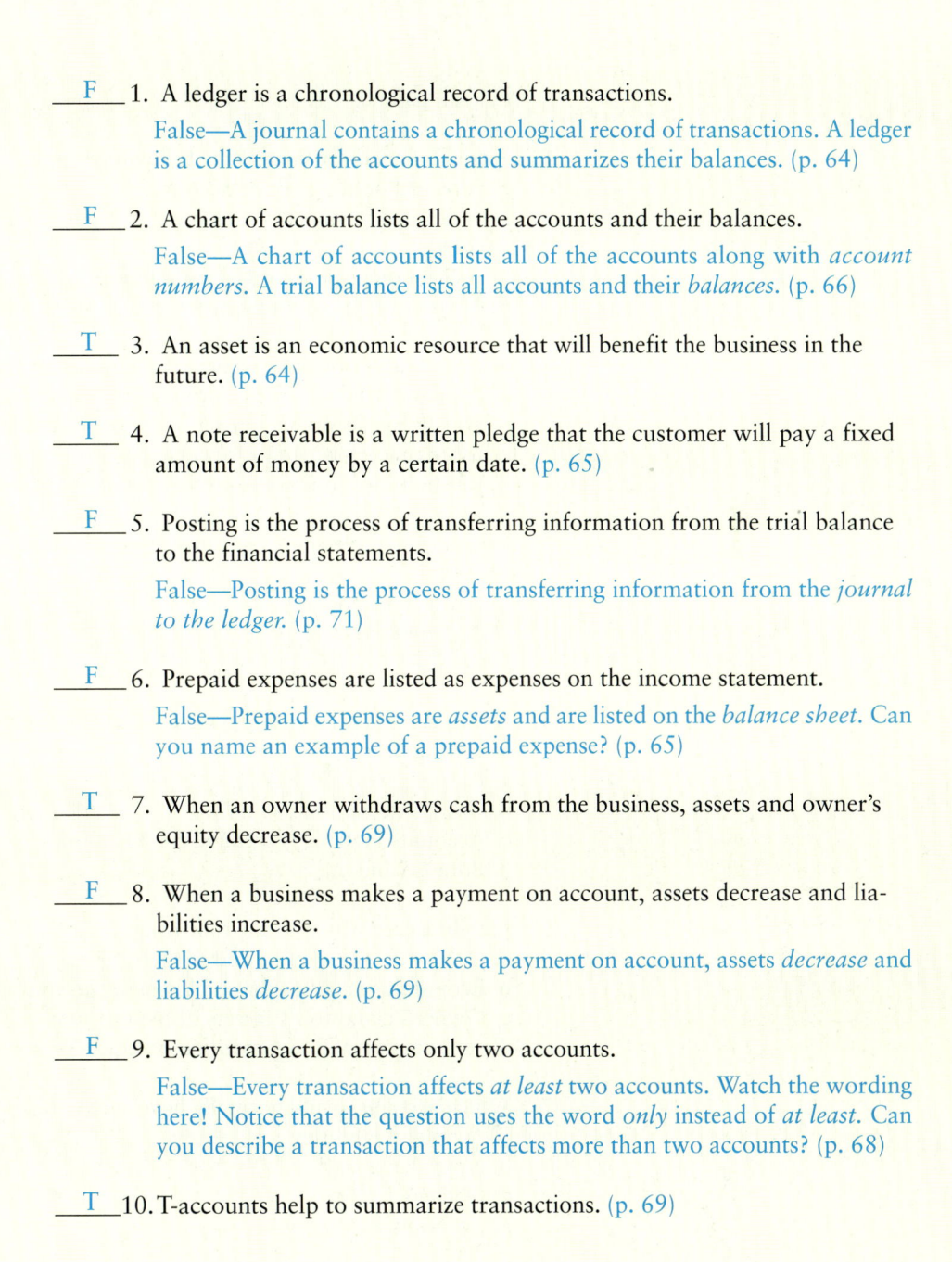

__F__ 1. A ledger is a chronological record of transactions.

    False—A journal contains a chronological record of transactions. A ledger is a collection of the accounts and summarizes their balances. (p. 64)

__F__ 2. A chart of accounts lists all of the accounts and their balances.

    False—A chart of accounts lists all of the accounts along with *account numbers*. A trial balance lists all accounts and their *balances*. (p. 66)

__T__ 3. An asset is an economic resource that will benefit the business in the future. (p. 64)

__T__ 4. A note receivable is a written pledge that the customer will pay a fixed amount of money by a certain date. (p. 65)

__F__ 5. Posting is the process of transferring information from the trial balance to the financial statements.

    False—Posting is the process of transferring information from the *journal to the ledger*. (p. 71)

__F__ 6. Prepaid expenses are listed as expenses on the income statement.

    False—Prepaid expenses are *assets* and are listed on the *balance sheet*. Can you name an example of a prepaid expense? (p. 65)

__T__ 7. When an owner withdraws cash from the business, assets and owner's equity decrease. (p. 69)

__F__ 8. When a business makes a payment on account, assets decrease and liabilities increase.

    False—When a business makes a payment on account, assets *decrease* and liabilities *decrease*. (p. 69)

__F__ 9. Every transaction affects only two accounts.

    False—Every transaction affects *at least* two accounts. Watch the wording here! Notice that the question uses the word *only* instead of *at least*. Can you describe a transaction that affects more than two accounts? (p. 68)

__T__ 10. T-accounts help to summarize transactions. (p. 69)

Multiple Choice

1. A business transaction is first recorded in which of the following? (p. 64)
   a. Chart of accounts
   b. Journal
   c. Ledger
   d. Trial balance

2. A trial balance is which of the following? (p. 64)
   a. A record holding all the accounts
   b. A detailed record of the changes in a particular asset, liability, or owner's equity
   c. A chronological record of transactions
   d. A list of all the accounts with their balances

3. Which sequence of actions correctly summarizes the accounting process? (p. 64)
   a. Prepare a trial balance, journalize transactions, post to the accounts
   b. Post to the accounts, journalize the transactions, prepare a trial balance
   c. Journalize transactions, post to the accounts, prepare a trial balance
   d. Journalize transactions, prepare a trial balance, post to the accounts

4. Which of the following accounts increase with a credit? (p. 69)
   a. Cash
   b. Owner's Capital
   c. Accounts Payable
   d. Both (b) and (c) increase when credited

5. A business makes a cash payment of $12,000 to a creditor. Which of the following occurs? (p. 69)
   a. Cash is credited for $12,000.
   b. Cash is debited for $12,000.
   c. Accounts Payable is credited for $12,000.
   d. Both (a) and (c).

6. Liabilities are which of the following? (p. 65)
   a. Debts or obligations owed to creditors
   b. Economic resources that will benefit the entity in the future
   c. Owner's claim to the assets of the business
   d. Amounts earned by providing products or services

7. Which account would normally have a debit balance? (p. 73)
   a. Accrued Liabilities
   b. Notes Payable
   c. Owner's Capital
   d. Accounts Receivable

8. Which of the following is the correct journal entry for a purchase of equipment for $50,000 cash? (p. 69)

	Accounts	Dr	Cr
a.	Equipment	50,000	
	Cash		50,000
b.	Equipment	50,000	
	Owner's capital		50,000
c.	Accounts receivable	50,000	
	Equipment		50,000
d.	Cash	50,000	
	Equipment		50,000

9. Which of the following is the correct journal entry for purchasing $5,000 worth of supplies on account? (p. 76)

	Accounts	Dr	Cr
a.	Supplies	5,000	
	Cash		5,000
b.	Accounts payable	5,000	
	Supplies		5,000
c.	Supplies	5,000	
	Accounts payable		5,000
d.	Cash	5,000	
	Supplies		5,000

10. Which of the following is the correct journal entry for providing $20,000 worth of consulting services for cash? (p. 77)

	Accounts	Dr	Cr
a.	Service revenue	20,000	
	Cash		20,000
b.	Accounts receivable	20,000	
	Service revenue		20,000
c.	Accounts receivable	20,000	
	Cash		20,000
d.	Cash	20,000	
	Service revenue		20,000

Quick Exercise

2-1. Indicate whether a debit or credit is required to record an increase for each of these accounts. (p. 73)

Dr	Cash	Dr	Prepaid Rent
Dr	Owner, Withdrawals	Cr	Notes Payable
Dr	Salaries Expense	Dr	Land
Cr	Service Revenue	Dr	Utilities Expense

2-2. Write a brief explanation for the following transactions: (p. 70)

	Accounts	Debit	Credit
a.	Cash	10,000	
	Owner, capital		10,000

a. Owner investment of cash.

	Accounts	Debit	Credit
b.	Supplies	500	
	Accounts payable		500

b. Purchased supplies on account.

	Accounts	Debit	Credit
c.	Cash	3,000	
	Service revenue		3,000

c. Received cash for services performed.

	Accounts	Debit	Credit
d.	Accounts receivable	2,000	
	Service revenue		2,000

d. Performed services on account.

	Accounts	Debit	Credit
e.	Accounts payable	300	
	Cash		300

     e.   Paid cash on account.

2-3.   Identify the following as an asset, liability, owner's equity, revenue, or expense account. Also indicate the normal balance as a debit or a credit. (p. 69)

	Account	Normal Balance
a. Building	Asset	Debit
b. Accounts Payable	Liability	Credit
c. Cash	Asset	Debit
d. Accounts Receivable	Asset	Debit
e. Prepaid Insurance	Asset	Debit
f. Supplies	Asset	Debit
g. Utilities Expense	Expense	Debit
h. Owner, Capital	Owner's Equity	Credit
i. Owner, Withdrawals	Owner's Equity	Debit

2-4.   Journalize the transactions for the Reid Public Relations Company using these accounts: Cash, Accounts Receivable, Notes Receivable, Supplies, Prepaid Insurance, Accounts Payable, Notes Payable, Reid Capital, Reid Withdrawals, Service Revenue, Salaries Expense, Rent Expense, Insurance Expense. (pp. 74–80)

March 1   **J. Reid invested $25,000 cash to begin her public relations company.**

Date	Accounts	Debit	Credit
Mar 1	Cash	25,000	
	Reid capital		25,000

March 2 Paid $3,000 for March rent.

Date	Accounts	Debit	Credit
Mar 2	Rent expense	3,000	
	Cash		3,000

March 4 Purchased $825 of supplies on account.

Date	Accounts	Debit	Credit
Mar 4	Supplies	825	
	Accounts payable		825

March 5 Performed $10,000 of services for a client on account.

Date	Accounts	Debit	Credit
Mar 5	Accounts receivable	10,000	
	Service revenue		10,000

March 8 Paid salaries of $2,500.

Date	Accounts	Debit	Credit
Mar 8	Salaries expense	2,500	
	Cash		2,500

March 15 Paid the semiannual insurance premium of $1,800 for the period March 15 to September 15.

Date	Accounts	Debit	Credit
Mar 15	Prepaid insurance	1,800	
	Cash		1,800

March 20   Signed a bank note and borrowed $20,000 cash.

Date	Accounts	Debit	Credit
Mar 20	Cash	20,000	
	Notes payable		20,000

March 25   Received $10,000 from customers on account. (See March 5.)

Date	Accounts	Debit	Credit
Mar 25	Cash	10,000	
	Accounts receivable		10,000

2-5. Find the errors in the trial balance that follows and prepare a corrected trial balance. (p. 82)

COLEMAN COPY CENTER
Trial Balance
March 31, 2011

Account Title	Balance Debit	Balance Credit
Cash	$30,000	
Accounts receivable	2,000	
Supplies	600	
Land	50,000	
Accounts payable		$ 2,600
Note payable		35,000
Jo Coleman, capital		42,550
Jo Coleman, withdrawals	2,400	
Service revenue		9,300
Salary expense	2,500	
Rent expense	1,200	
Interest expense	500	
Utilities expense	250	
Total	$89,450	$89,450

Do It Yourself! Question 1 Solutions

Debit/Credit Transaction Analysis

Requirements

1. Journalize each of the following transactions. Key journal entries by transaction letter.

		Accounts Title	Debit	Credit
a.		Cash	800	
		Accounts receivable	1,500	
		Service revenue		2,300
		Performed services on account and for cash.		

		Accounts Title	Debit	Credit
b.		Supplies	200	
		Cash		200
		Purchased supplies.		

		Accounts Title	Debit	Credit
c.		Cash	2,000	
		Loans payable		2,000
		Took out a loan for cash.		

		Accounts Title	Debit	Credit
d.		Repair tools	3,000	
		Cash		3,000
		Purchased repair tools.		

		Accounts Title	Debit	Credit
e.		Interest expense	75	
		Rent expense	825	
		Salary expense	1,000	
		Cash		1,900
		Purchased repair tools.		

		Accounts Title	Debit	Credit
f.		Utilities expense	100	
		Accounts payable		100
		Received utility bill.		

	Accounts Title	Debit	Credit
g.	Accounts payable	500	
	Cash		500
	Paid on account.		

	Accounts Title	Debit	Credit
h.	Cash	1,100	
	Accounts receivable		1,100
	Received cash on account.		

	Accounts Title	Debit	Credit
i.	Ted Johnson, withdrawals	1,300	
	Cash		1,300
	Owner withdrawal.		

2. Open the following accounts, with the balances indicated, in the ledger of Ted's Repair Shop. Use the T-account format.

- **Assets**—Cash, $6,000; Accounts Receivable, $1,200; Supplies, no balance; Repair Tools, no balance
- **Liabilities**—Accounts Payable, $700; Loans Payable, no balance
- **Owner's Equity**—Ted Johnson, Capital, $6,500; Ted Johnson, Withdrawals, no balance
- **Revenues**—Service Revenue, no balance
- **Expenses**—(none have balances) Interest Expense, Rent Expense, Salary Expense, Utilities Expense

3. Post all transactions in Requirement 1 to the ledger.

ASSETS

Cash			
Bal	6,000		
a.	800		
		b.	200
c.	2,000		
		d.	3,000
		e.	1,900
		g.	500
h.	1,100		
		i.	1,300
Bal	3,000		

Accounts receivable			
Bal	1,200		
a.	1,500		
		h.	1,100
Bal	1,600		

Supplies			
b.	200		
Bal	200		

Repair tools			
d.	3,000		
Bal	3,000		

LIABILITIES

Accounts payable			
		Bal	700
		f.	100
g.	500		
		Bal	300

Loans payable			
		c.	2,000
		Bal	2,000

OWNER'S EQUITY

Ted Johnson, capital			
		Bal	6,500
		Bal	6,500

Ted Johnson, withdrawals			
i.	1,300		
Bal	1,300		

REVENUES

Service revenue			
		a.	2,300
		Bal	2,300

EXPENSES

Interest expense			
e.	75		
Bal	75		

Rent expense			
e.	825		
Bal	825		

Salary expense			
e.	1,000		
Bal	1,000		

Utilities expense			
f.	100		
Bal	100		

4. Prepare the trial balance of Ted's Repair Shop at September 30, 2011.

TED'S REPAIR SHOP
Trial Balance
September 30, 2011

Account Title	Debit	Credit
Cash	$ 3,000	
Accounts receivable	1,600	
Supplies	200	
Repair tools	3,000	
Accounts payable		$ 300
Loans payable		2,000
Ted Johnson, capital		6,500
Ted Johnson, withdrawals	1,300	
Service revenue		2,300
Interest expense	75	
Rent expense	825	
Salary expense	1,000	
Utilities expense	100	
Total	$11,100	$11,100

The Power of Practice

For more practice using the skills learned in this chapter, visit MyAccountingLab. There you will find algorithmically generated questions that are based on these Demo Docs and your main textbook's Review and Assess Your Progress sections.

Go to MyAccountingLab and follow these steps:

1. Direct your URL to www.myaccountinglab.com.
2. Log in using your name and password.
3. Click the MyAccountingLab link.
4. Click Study Plan in the left navigation bar.
5. From the table of contents, select Chapter 2, Recording Business Transactions.
6. Click a link to work tutorial exercises.

3 The Adjusting Process

WHAT YOU PROBABLY ALREADY KNOW

When you receive your car insurance bill, the period of coverage is always in the future. The bill may indicate that your payment must be received no later than 12:01 a.m. on the day after your current coverage expires to maintain your policy. Your payment is actually a *prepayment*, Prepaid Insurance. Prepaid Insurance is an asset because the insurance coverage is a future benefit. But every day that the car is protected by the insurance policy, part of the benefit is used up. When an asset is used up, it becomes an expense. Technically, every day you are incurring an expense of 1/365 of your annual premium. Assume that you paid $730 for an annual insurance policy in December 2010 for the period covering January 1–December 31, 2011. Each day beginning January 1, you are using up $2 ($730/365 days) of the prepaid insurance and incurring an expense or benefit of $2. At the end of January 1, what is your future benefit? It is $728 because you've benefited from the insurance coverage service you received that day. Technically, you have prepaid insurance with a reduced value of $728 and an expense of $2; the total $730 payment is split between the two accounts. Each day there is an additional $2 expense and $2 less future value in the asset account. Although it would be too cumbersome to "adjust" these accounts on a daily basis, businesses will make adjustments to their records whenever financial statements are prepared.

Learning Objectives/Success Keys

1 Differentiate between accrual and cash-basis accounting.

Consider this example: Assume that you have a pet care business; you care for pets in their owners' absence. You had a customer who went away the last week of December and returned on January 1. You charge $140 for the weekly service and are paid on January 1.

- If you are using **cash-basis accounting**, how much revenue would you record in December? In January? Because the cash is **received** in January, $140 would be recorded as revenue in January and none in December.

- If you are using **accrual-basis accounting**, how much revenue would you record in December? In January? Because the revenue is **earned** in December when you performed the services, that is the month you would record $140 of revenue and none in January.

Review Exhibit 3-1 (p. 127) in the main text to reinforce the difference between the two methods of accounting.

2 **Define and apply the accounting period concept, revenue, and matching principles.**

Consider this example: Assume that the Cool Clothing store opened for business on May 15 and pays employees on the 1st and 15th of each month. Employees who worked May 15–31 will be paid on June 1; no payroll payments are made in May. Does this mean that there should be no wage or salary expense for the month of May? Is it fair that Cool Clothing reports the revenue from selling clothing without the related payroll expense? Customers would not be able to view and purchase the clothing without employees to stock the shelves and check out the customers. It makes sense to **match** the payroll expense for the month of May with the sales revenue. *This is a basic concept that is crucial to understand. See Exhibit 3-2 (p. 128) in the main text for a sample business transaction illustrating the appropriate revenue recognition timing. Exhibit 3-3 (p. 129) illustrates the matching principle.*

3 **Explain why adjusting entries are needed.**

An unadjusted trial balance is unfinished because it omits various revenue and expense transactions for the period. The adjusting process is to add in these additional transactions so that we can obtain the correct balances in the accounts for our end of period financial statements.

4 **Journalize and post adjusting entries.**

The following two-step process will facilitate preparing the adjusting journal entries:

1. Determine whether a revenue account needs to be recorded (credited) or an expense account needs to be recorded (debited.)

2. The other account in the entry MUST be either an asset or a liability account.

If you have determined that revenue needs to be credited, then an asset account must be debited (increased) or a liability account must be debited (decreased). If you have determined that an expense needs to be debited, then an asset account must be credited (decreased) or a liability must be credited (increased). **WATCH OUT:** Cash will **NEVER** be included in an adjusting journal entry. *Review Exhibits 3-7 through 3-10 (pp. 140–143) carefully for a review of the adjusting journal entry process.*

5 **Explain the purpose of and prepare an adjusted trial balance.**

Business transactions are journalized and posted; then a trial balance is prepared. After the adjusting journal entries are journalized, they are posted and an adjusted trial balance is prepared. The list of updated account balances is prepared to determine that debits equal credits before preparing the financial statements. *Exhibit 3-10 (p. 143) shows the flow of information from the trial balance to the adjusted trial balance on the work sheet.*

6 **Prepare the financial statements from the adjusted trial balance.**

Follow the flow of data from the adjusted trial balance in Exhibit 3-10 (p. 143) to the financial statements in *Exhibits 3-11 through 3-13 (p. 145)*.

Demo Doc 1

Adjusting Entries for Accrual Accounting

Learning Objectives 1–6

Woodson Services August 31 (year-end) trial balance (before adjustments) is as follows:

WOODSON SERVICES
Trial Balance
Year Ended August 31, 2011

Account Title	Debit	Credit
Cash	$10,600	
Accounts receivable	14,000	
Supplies	1,200	
Prepaid rent	3,000	
Furniture	15,000	
Accumulated depreciation—Furniture		$ 4,500
Accounts payable		2,600
Salary payable		0
Daniel Woodson, capital		40,000
Daniel Woodson, withdrawals	11,500	
Service revenue		24,000
Rent expense	5,000	
Salary expense	10,000	
Depreciation expense	0	
Supplies expense	800	
Total	$71,100	$71,100

Requirements

1. Open the T-accounts and enter their unadjusted balances.

2. Journalize the following adjusting entries at August 31, 2011. Key the entries by letter.

   a. Employees are paid $200 every Friday for the previous five days of work. August 31, 2011, is a Wednesday.
   b. Depreciation on the furniture is $1,500 for the year.
   c. Supplies on hand at August 31, 2011, are $400.
   d. Six months of rent ($3,000) was paid in advance on July 1, 2011. No adjustment has been made to the Prepaid Rent account since then.
   e. Accrued revenue of $1,800 must be recorded.

3. Post the adjusting entries.

4. Write the trial balance on a work sheet, enter the adjusting entries, and prepare an adjusted trial balance.

5. Prepare the income statement, statement of owner's equity, and balance sheet for Woodson Services.

6. Would any of these entries be made under the cash basis of accounting? Why or why not?

7. What would be the problem if the adjusting entries in this question were not made?

Demo Doc 1 Solutions

Requirement 1

Open the T-accounts and enter their unadjusted balances.

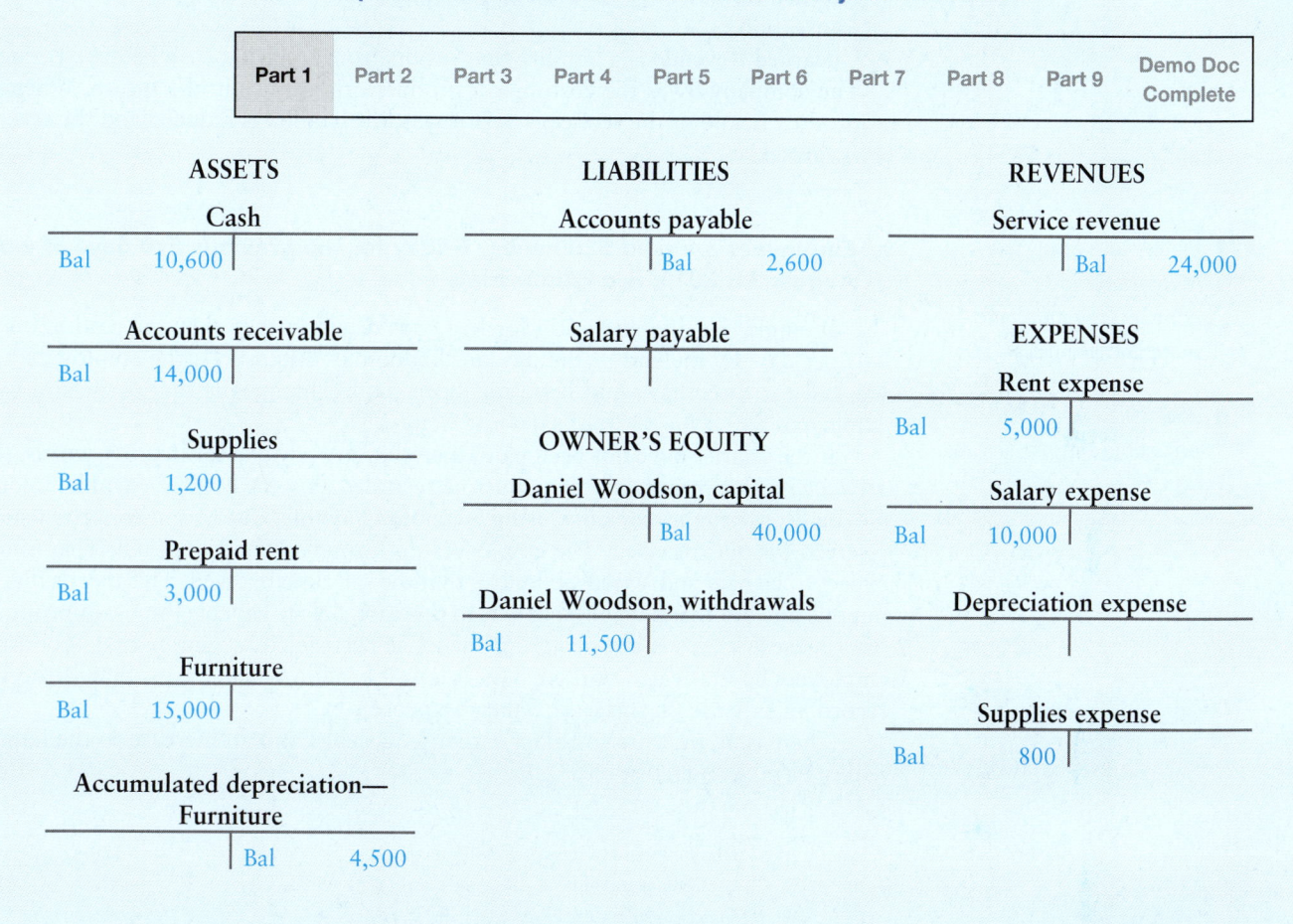

| Part 1 | Part 2 | Part 3 | Part 4 | Part 5 | Part 6 | Part 7 | Part 8 | Part 9 | Demo Doc Complete |

ASSETS

Cash
| Bal | 10,600 | |

Accounts receivable
| Bal | 14,000 | |

Supplies
| Bal | 1,200 | |

Prepaid rent
| Bal | 3,000 | |

Furniture
| Bal | 15,000 | |

Accumulated depreciation—Furniture
| | | Bal | 4,500 |

LIABILITIES

Accounts payable
| | | Bal | 2,600 |

Salary payable

OWNER'S EQUITY

Daniel Woodson, capital
| | | Bal | 40,000 |

Daniel Woodson, withdrawals
| Bal | 11,500 | |

REVENUES

Service revenue
| | | Bal | 24,000 |

EXPENSES

Rent expense
| Bal | 5,000 | |

Salary expense
| Bal | 10,000 | |

Depreciation expense

Supplies expense
| Bal | 800 | |

Requirement 2

Journalize the following adjusting entries at August 31, 2011. Key the entries by letter.

| Part 1 | Part 2 | Part 3 | Part 4 | Part 5 | Part 6 | Part 7 | Part 8 | Part 9 | Demo Doc Complete |

There are five general types of adjusting entries.

- **Prepaid expenses** are assets that are paid for in advance and will be used up in the future like supplies, prepaid rent (see transaction **d**), and insurance. As the asset is used up, the asset account is reduced and an expense is recorded.
- **Depreciation** is the allocation of the plant asset cost over its useful life (see transaction **b**). All plant assets used in the operation of the business, except land, are depreciated. The asset loses usefulness over time and is reduced. The cost of the plant asset is not reduced directly. Accumulated Depreciation, a contra asset account, is used to record the loss of asset usefulness. Depreciation expense matches the revenue generated from sales made possible from the use of these assets that are depreciated.

- **Accrued Expenses** are expenses the business has incurred but not yet paid. Common examples may be salaries (see transaction a) and utilities.
- **Accrued Revenue** is a revenue that has been earned but not collected in cash (see transaction e).
- **Unearned Revenue** is a liability that results from receiving cash before earning it. The company owes the customer a product or a service in the future. When the product is sold or the service is performed, the liability is reduced and the revenue is earned.

2 Define and apply the revenue period concept, revenue, and matching principles

4 Journalize and post adjusting entries

a. Employees are paid $200 every Friday for the previous five days of work. August 31, 2011, is a Wednesday.

If employees are paid $200 for five days of work, then they are paid $200/5 = $40 per day. By the end of the day on Wednesday, August 31, the employees have worked for three days and have not been paid. This means that Woodson owes employees $40 × 3 = $120 of salary at August 31.

If the salaries have not been paid, then they are pay*able* (or in other words, they are *owed*). This means that they must be recorded as some kind of payable account. Normally, we might consider using Accounts Payable, but this account is usually reserved for *bills* received. The employees do not send Woodson a bill. They simply expect to be paid and Woodson knows that the salaries are owed. This means that we put this into another payable account. In this case, Salary Payable is most appropriate.

Because salary is not owed until work is performed, we know that Woodson's employees have already worked. This is a *past* benefit, which means that we need to record an expense (in this case, Salary Expense).

There is an increase to Salary Expense (a debit) and an increase to the liability Salary Payable (a credit) of $120

a.	Salary expense (3 days × $200/5 days)	120	
	Salary payable		120
	To accrue salary expense.		

4 Journalize and post adjusting entries

b. Depreciation on the furniture is $1,500 for the year.

The entry to record depreciation expense is *always* the same. It is only the *number* (dollar amount) in the entry that changes. There is always an increase to Depreciation Expense (a debit) and an increase to the contra asset account of Accumulated Depreciation (a credit). Because we are given the depreciation expense of $1,500, we simply write the entry with that amount.

b.	Depreciation expense	1,500	
	Accumulated depreciation—Furniture		1,500
	To record depreciation expense.		

2 Define and apply the revenue period concept, revenue, and matching principles

4 Journalize and post adjusting entries

c. Supplies on hand at August 31, 2011, are $400.

Before adjustments, there is $1,200 in the Supplies account. If only $400 of supplies remains, then the other $800 must have been used ($1,200 − $400 = $800).

Supplies are an asset, a *future* benefit to Woodson. Once the supplies are used, they are a *past* benefit. This means that they are no longer assets, so the Supplies asset must be decreased by $800 (a credit). *Past* benefits are expenses, so Supplies Expense must be increased (a debit).

c.	Supplies expense ($1,200 − $400)	800	
	Supplies		800
	To record supplies used.		

2 Define and apply the revenue period concept, revenue, and matching principles

4 Journalize and post adjusting entries

d. Six months of rent ($3,000) was paid in advance on July 1, 2011. No adjustment has been made to the Prepaid Rent account since then.

Woodson prepaid $3,000 for six months of rent on July 1. This means that Woodson pays $3,000/6 = $500 a month for rent. At August 31, two months have passed since the prepayment, so two months of the prepayment have been used. The amount of rent used is 2 × $500 = $1,000.

When something is prepaid, it is a *future* benefit (an asset) because the business is now entitled to receive goods or services. Once those goods or services are received (in this case, once Woodson has occupied the building being rented), this becomes a *past* benefit and, therefore, an expense. This means that Rent Expense must be increased (a debit) and the Prepaid Rent (an asset) must be decreased (a credit).

d.	Rent expense ($3,000 × 2 months/6 months)	1,000	
	Prepaid rent		1,000
	To record insurance expense.		

2 Define and apply the revenue period concept, revenue, and matching principles

4 Journalize and post adjusting entries

e. Accrued revenue of $1,800 must be recorded.

Accrued revenue is another way of saying "accounts receivable" (or payment in the future). If accrued revenue is recorded, it means that accounts receivable are also recorded (that is, customers received goods or services from the business, but the business has not yet received the cash). The business is entitled to these receivables because the revenue has been earned.

Note that not all revenue is *accrued* revenue. This is *only* the revenue that is earned but not immediately received from the customer (that is, the accounts receivable). Revenues that are earned and received immediately in cash are *not* accrued revenues.

Service Revenue must be increased by $1,800 (a credit) and the Accounts Receivable asset must be increased by $1,800 (a debit).

e.	Accounts receivable	1,800	
	Service revenue		1,800
	To accrue revenue earned.		

Demo Doc 1 Solutions | Chapter 3

4 Journalize and post adjusting entries

Requirement 3

Post the adjusting entries.

| Part 1 | Part 2 | **Part 3** | Part 4 | Part 5 | Part 6 | Part 7 | Part 8 | Part 9 | Demo Doc Complete |

ASSETS

Cash
Bal 10,600	

Accounts receivable
14,000	
e. 1,800	
Bal 15,800	

Supplies
1,200	c. 800
Bal 400	

Prepaid rent
3,000	d. 1,000
Bal 2,000	

Furniture
Bal 15,000	

Accumulated depreciation—Furniture
	4,500
	b. 1,500
	Bal 6,000

LIABILITIES

Accounts payable
	Bal 2,600

Salary payable
	a. 120
	Bal 120

OWNER'S EQUITY

Daniel Woodson, capital
	Bal 40,000

Daniel Woodson, withdrawals
Bal 11,500	

REVENUES

Service revenue
	24,000
	e. 1,800
	Bal 25,800

EXPENSES

Rent expense
5,000	
d. 1,000	
Bal 6,000	

Salary expense
10,000	
a. 120	
Bal 10,120	

Depreciation expense
b. 1,500	
Bal 1,500	

Supplies expense
800	
c. 800	
Bal 1,600	

5 Explain the purpose of and prepare an adjusted trial balance

Requirement 4

Write the trial balance on a work sheet, enter the adjusting entries, and prepare an adjusted trial balance.

| Part 1 | Part 2 | Part 3 | **Part 4** | Part 5 | Part 6 | Part 7 | Part 8 | Part 9 | Demo Doc Complete |

WOODSON SERVICES
Preparation of Adjusted Trial Balance
Year Ended August 31, 2011

Account Title	Trial Balance Debit	Trial Balance Credit	Adjustments Debit	Adjustments Credit	Adjusted Trial Balance Debit	Adjusted Trial Balance Credit
Cash	$10,600				$10,600	
Accounts receivable	14,000		e. $1,800		15,800	
Supplies	1,200			c. 800	400	
Prepaid rent	3,000			d. 1,000	2,000	
Furniture	15,000				15,000	
Accumulated depreciation—Furniture		$ 4,500		b. 1,500		$ 6,000
Accounts payable		2,600				2,600
Salary payable		0		a. 120		120
Daniel Woodson, capital		40,000				40,000
Daniel Woodson, withdrawals	11,500				11,500	
Service revenue		24,000		e. 1,800		25,800
Rent expense	5,000		d. 1,000		6,000	
Salary expense	10,000		a. 120		10,120	
Depreciation expense	0		b. 1,500		1,500	
Supplies expense	800		c. 800		1,600	
Total	$71,100	$71,100	$5,220	$5,220	$74,520	$74,520

6 Prepare the financial statements from the adjusted trial balance

Requirement 5

Prepare the income statement, statement of owner's equity, and balance sheet for Woodson Services.

| Part 1 | Part 2 | Part 3 | Part 4 | **Part 5** | Part 6 | Part 7 | Part 8 | Part 9 | Demo Doc Complete |

WOODSON SERVICES
Income Statement
Year Ended August 31, 2011

Revenue:		
Service revenue		$25,800
Expenses:		
Salary expense	$10,120	
Rent expense	6,000	
Supplies expense	1,600	
Depreciation expense	1,500	
Total expenses		19,220
Net income		$ 6,580

| Part 1 | Part 2 | Part 3 | Part 4 | Part 5 | **Part 6** | Part 7 | Part 8 | Part 9 | Demo Doc Complete |

Remember, the one account that has not yet been updated is Daniel Woodson, Capital. The amount of $40,000 in this account is the amount from the beginning of the year (January 1). To update the account, we need to prepare the statement of owner's equity.

| Part 1 | Part 2 | Part 3 | Part 4 | Part 5 | Part 6 | **Part 7** | Part 8 | Part 9 | Demo Doc Complete |

WOODSON SERVICES
Statement of Owner's Equity
Year Ended August 31, 2011

Daniel Woodson, capital, September 1, 2010	$ 40,000
Add: Net income for year	6,580
	46,580
Less: Withdrawals by owner	(11,500)
Daniel Woodson, capital, August 31, 2011	$ 35,080

We use this updated Daniel Woodson, Capital amount on the balance sheet.

WOODSON SERVICES
Balance Sheet
August 31, 2011

Assets			Liabilities	
Cash		$10,600	Accounts payable	$ 2,600
Accounts receivable		15,800	Salary payable	120
Prepaid rent		400	Total liabilities	2,270
Supplies		2,000		
Furniture	$15,000			
Less: Accumulated			Equity	
depreciation	(6,000)	9,000	Daniel Woodson, capital	33,080
Total assets		$37,800	Total liabilities and equity	$37,800

1 Differentiate between accrual and cash-basis accounting

Requirement 6

Would any of these entries be made under the cash basis of accounting? Why or why not?

| Part 1 | Part 2 | Part 3 | Part 4 | Part 5 | Part 6 | Part 7 | **Part 8** | Part 9 | Demo Doc Complete |

Cash-basis accounting *only* records a journal entry when cash is involved. This means that there must be a line for cash in the journal entry in order for it to be recorded under the cash basis of accounting.

Because none of these adjusting entries deal with cash, none of them are relevant (that is, none of them would be recorded) under the cash basis of accounting.

On the other hand, accrual-basis accounting records revenue when it is earned and expenses when they are incurred. Revenue is earned when services are performed or goods are sold. Expenses are incurred when the service is received or the asset is used up. This method is in accordance with generally accepted accounting principles.

Requirement 7

What would be the problem if the adjusting entries in this question were not made?

| Part 1 | Part 2 | Part 3 | Part 4 | Part 5 | Part 6 | Part 7 | Part 8 | **Part 9** | Demo Doc Complete |

If these adjusting entries were not made, the financial statements of Woodson Services would not be accurate or up to date. Users reading Woodson's financial statements would not have the appropriate information to make financial decisions about the business.

| Part 1 | Part 2 | Part 3 | Part 4 | Part 5 | Part 6 | Part 7 | Part 8 | Part 9 | **Demo Doc Complete** |

Demo Doc 1 Solutions | Chapter 3

Quick Practice Questions

True/False

_____ 1. Revenue is recorded when it is earned, usually when a good or service has been delivered to the customer.

_____ 2. The time-period concept provides for periodic reporting at regular intervals.

_____ 3. An accounting year that ends on a date other than December 31 is called an interim year.

_____ 4. The revenue principle requires that a cash deposit for future construction be recorded as revenue.

_____ 5. Adjusting journal entries are made at the end of the period.

_____ 6. The income statement is the first financial statement that should be prepared.

_____ 7. Every adjusting journal entry affects one income statement account and one balance sheet account.

_____ 8. An accrual is an expense that is recorded after it is paid.

_____ 9. Accumulated Depreciation is a liability account.

_____ 10. Unearned Service Revenue appears on the income statement.

Multiple Choice

1. What items should be matched according to the matching principle?
   a. Debits with credits
   b. Assets with liabilities
   c. Expenses with revenues
   d. Accruals with prepaids

2. When is revenue recorded under the cash-basis system of accounting?
   a. When cash is received
   b. When revenue is earned
   c. When cash is received only if related expenses have been incurred
   d. In the period the related expenses are paid

3. What do adjusting entries properly measure?
   a. Net income for the period
   b. The assets, liabilities, and owner's equity on the balance sheet
   c. Both a and b
   d. Neither a nor b

4. Which of the following entities would most likely have an Unearned Revenue account?
   a. A local pizza store
   b. An accounting firm
   c. A department store
   d. A magazine publisher

5. Georgia Industries paid $48,000 for two years of insurance coverage on July 1, 2010. The company prepares financial statements on July 31, 2010. What is the amount of insurance expense on July 31?
   a. $48,000
   b. $ 2,000
   c. $24,000
   d. $46,000

6. Using the information from question 5, what is the adjusted balance in Prepaid Insurance on December 31, 2010?
   a. $36,000
   b. $24,000
   c. $12,000
   d. $38,000

7. *Sports Illustrated* receives $120,000 on September 1, 2011, for one years worth of magazine subscriptions for the year beginning September 1, 2011. What is the journal entry to record the prepaid subscriptions?

	Accounts	Debit	Credit
a.	Accounts receivable	120,000	
	Unearned subscription revenue		120,000
b.	Cash	120,000	
	Subscription revenue		120,000
c.	Cash	120,000	
	Unearned subscription revenue		120,000
d.	Accounts receivable	120,000	
	Subscription revenue		120,000

8. Which of the following accounts is depreciated?
   a. Building
   b. Land
   c. Supplies
   d. Prepaid Insurance

9. What is book value?
   a. The sum of all the depreciation recorded for the asset
   b. The cost of the depreciable asset
   c. The cost of the depreciable asset divided by the useful life
   d. The cost of the depreciable asset minus Accumulated Depreciation

10. Mason Company has a weekly payroll of $5,000. Wages are paid every Friday for the work performed Monday through Friday of that week. Assuming that the accounting period ends on a Tuesday, what amount of Wages Expense should be recorded on that date?
    a. $1,000
    b. $2,000
    c. $3,000
    d. $4,000

Quick Exercises

3-1. Central University received $840,000 in tuition from students in August 2010. The tuition is for the four-month semester, September–December 2010. What is the amount of revenue that should be recorded for the month of September?

   a. $_____ assuming the cash basis of accounting.
   b. $_____ assuming the accrual basis of accounting.

3-2. For each of the following situations, indicate if an expense or revenue should be recorded and the amount of the adjustment at the end of the month on January 31, 2011.

	Revenue or Expense	Adjustment Amount
a. $1,500 of supplies is purchased during January. On January 31, there is $800 of supplies remaining.	_____	_____
b. The five-day weekly payroll is $6,000. Employees worked the last two days of January and have not been paid by January 31.	_____	_____
c. $750 of Unearned Revenue has been earned in January.	_____	_____
d. Depreciation on equipment is $3,600 for the year.	_____	_____
e. Services of $2,300 were performed on January 31 and have not been recorded.	_____	_____

3-3. Journalize the required adjusting journal entries using the information in 3-2.

a.

Date	Accounts	Debit	Credit

b.

Date	Accounts	Debit	Credit

c.

Date	Accounts	Debit	Credit

d.

Date	Accounts	Debit	Credit

e.

Date	Accounts	Debit	Credit

3-4. Following is the trial balance for Coleman Copy Center:

COLEMAN COPY CENTER
Trial Balance
March 31, 2011

Account Title	Debit	Credit
Cash	$30,000	
Accounts receivable	2,000	
Supplies	600	
Land	50,000	
Accounts payable		$ 2,600
Note payable		35,000
Jo Coleman, capital		42,550
Jo Coleman, withdrawals	2,400	
Service revenue		9,300
Salary expense	2,500	
Rent expense	1,200	
Interest expense	500	
Utilities expense	250	
Total	$89,450	$89,450

Prepare (a) an income statement and (b) a statement of owner's equity for the month ending March 31, 2011.

COLEMAN COPY CENTER
Income Statement
Month Ended March 31, 2011

COLEMAN COPY CENTER
Statement of Owner's Equity
Month Ended March 31, 2011

3-5. Using the trial balance for Coleman Copy Center in 3-4, prepare the balance sheet at March 31, 2011.

COLEMAN COPY CENTER
Balance Sheet
March 31, 2011

Do It Yourself! Question 1

Angela's Business Services has the following balances on its December 31 (year-end) trial balance (before adjustments):

ANGELA'S BUSINESS SERVICES
Trial Balance
December 31, 2011

Account Title	Debit	Credit
Cash	$ 40,400	
Prepaid insurance	4,800	
Supplies	13,000	
Office equipment	25,000	
Accumulated depreciation—Equipment		$ 7,500
Accounts payable		5,300
Salary payable		
Unearned revenue		6,800
Angela Waring, capital		60,000
Angela Waring, withdrawals	8,000	
Service revenue		80,000
Insurance expense	13,200	
Salary expense	45,000	
Depreciation expense		
Supplies expense	10,200	
Total	$159,600	$159,600

Requirements

1. Open the T-accounts and enter the unadjusted balances.

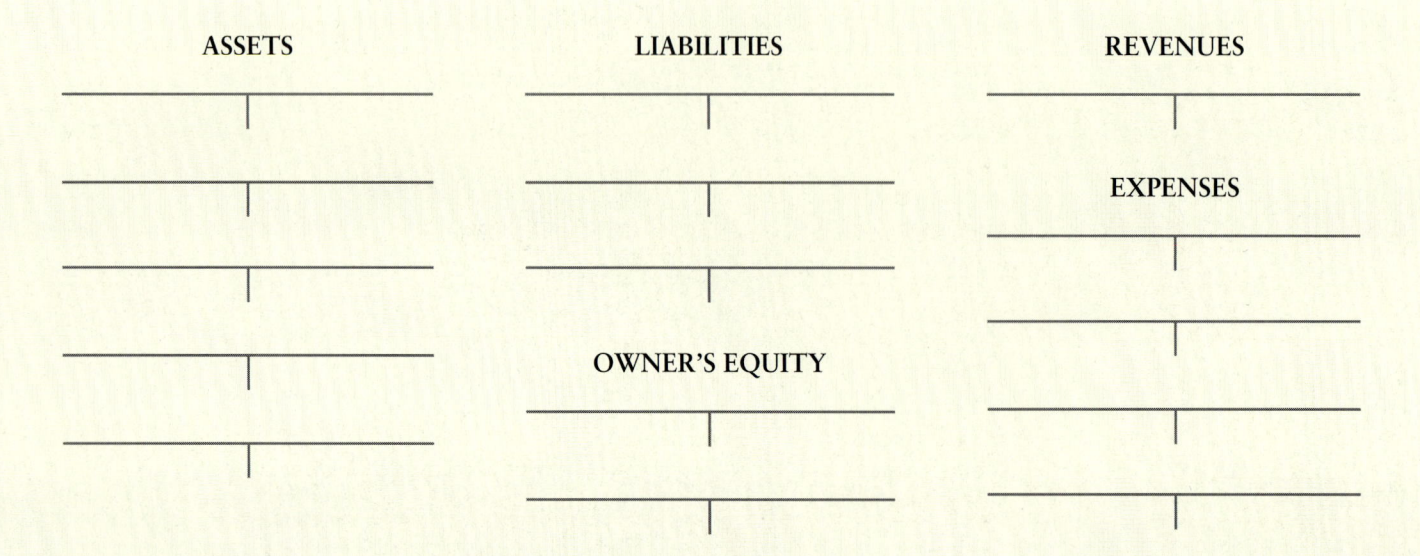

ASSETS　　　　　LIABILITIES　　　　　REVENUES

　　　　　　　　　　　　　　　　　　EXPENSES

　　　　　　　　OWNER'S EQUITY

2. Journalize the following adjusting entries at December 31, 2011. Key the entries by letter.

2 Define and apply the revenue period concept, revenue, and matching principles

4 Journalize and post adjusting entries

a. **Only $1,500 of the unearned revenue remains unearned.**

Date	Accounts	Debit	Credit

b. **Depreciation on the office equipment is $2,500 for the year.**

Date	Accounts	Debit	Credit

c. **Employees earned salaries of $4,000 that have not been paid.**

Date	Accounts	Debit	Credit

d. **$5,100 of supplies have been used.**

Date	Accounts	Debit	Credit

Do It Yourself! Question 1 | Chapter 3

e. Four months of insurance ($4,800) was paid in advance on December 1, 2011. No adjustment has been made to the Prepaid Insurance account since then.

Date	Accounts	Debit	Credit

5 Explain the purpose of and prepare an adjusted trial balance

3. Post the adjusting entries.

ASSETS

Cash

Prepaid insurance

Supplies

Office equipment

Accumulated depreciation—
Equipment

LIABILITIES

Accounts payable

Salary payable

Unearned revenue

OWNER'S EQUITY

Angela Waring, capital

Angela Waring, withdrawals

REVENUES

Service revenue

EXPENSES

Insurance expense

Salary expense

Depreciation expense

Supplies expense

82   Chapter 3 | Do It Yourself! Question 1

5 Explain the purpose of and prepare an adjusted trial balance

4. Write the trial balance on a work sheet, enter the adjusting entries, and prepare an adjusted trial balance.

6 Prepare the financial statements from the adjusted trial balance

5. Prepare the income statement, statement of owner's equity, and balance sheet for Angela's Business Services.

Do It Yourself! Question 1 | Chapter 3 **83**

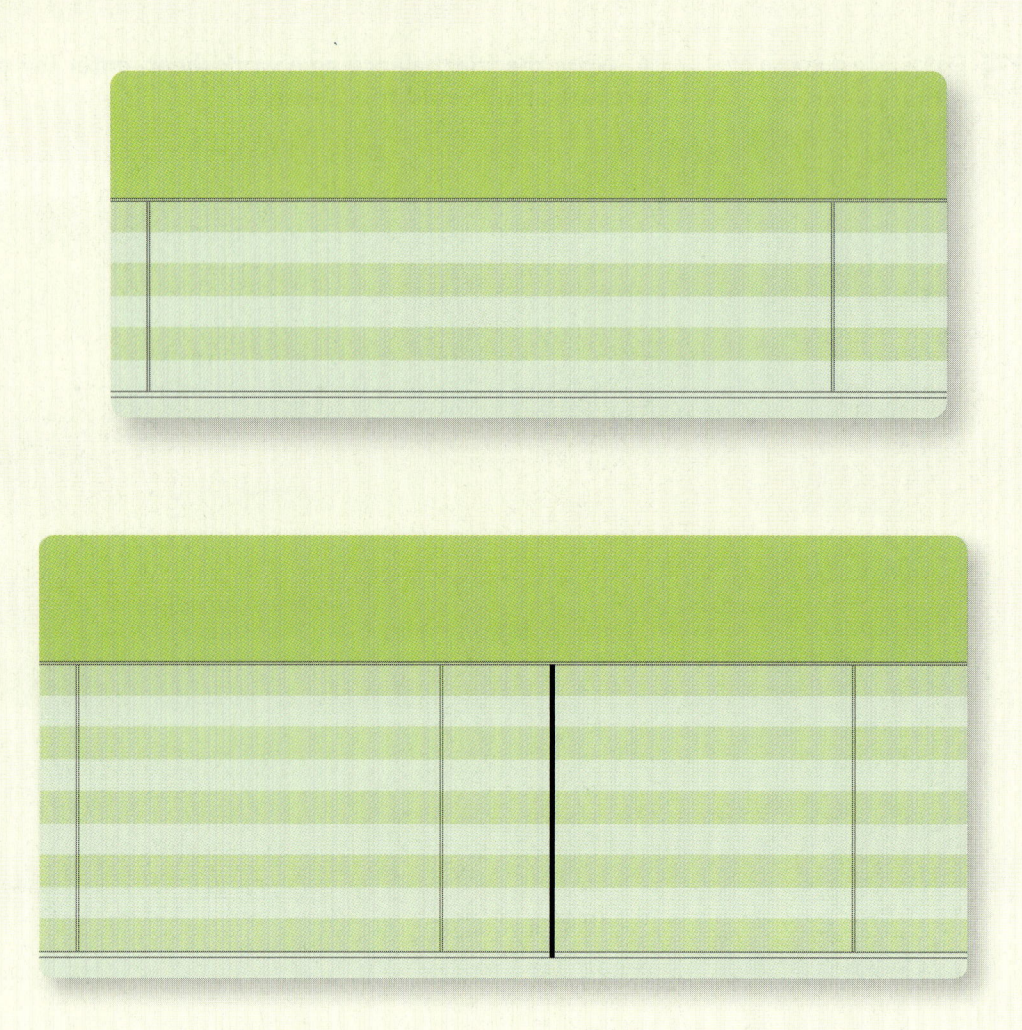

Chapter 3 | Do It Yourself! Question 1

Do It Yourself! Question 2

4 Journalize and post adjusting entries

Everly Industries is preparing its financial statements for the year ended March 31, 2011. Three accounting issues have been discovered.

Requirement

1. Make the necessary adjusting entry for each situation.

a. Employees work five days a week (Monday through Friday) and are paid $7,500 for the previous week of work each Friday. March 31, 2011, falls on a Thursday.

Date	Accounts	Debit	Credit

b. The T-account for supplies shows an unadjusted balance of $1,000. However, there is only $350 of supplies on hand at March 31, 2011.

Date	Accounts	Debit	Credit

c. The company has forgotten to record four months of interest expense ($80 per month) that has been incurred but not yet paid.

Date	Accounts	Debit	Credit

Quick Practice Solutions

True/False

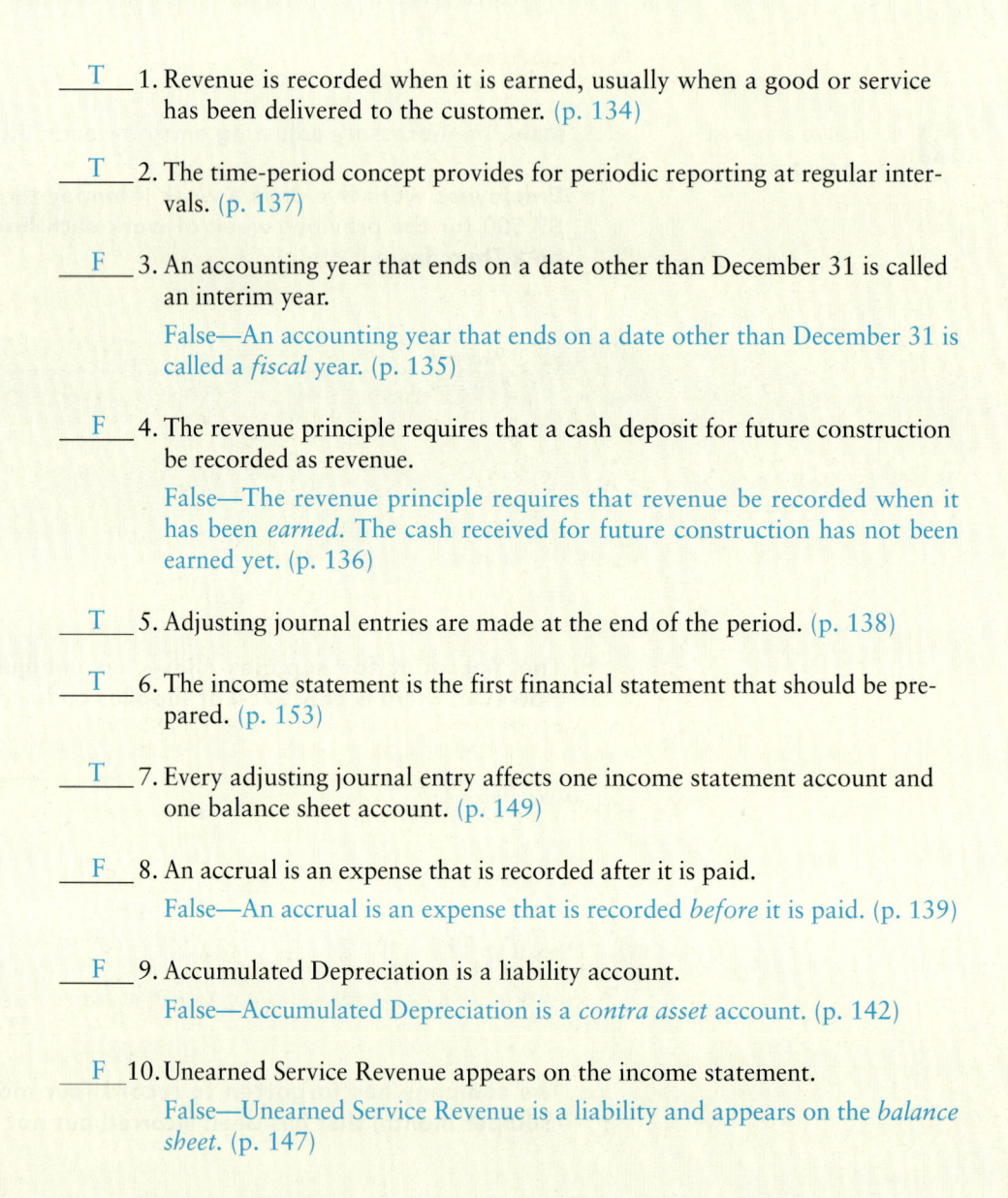

__T__ 1. Revenue is recorded when it is earned, usually when a good or service has been delivered to the customer. (p. 134)

__T__ 2. The time-period concept provides for periodic reporting at regular intervals. (p. 137)

__F__ 3. An accounting year that ends on a date other than December 31 is called an interim year.
False—An accounting year that ends on a date other than December 31 is called a *fiscal* year. (p. 135)

__F__ 4. The revenue principle requires that a cash deposit for future construction be recorded as revenue.
False—The revenue principle requires that revenue be recorded when it has been *earned*. The cash received for future construction has not been earned yet. (p. 136)

__T__ 5. Adjusting journal entries are made at the end of the period. (p. 138)

__T__ 6. The income statement is the first financial statement that should be prepared. (p. 153)

__T__ 7. Every adjusting journal entry affects one income statement account and one balance sheet account. (p. 149)

__F__ 8. An accrual is an expense that is recorded after it is paid.
False—An accrual is an expense that is recorded *before* it is paid. (p. 139)

__F__ 9. Accumulated Depreciation is a liability account.
False—Accumulated Depreciation is a *contra asset* account. (p. 142)

__F__ 10. Unearned Service Revenue appears on the income statement.
False—Unearned Service Revenue is a liability and appears on the *balance sheet*. (p. 147)

Multiple Choice

1. What items should be matched according to the matching principle? (p. 137)
   a. Debits with credits
   b. Assets with liabilities
   c. Expenses with revenues
   d. Accruals with prepaids

2. When is revenue recorded under the cash-basis system of accounting? (p. 134)
   a. When cash is received
   b. When revenue is earned
   c. When cash is received only if related expenses have been incurred
   d. In the period the related expenses are paid

3. What do adjusting entries properly measure? (p. 138)
   a. Net income for the period
   b. The assets, liabilities, and owner's equity on the balance sheet
   c. Both a and b
   d. Neither a nor b

4. Which of the following entities would most likely have an Unearned Revenue account? (p. 147)
   a. A local pizza store
   b. An accounting firm
   c. A department store
   d. A magazine publisher

5. Georgia Industries paid $48,000 for two years of insurance coverage on July 1, 2010. The company prepares financial statements on July 31, 2010. What is the amount of insurance expense on July 31? (p. 140)
   a. $48,000
   b. $ 2,000
   c. $24,000
   d. $46,000

6. Using the information from question 5, what is the adjusted balance in Prepaid Insurance on December 31, 2010? (p. 142)
   a. $36,000
   b. $24,000
   c. $12,000
   d. $38,000

7. *Sports Illustrated* receives $120,000 on September 1, 2011, for one year's worth of magazine subscriptions for the year beginning September 1, 2011. What is the journal entry to record the prepaid subscriptions? (p. 140)

	Accounts	Debit	Credit
a.	Accounts receivable	120,000	
	Unearned subscription revenue		120,000
b.	Cash	120,000	
	Subscription revenue		120,000
c.	Cash	120,000	
	Unearned subscription revenue		120,000
d.	Accounts receivable	120,000	
	Subscription revenue		120,000

Quick Practice Solutions | Chapter 3

8. Which of the following accounts is depreciated? (p. 142)
   a. Building
   b. Land
   c. Supplies
   d. Prepaid Insurance

9. What is book value? (p. 143)
   a. The sum of all the depreciation recorded for the asset
   b. The cost of the depreciable asset
   c. The cost of the depreciable asset divided by the useful life
   d. The cost of the depreciable asset minus Accumulated Depreciation

10. Mason Company has a weekly payroll of $5,000. Wages are paid every Friday for the work performed Monday through Friday of that week. Assuming that the accounting period ends on a Tuesday, what amount of Wages Expense should be recorded on that date? (p. 145)
    a. $1,000
    b. $2,000
    c. $3,000
    d. $4,000

Quick Exercise

3-1. Central University received $840,000 in tuition from students in August 2010. The tuition is for the four-month semester, September–December 2010. What is the amount of revenue that should be recorded for the month of September? (p. 146)

   a. $ 840,000 assuming the cash basis of accounting.
   b. $ 210,000 assuming the accrual basis of accounting.

3-2. For each of the following situations, indicate if an expense or revenue needs to be recorded and the amount of the adjustment at the end of the month on January 31, 2011. (p. 139)

	Revenue or Expense	Adjustment Amount
1. $1,500 of supplies is purchased during January. On January 31 $800 of supplies remain.	Expense	$700
2. The five-day weekly payroll is $6,000. Employees worked the last two days of January and have not been paid by January 31.	Expense	$2,400
3. $750 of Unearned Revenue has been earned in January.	Revenue	$750
4. Depreciation on equipment is $3,600 for the year.	Expense	$300
5. Services of $2,300 were performed on January 31 and have not been recorded.	Revenue	$2,300

3-3. Journalize the required adjusting journal entries using the information in 3-2. (p. 139)

a.

Date	Accounts	Debit	Credit
1/31/11	Supplies expense	700	
	Supplies		700

b.

Date	Accounts	Debit	Credit
1/31/11	Salary expense	2,400	
	Salary payable		2,400

c.

Date	Accounts	Debit	Credit
1/31/11	Unearned revenue	750	
	Service revenue		750

d.

Date	Accounts	Debit	Credit
1/31/11	Depreciation—Equipment	300	
	Accumulated depreciation—Equipment		300

e.

Date	Accounts	Debit	Credit
1/31/11	Accounts receivable	2,300	
	Service revenue		2,300

3-4. Following is the trial balance for Coleman Copy Center:

COLEMAN COPY CENTER
Trial Balance
March 31, 2011

Account Title	Balance Debit	Balance Credit
Cash	$30,000	
Accounts receivable	2,000	
Supplies	600	
Land	50,000	
Accounts payable		$ 2,600
Note payable		35,000
Jo Coleman, capital		42,550
Jo Coleman, withdrawals	2,400	
Service revenue		9,300
Salary expense	2,500	
Rent expense	1,200	
Interest expense	500	
Utilities expense	250	
Total	$89,450	$89,450

Prepare (a) an income statement and (b) a statement of owner's equity for the month ending March 31, 2011. (p. 153)

a.

COLEMAN COPY CENTER
Income Statement
Month Ended March 31, 2011

Revenue:		
Service revenue		$9,300
Expenses:		
Salary expense	2,500	
Rent expense	1,200	
Interest expense	500	
Utilities expense	250	
Total expenses	4,450	
Net income		$4,850

b.

COLEMAN COPY CENTER
Statement of Owner's Equity
Month Ended March 31, 2011

Jo Coleman, capital March 1, 2011	$42,550
Add: Net income	4,850
	47,400
Less: Withdrawals	(2,400)
Jo Coleman, capital, March 31, 2011	$45,000

3-5. Using the trial balance for Coleman Copy Center in 3-4, prepare the balance sheet at March 31, 2011. (p. 154)

COLEMAN COPY CENTER
Balance Sheet
March 31, 2011

Assets		Liabilities	
Cash	$30,000	Accounts payable	$ 2,600
Accounts receivable	2,000	Note payable	35,000
Supplies	600	Total liabilities	37,600
Land	50,000		
		Owner's Equity	
		Jo Coleman, capital	45,000
		Total liabilities and	
Total assets	$82,600	owner's equity	$82,600

Do It Yourself! Question 1 Solutions

Requirements

1. Open the ledger accounts with the unadjusted balances.

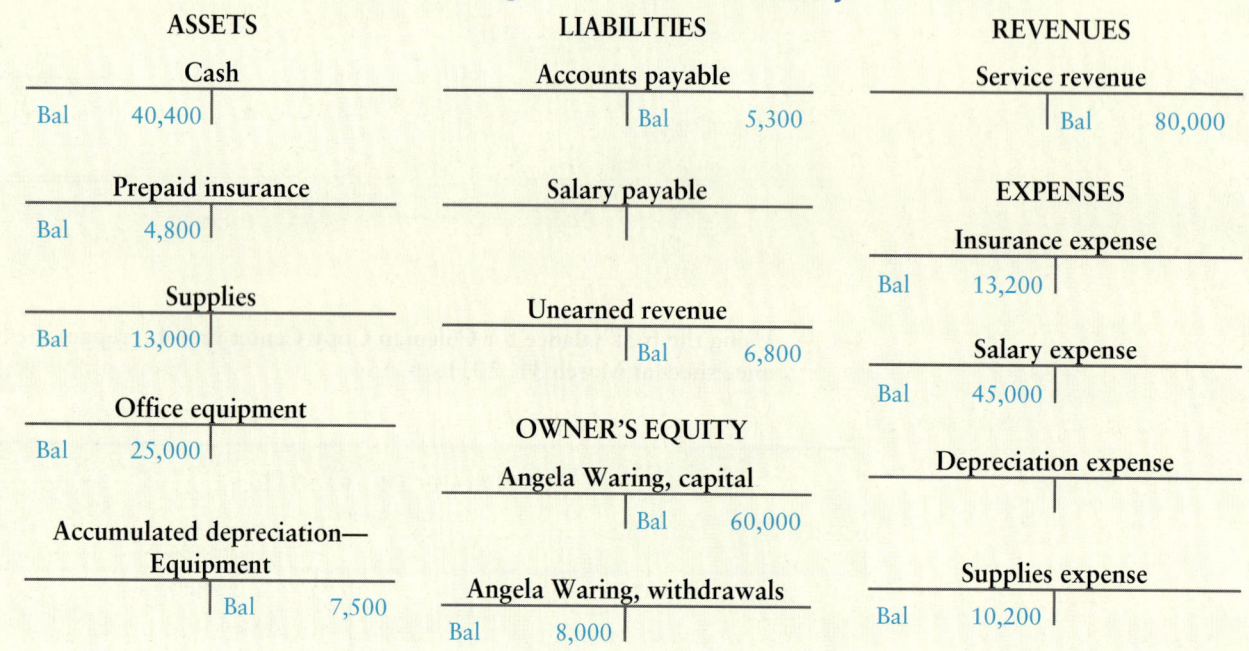

ASSETS	LIABILITIES	REVENUES
Cash	**Accounts payable**	**Service revenue**
Bal 40,400	Bal 5,300	Bal 80,000
Prepaid insurance	**Salary payable**	**EXPENSES**
Bal 4,800		**Insurance expense**
Supplies	**Unearned revenue**	Bal 13,200
Bal 13,000	Bal 6,800	**Salary expense**
Office equipment	**OWNER'S EQUITY**	Bal 45,000
Bal 25,000	**Angela Waring, capital**	**Depreciation expense**
Accumulated depreciation— Equipment	Bal 60,000	
	Angela Waring, withdrawals	**Supplies expense**
Bal 7,500	Bal 8,000	Bal 10,200

2. Journalize the following adjusting entries at December 31, 2011. Key the entries by letter.

a. Only $1,500 of the unearned revenue remains unearned.

a.	Unearned revenue ($6,800 − $1,500)	5,300	
	Service revenue		5,300
	To record service revenue collected in advance.		

b. Depreciation on the office equipment is $2,500 for the year.

b.	Depreciation expense	2,500	
	Accumulated depreciation—Equipment		2,500
	To record depreciation expense.		

c. Employees earned salaries of $4,000 that have not been paid.

c.	Salary expense	4,000	
	Salary payable		4,000
	To accrue salary expense.		

d. $5,100 of supplies have been used.

d.	Supplies expense	5,100	
	Supplies		5,100
	To record supplies used.		

e. Four months of insurance ($4,800) was paid in advance on December 1, 2011. No adjustment has been made to the Prepaid Insurance account since.

e.	Insurance expense ($4,800 × 1 month/4 months)	1,200	
	Prepaid insurance		1,200
	To record insurance expense.		

3. Post the adjusting entries.

ASSETS

Cash

Bal	40,400		

Prepaid insurance

	4,800	e.	1,200
Bal	3,600		

Supplies

	13,000	d.	5,100
Bal	7,900		

Office equipment

Bal	25,000		

Accumulated depreciation—Equipment

			7,500
		b.	2,500
		Bal	10,000

LIABILITIES

Accounts payable

		Bal	5,300

Salary payable

		c.	4,000
		Bal	4,000

Unearned revenue

Bal	5,300		6,800
		Bal	1,500

OWNER'S EQUITY

Angela Waring, capital

		Bal	60,000

Angela Waring, withdrawals

Bal	8,000		

REVENUES

Service revenue

			80,000
		a.	5,300
		Bal	85,300

EXPENSES

Insurance expense

	13,200		
e.	1,200		
Bal	14,400		

Salary expense

	45,000		
c.	4,000		
Bal	49,000		

Depreciation expense

b.	2,500		
Bal	2,500		

Supplies expense

	10,200		
d.	5,100		
Bal	15,300		

4. Write the trial balance on a work sheet, enter the adjusting entries, and prepare an adjusted trial balance.

ANGELA'S BUSINESS SERVICES
Preparation of Adjusted Trial Balance
Year Ended December 31, 2011

Account Title	Trial Balance Debit	Trial Balance Credit	Adjustments Debit	Adjustments Credit	Adjusted Trial Balance Debit	Adjusted Trial Balance Credit
Cash	$ 40,400				$ 40,400	
Prepaid insurance	4,800			(e) $ 1,200	3,600	
Supplies	13,000			(d) 5,100	7,900	
Office equipment	25,000				25,000	
Accumulated depreciation—Equipment		$ 7,500		(b) 2,500		$ 10,000
Accounts payable		5,300				5,300
Salary payable				(c) 4,000		4,000
Unearned revenue		6,800	(a) $ 5,300			1,500
Angela Waring, capital		60,000				60,000
Angela Waring, withdrawals	8,000				8,000	
Service revenue		80,000		(a) 5,300		85,300
Insurance expense	13,200		(e) 1,200		14,400	
Salary expense	45,000		(c) 4,000		49,000	
Depreciation expense			(b) 2,500		2,500	
Supplies expense	10,200		(d) 5,100		15,300	
Total	$159,600	$159,600	$18,100	$18,100	$166,100	$166,100

5. Prepare the income statement, statement of owner's equity, and balance sheet for Angela's Business Services.

ANGELA'S BUSINESS SERVICES
Income Statement
Year Ended December 31, 2011

Revenue:		
Service revenue		$85,300
Expenses:		
Salary expense	$49,000	
Supplies expense	15,300	
Insurance expense	14,400	
Depreciation expense	2,500	
Total expenses		81,200
Net income		$ 4,100

ANGELA'S BUSINESS SERVICES
Statement of Owner's Equity
Year Ended December 31, 2011

Angela Waring, capital, January 1, 2011	$60,000
Add: Net income for year	4,100
	64,100
Less: Withdrawals by owner	(8,000)
Angela Waring, capital, December 31, 2011	$56,100

ANGELA'S BUSINESS SERVICES
Balance Sheet
December 31, 2011

Assets			Liabilities	
Cash		$40,400	Accounts payable	$ 5,300
Prepaid insurance		3,600	Salary payable	4,000
Supplies		7,900	Unearned revenue	1,500
Office equipment	$25,000		Total liabilities	10,800
Less: Accumulated			**Equity**	
depreciation	(10,000)	15,000	Angela Waring, capital	56,100
Total assets		$66,900	Total liabilities and equity	$66,900

Do It Yourself! Question 2 Solutions

Requirement

1. Make the necessary adjusting entry for each situation.

a. Employees work five days a week (Monday through Friday) and are paid $7,500 for the previous week of work each Friday. March 31, 2011, falls on a Thursday.

$7,500/5 days = $1,500 salary per day of work

Monday through Thursday = 4 days of work

4 × $1,500 = $6,000

Salary expense ($7,500 × 4 days/5 days)	6,000	
Salary payable		6,000
To accrue salary expense.		

b. The T-account for supplies shows an unadjusted balance of $1,000. However, there is only $350 of supplies on hand at March 31, 2011.

$1,000 − $350 = $650 of supplies used

Supplies expense ($1,000 − $350)	650	
Supplies		650
To record supplies used.		

c. The company has forgotten to record four months of interest expense ($80 per month) that has been incurred but not yet paid.

4 months × $80 per month = $320

Interest expense (4 months × $80)	320	
Interest payable		320
To accrue interest expense.		

The Power of Practice

For more practice using the skills learned in this chapter, visit MyAccountingLab. There you will find algorithmically generated questions that are based on these Demo Docs and your main textbook's Review and Assess Your Progress sections.

Go to MyAccountingLab and follow these steps:

1. Direct your URL to www.myaccountinglab.com.
2. Log in using your name and password.
3. Click the MyAccountingLab link.
4. Click Study Plan in the left navigation bar.
5. From the table of contents, select Chapter 3, The Adjusting Process.
6. Click a link to work tutorial exercises.

4 Completing the Accounting Cycle

What You Probably Already Know

If you work, you have probably noticed that your pay stub includes year-to-date earnings. When a new year begins, the year-to-date totals from last year are gone and the year-to-date earnings include only the current year. Last year's records are not erased or unimportant. Earnings from last year are reported for each employee on a W-2 form, Wage and Tax Statement. This form is sent to employees in the new year to attach to their income tax return. The year-to-date earnings are zeroed out to be ready to accumulate earnings in the new year. The same thing happens in a business. At the end of the accounting year, the earnings and revenue accounts are zeroed out to get ready for the new year.

Learning Objectives/Success Keys

1 Prepare an accounting work sheet.

A **work sheet** is a multicolumned document or spreadsheet that is used to summarize accounting data at the end of the period. In Chapter 3, Exhibit 3-10 (p. 143) illustrated the first of three columns of data in the work sheet: the trial balance, adjusting journal entries, and the adjusted trial balance. The adjusted balances are brought forward to one of the last two sets of columns, either the income statement columns or the balance sheet columns. The income statement debit column includes expenses and the credit column includes revenue accounts. The balance sheet debit column includes assets and withdrawals; the credit column includes liabilities, owner's equity, and accumulated depreciation accounts. *Review Exhibits 4-2 through 4-6 (p. 208) to understand the flow of steps in preparing the work sheet.*

2 Use the work sheet to prepare financial statements.

The work sheet is a working document. It helps to make the adjusting entries, prepare financial statements, and close out the temporary accounts. *Review Exhibits 4-2 through 4-7 (p. 208 and 214) to understand the flow of information from the work sheet to the financial statements.*

3 Close the revenue, expense, and withdrawal accounts.

The revenue, expense, and withdrawal accounts are temporary accounts; the account balances are zeroed (closed) out at the end of the year to get ready for journalizing transactions in the new year. Income Summary is a temporary account that is used only for this process. The closing process also updates the ending Capital account balance for the net income or net loss and withdrawals during the year. *Review Exhibits 4-9 and 4-10 (pp. 217–218) to enhance your understanding of the closing process.*

4 Prepare the postclosing trial balance.

Once the revenues, expenses, and withdrawals are closed, one more postclosing trial balance can be prepared to list the accounts and their adjusted balances after closing. *See Exhibit 4-11 (p. 219) in the text for an example of a postclosing trial balance.*

5 Classify assets and liabilities as current or long-term.

It's important to remember that a liability (such as a mortgage or car loan) may be split between current and long-term liability classification on the balance sheet, such as when an installment on a loan is due within one year, but future installments are due thereafter.

Refer to Exhibits 4-12 or 4-13 (p. 221–222) to review the classified balance sheet.

6 Use the current ratio and the debt ratio to evaluate a company.

The current ratio is a key liquidity measure. It indicates the amount of current assets that is available for each dollar of current liabilities. A higher ratio is usually considered to be preferable.

The debt ratio is an indicator of the entity's ability to pay its debt. It measures the portion of assets that is financed with debt.

Demo Doc 1

Closing Entries

Learning Objectives 1–5

This question continues on from the Woodson Services problem given in Demo Doc 1 of Chapter 3 (see p. 69 of your Study Guide).

Use the data from Woodson Services adjusted trial balance at August 31, 2011:

WOODSON SERVICES
Adjusted Trial Balance
August 31, 2011

Account Title	Adjusted Trial Balance Debit	Adjusted Trial Balance Credit
Cash	$10,600	
Accounts receivable	15,800	
Supplies	400	
Prepaid rent	2,000	
Furniture	15,000	
Accumulated depreciation—Furniture		$ 6,000
Accounts payable		2,600
Salary payable		120
Daniel Woodson, capital		40,000
Daniel Woodson, withdrawals	11,500	
Service revenue		25,800
Rent expense	6,000	
Salary expense	10,120	
Depreciation expense	1,500	
Supplies expense	1,600	
Total	$74,520	$74,520

Requirements

1. Prepare Woodson's accounting work sheet showing the adjusted trial balance, the income statement accounts, and the balance sheet accounts.

2. Journalize and post the closing entries.

3. Prepare the postclosing trial balance.

4. Which assets are current? Which assets are long-term?

5. Which liabilities are current? Which liabilities are long-term?

6. Calculate Woodson's current and debt ratios.

Demo Doc 1 Solutions

Requirement 1

Prepare Woodson's accounting work sheet showing the adjusted trial balance, the income statement accounts, and the balance sheet accounts.

| Part 1 | Part 2 | Part 3 | Part 4 | Part 5 | Part 6 | Part 7 | Part 8 | Part 9 | Demo Doc Complete |

1 Prepare an accounting work sheet

2 Use the work sheet

The revenues and expenses belong on the income statement. All other accounts listed belong on the balance sheet.

Net income is calculated by subtracting the expenses from the revenues:

$$\$25,800 - \$19,220 = \$6,580$$

Net income is added to the credit side of the balance sheet to make total debits equal total credits. This is because net income increases the Capital account (as seen in Requirement 2 of this question, in which the closing entries are journalized).

WOODSON SERVICES
Work Sheet
August 31, 2011

Account Title	Adjusted Trial Balance Debit	Adjusted Trial Balance Credit	Income Statement Debit	Income Statement Credit	Balance Sheet Debit	Balance Sheet Credit
Cash	$10,600				$10,600	
Accounts receivable	15,800				15,800	
Supplies	400				400	
Prepaid rent	2,000				2,000	
Furniture	15,000				15,000	
Accumulated depreciation—Furniture		$ 6,000				$ 6,000
Accounts payable		2,600				2,600
Salary payable		120				120
Daniel Woodson, capital		40,000				40,000
Daniel Woodson, withdrawals	11,500				11,500	
Service revenue		25,800		$25,800		
Rent expense	6,000		$ 6,000			
Salary expense	10,120		10,120			
Depreciation expense	1,500		1,500			
Supplies expense	1,600		1,600			
Total	$74,520	$74,520	$19,220	$25,800	$55,300	$48,720
Net income			$ 6,580			$ 6,580
			$25,800	$25,800	$55,300	$55,300

102 Chapter 4 | Demo Doc 1 Solutions

3 Close the revenue, expense, and withdrawal accounts

Requirement 2

Journalize and post the closing entries.

| Part 1 | **Part 2** | Part 3 | Part 4 | Part 5 | Part 6 | Part 7 | Part 8 | Part 9 | Demo Doc Complete |

There are two reasons to prepare closing entries. First, we need to clear out the revenue, expense, and withdrawal accounts to a zero balance. This is because they need to begin the next year empty. Second, we need to update the Capital account.

In Chapter 1, we discussed the formula to calculate the balance in the Capital account:

> Beginning capital amount
> + Owner investments
> = Adjusted capital amount
> + Net income (or – net loss)
> – Owner withdrawals
> = Ending capital amount

	Capital
	Beginning capital amount
	Investments
	Adjusted capital amount
	Net income
Withdrawals	
	Ending capital amount

This formula is the key to preparing the closing entries. We will use this formula, but we will do it *inside* the Capital account T-account.

What is in the Capital account right now? From the trial balance, we can see that there is a balance of $40,000. But where did that balance come from? It is the adjusted capital amount. In this particular problem, because there are no investments (as seen from the problem in Chapter 3), it is also the ending balance from last period.

So we have an advantage: The first component of the formula (adjusted capital amount) is already in the T-account.

The next component is net income. This is *not* already in the Capital account. We do not have a T-account with net income in it, but we can *create* one.

We will create a new T-account called Income Summary. We will place in there all the components of net income and come out with the net income number at the bottom. From Chapter 1, remember the formula for net income:

> Revenues – Expenses = Net income

This means that we need to get all of the revenues and expenses into the Income Summary account.

Let's look at the Service Revenue T-account:

	Service revenue	
	Bal	25,800

Remember the first reason to prepare closing entries: We need to clear out the income statement accounts so that they are empty to begin the next year. What do we need to do to bring the Service Revenue account to zero? It has a *credit* balance of $25,800, so to bring that to zero, we need to *debit* $25,800.

This means that we have part of our first closing entry:

1.	Service revenue	25,800	
	???		25,800

What is the credit side of this entry? The reason we were looking at Service Revenue to begin with was to help calculate net income using the Income Summary. So the other side of the entry must go to the Income Summary:

1.	Service revenue	25,800	
	Income summary		25,800

	Service revenue		
			25,800
1.	25,800		
		Bal	0

| Part 1 | Part 2 | **Part 3** | Part 4 | Part 5 | Part 6 | Part 7 | Part 8 | Part 9 | Demo Doc Complete |

The next part of net income is the expenses. In this case, we have four different expenses:

Rent expense		Depreciation expense	
Bal	6,000	Bal	1,500

Salary expense		Supplies expense	
Bal	10,120	Bal	1,600

Each of these expenses has a *debit* balance. In order to bring these accounts to zero, we must *credit* them. The balancing debit will go to the Income Summary account:

2.	Income summary	19,220	
	Rent expense		6,000
	Salary expense		10,120
	Depreciation expense		1,500
	Supplies expense		1,600

Rent expense		Depreciation expense	
6,000		1,500	
	2. 6,000		2. 1,500
Bal 0		Bal 0	

Salary expense		Supplies expense	
10,120		1,600	
	2. 10,120		2. 1,600
Bal 0		Bal 0	

| Part 1 | Part 2 | Part 3 | **Part 4** | Part 5 | Part 6 | Part 7 | Part 8 | Part 9 | Demo Doc Complete |

Now let's look at the Income Summary account:

Income summary	
	1. 25,800
2. 19,220	
	Bal 6,580

The purpose of creating this account was to get a net income number. (If you did the Chapter 3 problem, note that this balance is the same net income number that appears on the income statement.)

We can now take this number and put it into the Capital account. How do we remove it from the Income Summary? The Income Summary has a *credit* balance of $6,580, which is the net income, so to remove this number, we must *debit* the Income Summary for $6,580:

3.	Income summary	6,580	
	???		6,580

Demo Doc 1 Solutions | Chapter 4 **105**

What is the credit side of this entry? The reason we created the Income Summary account to begin with was to help calculate the profit or loss for the Capital account. So the credit side of the entry must go to Daniel Woodson, Capital:

| 3. | Income summary | 6,580 | |
| | Daniel Woodson, capital | | 6,580 |

This adds the net income to the Capital account. Note that it also brings the Income Summary account to a zero balance.

Income summary

		1.	25,800
2.	19,220		
		Bal	0
3.	6,580		
		Bal	6,580

| Part 1 | Part 2 | Part 3 | Part 4 | **Part 5** | Part 6 | Part 7 | Part 8 | Part 9 | Demo Doc Complete |

The last component of the Capital account formula is withdrawals. There is already a Withdrawals account that exists:

Daniel Woodson, withdrawals

| Bal | 11,500 | |

What do we need to do to bring the Withdrawals account to zero? It has a *debit* balance of $11,500, so to bring that to zero we need to *credit* $11,500. The balancing debit will go to the Daniel Woodson, Capital account:

| 4. | Daniel Woodson, capital | 11,500 | |
| | Daniel Woodson, withdrawals | | 11,500 |

This subtracts the withdrawals from the Capital account.

The Capital account now has the following transactions:

Daniel Woodson, capital

				40,000	Beginning capital amount
			3.	6,580	Net income
Withdrawals	4.	11,500			
			Bal	35,080	Ending capital amount

106   Chapter 4 | Demo Doc 1 Solutions

The formula to update the capital amount has been recreated inside the Capital T-account.

	Daniel Woodson, withdrawals		
	11,500	4.	11,500
Bal	0		

	Daniel Woodson, capital		
		3.	40,000
			6,580
4.	11,500		
		Bal	35,080

Notice that all temporary accounts (that is, the revenue, the expense, the withdrawals, and the Income Summary accounts) now have a zero balance.

	Daniel Woodson, capital			
		3.	40,000	Beginning capital amount
			6,580	Net income
Withdrawals 4.	11,500			
		Bal	35,080	Ending capital amount

4 Prepare the postclosing trial balance

Requirement 3

Prepare the postclosing trial balance.

| Part 1 | Part 2 | Part 3 | Part 4 | Part 5 | **Part 6** | Part 7 | Part 8 | Part 9 | Demo Doc Complete |

Once the temporary accounts have been closed, we can prepare the trial balance again, listing the accounts with their new (postclosing) balances.

	Postclosing Trial Balance	
Account Title	**Debit**	**Credit**
Cash	10,600	
Accounts receivable	15,800	
Supplies	400	
Prepaid rent	2,000	
Furniture	15,000	
Accumulated depreciation—Furniture		6,000
Accounts payable		2,600
Salary payable		120
Daniel Woodson, capital		35,080
Total	$43,800	$43,800

Requirement 4

Classify assets and liabilities as current or long-term

Which assets are current? Which assets are long-term?

| Part 1 | Part 2 | Part 3 | Part 4 | Part 5 | Part 6 | **Part 7** | Part 8 | Part 9 | Demo Doc Complete |

Current assets are assets whose benefit will be realized within one year (or reporting period, whichever is longer). Typical current assets include cash, accounts receivable, prepaid expenses, and inventory. In this problem, the current assets are:

Cash—Cash is used constantly and its benefits are immediate.

Accounts Receivable—Generally, customers pay what they owe to the company in less than one year (reporting period).

Supplies—Supplies are usually purchased close to the time of use (benefit)—well within one year or reporting period.

Prepaid Rent—Generally, prepayments are not made more than one year (period) in advance. This means that the prepayments (benefits) will be used within one year (reporting period).

Total current assets = Cash + Accounts receivable + Supplies + Prepaid rent
= $10,600 + $15,800 + $400 + $2,000
= $28,800

Long-term assets are assets whose benefit will be realized in more than one year (or reporting period). Long-term assets include all asset accounts except for current assets. Some of the categories include long-term investments and property, plant, and equipment. In this problem, the only long-term asset is the **furniture**.

The furniture will be used (benefited from) for many years. We know this because the use of the furniture is represented as depreciation, which is being taken over many years.

Total long-term assets = Furniture(net) =
Furniture − Accumulated depreciation =
$15,000 − $6,000 = $9,000

Requirement 5

Classify assets and liabilities as current or long-term

Which liabilities are current? Which liabilities are long-term?

| Part 1 | Part 2 | Part 3 | Part 4 | Part 5 | Part 6 | Part 7 | **Part 8** | Part 9 | Demo Doc Complete |

108   Chapter 4 | Demo Doc 1 Solutions

Current liabilities are liabilities that will be paid (that is, obligations met) within one year (or reporting period, whichever is longer). In this problem, the current liabilities are:

Accounts Payable—Accounts Payable generally consists of bills from suppliers (such as utilities, providers of raw materials, and inventory). It is rare that such suppliers would be willing to wait a year (or reporting period) for payment. Most often, such bills are due within 30 days.

Salary Payable—Generally, employees are not willing to wait longer than a month to be paid.

$$\text{Total current liabilities} = \text{Accounts payable} + \text{Salary payable}$$
$$= \$2,600 + \$120$$
$$= \$2,720$$

Long-term liabilities include all obligations other than those classified as current liabilities. There are no long-term liabilities in this problem.

$$\text{Total long-term liabilities} = \$0$$

Requirement 6

6 Use the current ratio and the debt ratio to evaluate a company

Calculate Woodson's current and debt ratios.

| Part 1 | Part 2 | Part 3 | Part 4 | Part 5 | Part 6 | Part 7 | Part 8 | **Part 9** | Demo Doc Complete |

$$\text{Current ratio} = \frac{\text{Current assets}}{\text{Current liabilities}}$$

$$= \frac{\$28,800}{\$2,720}$$

$$= 10.59$$

$$\text{Debt ratio} = \frac{\text{Total liabilities}}{\text{Total assets}}$$

$$= \frac{\$2,720 + \$0}{\$28,800 + \$9,000}$$

$$= \frac{\$2,720}{\$37,800}$$

$$= 7.20\%$$

| Part 1 | Part 2 | Part 3 | Part 4 | Part 5 | Part 6 | Part 7 | Part 8 | Part 9 | Demo Doc Complete |

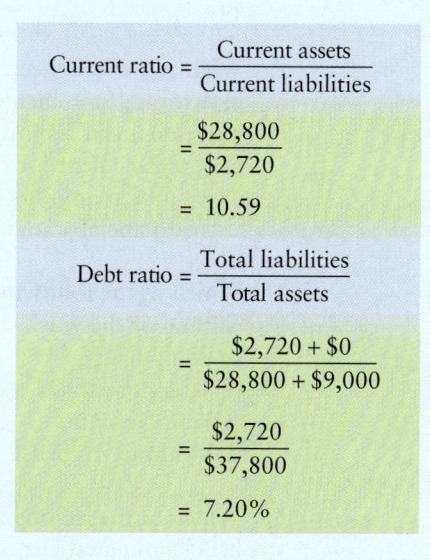

Demo Doc 1 Solutions | Chapter 4

Quick Practice Questions

True/False

_____ 1. The last step in the accounting cycle is preparing the financial statements.

_____ 2. The adjusted trial balance columns of a work sheet contain the account balances that appear on the financial statements.

_____ 3. If the sum of the work sheet income statement debit column is greater than the income statement credit column, there is net income.

_____ 4. Capital, revenue, expenses, and withdrawals are closed out at the end of the year.

_____ 5. The postclosing trial balance contains only balance sheet accounts.

_____ 6. A lower debt ratio is preferable to a higher debt ratio.

_____ 7. Long-term liabilities are debts that are not due for at least six months.

_____ 8. The capital in the balance sheet credit column of a work sheet represents the beginning capital amount plus any additional capital investments during the period.

_____ 9. Permanent accounts include revenue and expenses.

_____ 10. The difference between the debit and credit totals of the balance sheet columns of the work sheet is net income or net loss.

Multiple Choice

1. What is a work sheet?
   a. A formal statement issued to investors
   b. A document required by the Internal Revenue Service
   c. A replacement for the general journal
   d. A multicolumn document used by accountants to aid in the preparation of the financial statements

2. Which of the following accounts would appear in the balance sheet credit column of the work sheet?
   a. Equipment
   b. Salary Payable
   c. Rent Revenue
   d. Insurance Expense

3. Which of the following accounts is not closed out?
   a. Accumulated Depreciation
   b. Service Revenue
   c. Depreciation Expense
   d. Owner's Withdrawals

4. What is the measure of how quickly an item can be converted into cash?
   a. Contribution margin
   b. Liquidity
   c. Profitability
   d. Leverage

5. What type of asset is expected to be converted to cash, sold, or consumed during the next 12 months or within the business's normal operating cycle if longer than a year?
   a. Permanent assets
   b. Quick assets
   c. Current assets
   d. Cash-equivalent assets

6. What is the time span during which cash is used to acquire goods and services that are sold to customers and collected in cash?
   a. Operating cycle
   b. Cash-to-cash cycle
   c. Liquidity cycle
   d. Receivables-to-cash cycle

7. In what category would Inventory appear on a classified balance sheet?
   a. Long-term liability
   b. Plant asset
   c. Current asset
   d. Current liability

Use the following account balances for Philip's Rentals as of December 31, 2011, to answer questions 8–10:

Cash	$10,300	Prepaid rent	$ 3,600
Accounts payable	7,800	Equipment	15,000
Accumulated depreciation	2,000	Supplies	1,200
Philip Browning, capital	9,300	Unearned revenue	1,600
Philip Browning, withdrawals	2,200	Notes payable (due 12/31/2013)	7,500

8. What is the current ratio for Philip's Rentals?
   a. 1.61
   b. 1.03
   c. 1.29
   d. 1.38

9. What is the debt ratio for Philip's Rentals?
   a. 0.60
   b. 0.73
   c. 0.67
   d. 1.16

10. What are the total current assets and total assets, respectively, for Philip's Rentals?
    a. $15,100 and $30,100
    b. $13,900 and $27,100
    c. $15,100 and $28,100
    d. $13,700 and $30,100

Quick Exercises

4-1. For each of the following accounts, indicate whether it (a) normally has a debit or credit balance and (b) appears in the income statement or balance sheet columns of the work sheet.

	Normal Debit or Credit Balance	Income Statement or Balance Sheet
a. Equipment	_____	_____
b. Salary Expense	_____	_____
c. Unearned Revenue	_____	_____
d. Accumulated Depreciation	_____	_____
e. Accounts Payable	_____	_____
f. Service Revenue	_____	_____

4-2. Complete the work sheet information in the adjusted trial balance columns.

Account Title	Trial Balance Debit	Trial Balance Credit	Adjustments Debit	Adjustments Credit	Adjusted Trial Balance Debit	Adjusted Trial Balance Credit
Cash	$30,800					
Accounts receivable	5,800		(a) $6,000			
Prepaid insurance	2,400			(b) $1,200		
Building	17,000					
Accumulated depreciation—Building		$8,000		(c) 500		
Accounts payable		1,600				
Salary payable		1,000		(d) 2,400		
Daniel Woodson, capital		50,320				
Daniel Woodson, withdrawals	7,500					
Service revenue		25,800		(a) 6,000		
Insurance expense	2,500		(b) 1,200			
Rent expense	5,500					
Salary expense	11,120		(d) 2,400			
Depreciation expense	2,000		(c) 500			
Supplies expense	2,100					
Total	$86,720	$86,720	$10,100	$10,100		

4-3. Complete the remainder of the following work sheet:

Account Title	Adjusted Trial Balance Debit	Adjusted Trial Balance Credit	Income Statement Debit	Income Statement Credit	Balance Sheet Debit	Balance Sheet Credit
Cash	8,400					
Accounts receivable	10,100					
Supplies	2,400					
Prepaid rent	4,000					
Furniture	24,400					
Accumulated depreciation—Furniture		4,000				
Accounts payable		3,100				
Unearned revenue		2,420				
Daniel Woodson, capital		42,000				
Daniel Woodson, withdrawals	8,000					
Service revenue		25,000				
Rent expense	6,000					
Salary expense	9,820					
Depreciation expense	1,500					
Supplies expense	1,900					
Total	$76,520	$76,520				
Net income						

4-4. Given the following adjusted account balances, journalize the closing entries for Sports Unlimited on December 31, 2010.

Joseph Golf, capital	$ 85,000
Service revenue	104,400
Depreciation expense—Building	2,000
Salary expense	28,000
Supplies expense	8,500
Interest revenue	15,400
Rent expense	15,000
Joseph Golf, withdrawals	3,000

Date	Accounts	Debit	Credit

Quick Practice Questions | Chapter 4 **113**

Date	Accounts	Debit	Credit

Date	Accounts	Debit	Credit

Date	Accounts	Debit	Credit

4-5. Given the following adjusted account balances at December 31, 2010, calculate total (a) current assets, (b) current liabilities, (c) long-term assets, and (d) long-term liabilities.

Cash	$ 25,000
Accounts receivable	12,500
Land	100,000
Joseph Gold, capital	75,000
Accounts payable	15,200
Building	245,000
Accumulated depreciation—Bldg.	70,000
Salaries payable	1,500
Notes payable—due 12/31/12	39,000

Do It Yourself! Question 1

This question continues on from the Angela's Business Services problem given in Chapter 3.

Use the data from Angela's Business Services adjusted trial balance at December 31, 2011:

ANGELAS BUSINESS SERVICES
Adjusted Trial Balance
December 31, 2011

Account Title	Adjusted Trial Balance Debit	Adjusted Trial Balance Credit
Cash	$ 40,400	
Prepaid insurance	3,600	
Supplies	7,900	
Office equipment	25,000	
Accumulated depreciation—Equipment		$ 10,000
Accounts payable		5,300
Salary payable		4,000
Unearned revenue		1,500
Angela Waring, capital		60,000
Angela Waring, withdrawals	8,000	
Service revenue		85,300
Insurance expense	14,400	
Salary expense	49,000	
Depreciation expense	2,500	
Supplies expense	15,300	
Total	$166,100	$166,100

3 Close the revenue, expense, and withdrawal accounts

Requirement

1. Journalize and post the closing entries.

	Date	Accounts	Debit	Credit
1.				

	Date	Accounts	Debit	Credit
2.				

	Date	Accounts	Debit	Credit
3.				

	Date	Accounts	Debit	Credit
4.				

Do It Yourself! Question 2

Krake Theaters has the following data for 2011:

Total revenues	$10,000
Total expenses	13,000
Owner withdrawals	1,600
Owner investments	4,000

The Capital account had a balance of $8,200 at January 1, 2011.

Requirement

1. Journalize and post the closing entries.

	Date	Accounts	Debit	Credit
1.				

	Date	Accounts	Debit	Credit
2.				

	Date	Accounts	Debit	Credit
3.				

	Date	Accounts	Debit	Credit
4.				

Quick Practice Solutions

True/False Question

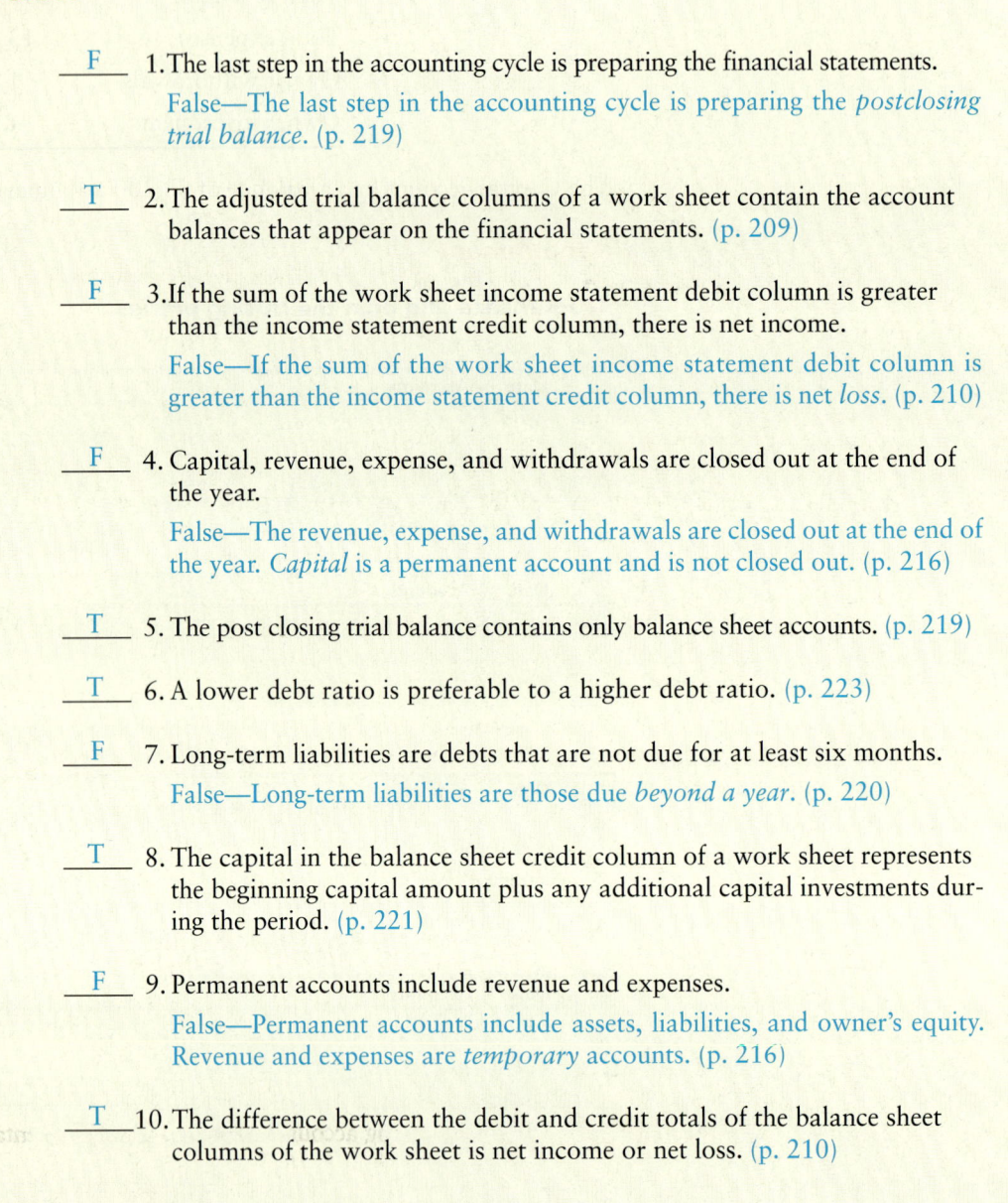

__F__ 1. The last step in the accounting cycle is preparing the financial statements.

False—The last step in the accounting cycle is preparing the *postclosing trial balance*. (p. 219)

__T__ 2. The adjusted trial balance columns of a work sheet contain the account balances that appear on the financial statements. (p. 209)

__F__ 3. If the sum of the work sheet income statement debit column is greater than the income statement credit column, there is net income.

False—If the sum of the work sheet income statement debit column is greater than the income statement credit column, there is net *loss*. (p. 210)

__F__ 4. Capital, revenue, expense, and withdrawals are closed out at the end of the year.

False—The revenue, expense, and withdrawals are closed out at the end of the year. *Capital* is a permanent account and is not closed out. (p. 216)

__T__ 5. The post closing trial balance contains only balance sheet accounts. (p. 219)

__T__ 6. A lower debt ratio is preferable to a higher debt ratio. (p. 223)

__F__ 7. Long-term liabilities are debts that are not due for at least six months.

False—Long-term liabilities are those due *beyond a year*. (p. 220)

__T__ 8. The capital in the balance sheet credit column of a work sheet represents the beginning capital amount plus any additional capital investments during the period. (p. 221)

__F__ 9. Permanent accounts include revenue and expenses.

False—Permanent accounts include assets, liabilities, and owner's equity. Revenue and expenses are *temporary* accounts. (p. 216)

__T__ 10. The difference between the debit and credit totals of the balance sheet columns of the work sheet is net income or net loss. (p. 210)

Multiple Choice Question

1. What is a work sheet? (p. 207)
   a. A formal statement issued to investors
   b. A document required by the Internal Revenue Service.
   c. A replacement for the general journal
   d. A multicolumn document used by accountants to aid in the preparation of the financial statements

2. Which of the following accounts would appear in the balance sheet credit column of the work sheet? (p. 208)
   a. Equipment
   b. Salary Payable
   c. Rent Revenue
   d. Insurance Expense

3. Which of the following accounts is not closed out? (p. 216)
   a. Accumulated Depreciation
   b. Service Revenue
   c. Depreciation Expense
   d. Owner's Withdrawals

4. What is the measure of how quickly an item can be converted into cash? (p. 220)
   a. Contribution margin
   b. Liquidity
   c. Profitability
   d. Leverage

5. What type of asset is expected to be converted to cash, sold, or consumed during the next 12 months or within the business's normal operating cycle if longer than a year? (p. 220)
   a. Permanent assets
   b. Quick assets
   c. Current assets
   d. Cash-equivalent assets

6. What is the time span during which cash is used to acquire goods and services that are sold to customers and collected in cash? (p. 220)
   a. Operating cycle
   b. Cash-to-cash cycle
   c. Liquidity cycle
   d. Receivables-to-cash cycle

7. In what category would Inventory appear on a classified balance sheet? (p. 220)
   a. Long-term liability
   b. Plant asset
   c. Current asset
   d. Current liability

Use the following account balances for Philip's Rentals as of December 31, 2011, to answer questions 8–10:

Cash	$10,300	Prepaid rent	$ 3,600
Accounts payable	7,800	Equipment	15,000
Accumulated depreciation	2,000	Supplies	1,200
Philip Browning, capital	9,300	Unearned revenue	1,600
Philip Browning, withdrawals	2,200	Notes payable (due 12/31/2013)	7,500

8. What is the current ratio for Philip's Rentals? (p. 223)
   a. 1.61
   b. 1.03
   c. 1.29
   d. 1.38

9. What is the debt ratio for Philip's Rentals? (p. 223)
   a. 0.60
   b. 0.73
   c. 0.67
   d. 1.16

10. What are the total current assets and total assets, respectively, for Philip's Rentals? (p. 223)
    a. $15,100 and $30,100
    b. $13,900 and $27,100
    c. $15,100 and $28,100
    d. $13,700 and $30,100

Quick Exercises

4-1. For each of the following accounts, indicate whether it (a) normally has a debit or credit balance and (b) appears in the income statement or balance sheet columns of the work sheet. (p. 209)

		Normal Debit (Dr.) or Credit (Cr.) Balance	Income Statement (I/S) or Balance Sheet (B/S)
a.	Equipment	Dr.	B/S
b.	Salary Expense	Dr.	I/S
c.	Unearned Revenue	Cr.	B/S
d.	Accumulated Depreciation	Cr.	B/S
e.	Accounts Payable	Cr.	B/S
f.	Service Revenue	Cr.	I/S

4-2. Complete the work sheet information that follows through the adjusted trial balance columns. (p. 208)

Account Title	Trial Balance Debit	Trial Balance Credit	Adjustments Debit	Adjustments Credit	Adjusted Trial Balance Debit	Adjusted Trial Balance Credit
Cash	$30,800				$30,800	
Accounts receivable	5,800		(a) $6,000		11,800	
Prepaid insurance	2,400			(b) $1,200	1,200	
Building	17,000				17,000	
Accumulated depreciation—Building		$8,000		(c) 500		$8,500
Accounts payable		1,600				1,600
Salary payable		1,000		(d) 2,400		3,400
Daniel Woodson, capital		50,320				50,320
Daniel Woodson, withdrawals	7,500				7,500	
Service revenue		25,800		(a) 6,000		31,800
Insurance expense	2,500		(b) 1,200		3,700	
Rent expense	5,500				5,500	
Salary expense	11,120		(d) 2,400		13,520	
Depreciation expense	2,000		(c) 500		2,500	
Supplies expense	2,100				2,100	
Total	$86,720	$86,720	$10,100	$10,100	$95,620	$95,620

4-3. Complete the remainder of the following work sheet: (p. 212)

Account Title	Adjusted Trial Balance Debit	Adjusted Trial Balance Credit	Income Statement Debit	Income Statement Credit	Balance Sheet Debit	Balance Sheet Credit
Cash	$8,400				$8,400	
Accounts receivable	10,100				10,100	
Supplies	2,400				2,400	
Prepaid rent	4,000				4,000	
Furniture	24,400				24,400	
Accumulated depreciation—Furniture		$4,000				$4,000
Accounts payable		3,100				3,100
Unearned revenue		2,420				2,420
Daniel Woodson, capital		52,000				52,000
Daniel Woodson, withdrawals	8,000				8,000	
Service revenue		25,000		$25,000		
Rent expense	6,000		$6,000			
Salary expense	9,820		9,820			
Depreciation expense	1,500		1,500			
Supplies expense	1,900		1,900			
Total	$76,520	$76,520	$19,220	$25,000	$57,300	$51,520
Net income			$6,220			$5,780
			$25,000	$25,000	$57,300	$57,300

Quick Practice Solutions | Chapter 4

4-4. Given the following adjusted account balances, journalize the closing entries for Sports Unlimited on December 31, 2010. (p. 217)

Joseph Golf, capital	$ 85,000
Service revenue	104,400
Depreciation expense—Building	2,000
Salary expense	28,000
Supplies expense	8,500
Interest revenue	15,400
Rent expense	15,000
Joseph Golf, withdrawals	3,000

Date	Accounts	Debit	Credit
12/31/10	Service revenue	104,400	
	Interest revenue	15,400	
	Income summary		119,800
	To close out revenue accounts into Income summary.		

Date	Accounts	Debit	Credit
	Income summary	53,500	
	Depreciation expense—Building		2,000
	Salary expense		28,000
	Supplies expense		8,500
	Rent expense		15,000
	To close out expense accounts into Income summary.		

Date	Accounts	Debit	Credit
	Income summary	66,300	
	Joseph Golf, capital		66,300
	To close out Income summary into Capital		

Date	Accounts	Debit	Credit
	Joseph Golf, withdrawals	3,000	
	Joseph Golf, capital		3,000
	To close out Withdrawals into Capital		

4-5. Given the following adjusted account balances at December 31, 2010, calculate total (a) current assets, (b) current liabilities, (c) long-term assets, and (d) long-term liabilities. (p. 220)

Cash	$ 25,000
Accounts receivable	12,500
Land	100,000
Joseph Golf, capital	75,000
Accounts payable	15,200
Building	245,000
Accumulated depreciation—Bldg.	70,000
Salaries payable	1,500
Notes payable—due 12/31/12	39,000

a.
Cash	$25,000
Accounts receivable	12,500
Total current assets	$37,500

b.
Accounts payable	$15,200
Salaries payable	1,500
Total current liabilities	$16,700

c.
Land	$100,000
Building	245,000
Less: Accumulated dep.—Bldg.	(70,000)
Total long-term assets	$275,000

d.
Notes payable—due 12/31/12	$39,000
Total long-term liabilities	$39,000

Do It Yourself! Question 1 Solutions

Requirement

1. Journalize and post the closing entries.

Date	Accounts	Debit	Credit
1.	Accounts receivable	85,300	
	Unearned subscription revenue		85,300

Date	Accounts	Debit	Credit
2.	Income summary	81,200	
	Insurance expense		14,400
	Salary expense		49,000
	Depreciation expense		2,500
	Supplies expense		15,300

Date	Accounts	Debit	Credit
3.	Income summary	4,100	
	Angela Waring, capital		4,100

Date	Accounts	Debit	Credit
4.	Angela Waring, capital	8,000	
	Angela Waring, withdrawals		8,000

Service revenue			Depreciation expense			Angela Waring, withdrawals		
		85,300	2,500			8,000		
1.	85,300			2.	2,500		4.	8,000
	Bal	0	Bal	0		Bal	0	

Insurance expense			Supplies expense			Angela Waring, capital		
14,400			15,300					60,000
	2.	14,400		2.	15,300		3.	4,100
Bal	0		Bal	0		4.	8,000	
							Bal	56,100

Salary expense			Income summary		
49,000				1.	85,300
	2.	49,000	2.	81,200	
Bal	0			Bal	4,100
			3.	4,100	
				Bal	0

Do It Yourself! Question 2 Solutions

Requirement

1. Journalize and post the closing entries.

	Date	Accounts	Debit	Credit
1.		Revenues	10,000	
		Income summary		10,000

	Date	Accounts	Debit	Credit
2.		Income summary	13,000	
		Expenses		13,000

	Date	Accounts	Debit	Credit
3.		Capital	3,000	
		Income summary		3,000

	Date	Accounts	Debit	Credit
4.		Capital	1,600	
		Withdrawals		1,600

```
           Revenues                         Income summary
                        10,000                             1.    10,000
    1.    10,000                      2.    13,000
              | Bal      0            Bal    3,000
                                                           3.     3,000
           Expenses                         Bal       0
          13,000
                   2.   13,000              Withdrawals
    Bal       0                             1,600
                                                           4.    1,600
                                            Bal      0

                       Capital
                                      8,200    Beginning capital amount
                                      4,000    Owner investments
                              Bal    12,200    Ending capital amount
     Net loss      3.   3,000
     Withdrawals   4.   1,600
                              Bal     7,600    Ending capital amount
```

Do It Yourself! Question 2 Solutions | Chapter 4

The Power of Practice

For more practice using the skills learned in this chapter, visit MyAccountingLab. There you will find algorithmically generated questions that are based on these Demo Docs and your main textbook's Review and Assess Your Progress sections.

Go to MyAccountingLab and follow these steps:

1. Direct your URL to www.myaccountinglab.com.
2. Log in using your name and password.
3. Click the MyAccountingLab link.
4. Click Study Plan in the left navigation bar.
5. From the table of contents, select Chapter 4, Completing the Accounting Cycle.
6. Click a link to work tutorial exercises.

5 Merchandising Operations

WHAT YOU PROBABLY ALREADY KNOW

You want to order a pair of pants from a mail-order catalog. The price listed in the catalog is $50. There is a 10% off coupon in the catalog for first-time customers that you plan to use. You also see that there will be a $6.95 shipping and handling charge for an order of this size. How much will the pair of pants cost you? Although the selling price listed is $50, that is not the cost to you. The 10% coupon results in a $5 discount ($50 × .10) *decreasing* the cost to $45 ($50 − 5). However, the shipping and handling charge of $6.95 *adds* to the cost of the pants. The required cost for the pants is $51.95 ($50.00 − 5.00 + 6.95).

Businesses calculate the cost of assets purchased in the same manner. When inventory is acquired, the cost is calculated as

1. the purchase price on the invoice
2. *plus* the cost of shipping or freight
3. *less* discounts taken

Learning Objectives/Success Keys

1 Describe and illustrate merchandising operations and the two types of inventory systems.

Merchandising consists of buying and selling *products* rather than services. *See the Operating Cycle of a merchandising company in the text in Exhibit 5-2 (p. 273).*

There are two types of inventory accounting systems:

- The periodic system requires a physical inventory count to be taken periodically to determine the amount of inventory on hand. The Inventory (asset) account is not continually updated for the increase in inventory owing to purchases or the decreases in inventory owing to sales.

- The perpetual system continuously updates the Inventory account and Cost of Goods Sold account for purchases and sales. The Inventory (asset) account is debited to record the purchase of inventory. A physical inventory count is still performed to verify the accuracy of the inventory balance.

2 Account for the purchase of inventory using a perpetual system.

In a perpetual system, the Inventory account is debited when inventory is purchased. *See Exhibit 5-3 (p. 275) in the text for an example of a purchase invoice.*

Review the "Inventory Systems: Perpetual and Periodic" section in the main text.

3 Account for the sale of inventory using a perpetual system.

Two entries must be recorded when inventory is sold under a perpetual system. One entry records the revenue amount charged to the customer and the cash or accounts receivable. The other records the cost of goods sold expense and the decrease in the cost of inventory. Sales Discounts and Sales Returns and Allowances are contra revenue, debit balance accounts. *Review the "Sale of Inventory" section of the main text.*

4 Adjust and close the accounts of a merchandising business.

The Inventory account should be adjusted, as necessary, to the actual amount of inventory on hand. Cost of Goods Sold will be affected by the inventory adjustment. The closing entries are similar to those studied in Chapter 4. All of the temporary accounts will be closed out, including the new ones introduced in this chapter: Sales, Sales Discounts, Sales Returns and Allowances and Cost of Goods Sold. *Review the closing entries in Exhibit 5-7 (p. 287).*

5 Prepare a merchandiser's financial statements.

The income statement of a merchandiser may be prepared in two formats. A single-step income statement lists all revenues followed by all expenses to determine net income or loss. The multi-step income statement shows various subtotals as gross profit and income from operations. The other statements are very similar to those for a service company. *Review a merchandiser's multi-step income statement in Exhibit 5-6 and a single-step statement in Exhibit 5-9 (pp. 280–291).*

6 Use gross profit percentage and inventory turnover to evaluate a business.

Two ratios that provide important information for a merchandiser are the gross profit percentage and inventory turnover. *Review the "Two Ratios for Decision Making" section in the main text.*

Demo Doc 1

Inventory Transaction Analysis (perpetual system)

Learning Objectives 1–6

Danner Company began operations on January 1, 2011. Danner had the following transactions during the year:

Jan. 1	Purchased inventory for $400 with credit terms of 2/15 net 30.
Jan. 12	Paid for the January 1 purchase in full.
Feb. 1	Sold 10 units costing $21 each to a customer for $360 on account. This sale had credit terms of 1/15 net 30.
Feb. 9	Customer returned three units from his February 1 order because he did not like the color of the goods.
Feb. 18	Customer paid for the February 1 order (less returns) in full.
May 5	Purchased inventory for $250 with credit terms of 2/10 net 30.
May 6	Paid special freight costs of $30 on the May 5 inventory purchase in cash.
May 14	Found that 15% of the goods purchased on May 5 were defective. Danner returned these goods.
Jun. 1	Paid for the May 5 purchase (less returns) in full.
Oct. 1	Sold $160 of goods to a customer for $220 with credit terms of 1/20 net 40.
Oct. 19	Received cash payment in full for the October 1 sale.

Requirements

1. Journalize these transactions using the perpetual method. Explanations are not required.

2. Show the Inventory and COGS T-accounts for the year.

3. Inventory on hand at December 31, 2011 (as per count) was $325. Make any necessary adjustments.

4. Prepare the top portion of Danner's 2011 income statement (ending with gross profit).

5. Calculate Danner's inventory turnover for 2011.

Demo Doc 1 Solutions

Requirement 1

Journalize these transactions using the perpetual method. Explanations are not required.

| Part 1 | Part 2 | Part 3 | Part 4 | Part 5 | Demo Doc Complete |

Jan. 1 Purchased inventory for $400 with credit terms of 2/15 net 30.

1 Describe and illustrate merchandising operations and the two types of inventory systems

2 Account for the purchase of inventory using a perpetual system

The Inventory account is involved here because inventory was purchased. Inventory is increased by $400 (a debit). Because the inventory was not paid for in cash (it was purchased on account), Accounts Payable must also be increased by $400 (a credit).

Note that the actual credit terms do not matter at this point, only that the purchase was not made in cash.

However, note that 2/15 net 30 means that the customer will get a 2% discount if the full amount is paid within 15 days. Otherwise, full payment is due in 30 days.

| Jan 1 | Inventory | 400 | |
| | Accounts payable | | 400 |

Jan. 12 Paid for the January 1 purchase in full.

1 Describe and illustrate merchandising operations and the two types of inventory systems

2 Account for the purchase of inventory using a perpetual system

Remember that 2/15 means that if full payment is made within 15 days, the customer gets a 2% discount.

We are paying the supplier, so we can decrease our Accounts Payable by $400 (a debit). Cash also decreases (a credit). But by how much? January 12 is within 15 days of the original purchase, so Danner is entitled to take the discount. Therefore, Danner only has to pay 100% − 2% = 98% of the purchase price to satisfy the debt owed. So the cash paid is:

$$98\% \times \$400 = \$392$$

The difference is an adjustment to the Inventory account. The cost principle says that we should record assets at cost. The true cost of the inventory is now less than we originally thought. So Inventory is decreased (a credit) by this difference.

Jan 12	Accounts payable	400	
	Inventory (to balance*)		8
	Cash [(100% − 2%) × $400]		392

*$400 − $392 = $8

The amount of the adjustment to Inventory was made to balance the entry. In all journal entries, total debits = total credits.

The amount of the adjustment to Inventory is the amount needed to make the total debits in the entry equal to the total credits in the entry. In this case, a credit of 400 − 392 = 8 is required.

1 Describe and illustrate merchandising operations and the two types of inventory systems

3 Account for the sale of inventory using a perpetual system

Feb. 1 **Sold 10 units costing $21 each to a customer for $360 on account. This sale had credit terms of 1/15 net 40.**

There are two parts to this transaction. First, Danner is earning sales revenue of $360. This will cause an increase to Sales Revenue (a credit) and (because it is not paid for in cash but rather sold on account) an increase to Accounts Receivable (a debit).

Second, Danner is also selling inventory. This means that Inventory will decrease (a credit) and COGS will increase (a debit) by:

$$10 \times \$21 = \$210$$

Remember that 1/15 net 40 means that the customer will get a 1% discount if the full amount is paid within 15 days. Otherwise, full payment is due in 40 days.

Feb 1	Accounts receivable	360	
	Sales revenue		360
	COGS (10 units × $21)	210	
	Inventory		210

1 Describe and illustrate merchandising operations and the two types of inventory systems

3 Account for the sale of inventory using a perpetual system

Feb. 9 **Customer returned three units from his February 1 order because he did not like the color of the goods.**

Because the customer is returning goods (and the goods are not defective) to the company, Danner's Inventory will increase (a debit) by $3 \times \$21 = \$63$. This then causes the COGS to decrease (a credit) by $63.

The customer has not yet paid, so this will decrease the amount of Accounts Receivable Danner can collect from the customer (a credit) by $(3/10) \times \$360 = \$108$. Instead of decreasing Sales Revenue, we will increase Sales Returns and Allowances (a debit) by $108. This allows Danner to keep track of sales returns and make better business decisions.

Feb 9	Inventory (3 × $21)	63	
	COGS		63
	Sales returns and allowances ([3/10] × $360)	108	
	Accounts receivable		108

1 Describe and illustrate merchandising operations and the two types of inventory systems

3 Account for the sale of inventory using a perpetual system

Feb. 18 **Customer paid for the February 1 order (less returns) in full.**

Remember that 1/15 means that if full payment is made within 15 days, the customer gets a 1% discount.

However, the customer is paying 18 days after the sale, which is longer than the 15 days the discount allows. Therefore, the customer must pay the *full* amount.

Demo Doc 1 Solutions | Chapter 5   **131**

Cash is increased (a debit) by $360 − $108 = $252 (original sale of $360 less the sales return of $108). Because the customer is paying Danner, Accounts Receivable is also decreased (a credit) by $252.

Feb 18	Cash ($360 − $108)	252	
	Accounts receivable		252

1 Describe and illustrate merchandising operations and the two types of inventory systems

2 Account for the purchase of inventory using a perpetual system

May 5   Purchased inventory for $250 with credit terms of 2/10 net 30.

Inventory is increasing by $250 (a debit). Because the inventory was not paid for in cash but rather on account, Accounts Payable must also be increased by $250 (a credit).

Remember that 2/10 net 30 means that the customer will get a 2% discount if the full amount is paid within 10 days. Otherwise, full payment is due in 30 days.

May 5	Inventory	250	
	Accounts payable		250

May 6   Paid special freight costs of $30 on the May 5 inventory purchase in cash.

The *total cost* of the inventory is the purchase price *plus* any additional purchasing costs (such as shipping or taxes). Therefore, we include the extra $30 of freight as part of the cost of the inventory.

Inventory is increased by $30 (a debit). Because these costs are being paid in cash, the Cash account is decreased (a credit) by $30.

May 6	Inventory	30	
	Cash		30

1 Describe and illustrate merchandising operations and the two types of inventory systems

2 Account for the purchase of inventory using a perpetual system

May 14   Found that 15% of the goods purchased on May 5 were defective. Danner returned these goods.

When the goods are returned to the supplier, they are taken out of inventory. This decreases Inventory (a credit) by 15% × $250 = $37.50. Because Danner has not yet paid for the goods, Accounts Payable is decreased for the related amount (a debit).

May 14	Accounts payable (15% × $250)	37.50	
	Inventory		37.50

132   Chapter 5 | Demo Doc 1 Solutions

> **1** Describe and illustrate merchandising operations and the two types of inventory systems
>
> **2** Account for the purchase of inventory using a perpetual system

Jun. 1 Paid for the May 5 purchase (less returns) in full.

Remember that 2/10 means that if full payment is made within 10 days, the customer gets a 2% discount.

Accounts Payable decreases by the original payable less returns made: $250 − $37.50 = $212.50 (a debit). Cash also decreases (a credit). June 1 is 27 days after the original purchase. This is within the deadline for payment of 30 days, but it is *not* early enough to take the discount. Therefore, the cash paid is the full amount of $212.50. In order for Danner to be entitled to take the discount, the payment would have had to have been made on May 15 (May 5 plus 10 days).

Jun 1	Accounts payable	212.50	
	Cash		212.50

> **1** Describe and illustrate merchandising operations and the two types of inventory systems
>
> **3** Account for the sale of inventory using a perpetual system

Oct. 1 Sold $160 of goods to a customer for $220 with credit terms of 1/20 net 40.

The company is earning sales revenue of $220. This will cause an increase to Sales Revenue (a credit) and (because it is not paid for in cash) an increase to Accounts Receivable (a debit).

The company is also selling inventory. This means that Inventory will decrease (a credit) and COGS will increase (a debit) by $160.

Note that the actual credit terms do not matter at this point, only that the sale was not made in cash.

However, note that 1/20 net 40 means that the customer will get a 1% discount if the full amount is paid within 20 days. Otherwise, full payment is due in 40 days.

Even though the sale was on account, the actual sale must be recorded at this time.

Oct 1	Accounts receivable	220	
	Sales revenue		220
	COGS	160	
	Inventory		160

> **1** Describe and illustrate merchandising operations and the two types of inventory systems
>
> **3** Account for the sale of inventory using a perpetual system

Oct. 19 Received cash for payment in full of the October 1 sale.

This payment is within the 20-day period, so the customer is entitled to take the discount. The customer will pay 100% − 1% = 99% of the receivable amount, or 99% × $220 = $217.80.

Accounts Receivable will be decreased by the *full* amount of $220 (a credit) because the bill has been paid and no more can be collected from the customer. Cash will increase by $217.80 (a debit) and the difference (the amount to balance) will go to Sales Discounts.

Oct 19	Cash [(100% − 1%) × $220]	217.80	
	Sales discounts (to balance*)	2.20	
	Accounts receivable		220

*$220 − 217.80 = 2.20

Demo Doc 1 Solutions | Chapter 5   **133**

4 Adjust and close the accounts of a merchandising business

Requirement 2

Show the Inventory and COGS T-accounts for the year.

| Part 1 | **Part 2** | Part 3 | Part 4 | Part 5 | Demo Doc Complete |

The entries are posted into the T-accounts (just as in previous chapters). However, for this question, we only want to see the Inventory and COGS T-accounts in detail:

Inventory					COGS			
Jan 1	400				Feb 1	210		
		Jan 12	8				Feb 9	63
		Feb 1	210		Oct 1	160		
Feb 9	63				Bal	307		
May 5	250							
May 6	30							
		May 14	37.50					
		Oct 1	160					
Bal	327.50							

4 Adjust and close the accounts of a merchandising business

Requirement 3

Inventory on hand at December 31, 2011 (as per count) was $325. Make any necessary adjustments.

| Part 1 | Part 2 | **Part 3** | Part 4 | Part 5 | Demo Doc Complete |

The balance of Inventory in the T-account is $327.50. Because the count shows less, there must be inventory shrinkage.

The number for Inventory on the balance sheet must *always* be the number from the actual physical *count*. This means that we need to adjust the Inventory balance to the count number of $325. This will require a decrease (credit) of $327.50 − $325 = $2.50 to Inventory. The balance to this entry is an increase (debit) to COGS for $2.50.

Dec 31	COGS ($327.50 − $325)	2.50	
	Inventory		2.50

The updated Inventory and COGS T-accounts are:

Inventory				COGS			
Jan 1	400			Feb 1	210		
		Jan 12	8			Feb 9	63
		Feb 1	210	Oct 1	160		
Feb 9	63			Bal	307		
May 5	250			Dec 31	2.50		
May 6	30			Bal	309.50		
		May 14	37.50				
		Oct 1	160				
Bal	327.50						
		Dec 31	2.50				
Bal	325						

5 Prepare a merchandiser's financial statements

Requirement 4

Prepare the top portion of Danner's 2011 income statement (ending with gross profit).

| Part 1 | Part 2 | Part 3 | **Part 4** | Part 5 | Demo Doc Complete |

DANNER COMPANY
Income Statement
Year Ended December 31, 2011

Sales revenue			$580.00*
Less: Sales discounts	$ (2.20)		
Sales returns and allowances	(108.00)	(110.20)	
Net sales revenue			$469.80
Cost of goods sold			(309.50)
Gross profit			160.30

*$360 + $220

Sales Discounts and Sales Returns and Allowances are *contra accounts* to Sales Revenue. As we did with Accumulated Depreciation, these contra accounts must be shown on the financial statements, then combined with their associated account to create the *net* value (in this case, net sales revenue).

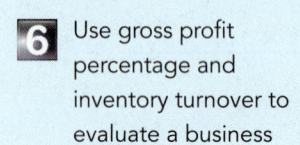

6 Use gross profit percentage and inventory turnover to evaluate a business

Requirement 5

Calculate Danner's inventory turnover for 2011.

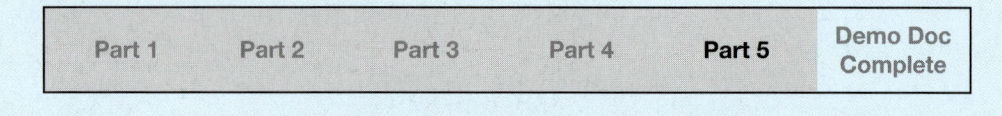

| Part 1 | Part 2 | Part 3 | Part 4 | **Part 5** | Demo Doc Complete |

Inventory turnover = COGS/Average inventory

Average (when used in a financial ratio) generally means the beginning balance plus the ending balance divided by 2.

2011 Inventory turnover
= $309.50/[($0 + $325)/2]
= $309.50/$162.50
= **1.9 times**

| Part 1 | Part 2 | Part 3 | Part 4 | Part 5 | **Demo Doc Complete** |

Quick Practice Questions

True/False

____ 1. Cost of Goods Sold is included in a merchandiser's income statement but excluded from a service company income statement.

____ 2. Under the periodic inventory system, the only way to determine the cost of goods sold is to take a physical count of the merchandise on hand.

____ 3. Most businesses use the periodic inventory system because it offers management more control over inventory.

____ 4. A sales return requires two entries to be journalized if the seller uses a perpetual inventory system.

____ 5. Sales Returns and Allowances is an expense account.

____ 6. The single-step income statement shows gross profit and income from operations.

____ 7. An inventory count is not performed if the perpetual inventory system is used.

____ 8. Advertising expenses would be considered general expenses on the income statement.

____ 9. A higher inventory turnover is preferable to a lower turnover.

____ 10. A company with a gross profit percentage of 40% must have a higher net income than one with a gross profit percentage of 30%.

Multiple Choice

1. What do credit terms 1/10 n/30 indicate?
    a. A 10% discount is available if payment is made within 30 days
    b. A 1% discount is available if payment is made within 10 days
    c. A 1% discount is available if payment is made within 30 days
    d. A 30% discount is available if payment is made within 10 days

2. Which of the following is necessary to record the purchase of merchandise on account under a perpetual inventory system?
    a. A credit to Cash
    b. A debit to Accounts payable
    c. A credit to Inventory
    d. A debit to Inventory

3. What account is credited when a discount is taken for prompt payment under a perpetual inventory system?
    a. Accounts payable
    b. Accounts receivable
    c. Purchase discounts
    d. Inventory

4. What is the entry required to record the payment of a $200 freight bill, assuming the shipping terms are FOB shipping point, under a perpetual inventory system?
   a. Debit inventory and credit Cash
   b. Debit Accounts payable and credit Inventory
   c. Debit Inventory and credit Purchase discounts
   d. Debit Purchase discounts and credit Inventory

5. How does the purchaser account for transportation charges when goods are shipped to them FOB destination?
   a. No journal entry would be recorded for the transportation charges.
   b. Debit Delivery expense for the amount of the transportation charges.
   c. Debit Freight-in for the amount of the transportation charges.
   d. Debit Inventory for the amount of the transportation charges.

6. Which of the following accounts has a normal debit balance?
   a. Sales revenue
   b. Sales returns and allowances
   c. Net sales revenue
   d. Gross profit

7. When the seller is liable for the shipping costs, what account is debited when payment is made?
   a. Delivery expense
   b. Freight-in
   c. Inventory
   d. Cash

8. Which of the following is necessary to record an adjustment to account for inventory shrinkage under a perpetual system?
   a. A credit to Miscellaneous expense
   b. A credit to Cost of goods sold
   c. A credit to Inventory
   d. A debit to Miscellaneous expense

9. Which of the following accounts should be closed to Income Summary?
   a. Beginning inventory
   b. Sales returns and allowances
   c. Owner withdrawals
   d. Ending inventory

10. What does inventory turnover indicate?
    a. How quickly inventory is received from the supplier after the order is placed
    b. How many days it takes the inventory to travel between the seller's warehouse and the buyer's warehouse
    c. How rapidly inventory is sold
    d. How many days it takes from the time an order is received until the day it is shipped

Quick Exercises

5-1. Werner Company purchased $11,000 of merchandise. The purchase invoice is for $11,200, which includes transportation charges of $200. The company returned $2,900 of the goods received before paying the invoice. The company paid the invoice within the discount terms, 2/10 n/30.

Requirement

1. Compute the following amounts:

   a. The amount of the discount

   b. The total amount for the merchandise recorded in the Inventory account

   c. The amount that the purchaser would remit if paid after the discount period

5-2. Select whether the following accounts are:

   (A) Closed out with a debit to the account
   (B) Closed out with a credit to the account
   (C) Not closed out at all

   a. _____ Sales revenue
   b. _____ Sales returns and allowances
   c. _____ Salary expense
   d. _____ Inventory
   e. _____ Depreciation expense
   f. _____ Accumulated depreciation
   g. _____ Accounts receivable
   h. _____ Interest revenue
   i. _____ Interest expense
   j. _____ Cost of goods sold

5-3. Moyer Company had the following transactions during August 2010. Assuming that the perpetual inventory system is used, prepare the journal entries to record these transactions.

Aug. 5   Purchased $2,900 of merchandise on account from Ryan Company, terms 3/15 n/60.

Aug. 9   Paid transportation cost of $440 directly to the trucking company for the August 5 purchase.

Aug. 10   Returned $600 of unwanted merchandise purchased on August 5.

Aug. 15   Paid for the August 5 purchase, less the return and the discount.

Date	Accounts	Debit	Credit

Date	Accounts	Debit	Credit

Date	Accounts	Debit	Credit

Date	Accounts	Debit	Credit

5-4. Prepare the necessary journal entries for Ryan Company using the transactions in 5-3. Assume that the cost of goods sold is 50% of the sales price.

Date	Accounts	Debit	Credit

Date	Accounts	Debit	Credit

Date	Accounts	Debit	Credit

Date	Accounts	Debit	Credit

Date	Accounts	Debit	Credit

Date	Accounts	Debit	Credit

Do It Yourself! Question 1

Franco Bros. began operations on January 1, 2011. Franco had the following transactions during the year:

Jan. 1	Purchased inventory for $150 under credit terms 2/10 net 30.
Jan. 8	Paid for the January 1 purchase in full.
Mar. 1	Purchased inventory for $240 under credit terms 2/20 net 45.
Apr. 1	Paid for the March 1 purchase in full.
July 1	Sold $80 worth of goods to a customer for $120 under credit terms 5/15 net eom (end of month).
July 12	Received cash payment in full for the July 1 sale.
Sept. 1	Found that 10% of the goods purchased on March 1 were defective. Franco Bros. returned these goods.
Oct. 1	Received cash refund for the goods returned on September 1.
Dec. 1	Sold $210 worth of goods to a customer for $320 under credit terms 1/15 net eom (end of month).
Dec. 6	Customer returned 20% of his December 1 order because he did not like the color of the goods.
Dec. 12	Customer paid for the December 1 order (less returns) in full.

Requirements

1 Describe and illustrate merchandising operations and the two types of inventory systems

1. Journalize these transactions using the perpetual system. Explanations are not required.

Date	Accounts	Debit	Credit
Jan 1			

2 Account for the purchase of inventory using a perpetual system

Date	Accounts	Debit	Credit
Jan 8			

3 Account for the sale of inventory using a perpetual system

Date	Accounts	Debit	Credit
Mar 1			

Date	Accounts	Debit	Credit
Apr 1			

Date	Accounts	Debit	Credit
Jul 1			

Date	Accounts	Debit	Credit
Jul 12			

Date	Accounts	Debit	Credit
Sep 1			

Date	Accounts	Debit	Credit
Oct 1			

Date	Accounts	Debit	Credit
Dec 1			

Date	Accounts	Debit	Credit
Dec 6			

Date	Accounts	Debit	Credit
Dec 12			

4 Adjust and close the accounts of a merchandising business

2. Show the Inventory and COGS T-accounts for the year.

4 Adjust and close the accounts of a merchandising business

3. Inventory on hand at December 31, 2011 (as per count) was $110. Make any necessary adjustments.

Date	Accounts	Debit	Credit

5 Prepare a merchandiser's financial statements

4. Prepare the top portion of Franco's 2011 income statement (ending with gross profit).

Quick Practice Solutions

True/False

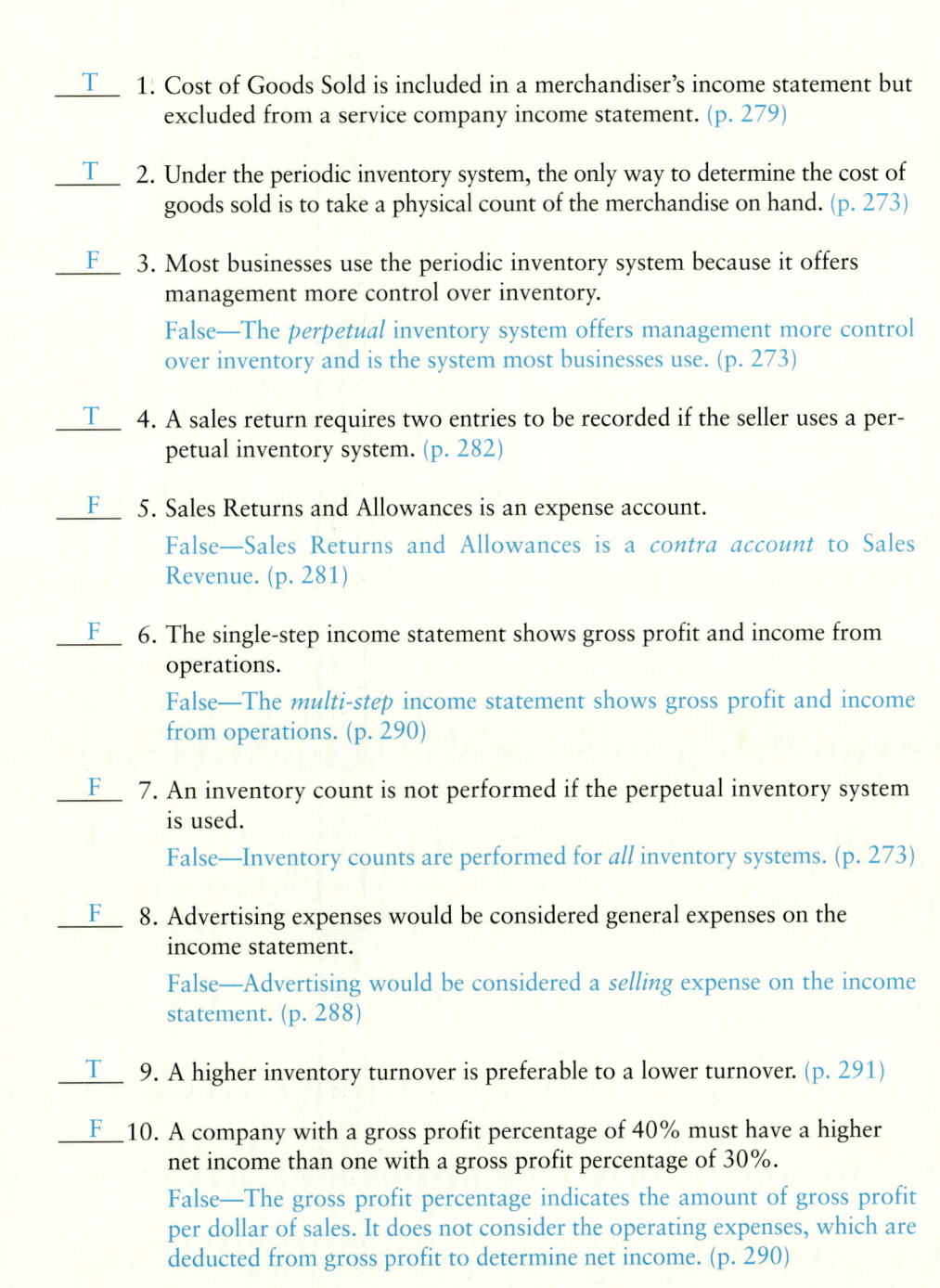

__T__ 1. Cost of Goods Sold is included in a merchandiser's income statement but excluded from a service company income statement. (p. 279)

__T__ 2. Under the periodic inventory system, the only way to determine the cost of goods sold is to take a physical count of the merchandise on hand. (p. 273)

__F__ 3. Most businesses use the periodic inventory system because it offers management more control over inventory.

False—The *perpetual* inventory system offers management more control over inventory and is the system most businesses use. (p. 273)

__T__ 4. A sales return requires two entries to be recorded if the seller uses a perpetual inventory system. (p. 282)

__F__ 5. Sales Returns and Allowances is an expense account.

False—Sales Returns and Allowances is a *contra account* to Sales Revenue. (p. 281)

__F__ 6. The single-step income statement shows gross profit and income from operations.

False—The *multi-step* income statement shows gross profit and income from operations. (p. 290)

__F__ 7. An inventory count is not performed if the perpetual inventory system is used.

False—Inventory counts are performed for *all* inventory systems. (p. 273)

__F__ 8. Advertising expenses would be considered general expenses on the income statement.

False—Advertising would be considered a *selling* expense on the income statement. (p. 288)

__T__ 9. A higher inventory turnover is preferable to a lower turnover. (p. 291)

__F__ 10. A company with a gross profit percentage of 40% must have a higher net income than one with a gross profit percentage of 30%.

False—The gross profit percentage indicates the amount of gross profit per dollar of sales. It does not consider the operating expenses, which are deducted from gross profit to determine net income. (p. 290)

Multiple Choice

1. What do credit terms 1/10 n/30 indicate? (p. 274)
    a. A 10% discount is available if payment is made within 30 days
    b. A 1% discount is available if payment is made within 10 days
    c. A 1% discount is available if payment is made within 30 days
    d. A 30% discount is available if payment is made within 10 days

2. Which of the following is necessary to record the purchase of merchandise on account under a perpetual inventory system? (p. 274)
   a. A credit to cash
   b. A debit to accounts payable

3. What account is credited when a discount is taken for prompt payment under a perpetual inventory system? (p. 275)
   a. Accounts payable
   b. Accounts receivable
   c. Purchase discounts
   d. Inventory

4. What is the entry required to journalize the payment of a $200 freight bill, assuming the shipping terms are FOB shipping point, under a perpetual inventory system? (p. 278)
   a. Debit Inventory and credit Cash
   b. Debit Accounts payable and credit Inventory
   c. Debit Inventory and credit Purchase discounts
   d. Debit Purchase discounts and credit Inventory

5. How does the purchaser account for transportation charges when goods are shipped to the FOB destination? (p. 278)
   a. No journal entry would be recorded for the transportation charges.
   b. Debit Delivery expense for the amount of the transportation charges.
   c. Debit Freight-in for the amount of the transportation charges.
   d. Debit Inventory for the amount of the transportation charges.

6. Which of the following accounts has a normal debit balance? (p. 281)
   a. Sales revenue
   b. Sales returns and allowances
   c. Net sales revenue
   d. Gross profit

7. When the seller is liable for the shipping costs, what account is debited when payment is made? (p. 278)
   a. Delivery expense
   b. Freight-in
   c. Inventory
   d. Cash

8. Which of the following is necessary to record an adjustment to account for inventory shrinkage under a perpetual system? (p. 286)
   a. A credit to Miscellaneous expense
   b. A credit to Cost of goods sold
   c. A credit to Inventory
   d. A debit to Miscellaneous expense

9. Which of the following accounts should be closed to Income Summary? (p. 287)
   a. Beginning inventory
   b. Sales returns and allowances
   c. Owner withdrawals
   d. Ending inventory

10. What does inventory turnover indicate? (p. 291)
    a. How quickly inventory is received from the supplier after the order is placed
    b. How many days it takes the inventory to travel between the seller's warehouse and the buyer's warehouse
    c. How rapidly inventory is sold
    d. How many days it takes from the time an order is received until the day it is shipped

Quick Exercises

5-1. Werner Company purchased $11,000 of merchandise. The purchase invoice is for $11,200, which includes transportation charges of $200. The company returned $2,900 of the goods received before paying the invoice. The company paid the invoice within the discount terms, 2/10 n/30. (p. 275)

Requirement

Compute the following amounts.

a. The amount of the discount

$$\$11,000 - 2,900 = \$8,100 \text{ net sales}$$
$$\$8,100 \times 0.02 = \$162$$

b. The total amount for the merchandise recorded in the Inventory account

$$\$11,200 - 2,900 - \$162 = \$8,138$$

c. The amount that the purchaser would remit if paid after the discount period

$$\$11,200 - 2,900 = \$8,300$$

5-2. Select whether the following accounts are (p. 287):

(A) Closed out with a debit to the account
(B) Closed out with a credit to the account
(C) Not closed out at all

    a.   A   Sales revenue
    b.   B   Sales returns and allowances
    c.   B   Salary expense
    d.   C   Inventory
    e.   B   Depreciation expense
    f.   C   Accumulated depreciation
    g.   C   Accounts receivable
    h.   A   Interest revenue
    i.   B   Interest expense
    j.   B   Cost of goods sold

5-3. Moyer Company had the following transactions during August 2010. Assuming that the perpetual inventory system is used, prepare the journal entries to record these transactions. (p. 274–276)

Aug. 5 Purchased $2,900 of merchandise on account from Ryan Company, terms 3/15 n/60.

Aug. 9 Paid transportation cost of $440 directly to the trucking company for the August 5 purchase.

Aug. 10 Returned $600 of unwanted merchandise purchased on August 5.

Aug. 15 Paid for the August 5 purchase, less the return and the discount.

Date	Accounts	Debit	Credit
Aug 5	Inventory	2,900	
	Accounts payable		2,900

Date	Accounts	Debit	Credit
Aug 9	Inventory	440	
	Cash		440

Date	Accounts	Debit	Credit
Aug 10	Accounts payable	600	
	Inventory		600

Date	Accounts	Debit	Credit
Aug 15	Accounts payable	2,300	
	Inventory		69
	Cash		2,231

5-4. Prepare the necessary journal entries for Ryan Company using the transactions in 5-3. Assume that the cost of good sold is 50% of the sales price. (p. 280–283)

Date	Accounts	Debit	Credit
Aug 5	Accounts receivable	2,900	
	Cash		2,900

Date	Accounts	Debit	Credit
Aug 5	Cost of goods sold	1,450	
	Inventory		1,450

Date	Accounts	Debit	Credit
Aug 9	No entry required		

Date	Accounts	Debit	Credit
Aug 10	Sales returns and allowances	600	
	Accounts receivable		600

Date	Accounts	Debit	Credit
Aug 10	Inventory	300	
	Cost of goods sold		300

Date	Accounts	Debit	Credit
Aug 15	Cash	2,231	
	Sales discounts	69	
	Accounts receivable		2,300

Do It Yourself! Question 1 Solutions

Requirements

1. Journalize these transactions. Explanations are not required.

Date	Accounts	Debit	Credit
Jan 1	Inventory	150	
	Accounts payable		150

Date	Accounts	Debit	Credit
Jan 8	Accounts payable	150	
	Inventory (to balance*)		3
	Cash [(100% − 2%) × $150]		147

* = $150 − $147 = 3

Date	Accounts	Debit	Credit
Mar 1	Inventory	240	
	Accounts payable		240

Date	Accounts	Debit	Credit
Apr 1	Accounts payable	240	
	Cash		240

Date	Accounts	Debit	Credit
Jul 1	Accounts receivable	120	
	Sales revenue		120
	COGS	80	
	Inventory		80

Date	Accounts	Debit	Credit
Jul 12	Cash [(100% − 5%) × $120]	114	
	Sales discounts (to balance*)	6	
	Accounts receivable		120

* = $120 − $114 = 6

Date	Accounts	Debit	Credit
Sep 1	Accounts receivable (10% × $240)	24	
	Inventory		24

Date	Accounts	Debit	Credit
Oct 1	Cash	24	
	Accounts receivable		24

Date	Accounts	Debit	Credit
Dec 1	Accounts receivable	320	
	Sales revenue		320
	COGS	210	
	Inventory		210

Date	Accounts	Debit	Credit
Dec 6	Inventory (20% × $210)	42	
	COGS		42
	Sales returns and allowances (20% × $320)	64	
	Accounts receivable		64

Date	Accounts	Debit	Credit
Dec 12	Cash ($320 − $64)	256	
	Accounts receivable		256

2. Show the Inventory and COGS T-accounts for the year.

Inventory					COGS			
Jan 1	150				Jul 1	80		
		Jan 8	3		Dec 1	210		
Mar 1	240						Dec 6	42
		Jul 1	80		Bal	248		
		Sep 1	24					
		Dec 1	210					
Dec 6	42							
Bal	115							

3. Inventory on hand at December 31, 2011 (as per count) was $110. Make any necessary adjustments.

Dec 31	COGS ($115 – $110)	5	
	Inventory		5

Inventory				COGS			
Jan 1	150			Jul 1	80		
		Jan 8	3	Dec 1	210		
Mar 1	240					Dec 6	42
		Jul 1	80	Bal	248		
		Sep 1	24	Dec 31	5		
		Dec 1	210	Bal	253		
Dec 6	42						
Bal	115						
		Dec 31	5				
Bal	110						

4. Prepare the top portion of Franco's 2011 income statement (ending with gross profit).

FRANCO BROS.
Income Statement
Year Ended December 31, 2011

Sales revenue			$440*
Less: Sales discounts	$ (6)		
Sales returns & allowances	(64)	(70)	
Net sales revenue			$370
Cost of goods sold			(253)
Gross profit			$117

*$120 + $320

The Power of Practice

For more practice using the skills learned in this chapter, visit MyAccountingLab. There you will find algorithmically generated questions that are based on these Demo Docs and your main textbook's Review and Assess Your Progress sections.

Go to MyAccountingLab and follow these steps:

1. Direct your URL to www.myaccountinglab.com.
2. Log in using your name and password.
3. Click the MyAccountingLab link.
4. Click Study Plan in the left navigation bar.
5. From the table of contents, select Chapter 5, Merchandising Operations.
6. Click a link to work tutorial exercises.

6 Merchandise Inventory

WHAT YOU PROBABLY ALREADY KNOW

Assume that you want to invest in the stock market. You purchase 100 shares of a stock mutual fund in January at $24/share, another 100 shares in February at $27/share, and another 100 shares in April at $30/share. In December, you decide to sell 200 shares of stock to purchase a used car. The market value of the stock at the date of sale is $35/share. You know that you will receive $7,000 (200 shares × $35/share) and that the market price of the shares is higher than what you paid, so you have a gain. To compute the amount of the gain you will have to report on your tax return, you must determine the cost of the shares. Because there were purchases over a period of time at several different prices, how is the cost computed for the 200 shares sold? Can we assume that the shares sold were the first 100 shares purchased at $24/share plus the next 100 shares purchased at $27/share for a total cost of $5,100, that is, (100 shares × $24) + (100 shares × $27)? Can we calculate the cost using an average? Yes, either of these methods is allowed by the Internal Revenue Service. The same problem exists for businesses to determine the cost of the inventory units sold when the unit cost varies. Generally accepted accounting principles (GAAP) also allows a choice from several methods to calculate the cost of goods sold.

Learning Objectives/Success Keys

1 Define accounting principles related to inventory.

The following accounting principles can have an impact on inventory.

- The **consistency principle** states that businesses should use the same accounting methods from period to period.

- The **disclosure principle** holds that a company should report enough information for outsiders to make wise decisions about the company.

- The **materiality concept** states that a company must perform strictly proper accounting *only* for significant items.

- **Conservatism** in accounting means exercising caution in reporting items in the financial statements.

2 Define inventory costing methods.

Under the FIFO (First-In, First-Out) method, the cost of goods sold is based on the oldest purchases. Under the LIFO (Last-in, First-Out) method, ending inventory comes from the oldest costs (first purchases) of the period. Under the average-cost method, the business computes a new average cost per unit after each purchase.

3 Account for perpetual inventory by the three most common costing methods.

The inventory cost method selected for use is an *assumed* outflow of goods to determine the cost of goods sold expense and ending inventory; the actual physical outflow of goods sold may differ. **FIFO** is a popular method that *assumes the oldest goods are sold first leaving the newest goods in ending inventory.* **LIFO** is the opposite assumption; it *assumes that the newest goods are sold first leaving the oldest goods in ending inventory.* **Average cost** assumes that the goods sold as well as those in ending inventory have the same cost.

$$\frac{\text{Total Cost of goods available for sale (Beginning inventory + Purchases)}}{\text{Total Quantity of goods available for sale}} = \frac{\text{Average cost}}{\text{per unit of inventory}}$$

Review the inventory records and cost flows for these methods in Exhibits 6-2 through 6-6 (pp. 334–340).

4 Compare the effects of the three most common costing methods.

The cost of goods sold will usually be different for each of the methods. However, the sum of the cost of goods sold plus the cost of ending inventory will equal the cost of goods available for sale for all methods. In times of inflation, FIFO will result in higher net income and higher ending inventory amounts than LIFO. The average-cost method falls between FIFO and LIFO results. *Review the comparative results of these methods in Exhibit 6-8 (p. 342).*

5 Apply the lower-of-cost-or-market rule to inventory.

The inventory amount on the balance sheet is reduced to the market value if that amount is lower than the cost. This is an application of the conservatism concept. *Review the "Lower-of-Cost-or-Market Rule" section in the main text (p. 346). Note the required journal entry and balance sheet presentation.*

6 Measure the effects of inventory errors.

When measuring the effects of inventory errors, it is helpful to remember that:

> Cost of goods sold + Cost of ending inventory = Cost of goods available

The cost of goods available is a defined amount. Therefore, if the cost of ending inventory is understated, the cost of goods sold must be overstated by the same amount to compensate for the error. **Understating ending inventory results in an understatement of net income.** The reverse is also true; **overstating ending inventory results in an overstatement of net income.**

The ending inventory for one period becomes the beginning inventory for the next. An error in ending inventory is carried over into the succeeding period. **Whatever effect the ending inventory error had on the income statement in the initial period causes the opposite effect on net income in the next period.** *Review the impact of ending inventory errors in Exhibits 6-9 and 6-10 (p. 348).*

7 Estimate ending inventory by the gross profit method.

Sometimes a business may need to estimate its ending inventory. If there is a natural disaster and the inventory is destroyed, an estimate must be determined for insurance purposes.

To calculate the estimate of inventory:

a. Determine the cost of goods available for sale (Beginning inventory + Purchases).

b. Estimate the cost of goods sold; Net sales − (Normal gross profit rate × Net sales).

c. Subtract the estimate of cost of goods sold (b) from the cost of goods available for sale (a) to determine the *estimated cost of ending inventory.*

Review the gross profit method of estimating inventory in Exhibit 6-11 (p. 349).

Demo Doc 1

Inventory Costing Methods and Lower of Cost or Market

Learning Objectives 1–5

Collins Company's inventory records show the following data for 2011:

Inventory at January 1	400 units @	$2 each
Inventory purchases, March	200 units @	$3 each
Sales, May	160 units @	
Inventory purchases, July	100 units @	$4 each
Sales, September	460 units @	
Inventory purchases, November	250 units @	$5 each

Assume there is no inventory shrinkage.

Requirements

1. Calculate COGS for the year ended December 31, 2011, and inventory at December 31, 2011, under each of the following assumptions:

- FIFO
- Perpetual LIFO
- Perpetual Average Cost

2. Sales revenues were $4,000 for 2011. Calculate gross profit under each method.

3. Which method would maximize net income? Which method would minimize income taxes? Which method has the most conservative value for net income?

4. Assume that Collins is using FIFO. The ending inventory has a market price of $4.50 per unit. Calculate the lower of cost or market and make any necessary adjustment.

Demo Doc 1 Solutions

Requirement 1

Calculate COGS for the year ended December 31, 2011, and inventory at December 31, 2011, under each of the following assumptions.

- **FIFO**
- **Perpetual LIFO**
- **Perpetual Average Cost**

Part 1	Part 2	Part 3	Part 4	Part 5	Part 6	Part 7	Demo Doc Complete

Before doing any costing calculations, it is important to determine the goods available for sale (both in units and dollars). We must also determine the number of units that were sold and the number of units in ending inventory.

Goods available for sale = Beginning inventory + Purchases

Beginning Inventory
- 400 units @ $2 = $ 800

Inventory Purchases
- 200 units @ $3 = $ 600
- 100 units @ $4 = $ 400
- 250 units @ $5 = 1,250
- **950 units** $3,050

= Goods available for sale

Number of units sold = 160 in May + 460 in September
= 620 units for the year

COGS = Beginning inventory + Inventory purchases − Ending inventory

OR

COGS = Goods available for sale − Ending inventory

Demo Doc 1 Solutions | Chapter 6

This formula is expressed in *dollars*, but it also works in *units*:

Units sold = Units in Beginning inventory + Units purchased − Units in Ending inventory

OR

Units sold = Units available for sale − Units in Ending inventory

620 units = 950 units − Units in Ending inventory

Units in Ending inventory = 330

2 Define inventory costing methods

3 Account for perpetual inventory by the three most common costing methods

4 Compare the effects of the three most common costing methods

FIFO

| Part 1 | **Part 2** | Part 3 | Part 4 | Part 5 | Part 6 | Part 7 | Demo Doc Complete |

We are using the FIFO method. This means *first in, first out*. In other words, we always sell the *oldest* item we have. So what is left in inventory? The *newest* units.

There were 620 units sold. Under FIFO, these are the *oldest* inventory items. The oldest inventory is the beginning inventory of 400 units @ $2/unit. They must be part of COGS.

There are 620 − 400 = 220 other units that were sold. Some of these must be from the next oldest inventory: the March purchase of 200 units @ $3/unit.

There are 220 − 200 = 20 other units that were also sold (that were not part of beginning inventory or the March purchase).

These other units must have come from the July purchase of 100 units @ $4/unit (the next oldest units).

So we can calculate COGS as:

From Beginning inventory:
400 units × $2 per unit = $ 800
From March purchase:
200 units × $3 per unit = 600
From July purchase:
20 units × $4 per unit = 80
COGS $1,480

There are 330 units in ending inventory. These are the 330 *newest* units the company has.

The newest units are the ones purchased in November of 250 units @ $5 per unit. They must be part of the ending inventory.

There are 330 – 250 = 80 other units that are also part of ending inventory (that were not from the November purchase). These other units must have come from the July purchase of 100 units @ $4 per unit (the next newest units). So we can calculate ending inventory as:

From November purchase:
250 units × $5 per unit = $1,250
From July purchase:
80 units × $4 per unit = 320
Ending inventory $1,570

So under FIFO, COGS = $1,480 and inventory at December 31, 2011 = $1,570.

Perpetual LIFO

| Part 1 | Part 2 | **Part 3** | Part 4 | Part 5 | Part 6 | Part 7 | Demo Doc Complete |

What differs under LIFO is the *dollar* amount of ending inventory and COGS. The *number* of units sold and the *number* of units in ending inventory are still the same at 620 and 330 units, respectively. LIFO sells the newest units, but we must track *each sale individually* with the perpetual recording system. It is also important to remember that under perpetual inventory recording, we are keeping up-to-date track of inventory. We cannot sell units that *we have not yet acquired*.

The first sale is in May when 160 units are sold. At this time, what were the newest units in stock? The 200 units @ $3 per unit purchased in March. So the 160 units sold must have come from this group. This means that:

May COGS = 160 × $3
= $480

The second sale was in September when 460 units were sold. At that time, what were the newest units in stock? The 100 units @ $4 per unit purchased in July. But this is not enough to cover the entire sale. There were another 460 – 100 = 360 units sold.

Some of these other units must have come from the next newest group, the 200 units @ $3 per unit purchased in March. However, there are only 40 of these units left after the sale in May. There were another 360 – 40 = 320 units sold.

These other units must come from the beginning inventory of 400 units @ $2 per unit. This means that September COGS is calculated as:

From July purchase:
100 units × $4 per unit = $ 400
From March purchase:
40 units × $3 per unit = 120
From Beginning inventory:
320 units × $2 per unit = 640
September COGS $1,160

Total COGS for the period is the COGS for all sales added together:

May COGS + September COGS = Total COGS
$480 + $1,160 = $1,160

Inventory at December 31 is whatever remains.

There were 400 − 320 = 80 units of the beginning inventory (@ $2 per unit) that were not sold.

The entire March purchase of 200 units @ $3 per unit was sold in May (160 units) and September (40 units), so there is none of this inventory left unsold.

The entire July purchase of 100 units @ $4 per unit was sold in September.

None of the units from the November purchase of 250 units @ $5 per unit were sold. This means that all of these units are part of ending inventory. So we can calculate ending inventory as:

From Beginning inventory:
80 units × $2 per unit = $ 160
From November purchase:
250 units × $5 per unit = 1,250
Ending inventory $1,410

These same calculations can also be done in chart format:

	Purchases			Cost of Goods Sold			Inventory on Hand		
Date	Quantity	Unit Cost	Total Cost	Quantity	Unit Cost	Total Cost	Quantity	Unit Cost	Total Cost
January							400	$2	$ 800
March	200	$3	$ 600				400	$2	$ 800
							200	$3	$ 600
May				160	$3	$ 480	400	$2	$ 800
							40	$3	$ 120
July	100	$4	$ 400				400	$2	$ 800
							40	$3	$ 120
							100	$4	$ 400
September				100	$4	$ 400			
				40	$3	$ 120			
				320	$2	$ 640	80	$2	$ 160
November	250	$5	$1,250				80	$2	$ 160
							250	$5	$1,250
December				600		$1,640	330		$1,410

So under perpetual LIFO, COGS = $1,640 and inventory at December 31, 2011 = $1,410.

2 Define inventory costing methods

3 Account for inventory by the three most common costing methods

4 Compare the effects of the three most common costing methods

Perpetual Average Cost

| Part 1 | Part 2 | Part 3 | **Part 4** | Part 5 | Part 6 | Part 7 | Demo Doc Complete |

This method calculates the average cost per unit with *every* sale.

The first sale is in May. At that time in inventory, we have:

400 units × $2 per unit = $ 800
200 units × $3 per unit =   600
600 units $1,400

So at this time, the average cost per unit is:

$$\text{Average cost per unit} = \frac{\text{Cost of units in inventory}}{\text{Units in inventory}}$$

$$\text{Average cost per unit} = \frac{\$1,400}{600 \text{ units}}$$

$$= \$2.33 \text{ per unit}$$

Demo Doc 1 Solutions | Chapter 6 **163**

The COGS for the May sale is:

$$160 \text{ units} \times \$2.33 \text{ per unit} = \$373$$

We have 600 units − 160 units = 440 units left in inventory @ $2.33 per unit = $1,025.

The next sale is in September. At this time in inventory, we have:

440 units × $2.33 per unit	=	$1,025
100 units × $4 per unit	=	400
540 units		$1,425

So at this time, the average cost per unit is:

$$\text{Average cost per unit} = \frac{\$1,425}{540 \text{ units}}$$

$$= \$2.64 \text{ per unit}$$

$$\text{September COGS} = 460 \text{ units} \times \$2.64 \text{ per unit}$$

$$= \$1,214$$

There are now 540 units − 460 units = 80 units left in inventory at the average cost of $2.64 = $211.

Total COGS for the period is the COGS for all sales added together:

May COGS	+	September COGS	=	Total COGS
$373	+	$1,214	=	$1,587

Inventory at December 31, 2011, is the units left over after the September sale plus those purchased in November:

80 units × $2.64 per unit	=	$ 211
250 units × $5 per unit		1,250
330 units in ending inventory	=	$1,461

These same calculations can also be done in chart format:

	Purchases			Cost of Goods Sold			Inventory on Hand		
Date	Quantity	Unit Cost	Total Cost	Quantity	Unit Cost	Total Cost	Quantity	Unit Cost	Total Cost
January				400	$2.00	$ 800			
March	200	$3	$ 600				400	$2.00	$ 800
							200	$3.00	$ 600
May				160	$2.33	$ 373	440	$2.33	$1,025
July	100	$4	$ 400				440	$2.33	$1,025
							100	$4.00	$ 400
September				460	$2.64	$1,214	80	$2.64	$ 211
November	250	$5	$1,250				80	$2.61	$ 211
							250	$5.00	$1,250
December				620		$1,587	330		$1,461

So under moving average, COGS = $1,587 and inventory at December 31, 2011 = $1,461.

Requirement 2

4 Compare the effects of the three most common costing methods

Sales revenues were $4,000 for 2011. Calculate gross profit under each method.

| Part 1 | Part 2 | Part 3 | Part 4 | **Part 5** | Part 6 | Part 7 | Demo Doc Complete |

Gross profit = Sales revenue − COGS

	FIFO	Perpetual LIFO	Perpetual Average Cost
Sales revenue	$4,000	$4,000	$4,000
− COGS	1,480	1,640	1,587
Gross profit	$2,520	$2,360	$2,413

Requirement 3

1 Define accounting principles related to inventory

4 Compare the effects of the three most common costing methods

Which method would maximize net income? Which method would minimize income taxes? Which method has the most conservative value for net income?

| Part 1 | Part 2 | Part 3 | Part 4 | Part 5 | **Part 6** | Part 7 | Demo Doc Complete |

Demo Doc 1 Solutions | Chapter 6   **165**

For the three methods, we have the following COGS:

FIFO	$1,480
LIFO	1,640
Average Cost	1,587

Of these, FIFO is the lowest and LIFO is the highest. Note that FIFO and LIFO will usually be the extremes with average cost being somewhere in the middle.

FIFO gives the lowest COGS, which means that it gives the highest gross profit. You can see this result in Requirement 2 of this question. This means that FIFO would maximize net income.

LIFO gives the highest COGS, which means that it gives the lowest gross profit. You can also see this result in Requirement 2 of this question. This means that LIFO would minimize net income, which in turn would minimize income taxes. This would also be the most conservative value for net income.

Note that if prices are decreasing over time (such as for high-tech items that quickly become obsolete), then the reverse of this analysis is true (FIFO gives highest COGS).

Requirement 4

[5] Apply the lower-of-cost-or-market rule to inventory

Assume that Collins is using FIFO. The ending inventory has a market price of $4.50 per unit. Calculate the lower of cost or market and make any necessary adjustment.

| Part 1 | Part 2 | Part 3 | Part 4 | Part 5 | Part 6 | **Part 7** | Demo Doc Complete |

We have already determined that there are 330 units in ending inventory. Under FIFO, the cost of these units is $1,570. The market price of these units is:

$$330 \text{ units} \times \$4.50 \text{ per unit} = \$1,485$$

If cost is $1,570 and market price is $1,485, the lower of cost or market is $1,485 (the market value of the inventory).

The balance in the inventory T-account is currently the cost of $1,570. Therefore, Inventory must be decreased to the market value of $1,485. So Inventory is decreased (a credit) by $1,570 − $1,485 = $85. The other side of the journal entry is an adjustment to COGS. This will have to be a debit to balance out the credit to Inventory.

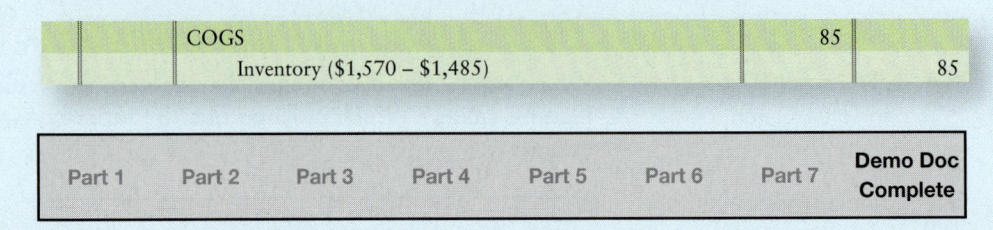

	COGS		85	
	Inventory ($1,570 − $1,485)			85

| Part 1 | Part 2 | Part 3 | Part 4 | Part 5 | Part 6 | Part 7 | **Demo Doc Complete** |

Demo Doc 2

Gross Profit Method and Inventory Errors

Learning Objectives 6, 7

On December 31, 2011, Talon Company's warehouse and accounting records were destroyed in a flood. For insurance purposes, Talon must estimate the value of the inventory lost.

Through records from its bank and suppliers, Talon has been able to compile the following information:

Sales Revenue for 2011	$20,000
Inventory at December 31, 2011	6,000
Inventory Purchases for 2011	23,000

Talon has historically had gross profit of 10%.

Requirements

1. Estimate Talon's ending inventory value for 2011 using the gross profit method.

2. Assume that the actual value of inventory lost was $12,000. What is Talon's true COGS? Is COGS overstated or understated? How will this impact Talon's estimate of net income for 2011?

Demo Doc 2 Solutions

Requirement 1

7 Estimate ending inventory by the gross profit method

Estimate Talon's ending inventory value for 2011 using the gross profit method.

| Part 1 | Part 2 | Demo Doc Complete |

The gross profit method uses the COGS formula:

$$\text{COGS} = \text{Beginning inventory} + \text{Inventory purchases} - \text{Ending inventory}$$

We are given information about purchases and beginning inventory, but to calculate ending inventory we will need an estimate for COGS.

The formula for the gross profit percentage is:

$$\text{Gross profit percentage} = \frac{\text{Gross profit}}{\text{Sales revenue}} = \frac{\text{Sales} - \text{COGS}}{\text{Sales}}$$

So we know that 10% = ($20,000 − COGS)/$20,000.
From this, we can calculate COGS = $18,000. Using this in the COGS formula:

$$\$18{,}000 = \$6{,}000 + \$23{,}000 - \text{Ending inventory}$$

From this, we can calculate ending inventory = $11,000.

Requirement 2

6 Measure the effects of inventory errors

Assume that the actual value of inventory lost was $12,000. What is Talon's true COGS? Is COGS overstated or understated? How will this impact Talon's estimate of net income for 2011?

| Part 1 | **Part 2** | Demo Doc Complete |

Using the actual value of $12,000 for ending inventory, we can recalculate COGS.

$$\text{COGS} = \$6{,}000 + \$23{,}000 - \$12{,}000$$
$$= \$17{,}000$$

Because Talon is estimating COGS of $18,000, COGS is overstated by $18,000 − $17,000 = $1,000. If Talon uses the wrong COGS number of $18,000 to calculate net income, then net income will be understated by $1,000.

| Part 1 | Part 2 | **Demo Doc Complete** |

Quick Practice Questions

True/False

_____ 1. Under FIFO, the ending inventory cost comes from the oldest purchases.

_____ 2. FIFO is the opposite of LIFO.

_____ 3. The LIFO method can result in misleading inventory costs on the balance sheet because the oldest prices are left in ending inventory.

_____ 4. When inventory costs are rising, LIFO will result in the lowest gross profit.

_____ 5. When using a perpetual inventory system, a business will debit Inventory and credit Cost of Goods Sold each time a sale is recorded.

_____ 6. If a company had 10 units of beginning inventory with a unit cost of $10 and a subsequent purchase of 15 units with a unit cost of $12, the average cost of one unit sold would be $11.

_____ 7. When applying lower-of-cost-or-market rules to ending inventory valuation, market value generally refers to the company's current selling price for its inventory.

_____ 8. Understating beginning inventory in the current year will understate cost of goods sold in the current year.

_____ 9. Overstating ending inventory in 2010 will overstate net income for 2011.

_____ 10. The gross profit method is an estimate of inventory that can be used to estimate losses for insurance claims due to a fire or natural disaster.

Multiple Choice

1. Anticipating no gains but providing for all probable losses can be most closely associated with which of the following?
   a. Conservatism
   b. Disclosure principle
   c. Consistency principle
   d. Materiality concept

2. Which of the following are required to record the sale of merchandise on credit under a perpetual inventory system?
   a. Debit Accounts Receivable; credit Sales Revenue
   b. Debit Cost of Goods Sold; credit cash
   c. Debit Cost of Goods Sold; credit Inventory
   d. Both (a) and (c) are necessary entries

3. What is the effect of using FIFO during a period of rising prices under a perpetual inventory system?
   a. Less net income than LIFO
   b. Less operating expenses than LIFO
   c. Higher gross profit than LIFO
   d. Higher cost of goods sold than average costing

4. Which of the following is NOT a reason for choosing the LIFO method?
   a. LIFO reports the most up-to-date inventory values on the balance sheet.
   b. LIFO uses more current costs in calculating cost of goods sold.
   c. LIFO allows owners and managers to manage reported income.
   d. LIFO generally results in lower income taxes paid.

5. Which of the following is true for ending inventory when prices are falling and the LIFO inventory system is used?
   a. LIFO ending inventory is less than FIFO.
   b. LIFO ending inventory is greater than FIFO.
   c. LIFO ending inventory is equal to FIFO.
   d. LIFO ending inventory is equally likely to be higher or lower than FIFO.

6. The following data are for Daisy's Florist Shop for the first seven months of its fiscal year:

Beginning inventory	$53,500
Purchases	75,500
Net sales revenue	93,700
Normal gross profit percent	30%

   What is the estimated inventory on hand as determined by the gross profit method?
   a. $28,110
   b. $63,410
   c. $65,590
   d. $100,890

7. Which of the following statements is true about a company making an accounting change in its financial statements?
   a. It is generally entitled to make one accounting change per year.
   b. It must report the change in accounting method.
   c. Companies can never make accounting changes because of the consistency principle.
   d. It must petition the Financial Accounting Standards Board for permission to make the change.

8. When is an item considered material?
   a. When it facilitates comparison with the financial statements of another company in the same industry
   b. When its inclusion in the financial statements would cause a statement user to change a decision
   c. When its dollar value is greater than 10% of net income
   d. When it is accounted for using a treatment that is not normally allowed by generally accepted accounting principles

9. Ending inventory for Commodity X consists of 20 units. Under the FIFO method, the cost of the 20 units is $5 each. Current replacement cost is $4.50 per unit. Using the lower-of-cost-or-market rule to value inventory, the balance sheet would show ending inventory at what amount?
   a. $4.75
   b. $5.00
   c. $90.00
   d. $100.00

10. Inventory at the end of the current year is overstated by $20,000. What effect will this error have on the following year's net income?
    a. Net income will be overstated $20,000.
    b. Net income will be understated $20,000.
    c. Net income will be correctly stated.
    d. Net income will be understated $40,000.

Quick Exercises

6-1. Compute the missing income statement amounts for each of the following independent companies:

Company	Net Sales	Beginning Inventory	Purchases	Ending Inventory	Cost of Goods Sold	Gross Profit
A	$ 93,000	$14,600	$65,000	(a)	$58,300	(b)
B	(c)	$31,600	(d)	$23,600	$96,200	$52,500
C	$ 89,300	$23,600	$54,000	(f)	(e)	$23,900
D	$105,000	$11,200	(h)	$ 9,400	(g)	$48,200

a. _____
b. _____
c. _____
d. _____
e. _____
f. _____
g. _____
h. _____

6-2. Which inventory method would best meet the specific goal of management stated below? Show your answer by inserting the proper letter beside each statement.

a. Specific unit cost
b. LIFO
c. FIFO
d. Average cost

_____ 1. Management desires to properly match net sales revenue with the most recent cost of goods.
_____ 2. Management desires to minimize the company's ending inventory balance during a period of falling prices.
_____ 3. The company sells rare antique items.
_____ 4. Management desires to show the current value of inventory on the balance sheet.
_____ 5. Management desires to minimize the company's tax liability during a period of rising prices.

6-3. Plastic Products Company lost some of its inventory due to a flood and needs to determine the amount of the inventory lost. The following data are available for 2011:

Sales revenue	$400,000
Estimated gross profit rate	35%
January 1, beginning inventory	11,600
Net purchases	275,000
Inventory on hand, after flood	6,500

Requirements

1. Compute what the estimated ending inventory should be using the gross profit method.

2. Calculate the amount of the inventory loss.

6-4. Determine the effect on cost of goods sold and net income for the current year of the following inventory errors. Indicate your answer with either a + (overstated) or a − (understated).

Item	Error	Effect on Cost of Goods Sold	Effect on Net Income
1	Beginning inventory is understated.		
2	Ending inventory is understated.		
3	Beginning inventory is overstated.		
4	Ending inventory is overstated.		

Do It Yourself! Question 1

Sam Company's inventory records show the following data for July 2011:

Inventory at July 1	10 units	@	$1 each
Inventory Purchases, July 5	80 units	@	$2 each
Sales, July 10	50 units	@	
Inventory Purchases, July 15	20 units	@	$3 each
Sales, July 20	40 units	@	
Inventory Purchases, July 25	30 units	@	$4 each

Assume there is no inventory shrinkage.

Requirements

3 Account for inventory by the three most common costing methods

1. **Calculate COGS for the month ended July 31, 2011, and inventory at July 31, 2011, using the FIFO costing method.**

4 Compare the effects of the three most common costing methods

2. **Calculate COGS for the month ended July 31, 2011, and inventory at July 31, 2011, using the perpetual LIFO costing method.**

3. **Calculate COGS for the month ended July 31, 2011, and inventory at July 31, 2011, using the moving average (perpetual average cost) costing method.**

4. **Sales revenues were $500 for July 2011. Calculate gross profit under each method.**

5 Apply the lower-of-cost-or-market rule to inventory

5. **The market value of ending inventory is $130. If Sam uses perpetual LIFO, give any necessary adjustment for the lower-of-cost-or-market rule.**

Journal				Page 1
Date	Accounts		Debit	Credit

Do It Yourself! Question 1 | Chapter 6   **173**

Do It Yourself! Question 2

On December 31, 2011, Virga Brothers lost all of its inventory during a hurricane. Virga was able to gather the following information.

Inventory at January 1, 2011	$ 40,000
Inventory purchases for 2011	90,000
Sales revenue for 2011	180,000

Historically, Virga has had gross profit of 40%.

Requirement

7 Estimate ending inventory by the gross profit method

1. Estimate the value of Virga's lost inventory.

Quick Practice Solutions

True/False

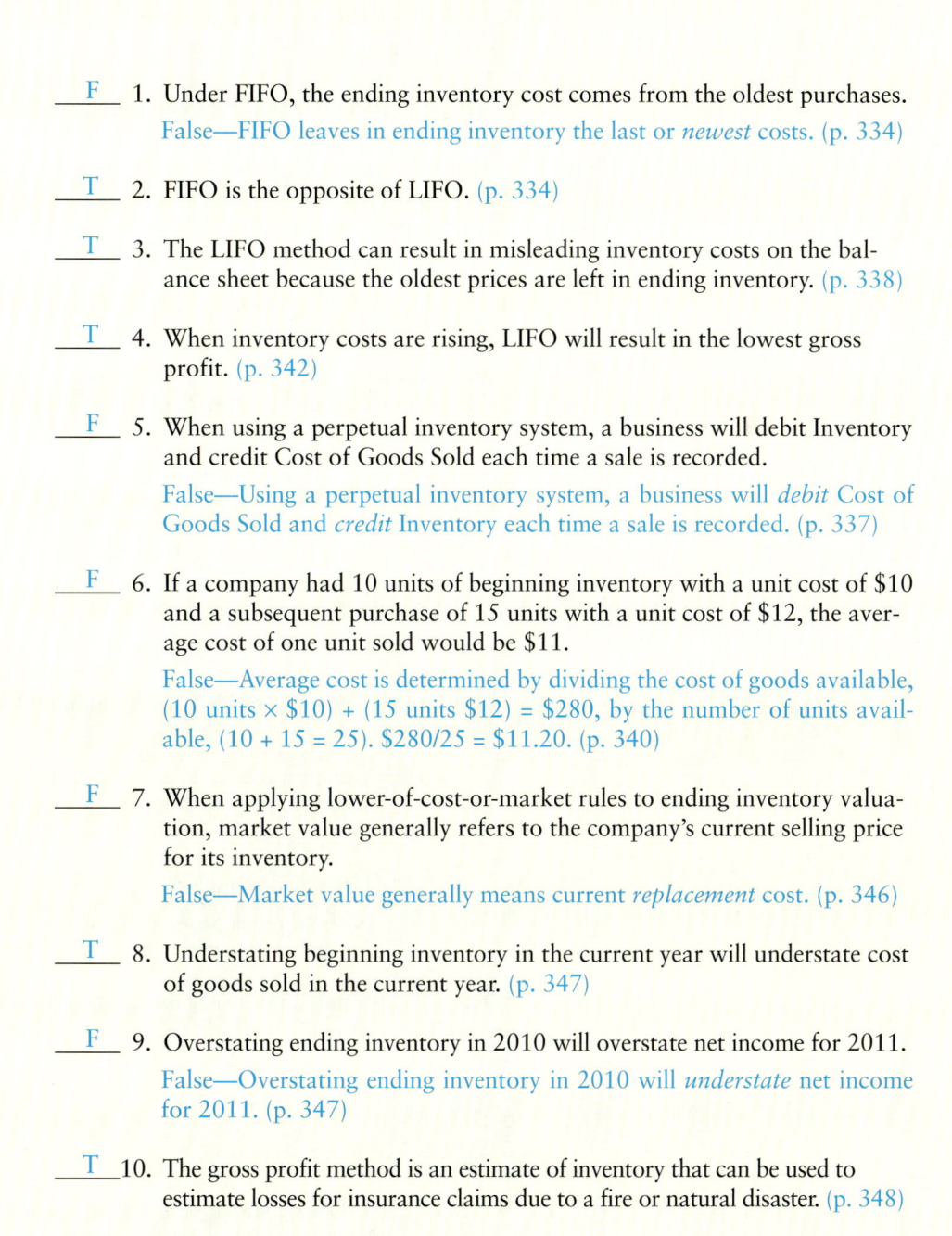

__F__ 1. Under FIFO, the ending inventory cost comes from the oldest purchases.

False—FIFO leaves in ending inventory the last or *newest* costs. (p. 334)

__T__ 2. FIFO is the opposite of LIFO. (p. 334)

__T__ 3. The LIFO method can result in misleading inventory costs on the balance sheet because the oldest prices are left in ending inventory. (p. 338)

__T__ 4. When inventory costs are rising, LIFO will result in the lowest gross profit. (p. 342)

__F__ 5. When using a perpetual inventory system, a business will debit Inventory and credit Cost of Goods Sold each time a sale is recorded.

False—Using a perpetual inventory system, a business will *debit* Cost of Goods Sold and *credit* Inventory each time a sale is recorded. (p. 337)

__F__ 6. If a company had 10 units of beginning inventory with a unit cost of $10 and a subsequent purchase of 15 units with a unit cost of $12, the average cost of one unit sold would be $11.

False—Average cost is determined by dividing the cost of goods available, (10 units × $10) + (15 units $12) = $280, by the number of units available, (10 + 15 = 25). $280/25 = $11.20. (p. 340)

__F__ 7. When applying lower-of-cost-or-market rules to ending inventory valuation, market value generally refers to the company's current selling price for its inventory.

False—Market value generally means current *replacement* cost. (p. 346)

__T__ 8. Understating beginning inventory in the current year will understate cost of goods sold in the current year. (p. 347)

__F__ 9. Overstating ending inventory in 2010 will overstate net income for 2011.

False—Overstating ending inventory in 2010 will *understate* net income for 2011. (p. 347)

__T__ 10. The gross profit method is an estimate of inventory that can be used to estimate losses for insurance claims due to a fire or natural disaster. (p. 348)

Multiple Choice

1. Anticipating no gains but providing for all probable losses can be most closely associated with which of the following? (p. 333)
   a. Conservatism
   b. Disclosure principle
   c. Consistency principle
   d. Materiality concept

2. Which of the following are required to record the sale of merchandise on credit under a perpetual inventory system? (p. 337)
   a. Debit Accounts Receivable; credit Sales Revenue
   b. Debit Cost of Goods Sold; credit cash
   c. Debit Cost of Goods Sold; credit Inventory
   d. Both (a) and (c) are necessary entries

3. What is the effect of using FIFO during a period of rising prices under a perpetual inventory system? (p. 342)
   a. Less net income than LIFO
   b. Less operating expenses than LIFO
   c. Higher gross profit than LIFO
   d. Higher cost of goods sold than average costing

4. Which of the following is NOT a reason for choosing the LIFO method? (p. 338)
   a. LIFO reports the most up-to-date inventory values on the balance sheet.
   b. LIFO uses more current costs in calculating cost of goods sold.
   c. LIFO allows owners and managers to manage reported income.
   d. LIFO generally results in lower income taxes paid.

5. Which of the following is true for ending inventory when prices are falling and the LIFO inventory system is used? (p. 342)
   a. LIFO ending inventory is less than FIFO.
   b. LIFO ending inventory is greater than FIFO.
   c. LIFO ending inventory is equal to FIFO.
   d. LIFO ending inventory is equally likely to be higher or lower than FIFO.

6. The following data are for Daisy's Florist Shop for the first seven months of its fiscal year:

Beginning inventory	$53,500
Purchases	75,500
Net sales revenue	93,700
Normal gross profit percent	30%

   What is the estimated inventory on hand as determined by the gross profit method? (p. 348)
   a. $28,110
   b. $63,410
   c. $65,590
   d. $100,890

7. Which of the following statements is true about a company making an accounting change in its financial statements? (p. 333)
   a. It is generally entitled to make one accounting change per year.
   b. It must report the change in accounting method.
   c. Companies can never make accounting changes because of the consistency principle.
   d. It must petition the Financial Accounting Standards Board for permission to make the change.

8. When is an item considered material? (p. 333)
   a. When it facilitates comparison with the financial statements of another company in the same industry
   b. When its inclusion in the financial statements would cause a statement user to change a decision
   c. When its dollar value is greater than 10% of net income
   d. When it is accounted for using a treatment that is not normally allowed by generally accepted accounting principles

9. Ending inventory for Commodity X consists of 20 units. Under the FIFO method, the cost of the 20 units is $5 each. Current replacement cost is $4.50 per unit. Using the lower-of-cost-or-market rule to value inventory, the balance sheet would show ending inventory at what amount? (p. 346)
   a. $4.75
   b. $5.00
   c. $90.00
   d. $100.00

10. Inventory at the end of the current year is overstated by $20,000. What effect will this error have on the following year's net income? (p. 347)
    a. Net income will be overstated $20,000.
    b. Net income will be understated $20,000.
    c. Net income will be correctly stated.
    d. Net income will be understated $40,000.

Quick Exercises

6-1. Compute the missing income statement amounts for each of the following independent companies: (p. 332)

Company	Net Sales	Beginning Inventory	Purchases	Ending Inventory	Cost of Goods Sold	Gross Profit
A	$93,000	$14,600	$65,000	(a)	$58,300	(b)
B	(c)	$31,600	(d)	$23,600	$96,200	$52,500
C	$89,300	$23,600	$54,000	(f)	(e)	$23,900
D	$105,000	$11,200	(h)	$9,400	(g)	$48,200

(a) $14,600 + $65,000 − $58,300 = $ 21,300
(b) $93,000 − $58,300 = $ 34,700
(c) $96,200 + $52,500 = $148,700
(d) $23,600 + $96,200 − $31,600 = $ 88,200
(e) $89,300 − $23,900 = $ 65,400
(f) $23,600 + $54,000 − $65,400 = $ 12,200
(g) $105,000 − $48,200 = $ 56,800
(h) $9,400 + $56,800 − $11,200 = $ 55,000

6-2. Which inventory method would best meet the specific goal of management stated below? Show your answer by inserting the proper letter beside each statement. (p. 334)

a. Specific unit cost
b. LIFO
c. FIFO

__b__ 1. Management desires to properly match net sales revenue with the most recent cost of goods.

__c__ 2. Management desires to minimize the company's ending inventory balance during a period of falling prices.

__a__ 3. The company sells rare antique items.

__c__ 4. Management desires to show the current value of inventory on the balance sheet.

__b__ 5. Management desires to minimize the company's tax liability during a period of rising prices.

6-3. Plastic Products Company lost some of its inventory due to a flood and needs to determine the amount of the inventory lost. The following data are available for 2011: (p. 349)

Net sales revenue	$400,000
Estimated gross profit rate	35%
January 1, beginning inventory	11,600
Net purchases	275,000
Inventory on hand, after flood	6,500

Requirements

1. Compute what the estimated ending inventory should be using the gross profit method.

Beginning inventory		$ 11,600
Net purchases		275,000
Cost of goods available		286,600
Estimated cost of goods sold:		
Net sales revenue	400,000	
Less: Estimated gross profit of 35%	(140,000)	
Estimated cost of goods sold		260,000
Estimated cost of ending inventory		$ 26,600

2. Calculate the amount of the inventory loss.

Estimated cost of ending inventory	$ 26,600
Less: Inventory on hand, after flood	6,500
Amount of inventory loss	$ 20,100

6-4   Determine the effect on cost of goods sold and net income for the current year of the following inventory errors. Indicate your answer with either a + (overstated) or a − (understated). (p. 347)

Item	Error	Effect on Cost of Goods Sold	Effect on Net Income
1	Beginning inventory is understated.	−	+
2	Ending inventory is understated.	+	−
3	Beginning inventory is overstated.	+	−
4	Ending inventory is overstated.	−	+

Do It Yourself! Question 1 Solutions

Requirements

1. Calculate COGS for the month ended July 31, 2011, and inventory at July 31, 2011, using the FIFO costing method.

Beginning inventory	10 units	@	$1 per unit	=	$ 10
Inventory purchases					
July 5	80 units	@	$2 per unit	=	160
July 15	20 units	@	$3 per unit	=	60
July 25	30 units	@	$4 per unit	=	120
Goods available for sale	130 units				$350

Number of units sold = 50 on July 10 + 40 on July 20
= 90 units

90 units = 10 units + 130 units − Units in ending inventory
90 units = 140 units − Units in ending inventory
50 units = Units in ending inventory

From beginning inventory:
10 units × $1 per unit   = $ 10
From July 5 purchase:
80 units × $2 per unit   =   160
COGS $170

From July 25 purchase:
30 units × $4 per unit   = $120
From July 15 purchase:
20 units × $3 per unit   =   60
Ending inventory $180

2. Calculate COGS for the month ended July 31, 2011, and inventory at July 31, 2011, using the perpetual LIFO costing method.

July 10 COGS = 50 × $2 (from July 5 purchase)
= $100

From July 25 purchase:
30 units × $3 per unit = $ 60
From July 5 purchase:
20 units × $2 per unit = 40
July 20 COGS $100

July 10 COGS + July 20 COGS = Total COGS

$100 + $100 = $200

From beginning inventory:
10 units × $1 per unit = $ 10
From July 5 purchase:
10 units × $2 per unit = 20
From July 25 purchase:
30 units × $4 per unit = 120
Ending inventory $150

These same calculations can also be done in chart format:

	Purchases			Cost of Goods Sold			Inventory on Hand		
Date	Quantity	Unit Cost	Total Cost	Quantity	Unit Cost	Total Cost	Quantity	Unit Cost	Total Cost
July 1							10	$1	$ 10
July 5	80	$2	$160				10	$1	$ 10
							80	$2	$160
July 10				50	$2	$100	10	$1	$ 10
							30	$2	$ 60
July 15	20	$3	$ 60				10	$1	$ 10
							30	$2	$ 60
							20	$3	$ 60
July 20				20	$3	$ 60	10	$1	$ 10
				20	$2	$ 40	10	$2	$ 20
July 25	30	$4	$120				10	$1	$ 10
							10	$2	$ 20
							30	$4	$120
July 31				90		$200	50		$150

3. Calculate COGS for the month ended July 31, 2011, and inventory at July 31, 2011, using the perpetual average cost costing method.

July 9 inventory:

10 units × $1 per unit	=	$ 10
80 units × $2 per unit	=	160
90 units		$170

For July 10 Sale:

$$\text{Average cost per unit} = \frac{\$170}{90 \text{ units}}$$

$$= \$1.89 \text{ per unit}$$

July 10 COGS = 50 units × $1.89 per unit
= $94

Inventory after July 10 sale = 40 units × $1.89 per unit
= $76

July 19 inventory:

40 units × $1.89 per unit	=	$ 76
20 units × $3 per unit	=	60
60 units		$136

For July 20 Sale:

$$\text{Average cost per unit} = \frac{\$136}{60 \text{ units}}$$

$$= \$2.27 \text{ per unit}$$

July 20 COGS = 40 units × $2.27 per unit
= $91

Inventory after July 20 sale = 20 units × $2.27 per unit
= $45

July 10 COGS	+	July 20 COGS	=	Total COGS
$94	+	$91	=	$185

From beginning after previous sale:
20 units × $2.27 per unit = $ 45
From July 25 purchase:
30 units × $4 per unit = 120
Ending inventory $150

These same calculations can also be made in chart format:

	Purchases			Cost of Goods Sold			Inventory on Hand		
Date	Quantity	Unit Cost	Total Cost	Quantity	Unit Cost	Total Cost	Quantity	Unit Cost	Total Cost
July 1							10	$1.00	$ 10
July 5	80	$2.00	$160				10	$1.00	$ 10
							80	$2.00	$160
July 10				50	$1.89	$ 94	40	$1.89	$ 76
July 15	20	$3.00	$ 60				40	$1.89	$ 76
							20	$3.00	$ 60
July 20				40	$2.27	$ 91	20	$2.27	$ 45
July 25	30	$4.00	$120				20	$2.27	$ 45
							30	$4.00	$120
July 31				90		$185	50		$165

4. Sales revenues were $500 for 2011. Calculate gross profit under each method.

	FIFO	Perpetual LIFO	Perpetual Average Cost
Sales Revenue	$500	$500	$500
– COGS	170	$200	185
Gross Profit	$330	$300	$315

5. The market value of ending inventory is $130. If Sam uses perpetual LIFO, give any necessary adjustment for the lower-of-cost-or-market rule.

Cost (under perpetual LIFO) = $150   Market = $130
Lower of cost or market = $130

COGS		20	
Inventory ($150 – $130)			20

Do It Yourself! Question 2 Solutions

Requirement

1. Estimate the value of Virga's lost inventory.

$$\text{Gross profit percentage} + \frac{\text{Gross profit}}{\text{Sales revenue}} = \frac{\text{Sales} - \text{COGS}}{\text{Sales}}$$

40% = ($180,000 − COGS) / $180,000
COGS = $108,000

$$\text{COGS} = \text{Beginning inventory} + \text{Inventory purchases} - \text{Ending inventory}$$

$108,000 = $40,000 + $90,000 − Ending inventory
Ending inventory = $22,000

The Power of Practice

For more practice using the skills learned in this chapter, visit MyAccountingLab. There you will find algorithmically generated questions that are based on these Demo Docs and your main textbook's Review and Assess Your Progress sections.

Go to MyAccountingLab and follow these steps:

1. Direct your URL to www.myaccountinglab.com.
2. Log in using your name and password.
3. Click the MyAccountingLab link.
4. Click Study Plan in the left navigation bar.
5. From the table of contents, select Chapter 6, Merchandise Inventory.
6. Click a link to work tutorial exercises.

7 Internal Control and Cash

What You Probably Already Know

When you shop in a department store, you have probably noticed that there are electronic tags on some of the goods. The cashier will remove the tag upon purchase to avoid sounding an alarm when exiting the store through the security gates. You may also have noticed that fine jewelry is likely displayed in a locked case that can only be opened by an employee. The employee will stay with you until the item is returned to the case and locked or purchased. Cartons of cigarettes are also usually secured behind locked doors or cabinets.

If you work as a cashier, it's likely that you have your own cash drawer. Periodically there may be times when cash is collected and deposited in a safe or taken to the bank. At the end of the shift, the cash is counted and compared to the sales rung up for the period to determine that the appropriate amount of cash is in the drawer. These observations are just a few of the procedures and policies that businesses employ to achieve a good system of internal control.

Learning Objectives/Success Keys

1 Define internal control.

Internal control is the entity's plan to safeguard assets, encourage employees to follow company policy, promote operational efficiency, and ensure accurate and reliable accounting records.

2 Explain the Sarbanes-Oxley Act.

Strong controls are more important than ever owing to the overstatement of net income that occurred in companies like Enron and WorldCom. As a result of these misstatements, public companies are now required to issue an internal control report and the outside auditor must evaluate the company's controls.

3 List and describe the components of internal control and control procedures.

Business owners and managers must be acutely aware of the need to have adequate policies and procedures in place to protect the company. Hiring competent, reliable, and ethical personnel and paying them a fair salary; assigning employees responsibilities and making them accountable; and separating responsibility for the custody of assets from the accounting and the operating departments are some of the ways employers address this need. They also engage in periodic internal and external audits, use prenumbered source documents, and use electronic devices to safeguard assets. *Review the "Internal Control Procedures" section of the main text carefully. This topic is critical for business owners and managers.*

4 Explain control procedures unique to e-commerce.

E-commerce can unknowingly create pathways for hackers to access private information. Special care must be taken to alleviate the risk of stolen account numbers, stolen passwords, Trojan horses, phishing, and computer viruses. *Review Internal Controls for E-Commerce in the text to see how these risks can be alleviated.*

5 Demonstrate the use of a bank account as a control device.

Keeping cash in a bank account helps control cash because banks have established practices for safeguarding customers' money. Banks use various documents, such as checks and bank statements, to help protect their customers' cash. *See Exhibits 7-2 and 7-3 (p. 387) in the text for examples of such documents.*

6 Prepare a bank reconciliation and journalize the related journal entries.

Review the format of the bank reconciliation in Exhibit 7-5, Panel B (p. 390). Take note that the ending "Adjusted bank balance" and "Adjusted book balance" are the same amount. These amounts represent the correct book balance. As you review Exhibit 7-5, think about the objective of the bank reconciliation, which is to arrive at the correct book balance. This focus should help you to understand the rationale for why the various items are added to or subtracted from the balance per bank and the balance per books. When these balances differ, journal entries record all the items that appear between those two amounts to obtain the correct balance. Continue to review the journal entries related to Exhibit 7-5.

7 Apply internal controls to cash receipts.

The assignment and separation of employee responsibilities is important for handling cash. Cashiers should each use a separate drawer. The cash should be counted and checked against the sales register information. Remittances that are mailed in are opened and the checks and source documentation are forwarded to two separate individuals. A third party verifies that the amount deposited agrees with the source documentation. *Review the cash receipt controls in Exhibits 7-8 and 7-9 (pp. 396–397).*

8 Apply internal controls to cash payments.

Three documents are required to be in agreement and approved before a check will be disbursed: receiving report, purchase invoice, and purchase order. Separate individuals must be responsible for approving the purchase, verifying that the services or goods have been received, and approving the invoice for payment. *Review the description of these documents shown in Exhibit 7-11 (p. 398) and the process description in Exhibit 7-10 (p. 398) of the main text.*

9 Explain and journalize petty cash transactions.

Petty cash is small amounts of currency set held on the business' premises to take care of unexpected cash expenses. The usual bank controls are not in place, so petty cash requires its own special controls, such as a petty cash custodian and the use of petty cash tickets. *Review The Petty Cash Fund in the text to see examples of how to account for petty cash.*

10 Describe ethical business issues related to accounting.

Ethical business practices have always been important, but they have taken on renewed emphasis due to the recent accounting scandals of Enron and other companies. Employees are often held to the code of ethics of their employers. Accountants are subject to higher standards than others and must comply with the code of ethics of various professional accounting associations.

Demo Doc 1

Bank Reconciliations

Learning Objectives 1–7

Hunter Company has the following information for July 2011:

Cash			
July 1 Bal	2,100		
		July 8	400
July 14	300		
		July 25	900
July 29	120		
		July 30	500
July 31 Bal	720		

Bank Statement for July 2011		
Balance, July 1, 2011		2,100
Deposits		
July 14		300
Checks		
July 8	400	
July 10	230*	
July 25	900	(1,530)
Other items:		
NSF check from Jim Andrews		(150)
Interest on account balance		25
EFT — collection of installment payments from customers		800
EFT — monthly rent expense		(700)
Service charges		(75)
Balance, July 31, 2011		770

*The July 10 check was not written by Hunter. It was written by another bank customer and taken from Hunter's account in error.

Hunter deposits all cash receipts and makes all payments by check.

Requirements

1. How does a bank statement assist with internal control?

2. Prepare Hunter's bank reconciliation at July 31, 2011.

3. Journalize any entries required by Hunter and update Hunter's Cash T-account. Explanations are not required.

4. The employee at Hunter who opens the mail and physically collects the cash is the same person who updates the cash receipts journal and prepares the bank reconciliation. Is this a good internal control system?

5. How does the law ensure that companies have good internal controls?

Demo Doc 1 Solutions

Requirement 1

5 Demonstrate the use of a bank account as a control device

How does a bank statement assist with internal control?

| Part 1 | Part 2 | Part 3 | Part 4 | Part 5 | Part 6 | Demo Doc Complete |

A bank statement is essentially a synopsis of the bank's view of the transactions that affected a specific bank account. The issuance of the bank statement allows a bank account holder to perform a bank reconciliation, which better allows them to find and address any potential problems (such as errors or fraud).

Requirement 2

6 Prepare a bank reconciliation and journalize the related entries

Prepare Hunter's bank reconciliation at July 31, 2011.

| Part 1 | Part 2 | Part 3 | Part 4 | Part 5 | Part 6 | Demo Doc Complete |

When you receive a monthly bank statement, the cash balance on your records is often different from the amount on the bank statement. The bank reconciliation reconciles, or brings into agreement, the checking account balance on the depositor's records and the bank's records.

In this case, to prepare the bank reconciliation we need to add reconciling items to both the bank balance and Hunter's cash balance. First, we must determine what these adjustments are. To more easily calculate the impact of these adjustments, we begin with a work sheet.

Make three columns: one for Hunter, one for the bank, and one for reconciling items in the middle. Begin with the balance both sides have for cash at July 31, 2011.

Hunter	Reconciling Items	Bank
720	July 31 Balance	770

A reconciling item arises because a valid transaction has not been recorded by both parties. For example, if the bank records service charges and Hunter does not, a reconciling item is required to bring Hunter's cash balance to the correct amount.

For each reconciling item, we will describe it in the Reconciling Items column and add it to or subtract it from the column of the party that has *not* yet recorded that transaction/entry.

6 Prepare a bank reconciliation and journalize the related entries

Deposits in Transit

According to the Cash T-account, Hunter made two deposits.

Cash

Jul 1 Bal	2,100	Jul 8	400
Jul 14	300	Jul 25	900
Jul 29	120	Jul 30	500
Jul 31 Bal	720		

The two deposits are:

July 31	300
July 29	120

However, the bank statement only shows one (the July 14 deposit for $300). The July 29 deposit for $120 has not yet been recorded by the bank. This is a deposit in transit and will *increase* the bank account when the bank processes and records the deposit.

Outstanding Checks and Bank Error

6 Prepare a bank reconciliation and journalize the related entries

According to the Cash T-account, Hunter wrote three checks.

Cash			
Jul 1 Bal	2,100		
		Jul 8	400
Jul 14	300		
		Jul 25	900
Jul 29	120		
		Jul 30	500
Jul 31 Bal	720		

The three checks are:

July 8	400
July 25	900
July 30	500

The bank statement shows three checks; however, only two (the July 8 check for $400 and the July 25 check for $900) are valid.

The July 10 check for $230 shown on the bank statement is a bank error and does not relate to Hunter. This error needs to be corrected by the bank (it would be a good idea for Hunter to contact the bank to confirm that it is correcting this mistake). This is an *increase* to Cash on the bank's side.

The bank statement does not show the third valid check: The July 30 check for $500 has not yet been recorded by the bank. This is an outstanding check and will *decrease* the bank account when it is recorded. The bank will record this check in the (near) future when it is cashed.

NSF Check

6 Prepare a bank reconciliation and journalize the related entries

A check deposited by Hunter for $150 was returned to the bank for insufficient funds. Hunter has not yet recorded the return of this customer check.

The $150 the customer owed has *not* been paid because Hunter was unable to cash the customer's check. The account receivable must be reinstated and Hunter's Cash account must be *decreased*.

Interest Earned

Interest revenue of $25 has been earned on Hunter's bank balance but has not yet been recorded by Hunter. This will *increase* Hunter's Cash account.

Installment Payments Received

Installment payments from customers of $800 have been collected by the bank via EFT but have not yet been recorded by Hunter. This will *increase* Hunter's Cash account.

Rent Expense

The rent payment of $700 was made by the bank (on Hunter's behalf) but has not yet been recorded by Hunter. This will *decrease* Hunter's Cash account.

Service Charges

Service charges of $75 have been incurred with the bank but have not yet been recorded by Hunter. This will *decrease* Hunter's Cash account.

Put all of these reconciling items into the work sheet.

Notice that the only items showing in the bank's column are deposits in transit, outstanding checks, and bank errors. Generally, these are the only reconciling items that will be on the bank's side of the reconciliation. Almost all other items will be on the company's side of the reconciliation. It is easier to remember potential reconciling items for the bank with the acronym DOE:

D		Deposits in Transit
O		Outstanding Checks
E		Bank Errors

Hunter	Reconciling Items	Bank
720	July 31 Balance	770
	Deposits in transit	120
	Outstanding checks	−500
	Bank error (July 10 check)	230
−150	NSF check	
25	Interest earned	
800	Installment payments collected	
−700	Rent payment	
−75	Service charges	
620	Total	620

Notice that both columns in the work sheet have the same total. This is a good check to ensure that all calculations are correct. If these totals were not the same, there would be an error and/or some data would be missing.

| Part 1 | Part 2 | **Part 3** | Part 4 | Part 5 | Part 6 | Demo Doc Complete |

We can now take these reconciling items and prepare the formal bank reconciliation. We list all additions and subtractions required for the bank and Hunter.

HUNTER COMPANY
Bank Reconciliation
July 31, 2011

Bank:			
Balance, July 31, 2011			770
Add: July 29 Deposit in transit			120
Bank error (July 10 check not belonging to Hunter)			230
			1,120
Less: July 30 outstanding check			(500)
Adjusted bank balance, July 31, 2011			620
Books:			
Balance, July 31, 2011			720
Add: Bank collection of installment payments			800
Interest earned on account			25
			1,545
Less: Rent payment		700	
NSF check		150	
Service charges		75	(925)
Adjusted book balance, July 31, 2011			620

Requirement 3

6 Prepare a bank reconciliation and journalize the related entries

Journalize any entries required by Hunter and update Hunter's Cash T-account. Explanations are not required.

| Part 1 | Part 2 | Part 3 | **Part 4** | Part 5 | Part 6 | Demo Doc Complete |

Any reconciling items on Hunter's side for the bank reconciliation should be journalized. Usually, these entries are made in the order in which they appear on the bank reconciliation.

Demo Doc 1 Solutions | Chapter 7   **195**

6 Prepare a bank reconciliation and journalize the related entries

Installment Payments

Cash increases (a debit) and Accounts Receivable decreases (a credit) by $800.

Jul 31	Cash	800	
	Accounts receivable		800

6 Prepare a bank reconciliation and journalize the related entries

Interest Earned

Cash increases (a debit) and Interest Revenue increases (a credit) by $25.

Jul 31	Cash	25	
	Interest revenue		25

6 Prepare a bank reconciliation and journalize the related entries

Rent Payment

Cash decreases (a credit) and Rent Expense increases (a debit) by $700.

Jul 31	Rent expense	700	
	Cash		700

6 Prepare a bank reconciliation and journalize the related entries

NSF Check

Cash decreases (a credit) and Accounts Receivable increases (a debit) by $150.

Jul 31	Cash	800	
	Accounts receivable		800

6 Prepare a bank reconciliation and journalize the related entries

Service Charges

Cash decreases (a credit) and Misc. Expense increases (a debit) by $75.

Jul 31	Accounts receivable—J. Andrews	150	
	Cash		150

Post these adjustments to the Cash T-account:

Cash

Jul 1 Bal	720		
	800		
	25		
		Jul 31	700
			150
			75
Jul 31 Bal	620		

The final cash balance is $620, which is also the total on the bank reconciliation. Both totals must agree, so this is a good check to make sure that everything was done correctly.

Requirement 4

The employee at Hunter who opens the mail and physically collects the cash is the same person who updates the cash receipts journal and prepares the bank reconciliation. Is this a good internal control system?

| Part 1 | Part 2 | Part 3 | Part 4 | **Part 5** | Part 6 | Demo Doc Complete |

If an employee collects the cash *and* records the receipt of the cash *and* performs the bank reconciliation, then there is an opportunity for fraud.

The employee could steal the cash and delay recording the cash receipt or perhaps never record the cash receipt. The employee could hide his or her act for a long period of time by manipulating the bank reconciliations.

To avoid this problem, most internal control systems require <u>separation of duties</u>; that is, the employees who handle cash (both receipts and payments) are *not* the same employees who maintain the accounting records and prepare the bank reconciliations.

In an E-Commerce business, the issue may also result in decreased pricacy of customer information. Having such information monitored by two employees decreases the chance for hackers to gain unauthorized access.

Requirement 5

How does the law ensure that companies have good internal controls?

| Part 1 | Part 2 | Part 3 | Part 4 | Part 5 | **Part 6** | Demo Doc Complete |

The Sarbanes-Oxley Act was passed by Congress to address the issue of internal controls. Some of its provisions include: auditors must evaluate internal controls, and companies must issue internal control reports. There are stiff fines and penalties, and potentially even jail time, for company managers who violate this Act.

| Part 1 | Part 2 | Part 3 | Part 4 | Part 5 | Part 6 | **Demo Doc Complete** |

Demo Doc 1 Solutions | Chapter 7

Demo Doc 2

Petty Cash

Learning Objectives 1, 3, 8–10

Young Brothers established a $300 petty cash fund on July 1, 2011. On July 31, 2011, the petty cash box contained $80 cash and the following receipts:

July 5	Travel expenses	$80
July 12	Donuts for client meeting	50
July 23	Office supplies	60
July 29	Delivery charges	40

On August 1, 2011, the petty cash balance was replenished.

Requirements

1. Journalize the entry to establish the fund.

2. What is the total cash amount paid from petty cash in July? How does this compare to the amount remaining in the petty cash box?

3. What is the problem with petty cash in July? Why did this problem occur? How can it be fixed?

4. Journalize the entry to record the expenses incurred from petty cash during July. (Assume all charges are recorded as supplies expense, delivery expense, travel expense, or catering expense.) On what date(s) are these expenses recorded?

5. A Young employee notices that there have been several months in a row in which the petty cash has been short. Although the amounts involved are small (immaterial), the trend is consistent. What should the employee do?

Demo Doc 2 Solutions

8 Apply internal controls to cash payments

9 Explain and journalize petty cash transactions

Requirement 1

Journalize the entry to establish the fund.

| Part 1 | Part 2 | Part 3 | Part 4 | Part 5 | Demo Doc Complete |

When the fund is established, cash is withdrawn from Young's bank accounts and put into the petty cash box. This increases Petty Cash (a debit) and decreases Cash in Bank (a credit) by $300.

Jul 1	Petty cash		300	
	Cash in bank			300

Requirement 2

What is the total cash amount paid from petty cash in July? How does this compare to the amount remaining in the petty cash box?

| Part 1 | **Part 2** | Part 3 | Part 4 | Part 5 | Demo Doc Complete |

The receipts in the petty cash box total $80 + $50 + $60 + $40 = $230. This means that there should be $300 − $230 = $70 left in the petty cash box. However, there is actually $80 of cash remaining. This is a cash overage.

Requirement 3

What is the problem with petty cash in July? Why did this problem occur? How can it be fixed?

| Part 1 | Part 2 | **Part 3** | Part 4 | Part 5 | Demo Doc Complete |

As stated in Requirement 2, there is a cash overage of $80 − $70 = $10. This could be because a receipt is in error or cash was put into petty cash and not recorded.

Young should implement some internal controls to better monitor petty cash. These could include requiring the use of petty cash tickets with an authorized signature (the person signing would presumably review the receipts for correctness).

Requirement 4

Journalize the entry to record the expenses incurred from petty cash during July. (Assume all charges are recorded as supplies expense, delivery expense, travel expense, or catering expense.) On what date(s) are these expenses recorded?

| Part 1 | Part 2 | Part 3 | **Part 4** | Part 5 | Demo Doc Complete |

These expenses are *not* recorded at the time they are incurred. The amounts involved are immaterial, so instead we can wait to record them until the petty cash is replenished:

Aug 1	Supplies expense	60	
	Delivery expense	40	
	Travel expense	80	
	Catering expense	50	
	Cash short (over)		10
	Cash		220

The missing $10 is recorded as *Cash Short (Over)*. The amount is for an overage, so this account is credited (as if it were "revenue").

Requirement 5

A Young employee notices that there have been several months in a row in which the petty cash has been short. Although the amounts involved are small (immaterial), the trend is consistent. What should the employee do?

| Part 1 | Part 2 | Part 3 | Part 4 | **Part 5** | Demo Doc Complete |

It is easy to have cash overages and shortages from month to month. Record-keeping for petty cash is often spotty because it is usually handled by someone who is not familiar with accounting. However, consistent shortages every month imply that there may be unethical behavior on the part of the petty cash handler.

Having someone review petty cash transactions periodically is a good internal control.

The employee who notices this trend should discuss it with the person responsible for petty cash. If the issue cannot be resolved, then the employee should report it to a supervisor.

| Part 1 | Part 2 | Part 3 | Part 4 | Part 5 | **Demo Doc Complete** |

Quick Practice Questions

True/False

_____ 1. A deposit in transit has been recorded by the company but not by the bank.

_____ 2. An NSF check would be recorded on the books by debiting Accounts Receivable.

_____ 3. The AICPA Code of Professional Conduct and the Standards of Ethical Conduct for Management Accountants set the minimum standards of conduct for members of the AICPA and the IMA.

_____ 4. Only accountants are held to a code of ethics.

_____ 5. Different people should perform various accounting duties to minimize errors and the opportunities for fraud.

_____ 6. Funds disbursed from the petty cash fund will be recorded as a credit to the Petty Cash account.

_____ 7. The person who prepares checks for payment would be a suitable employee to reconcile the bank account.

_____ 8. Encryption helps to secure confidential information in e-commerce.

_____ 9. Outstanding checks would include only those checks written for the current month that have not cleared or been canceled by the bank.

_____ 10. It is a good control to have just one person open the checks and deposit them in the bank.

Multiple Choice

1. Which of the following is not an objective of internal control?
   a. Help safeguard the assets a business uses in its operations
   b. Guarantee a company will not go bankrupt
   c. Encourage adherence to company policies
   d. Promote operational efficiency

2. Which of the following items used to reconcile cash does not require an adjusting entry?
   a. Bank service charge
   b. Interest earned
   c. A note collected by the bank
   d. Deposits in transit

3. Which of the following statements about bank reconciliations is correct?
   a. Should not be prepared by an employee who handles cash transactions
   b. Is part of a sound internal control system
   c. Is a formal financial statement
   d. Both (a) and (b) are correct

4. Which of the following items does not cause a difference between the cash balance per bank and book?
   a. NSF checks
   b. Deposits in transit
   c. Outstanding checks
   d. Canceled checks

5. The following data are available for Wonder Boutique for October:

Book balance, October 3	$5,575
Outstanding checks	584
Deposits in transit	2,500
Service charges	75
Interest revenue	25

   What is the adjusted book balance on October 31 for Wonder Boutique based on the preceding data?
   a. $5,500
   b. $5,525
   c. $5,550
   d. $7,466

6. The bank statement lists a $700 deposit as $70. On a bank reconciliation, this will appear as which of the following?
   a. Addition to the book balance
   b. Deduction from the book balance
   c. Addition to the bank balance
   d. Deduction from the bank balance

7. When the Cash Short (Over) account has a credit balance, it is treated as what type of account?
   a. Expense
   b. Liability
   c. Revenue
   d. Equity

8. For which items must journal entries be prepared?
   a. Any errors made on the books revealed by the bank reconciliation
   b. Any errors made by the bank revealed by the bank reconciliation
   c. All items on the bank's side
   d. Only outstanding checks

9. Which of the following is *not* a control over petty cash?
   a. Keeping an unlimited amount of cash on hand
   b. Supporting all fund disbursements with a petty cash ticket
   c. Replenishing the fund through normal cash disbursement procedures
   d. Designating one employee to administer the fund

10. If the petty cash fund is not replenished on the balance sheet date, which of the following will be true?
    a. Assets will be overstated
    b. Income will be overstated
    c. Neither (a) nor (b)
    d. Both (a) and (b)

Quick Exercises

7-1. Classify each of the following reconciling items of the Bread and Butter Company as one of the following:

   a. An addition to the bank balance
   b. A deduction from the bank balance
   c. An addition to the book balance
   d. A deduction from the book balance
   e. Not a reconciling item

   _____ 1. Collection of note receivable plus interest revenue by bank
   _____ 2. Bookkeeper recorded check #849 as $557 instead of the correct amount of $755
   _____ 3. Bank service charges
   _____ 4. Bank credited the account for interest revenue
   _____ 5. Bank added deposit to Bread and Butter's account in error
   _____ 6. Deposits in transit
   _____ 7. Bank withdrew $1,270 from Bread and Butter's account for a check written for $12,700
   _____ 8. Bookkeeper failed to record a check that was returned with the bank statement
   _____ 9. Check deposited and returned by the bank marked NSF
   _____ 10. Outstanding checks

7-2. On November 1, 2011, Heather Station established a $300 petty cash fund. At the end of November the petty cash fund contained:

Cash on hand		$ 45.00
Petty cash tickets for		
Postage	$73.50	
Office supplies	87.55	
Miscellaneous items	90.95	
		252.00
Total		$297.00

   a. Prepare the journal entry to establish the petty cash fund on November 1, 2011.

Journal				Page 1
Date	Accounts		Debit	Credit

b. Prepare the journal entry on November 30, 2011, to replenish the petty cash fund.

Journal			Page 1
Date	Accounts and Explanation	Debit	Credit

7-3. Using the following information, record the journal entries that would be necessary after preparing the bank reconciliation for Louis Brothers. Some items may not require an entry.

a. Outstanding checks total $1,533.25.

Journal			Page 1
Date	Accounts and Explanation	Debit	Credit

b. The bookkeeper recorded a $1,524 check as $15,240 in payment of the current month's rent.

Journal			Page 1
Date	Accounts and Explanation	Debit	Credit

c. A deposit of $300 from a customer was credited to Louis Brothers for $3,000 by the bank.

Journal			Page 1
Date	Accounts and Explanation	Debit	Credit

d. A customer's check for $1,380 was returned for nonsufficient funds.

Journal			Page 1
Date	Accounts and Explanation	Debit	Credit

e. The bank service charge based on the bank statement is $70.

Journal				Page 1
Date	Accounts and Explanation		Debit	Credit

7-4. The following data have been gathered for Ragpicker Company. Calculate the correct cash balance on February 28, 2011, by performing the part of the bank reconciliation beginning with the balance per bank as shown. NOTE: Not all of the following information may be needed.

a. The service charges for February amount to $90.
b. Outstanding checks amount to $650.
c. The bank erroneously credited Ragpicker Company's account for $300 for a deposit made by another company.
d. Check #665 for $3,000 for the cash purchase of office equipment was erroneously recorded by the bookkeeper as $2,080.
e. A deposit ticket correctly prepared for $975 appeared on the bank statement as a deposit for $795.
f. A customer's check for $560 was returned with the bank statement and stamped NSF.
g. Check #650 for $125 for utilities expense was erroneously recorded by the bookkeeper as $1,250.

RAGPICKER COMPANY
Bank Reconciliation
February 28, 2011

Bank:			
Balance, February 28, 2011			$ 7,975
Add:			
Less:			
Adjusted bank balance, February 28, 2011			

7-5. The following data have been gathered for Batter Company to assist you in preparing the September 30, 2011, bank reconciliation:

a. The September 30 bank balance was $5,460.
b. The bank statement included $30 of service charges.
c. There was an EFT deposit of $1,800 on the bank statement for the monthly rent due from a tenant.
d. Checks #541 and #543, for $205 and $420, respectively, were not among the canceled checks returned with the statement.
e. The September 30 deposit of $3,800 did not appear on the bank statement.
f. The bookkeeper had erroneously recorded a $500 check as $5,000. The check was payment for an amount due on account.
g. Included with the canceled checks was a check written by Bitter Company for $200, which was deducted from Batter Company's account.
h. The bank statement included an NSF check written by Tate Company for a $360 payment on account.
i. The Cash account showed a balance of $2,925 on September 30.

Prepare the September 30, 2011, bank reconciliation for Batter Company.

BATTER COMPANY
Bank Reconciliation
September 30, 2011

Bank:
Balance, September 30, 2011
Add:

Less:

Adjusted bank balance, September 30, 2011

Books:
Balance, September 30, 2011
Add:

Less:

Adjusted book balance, September 30, 2011

Do It Yourself! Question 1

Bank Reconciliations

Quint Company has the following information for May 2011:

Cash

May 1 Bal	4,500		
		May 4	900
May 9	600		
		May 12	2,300
May 18	1,000		
		May 22	1,500
May 28	700		
		May 30	500
May 31 Bal	1,600		

Bank Statement for May 2011

Balance, May 1, 2011		4,500
Deposits		
May 9	600	
May 18	1,000	1,600
Checks		
May 4	900	
May 12	2,300	
May 22	1,500	(4,700)
Other items:		
EFT — payment of loan payable		(1,300)
NSF check from Bennet Smith		(400)
Service charges		(100)
EFT — monthly rent collection		1,200
Interest on account balance		50
Balance, May 31, 2011		850

The loan payment includes principal of $950 and interest of $350.

The rent collection is from tenants leasing extra space in Quint's office building.

Quint deposits all cash receipts and makes all payments by check.

Requirements

6 Prepare a bank reconciliation and journalize the related entries

1. Prepare Quint's bank reconciliation at May 31, 2011.

Reconciling Items
Total

6 Prepare a bank reconciliation and journalize the related entries

2. Journalize any entries required by Quint and update Quint's Cash T-account. Explanations are not required.

Date	Accounts and Explanations	Debit	Credit

Date	Accounts and Explanations	Debit	Credit

Date	Accounts and Explanations	Debit	Credit

Date	Accounts and Explanations	Debit	Credit

Date	Accounts and Explanations	Debit	Credit

Do It Yourself! Question 1 | Chapter 7

Do It Yourself! Question 2

Petty Cash

Xander Co. established a $400 petty cash fund on May 1, 2011. On May 31, 2011, the petty cash box contained $80 cash and the following receipts:

May 6	Office supplies	$75
May 13	Delivery charges	90
May 24	Pizza for office party	70
May 30	Office supplies	85

On June 1, 2011, the petty cash balance was replenished.

Requirements

1. Journalize the entry to establish the fund.

Date	Accounts and Explanations	Debit	Credit

2. Journalize the entry to record the expenses incurred from petty cash during May. (Assume all charges are recorded as supplies expense, delivery expense, or catering expense.)

Date	Accounts and Explanations	Debit	Credit

Quick Practice Solutions

True/False

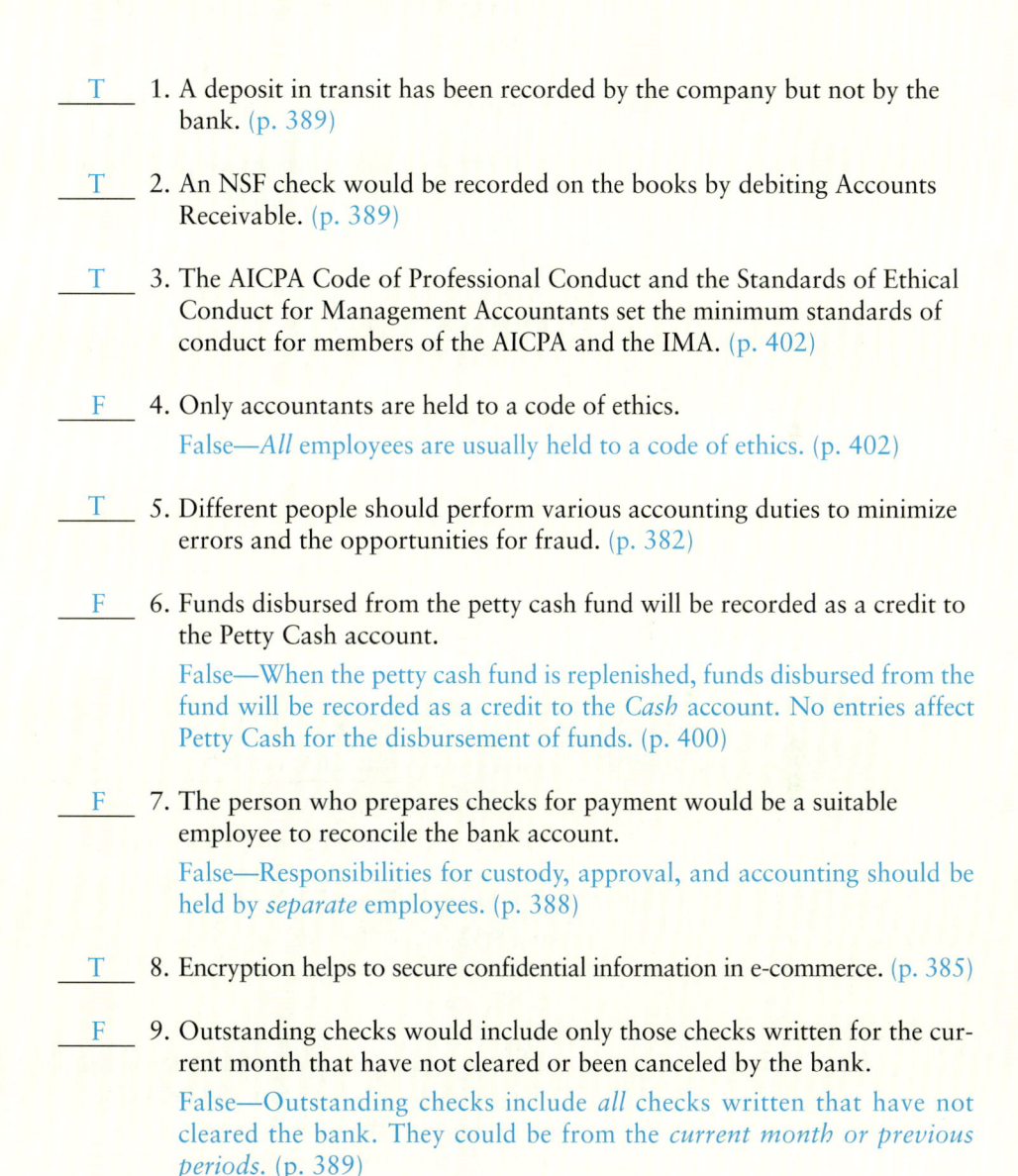

__T__ 1. A deposit in transit has been recorded by the company but not by the bank. (p. 389)

__T__ 2. An NSF check would be recorded on the books by debiting Accounts Receivable. (p. 389)

__T__ 3. The AICPA Code of Professional Conduct and the Standards of Ethical Conduct for Management Accountants set the minimum standards of conduct for members of the AICPA and the IMA. (p. 402)

__F__ 4. Only accountants are held to a code of ethics.

False—*All* employees are usually held to a code of ethics. (p. 402)

__T__ 5. Different people should perform various accounting duties to minimize errors and the opportunities for fraud. (p. 382)

__F__ 6. Funds disbursed from the petty cash fund will be recorded as a credit to the Petty Cash account.

False—When the petty cash fund is replenished, funds disbursed from the fund will be recorded as a credit to the *Cash* account. No entries affect Petty Cash for the disbursement of funds. (p. 400)

__F__ 7. The person who prepares checks for payment would be a suitable employee to reconcile the bank account.

False—Responsibilities for custody, approval, and accounting should be held by *separate* employees. (p. 388)

__T__ 8. Encryption helps to secure confidential information in e-commerce. (p. 385)

__F__ 9. Outstanding checks would include only those checks written for the current month that have not cleared or been canceled by the bank.

False—Outstanding checks include *all* checks written that have not cleared the bank. They could be from the *current month or previous periods*. (p. 389)

__F__ 10. It is a good control to have just one person open the checks and deposit them in the bank.

False—*Separate* individuals should be assigned custody, approval, and accounting tasks. (p. 382)

Multiple Choice

1. Which of the following is not an objective of internal control? (p. 379)
   a. Help safeguard the assets a business uses in its operations
   b. **Guarantee a company will not go bankrupt**
   c. Encourage adherence to company policies
   d. Promote operational efficiency

2. Which of the following items used to reconcile cash does not require an adjusting entry? (p. 389)
   a. Bank service charge
   b. Interest earned
   c. A note collected by the bank
   d. Deposits in transit

3. Which of the following statements about bank reconciliations is correct? (p. 388)
   a. Should not be prepared by an employee who handles cash transactions
   b. Is part of a sound internal control system
   c. Is a formal financial statement
   d. Both (a) and (b) are correct

4. Which of the following items does not cause a difference between the cash balance per bank and book? (p. 389)
   a. NSF checks
   b. Deposits in transit
   c. Outstanding checks
   d. Canceled checks

5. The following data are available for Wonder Boutique for October:

Book balance, October 31	$5,575
Outstanding checks	584
Deposits in transit	2,500
Service charges	75
Interest revenue	25

   What is the adjusted book balance on October 31 for Wonder Boutique based on the preceding data? (p. 394)
   a. $5,500
   b. $5,525
   c. $5,550
   d. $7,466

6. The bank statement lists a $700 deposit as $70. On a bank reconciliation, this will appear as which of the following? (p. 394)
   a. Addition to the book balance
   b. Deduction from the book balance
   c. Addition to the bank balance
   d. Deduction from the bank balance

7. When the Cash Short (Over) account has a credit balance, it is treated as what type of account? (p. 401)
   a. Expense
   b. Liability
   c. Revenue
   d. Equity

8. For which items must journal entries be prepared? (p. 388)
   a. Any errors made on the books revealed by the bank reconciliation
   b. Any errors made by the bank revealed by the bank reconciliation
   c. All items on the bank's side
   d. Only outstanding checks

9. Which of the following is *not* a control over petty cash? (pp. 399–400)
   a. Keeping an unlimited amount of cash on hand
   b. Supporting all fund disbursements with a petty cash ticket
   c. Replenishing the fund through normal cash disbursement procedures
   d. Designating one employee to administer the fund

10. If the petty cash fund is not replenished on the balance sheet date, which of the following will be true? (p. 400)
    a. Assets will be overstated
    b. Income will be overstated
    c. Neither (a) nor (b)
    d. Both (a) and (b)

Quick Exercises

7-1   Classify each of the following reconciling items of the Bread and Butter Company as one of the following: (p. 391)

   a. An addition to the bank balance
   b. A deduction from the bank balance
   c. An addition to the book balance
   d. A deduction from the book balance
   e. Not a reconciling item

c	1.	Collection of note receivable plus interest revenue by bank
d	2.	Bookkeeper recorded check #849 as $557 instead of the correct amount of $755
d	3.	Bank service charges
a	4.	Bank credited the account for interest revenue
b	5.	Bank added deposit to Bread and Butter's account in error
a	6.	Deposits in transit
b	7.	Bank withdrew $1,270 from Bread and Butter's account for a check written for $12,700
d	8.	Bookkeeper failed to record a check that was returned with the bank statement
d	9.	Check deposited and returned by the bank marked NSF
b	10.	Outstanding checks

7-2 On November 1, 2011, Heather Station established a $300 petty cash fund. At the end of November the petty cash fund contained: (p. 400)

Cash on hand		$ 45.00
Petty cash tickets for:		
Postage	$73.50	
Office supplies	87.55	
Miscellaneous items	90.95	
		252.00
Total		$297.00

a. Prepare the journal entry to establish the petty cash fund on November 1, 2011.
b. Prepare the journal entry on November 30, 2011, to replenish the petty cash fund.

Journal — Page 1

	Date	Accounts and Explanation	Debit	Credit
a.	Nov 1	Petty cash	300	
		Cash		300
		To establish the petty cash fund.		

Journal — Page 1

	Date	Accounts and Explanation	Debit	Credit
b.	Nov 30	Postage expense	73.50	
		Office supplies	87.55	
		Miscellaneous expense	90.95	
		Cash short and over	3.00	
		Cash		255.00
		To replenish petty cash.		

7-3 Using the following information, record the journal entries that would be necessary after preparing the bank reconciliation for Louis Brothers on May 31, 2011. Not all items will require an entry. (p. 391)

a. Outstanding checks total $1,533.25.
b. The bookkeeper recorded a $1,524 check as $15,240 in payment of the current month's rent.
c. A deposit of $300 from a customer was credited to Louis Brothers for $3,000 by the bank.
d. A customer's check for $1,380 was returned for nonsufficient funds.
e. The bank service charge based on the bank statement is $70.

Journal — Page 1

	Date	Accounts and Explanation	Debit	Credit
a.		No entry required.		

Journal — Page 1

	Date	Accounts and Explanation	Debit	Credit
b.	May 31	Cash	13,716	
		Rent expense		13,716

Journal — Page 1

	Date	Accounts and Explanation	Debit	Credit
c.		No entry required.		

Journal — Page 1

	Date	Accounts and Explanation	Debit	Credit
d.	May 31	Accounts receivable	1,380	
		Cash		1,380

Journal — Page 1

	Date	Accounts and Explanation	Debit	Credit
e.	May 31	Miscellaneous expense	70	
		Cash		70

7-4 The following data have been gathered for Ragpicker Company. Calculate the correct cash balance on February 28, 2011, by performing the part of the bank reconciliation beginning with the balance per bank as shown. NOTE: Not all of the following information may be needed. (p. 389)

a. The service charges for February amount to $90.
b. Outstanding checks amount to $650.
c. The bank erroneously credited Ragpicker Company's account for $300 for a deposit made by another company.
d. Check #665 for $3,000 for the cash purchase of office equipment was erroneously recorded by the bookkeeper as $2,080.
e. A deposit ticket correctly prepared for $975 appeared on the bank statement as a deposit for $795.
f. A customer's check for $560 was returned with the bank statement and stamped NSF.
g. Check #650 for $125 for utilities expense was erroneously recorded by the bookkeeper as $1,250.

RAGPICKER COMPANY
Bank Reconciliation
February 28, 2011

Bank:		
Balance, February 28, 2011		$ 7,975
Add:		
Bank error—deposit of $975 recorded as $795	$180	
		180
Less:		
Outstanding checks	650	
Bank Error	300	
		(950)
Adjusted bank balance, February 28, 2011		$7,205

NOTE: Remember that the adjusted bank balance is the correct book balance.

7-5 The following data have been gathered for Batter Company to assist you in preparing the September 30, 2011, bank reconciliation: (p. 391)

a. The September 30 bank balance was $5,460.
b. The bank statement included $30 of service charges.
c. There was an EFT deposit of $1,800 on the bank statement for the monthly rent due from a tenant.
d. Checks #541 and #543, for $205 and $420, respectively, were not among the canceled checks returned with the statement.
e. The September 30 deposit of $3,800 did not appear on the bank statement.
f. The bookkeeper had erroneously recorded a $500 check as $5,000. The check was payment for an amount due on account.
g. Included with the canceled checks was a check written by Bitter Company for $200, which was deducted from Batter Company's account.
h. The bank statement included an NSF check written by Tate Company for a $360 payment on account.
i. The Cash account showed a balance of $2,925 on September 30.

Prepare the September 30, 2011, bank reconciliation for Batter Company.

BATTER COMPANY
Bank Reconciliation
September 30, 2011

Bank:		
Balance, September 30, 2011		$5,460
Add: Deposit in transit	$3,800	
Bank error—Bitter Co. check	200	
		4,000
Less: Outstanding checks		
Check #541	205	
Check #543	420	
		(625)
Adjusted bank balance, September 30, 2011		$8,835
Books:		
Balance, September 30, 2011		$2,925
Add:		
EFT—rent deposit	$1,800	
Bookkeeper error ($5,000 − 500)	4,500	
		6,300
Less:		
Bank service charge	30	
NSF check	360	
		(390)
Adjusted book balance, September 30, 2011		$8,835

Do It Yourself! Question 1 Solutions

Requirement

1. Prepare Quint's bank reconciliation at May 31, 2011.

Quint	Reconciling Items	Bank
1,600	May 31 Balance	850
	Deposits in transit	700
	Outstanding checks	(500)
(1,300)	Mortgage payment	
(400)	NSF check	
(100)	Service charges	
1,200	Rent collection	
50	Interest earned	
1,050	Total	1,050

QUINT COMPANY
Bank Reconciliation
May 31, 2011

Bank:		
Balance, May 31, 2011		850
Add: May 28 deposit in transit		700
		1,550
Less: May 30 outstanding check		(500)
Adjusted bank balance, May 31, 2011		1,050
Books:		
Balance, May 31, 2011		1,600
Add: Bank collection of rent		1,200
Interest earned on account		50
		2,850
Less: Mortgage payment	1,300	
NSF check—B. Smith	400	
Service charges	100	(1,800)
Adjusted book balance, May 31, 2011		1,050

2. Journalize any entries required by Quint and update Quint's Cash T-account. Explanations are not required.

May 31	Cash		1,200	
	Rent revenue			1,200

May 31	Cash		50	
	Interest revenue			50

May 31	Mortgage payable		950	
	Interest expense		350	
	Cash			1,300

May 31	Accounts receivable—Bennet Smith		400	
	Cash			400

May 31	Miscellaneous expense		100	
	Cash			100

```
                       Cash
    May 31 Bal  1,600 |
                1,200 |
                   50 |
                      | May 31    1,300
                      |             400
                      |             100
    ──────────────────|───────────────
    May 31 Bal  1,050 |
```

Do It Yourself! Question 2 Solutions

Requirements

1. Journalize the entry to establish the fund.

May 1	Petty cash		400	
	Cash in bank			400

2. Journalize the entry to record the expenses incurred from petty cash during May.

Jun 1	Supplies expense ($75 + $85)		160	
	Delivery expense		90	
	Catering expense		70	
	Cash			320

The Power of Practice

For more practice using the skills learned in this chapter, visit MyAccountingLab. There you will find algorithmically generated questions that are based on these Demo Docs and your main textbook's Review and Assess Your Progress sections.

Go to MyAccountingLab and follow these steps:

1. Direct your URL to www.myaccountinglab.com.
2. Log in using your name and password.
3. Click the MyAccountingLab link.
4. Click Study Plan in the left navigation bar.
5. From the table of contents, select Chapter 7, Internal Control and Cash.
6. Click a link to work tutorial exercises.

8 Receivables

WHAT YOU PROBABLY ALREADY KNOW

You probably already know that if a friend borrows money from you, there is a *chance* you may not be repaid. You would not loan a friend money if you didn't believe that he or she is creditworthy and will likely repay the debt. However, until the money is received, there is no guarantee. If the friend asks to borrow more money before repaying the original loan, you may be more likely to refuse your friend because your risk of nonpayment is increased. There has been no history of successful repayment yet. If the friend never pays, you have incurred a loss equal to the amount of the loan.

The same concerns exist for a business. Sales on account are made only after a company has been approved by the credit department. Despite the most thorough investigation, there will always be some customers who may not pay the amount due. The uncollectible accounts receivable results in a reduction to the asset and to net income.

Learning Objectives/Success Keys

1 Define and explain common types of receivables.

The two most common types of receivables are accounts receivable and notes receivable. Accounts receivable are amounts to be collected from customers from sales made on credit. Notes receivable are more formal and usually longer in term than accounts receivable.

2 Design internal controls for receivables.

An important feature of a strong system of internal control is to separate responsibility for custody of assets from the accounting and operating departments. The individual handling cash should not be granting credit, nor should he or she be accounting for receivables.

3 Use the allowance method to account for uncollectibles.

The **allowance method** matches the sales revenues with the uncollectible accounts expense. An *estimate* of the uncollectible accounts expense must be made in the period of sale using either the aging of receivables or the percentage-of-sales methods. The entry required at the end of the period is:

Uncollectible accounts expense	X	
Allowance for doubtful accounts		X

The **Allowance for Doubtful Accounts** is a contra-asset account. This account is credited, rather than Accounts Receivable, because it is unknown on the entry date which specific customers will eventually not pay. When it is determined which customer's receivable is uncollectible, the Allowance account is reduced (debited) and the specific customer accounts receivable is reduced (credited). *Carefully review "Accounting for Uncollectibles (Bad Debts)" in the main text. This can be a challenging concept.*

4 Understand the direct write-off method for uncollectibles.

The **direct write-off method** is simple to employ, but the method is not in accordance with GAAP. No estimate of the uncollectible accounts expense is recorded. When it is determined which customer's receivable is uncollectible, the following entry is recorded:

Uncollectible accounts expense	X	
Accounts receivable		X

Check out "The Direct Write-Off Method" in the main text.

5 Report receivables on the balance sheet.

The amount reported for accounts receivables on the balance sheet is the amount the business expects to collect. This can be reported in one of two ways:

a. Accounts receivable is on the face of the balance sheet, followed by the allowance for uncollectible accounts as a deduction, leaving net Accounts Receivable.
b. Accounts receivable may be shown at the net amount on the face of the balance sheet with parenthetical disclosure of the allowance balance or in the footnotes.

6 Journalize credit-card, bankcard, and debit-card sales.

When consumers use credit-cards, bankcards, and debit-cards, the company from whom they are purchasing goods and services has a much lower risk of uncollectible accounts. *Review the journal entries to account for these kinds of receivables in the text in Credit-Card, Debit-Card and Bankcard Sales.*

7 Account for notes receivable.

A **note receivable** is a formal written promise to pay the amount borrowed by the debtor plus interest. Interest must be recorded for the period of indebtedness. *Study the key components of a note in Exhibit 8-4 (p. 440). Review "Computing Interest on a Note" in the main text and the interest revenue accrual journal entries that follow.*

8 Use the acid-test ratio and days' sales in receivables to evaluate a company.

A measure of liquidity is the acid-test ratio. The current assets most quickly converted into cash are compared to the total current liabilities. A higher result is usually more favorable. The ratio is calculated as follows:

$$\text{Acid-test ratio} = \frac{\text{Cash + Short-term investments + Net current receivables}}{\text{Total current liabilities}}$$

The **days' sales in receivables** indicates the number of days it takes on average to collect from customers. The objective is to minimize the collection period.

Review the ratio computations in "Using Accounting Information for Decision Making" in the main text.

Demo Doc 1

Learning Objectives 1–5

Hart Company's, December 31, 2010, balance sheet reported:

Accounts receivable	$800
Allowance for uncollectible accounts	(40)
Accounts receivable (net)	$760

Requirements

1. Is Hart using the allowance method or the direct write-off method to account for uncollectible receivables? How much of the December 31, 2010, balance of accounts receivable did Hart expect to collect?

2. During 2011, Hart wrote off accounts receivable totaling $35 from Amanda Blake. Journalize these write-offs as one transaction. How does this transaction affect the net accounts receivable balance? How would this transaction have been recorded if the direct write-off method were being used?

3. During 2011, Hart earned $2,800 of service revenues, all on account. Journalize these revenues as one transaction.

4. During 2011, Hart collected $2,745 cash from customers. Journalize this transaction and calculate the gross accounts receivable balance at December 31, 2011.

5. Assume that Hart estimates uncollectible account expense to be 1.5% of revenues. Journalize the entry to adjust the allowance at December 31, 2011. What is the December 31, 2011, balance in the allowance?

6. Ignoring Requirement 5, assume that Hart estimates that 5% of accounts receivable will turn out to be uncollectible. Gross accounts receivable at December 31, 2011, were $825. Journalize the entry to adjust the allowance at December 31, 2011. What is the December 31, 2011, balance in the allowance?

7. Ignoring Requirements 5 and 6, assume that Hart has the following information at December 31, 2011:

Age	Gross Accounts Receivable	Percentage Estimated Uncollectible
< 30 days	$100	2%
30–60 days	500	4%
> 60 days	220	10%
Total	$820	

Journalize the entry to adjust the allowance at December 31, 2011. What is the December 31, 2011, balance in the allowance? Show how accounts receivable would be reported on the balance sheet at December 31, 2011.

8. In 2012, Hart wrote off $48 of accounts receivable. On June 30, 2012, Hart estimated uncollectible accounts expense was $10 for the first six months of the year, based on the percentage-of-sales method. Journalize these transactions.

9. At December 31, 2012, based on the percentage-of-receivables method, Hart estimated the allowance balance to be $35. Journalize Hart's entry to adjust the allowance for the year-end financial statements. (Assume the December 31, 2011, balance in the allowance was $30.) What is total uncollectible account expense for 2012?

10. Calculate Hart's days' sales in accounts receivable for 2011. (Assume Hart uses the aging-of-accounts method in Requirement 7.) What does this ratio mean?

11. The employee at Hart who opens the mail and physically collects the cash is the same person who updates the cash receipts journal and accounts receivable ledger. Is this a good internal control system?

Demo Doc 1 Solutions

1 Define and explain common types of receivables

4 Understand the direct write-off method for uncollectibles

5 Report receivables on the balance sheet

Requirement 1

Is Hart using the allowance method or the direct write-off method to account for uncollectible receivables? How much of the December 31, 2010, balance of accounts receivable did Hart expect to collect?

Part 1	Part 2	Part 3	Part 4	Part 5	Part 6	Part 7	Part 8	Part 9	Part 10	Part 11	Demo Doc Complete

Hart is using the allowance method. We know this because an allowance for uncollectible accounts has been set up. If Hart were using the direct write-off method, there would be no allowance for uncollectible accounts.

Gross accounts receivable is the total amount of receivables that exist. For Hart, this is $800. The allowance is (by definition) the amount of receivables we do *not* expect to collect.

The total receivables minus the amount we do not expect to collect (that is, the gross accounts receivable minus the allowance) is the amount we *do* expect to collect (that is, the *net* accounts receivable).

Hart expects to collect $760 of the accounts receivable.

3 Use the allowance method to account for uncollectibles

4 Understand the direct write-off method for uncollectibles

Requirement 2

During 2011, Hart wrote off accounts receivable totaling $35 from Amanda Blake. Journalize these write-offs as one transaction. How does this transaction affect the net accounts receivable balance? How would this transaction have been recorded if the direct write-off method were being used?

Part 1	Part 2	Part 3	Part 4	Part 5	Part 6	Part 7	Part 8	Part 9	Part 10	Part 11	Demo Doc Complete

Writing off an account receivable means removing it from the accounting books/records because it has been determined that this specific amount will *not* be collected. This means that we have to reduce (credit) the Accounts Receivable. Additionally, now that we have found one of the accounts that will not be collected, we can take it out of our estimate of uncollectible accounts (the Allowance for Uncollectible Accounts). This results in a decrease to this account (a debit).

Allowance for uncollectible accounts		35	
Accounts receivable—Amanda Blake			35

This is the standard format to write off uncollectible Accounts Receivables when using the allowance method. The entry structure is always the same, only the amount changes.

Note that this entry does *not* change the *net* accounts receivable. Gross accounts receivable decreases, but so does the allowance. Overall the change is zero:

Gross accounts receivable	change of –$35
–Allowance for uncollectible accounts	(change of –$35)
Net accounts receivable	no change

The impact of this transaction is:

Gross accounts receivable	$800 – $35 = $765
–Allowance	($40 – $35 = $5)
Net accounts receivable	$760 – $0 = $760

There is no allowance under the direct write-off method, so the debit in the write-off entry is an increase to Uncollectible Accounts Expense.

	Uncollectible accounts expense	35	
	Accounts receivable—Amanda Blake		35

Requirement 3

During 2011, Hart earned $2,800 of service revenues, all on account. Journalize these revenues as one transaction.

| Part 1 | Part 2 | **Part 3** | Part 4 | Part 5 | Part 6 | Part 7 | Part 8 | Part 9 | Part 10 | Part 11 | Demo Doc Complete |

When revenues are earned, we increase the Revenues account (a credit). In this case, we are not receiving cash, so instead we increase Accounts Receivable (a debit) to show that we intend to collect this amount later from our customer(s).

	Accounts receivable	2,800	
	Service revenue		2,800

Requirement 4

During 2011, Hart collected $2,745 cash from customers. Journalize this transaction and calculate the gross accounts receivable balance at December 31, 2011.

| Part 1 | Part 2 | Part 3 | **Part 4** | Part 5 | Part 6 | Part 7 | Part 8 | Part 9 | Part 10 | Part 11 | Demo Doc Complete |

When cash is collected, we increase the Cash account (a debit) and decrease Accounts Receivable (a credit).

Cash	2,745	
Accounts receivable		2,745

From the initial data given in the question, we can see that *gross* accounts receivable had a balance of $800 at the beginning of the year ($760 is the *net* balance). Accounts Receivable increased in the year as revenues were earned. Accounts Receivable decreased when uncollectible accounts were written off and when cash was collected. Using this information, we can calculate the ending balance in (gross) Accounts Receivable:

Accounts receivable			
Dec 31, 2010 Bal	800		
2011 Revenues	2,800	2011 Write-offs	35
		2011 Cash collections	2,745
Dec 31, 2011 Bal	820		

Requirement 5

3 Use the allowance method to account for uncollectibles

Assume that Hart estimates uncollectible account expense to be 1.5% of revenues. Journalize the entry to adjust the allowance at December 31, 2011. What is the December 31, 2011, balance in the allowance?

| Part 1 | Part 2 | Part 3 | Part 4 | **Part 5** | Part 6 | Part 7 | Part 8 | Part 9 | Part 10 | Part 11 | Demo Doc Complete |

The problem states, "Hart estimates uncollectible account expense to be 1.5% of revenues." The key phrase here is "1.5% of revenues." This informs us that Hart is using the <u>percentage-of-sales</u> method to calculate the expense and allowance.

Under the percentage-of-sales method, the percentage of sales equals the uncollectible accounts expense. Therefore, we can calculate that 1.5% of $2,800 = $42 = the uncollectible accounts expense. This means that we record $42 of expense in our journal entry.

Recording the Uncollectible Accounts Expense increases that account (a debit) and also increases the total estimate of uncollectible accounts: the Allowance (a credit).

Uncollectible accounts expense ($2,800 × 1.5%)	42	
Allowance for uncollectible accounts		42

This is the standard journal entry format to record Uncollectible Accounts Expense and adjust the Allowance. The entry structure is always the same; only the amount changes.

The balance in the Allowance account must be calculated. The beginning balance in the allowance for 2011 is the ending balance for 2010 (the $40 shown at the beginning of the question, as shown in the balance sheet presentation on page 223).

During the year, write-offs will decrease the allowance ($35, as in Requirement 2) and the year-end adjustment will increase it ($42, as in this requirement). We can fill in this information to calculate an ending balance of $47 in the Allowance account.

Allowance for uncollectible accounts			
2011 Write-offs	35	Dec 31, 2010 Bal	40
		2011 Uncollectible accounts expense adjustment	42
		Dec 31, 2011 Bal	47

Requirement 6

3 Use the allowance method to account for uncollectibles

Ignoring Requirement 5, assume that Hart estimates that 5% of accounts receivable will turn out to be uncollectible. Gross accounts receivable at December 31, 2011, were $825. Journalize the entry to adjust the allowance at December 31, 2011. What is the December 31, 2011, balance in the allowance?

| Part 1 | Part 2 | Part 3 | Part 4 | Part 5 | **Part 6** | Part 7 | Part 8 | Part 9 | Part 10 | Part 11 | Demo Doc Complete |

The problem states, "*Hart estimates that 5% of accounts receivable will turn out to be uncollectible.*" The key phrase here is "*5% of accounts receivable.*"

This informs us that Hart is using the <u>percentage-of-receivables</u> method to calculate the allowance and *then* the expense.

Under the percentage-of-receivables method, the percentage of receivables equals the ending balance in the allowance. Therefore, we can calculate that 5% of $820 = $41 = the required (or target) ending balance in the allowance.

We need an additional credit in the T-account to make it balance (to make the total correct).

We can use the $41 target ending balance in the T-account (along with the beginning balance of $40 and the write-offs of $35) to calculate the Uncollectible Accounts Expense of **$36** ($41 required balance − $5 current credit balance = $36). This is the amount that must be used in the journal entry.

Allowance for uncollectible accounts			
2011 Write-offs	35	Dec 31, 2010 Bal	40
		2011 Uncollectible accounts expense	X
		Dec 31, 2011 Bal	41

So 40 − 35 + X = 41
X = 41 − 40 + 35 = 36

Demo Doc 1 Solutions | Chapter 8 **231**

Uncollectible accounts expense		36	
Allowance for uncollectible accounts			36

This is the standard journal entry format to record Uncollectible Accounts Expense and adjust the Allowance. The entry structure is always the same; only the amount changes.

Requirement 7

Ignoring Requirements 5 and 6, assume that Hart has the following information at December 31, 2011:

Age	Gross Accounts Receivable	Percentage Estimated Uncollectible
< 30 days	$100	2%
30–60 days	500	4%
> 60 days	220	10%
Total	$820	

> **3** Use the allowance method to account for uncollectibles

Journalize the entry to adjust the allowance at December 31, 2011. What is the December 31, 2011, balance in the allowance? Show how accounts receivable would be reported on the balance sheet at December 31, 2011.

| Part 1 | Part 2 | Part 3 | Part 4 | Part 5 | Part 6 | **Part 7** | Part 8 | Part 9 | Part 10 | Part 11 | Demo Doc Complete |

The problem does not explicitly state which method is being used; however, the table clearly shows estimated uncollectible percentages of *accounts receivable*. This informs us that Hart is using the percentage-of-receivables (aging-of-accounts) method to calculate the allowance and *then* the expense. In fact, *all* aging-of-accounts methods are a subset of the percentage-of-receivable method.

Under the percentage-of-receivables (aging-of-accounts) method, the percentage of receivables equals the ending balance in the allowance. Therefore, we can calculate that (2% of $100) + (4% of $500) + (10% of $220) = $44 = the required (or target) ending balance in the allowance.

Age	Gross Accounts Receivable		Percentage Estimated Uncollectible		Amount Estimated Uncollectible
< 30 days	$100	×	2%	=	$ 2
30–60 days	500	×	4%	=	20
> 60 days	220	×	10%	=	22
Total	$820	×			$44

Ending allowance balance

We need an additional credit in the T-account to make it balance (to make the total correct).

We can use the $44 ending balance in the T-account (along with the beginning balance of $40 and the write-offs of $35) to calculate the Uncollectible Accounts Expense of $39. This is the amount that must be used in the journal entry ($44 required balance − $5 credit balance = $39 amount for journal entry).

5 Report receivables on the balance sheet

Allowance for uncollectible accounts			
		Dec 31, 2010 Bal	40
2011 Write-offs	35		
		2011 Uncollectible accounts expense adjustment	X
		Dec 31, 2011 Bal	44

So 40 − 35 + X = 44
X = 44 − 40 + 35 = 39

Uncollectible accounts expense	39	
Allowance for uncollectible accounts		39

This is the standard journal entry format to record Uncollectible Accounts Expense and adjust the Allowance. The entry structure is always the same; only the amount changes.

On the balance sheet, we would see the gross accounts receivable combined with the Allowance contra account:

Accounts receivable	$ 820
Less Allowance for uncollectible accounts	(44)
Accounts receivable (net)	$776

Requirement 8

3 Use the allowance method to account for uncollectibles

In 2012, Hart wrote off $48 of accounts receivable. On June 30, 2012, Hart estimated uncollectible accounts expense was $10 for the first six months of the year, based on the percentage-of-sales method. Journalize these transactions.

| Part 1 | Part 2 | Part 3 | Part 4 | Part 5 | Part 6 | Part 7 | **Part 8** | Part 9 | Part 10 | Part 11 | Demo Doc Complete |

As in Requirement 2, we use the standard format to write off uncollectible Accounts Receivables:

Allowance for uncollectible accounts	48	
Accounts receivable		48

Demo Doc 1 Solutions | Chapter 8

We also use the standard format to record the Uncollectible Accounts Expense:

Uncollectible accounts expense	10	
Allowance for uncollectible accounts		10

Requirement 9

3 Use the allowance method to account for uncollectibles

At December 31, 2012, based on the percentage-of-receivables method, Hart estimated the allowance balance to be $35. Journalize Hart's entry to adjust the allowance for the year-end financial statements. (Assume the December 31, 2011, balance in the allowance was $30.) What is total uncollectible account expense for 2012?

| Part 1 | Part 2 | Part 3 | Part 4 | Part 5 | Part 6 | Part 7 | Part 8 | **Part 9** | Part 10 | Part 11 | Demo Doc Complete |

Because we only have the target balance in the allowance, we need to analyze the Allowance T-account in order to determine how much Uncollectible Accounts Expense to record for the remaining three months of the year.

So far, the Allowance has been affected in 2012 by write-offs and the Uncollectible Accounts Expense recorded in June:

Allowance for uncollectible accounts

		Dec 31, 2011 Bal	30
2012 Write-offs	48		
		June 2012 Expense Adjustment	10
Bal before Adj	8		
		Dec 31, 2012 Expense Adj	X
		Dec 31, 2012 Bal	35

So X − 8 = 35
X = 35 + 8 = 43

So the additional expense recorded on December 31, 2012, is $43. Again, we use the standard format to record Uncollectible Accounts Expense:

Uncollectible accounts expense	43	
Allowance for uncollectible accounts		43

Requirement 10

8 Use the acid-test ratio and days' sales in receivables to evaluate a company

Calculate Hart's days' sales in accounts receivable for 2011. (Assume Hart uses the aging-of-accounts method in Requirement 7.) What does this ratio mean?

| Part 1 | Part 2 | Part 3 | Part 4 | Part 5 | Part 6 | Part 7 | Part 8 | Part 9 | **Part 10** | Part 11 | Demo Doc Complete |

The days' sales ratio is calculated as:

$$\text{Days' sales in average accounts receivable} = \frac{\text{Average net accounts receivable} \times 365 \text{ days}}{\text{Net sales}}$$

From Requirement 3, we know that service revenues for 2011 are $2,800. From Requirement 7, we know that net accounts receivable were $760 on December 31, 2010, and $776 on December 31, 2011.

So for Hart:

$$\text{Days' sales in average accounts receivable} = \frac{\frac{1}{2} \times [\$760 + \$776] \times 365 \text{ days}}{\$2,800}$$

$$= 100.1 \text{ days}$$

The average amount of time that it takes Hart to collect an account receivable is 100.1 days (more than three months).

Requirement 11

2 Design internal controls for receivables

The employee at Hart who opens the mail and physically collects the cash is the same person who updates the cash receipts journal and accounts receivable ledger. Is this a good internal control system?

| Part 1 | Part 2 | Part 3 | Part 4 | Part 5 | Part 6 | Part 7 | Part 8 | Part 9 | Part 10 | **Part 11** | Demo Doc Complete |

If an employee collects the cash *and* records the receipt of the cash *and* updates the accounts receivable ledger, there is an opportunity for fraud. The employee could steal the cash and delay recording the cash receipt or perhaps never record the cash receipt. The employee could hide his or her act for a long period of time by manipulating the accounts receivable ledger.

To avoid this problem, most internal control systems require <u>separation of duties</u>; that is, the employees who handle cash (both receipts and payments) are *not* the same employees who maintain the accounting records.

| Part 1 | Part 2 | Part 3 | Part 4 | Part 5 | Part 6 | Part 7 | Part 8 | Part 9 | Part 10 | Part 11 | Demo Doc Complete |

Demo Doc 2

Notes Receivable

Learning Objectives 1, 7

On November 1, 2011, Jordan Company borrowed $1,800 cash from Donald Company. Jordan signed a three-month, 10% note. Jordan paid the note plus interest in full on the due date. Both Jordan and Donald have December 31 year-ends.

Requirements

1. When is the note due? What is the total interest that will be paid on this note? What is its maturity value?

2. Prepare all journal entries for this note for both companies from November 1, 2011, through the due date. Explanations are not required.

Demo Doc 2 Solutions

1 Define and explain common types of receivables

7 Account for notes receivable

Requirement 1

When is the note due? What is the total interest that will be paid on this note? What is its maturity value?

| Part 1 | Part 2 | Demo Doc Complete |

The note was issued on November 1, 2011. Because it is a three-month note, it is due three months from that date on February 1, 2012.

The amount of interest incurred over the entire life of the note is calculated as:

Interest incurred = Amount of debt × Annual interest rate × Time elapsed (in years)

So in this case:

$$\text{Interest incurred} = \$1{,}800 \times 10\% \times \frac{3 \text{ months}}{12 \text{ months}}$$
$$= \$45$$

The maturity value is calculated as:

Maturity value = Principal + Interest incurred over life of the note

So in this case:

$$\text{Maturity value} = \$1{,}800 + \$45$$
$$= \$1{,}845$$

Requirement 2

Prepare all journal entries for this note for both companies from November 1, 2011, through the due date. Explanations are not required.

| Part 1 | Part 2 | Demo Doc Complete |

7 Account for notes receivable

November 1, 2011: Jordan borrows $1,800 from Donald.

Jordan borrowed cash from Donald. This means that Donald has a decrease (a credit) to Cash of $1,800. Because Donald can expect to get this money back (that is, collect it) in the future, we can also set up a Notes Receivable asset (a debit) for $1,800.

Donald:

Nov 1	Notes receivable	1,800	
	Cash		1,800

Jordan has an increase to Cash (a debit) and because the money must be paid back, we can set up a Notes Payable liability (a credit) for $1,800.

Jordan:

Nov 1	Cash	1,800	
	Notes payable		1,800

7 Account for notes receivable

December 31, 2011: Accrue 10% interest on note.

Both companies have a December 31 year-end. This means that they need to adjust their accounting information on this date. By this time, the note has been outstanding for two months. This means that interest has been incurred on the note.

The amount of interest incurred is calculated as:

Interest incurred = Amount of debt × Annual interest rate × Time elapsed (in years)

So in this case:

$$\text{Interest incurred} = \$1,800 \times 10\% \times \frac{2 \text{ months}}{12 \text{ months}}$$
$$= \$30$$

Note that *all* interest rates that are given are assumed to be *annual* rates, unless specifically stated otherwise.

Donald has earned Interest Revenue (a credit) of $30. Because the cash has not yet been received, we must also set up an Interest Receivable account (a debit) of $30.

Donald:

Dec 31	Interest receivable	30	
	Interest revenue ($1,800 × 10% × 2/12)		30

Jordan has incurred Interest Expense (a debit) of $30. Because the cash has yet to be paid, we must also set up an Interest Payable account (a credit) of $30.

Jordan:

| Dec 31 | Interest expense | 30 | |
| | Interest payable | | 30 |

7 Account for notes receivable

February 1, 2012: Note and interest are paid in full.

On this day, the note and interest are fully paid. For Donald, this causes a decrease to Notes Receivable (a credit) of $1,800. Additionally, Donald is receiving the interest that was accrued on December 31, so there will also be a decrease to Interest Receivable of $30 (a credit).

However, there is *more* interest than this! Donald has also earned interest between December 31 and February 1 (one month):

$$\text{Interest incurred} = \$1,800 \times 10\% \times \frac{1 \text{ months}}{12 \text{ months}}$$
$$= \$15$$

So Donald records Interest Revenue (a credit) of $15.

All of these amounts are being paid in cash, so Donald's Cash account will be increased (a debit) by $1,800 + $30 + $15 = $1,845 (the maturity value).

Donald:

Feb 1	Cash (maturity value)	1,845	
	Notes receivable		1,800
	Interest receivable		30
	Interest revenue ($1,800 × 10% × 1/12)		15

With payment of the note and interest, Jordan will decrease Notes Payable by $1,800 and Interest Payable by $30 (debits). Jordan will also record additional interest expense of $15 (a debit) and decrease Cash (a credit) by $1,845.

Jordan:

Feb 1	Notes payable	1,800	
	Interest payable	30	
	Interest expense	15	
	Cash		1,845

| Part 1 | Part 2 | Demo Doc Complete |

Demo Doc 3

Credit-Card Receivables

Learning Objectives 1, 5, 6

Mack Company accepts credit-card payments from its customers. On May 4, 2011, a customer paid for $800 worth of services using his MasterCard credit card. MasterCard charges Mack a 3% fee to process the transaction. On May 10, 2011, Mack received the cash payment from MasterCard for this sale.

Requirements

1. What type of receivable is involved in these transactions? How does this type of receivable differ from a traditional account receivable?

2. Show Mack's journal entry to record the sale on May 4, 2011.

3. Show Mack's journal entry to record the cash receipt from MasterCard on May 10, 2011.

Demo Doc 3 Solutions

1 Define and explain common types of receivables

6 Journalize credit-card, bankcard and debit-card sales

5 Report receivables on the balance sheet

6 Journalize credit-card, bankcard and debit-card sales

Requirement 1

What type of receivable is involved in these transactions? How does this type of receivable differ from a traditional account receivable?

| Part 1 | Part 2 | Part 3 | Demo Doc Complete |

This transaction involves credit card receivables. These receivables are different because they are due from the credit card corporation, which is a financing organization. The credit card corporation will take care of all collections and bad debts (uncollectible accounts).

In comparison, traditional accounts receivable are due directly from the individual customers, and it is Mack who would bear the responsibility for collection and the cost of bad debts. However, Mack would not have to pay any credit card fees, as they would if Mastercard took on these responsibilities.

Requirement 2

Show Mack's journal entry to record the sale on May 4, 2011.

| Part 1 | Part 2 | Part 3 | Demo Doc Complete |

As with a non-credit-card sale, Mack will increase Accounts Receivable (a debit) and increase Service Revenue (a credit) by $800. However, the account receivable is not for the full $800, because not all of this amount will be collected. The 3% MasterCard fee must be deducted.

So Accounts Receivable = $800 × (1 − 3%) = $776.

The difference of $800 − $776 = $24 is recorded as an increase (debit) to Credit-Card Discount Expense.

Accounts receivable—MasterCard ($800 × [1 − 3%])	776	
Credit-card discount expense ($800 × 3%)	24	
Service revenue		800

5 Report receivables on the balance sheet

6 Journalize credit-card, bankcard and debit-card sales

Requirement 3

Show Mack's journal entry to record the cash receipt from MasterCard on May 10, 2011.

| Part 1 | Part 2 | **Part 3** | Demo Doc Complete |

The collection of the account receivable is similar to any other collection of an account receivable. Accounts Receivable is decreased (a credit) by $776 and Cash is increased (a debit) by $776.

| Cash | | 776 | |
| Accounts receivable—MasterCard | | | 776 |

| Part 1 | Part 2 | Part 3 | **Demo Doc Complete** |

242 Chapter 8 | Demo Doc 3 Solutions

Quick Practice Questions

True/False

_____ 1. The Allowance for Uncollectible Accounts is a contra account to Accounts Receivable.

_____ 2. Under the allowance method, the recovery of an account previously written off has no effect on net income.

_____ 3. Under the allowance method, the entry to write off an account that is determined to be uncollectible includes a credit to the Allowance for Uncollectible Accounts.

_____ 4. Under the allowance method, the entry to write off an account that has been deemed uncollectible has no effect on the total assets of the firm.

_____ 5. The direct write-off method is the preferred way to apply the accrual basis for measuring uncollectible accounts expense because it matches revenues and expenses on the income statement.

_____ 6. Under the direct write-off method, the entry to write off an account that has been deemed uncollectible has no effect on the total assets of the firm.

_____ 7. A written promise to pay a specified amount of money at a particular future date is referred to as a promissory note.

_____ 8. If the maker of a note does not pay at maturity, the maker is said to dishonor the note.

_____ 9. The acid-test ratio includes cash, inventory, and net accounts receivable in the numerator.

_____ 10. Nonbank credit-card sales are recorded as a debit to Accounts Receivable and a credit to Sales Revenue in the same amount.

Multiple Choice

1. Chuck Battle's account of $5,000 must be written off. Which of the following would be journalized assuming that the allowance method is used?
   a. A debit to Battle's Accounts Receivable and a credit to Allowance for Uncollectible Accounts
   b. A debit to Allowance for Uncollectible Accounts and a credit to Battle's Accounts Receivable
   c. A debit to Cash and a credit to Uncollectible Accounts Expense
   d. A debit to Cash and a credit to Battle's Accounts Receivable

2. The current credit balance in Allowance for Uncollectible Accounts before adjustment is $658. An aging schedule reveals $3,700 of uncollectible accounts. What is the ending balance in the Allowance for Uncollectible Accounts?
   a. $3,042
   b. $3,700
   c. $4,029
   d. $4,358

3. The current debit balance in Allowance for Uncollectible Accounts before adjustment is $742. An aging schedule reveals $3,500 of uncollectible accounts. What is the amount of the journal entry for Estimated Uncollectible Accounts?
   a. $742
   b. $2,758
   c. $3,500
   d. $4,242

4. What is the type of account and normal balance of Allowance for Uncollectible Accounts?
   a. Asset, debit
   b. Contra asset, credit
   c. Liability, credit
   d. Contra liability, debit

5. If the direct write-off method is used for uncollectible receivables, what account is debited when writing off a customer's account?
   a. Accounts Receivable
   b. Allowance for Uncollectible Accounts
   c. Uncollectible Accounts Expense
   d. Sales Returns and Allowances

6. What is the effect on the financial statements of writing off an uncollectible account under the direct write-off method?
   a. Increases expenses and decreases liabilities
   b. Decreases net income and decreases assets
   c. Decreases assets and increases owners' equity
   d. Increases expenses and increases assets

7. Which of the following is not avoided when a company uses national credit cards?
   a. Checking a customer's credit rating
   b. Keeping an accounts receivable subsidiary ledger for each customer
   c. Having to collect cash from customers
   d. Paying a credit-card discount expense

8. A 90-day, 12% note for $20,000, dated July 10, is received from a customer. What is the maturity value of the note?
   a. $20,000
   b. $20,600
   c. $21,200
   d. $22,400

9. Carolina Supply accepted an 8-month, $16,000 note receivable, with 8% interest, from Reading Company on August 1, 2011. Carolina Supply's year-end is December 31. What is the amount of interest to be accrued on December 31, 2011?
   a. $320
   b. $533
   c. $853
   d. $1,280

10. Which of the following is recorded on the payee's books when a debtor dishonors a note receivable?
    a. Debit Uncollectible Accounts Expense
    b. Debit Accounts Receivable
    c. No entry required
    d. Debit Notes Receivable

Quick Exercises

8-1. Prepare the adjusting journal entry on December 31, 2011, for the following independent situations:

   a. The Allowance for Uncollectible Accounts has a $700 credit balance prior to adjustment. Net credit sales during the year are $216,000 and 4% are estimated to be uncollectible.

Journal				Page 1
Date	Accounts		Debit	Credit

   b. The Allowance for Uncollectible Accounts has a $500 credit balance prior to adjustment. An aging schedule prepared on December 31 reveals an estimated uncollectible accounts amount of $7,300.

Journal				Page 1
Date	Accounts		Debit	Credit

c. The Allowance for Uncollectible Accounts has a $525 debit balance prior to adjustment. An aging schedule prepared on December 31 reveals an estimated uncollectible accounts amount of $5,100.

Journal				Page 1
Date	Accounts		Debit	Credit

d. The Allowance for Uncollectible Accounts has an $800 credit balance prior to adjustment. Net credit sales during the year are $229,000 and 3.5% are estimated to be uncollectible.

Journal				Page 1
Date	Accounts		Debit	Credit

8-2. Compute the ending balance in the Allowance for Uncollectible Accounts after the adjusting entries in 8-1 have been prepared for the four independent situations, a–d.

    a. _____
    b. _____
    c. _____
    d. _____

8-3. Record the following independent transactions assuming the allowance method is used.

    a. August 5, 2011—Wrote off Jones Corp. account receivable for $2,200 as uncollectible.

Date	Accounts	Debit	Credit

    b. August 17, 2011—Collected the $2,200 from Jones Corp. in full.

Date	Accounts	Debit	Credit

c. August 31, 2011—Recorded uncollectible accounts expense of $16,500.

Date	Accounts	Debit	Credit

8-4. On December 31, 2011, Rainbow Appliances has $275,000 in accounts receivable and an Allowance account with a credit balance of $240. Current period net credit sales are $771,000, and cash sales are $68,000.

Rainbow Appliances performs an aging schedule; the results follow, along with the appropriate percentages that Rainbow applies to the categories shown.

Age	Gross Accounts Receivable	Estimated Uncollectible
Not yet due	$150,000	1%
31–60 days past due	50,000	5%
61–90 days past due	40,000	10%
91–120 days past due	25,000	25%
Over 120 days past due	10,000	50%
Total	$275,000	

a. Assuming Rainbow uses the aging approach of accounting for uncollectible accounts, prepare the adjusting entry required at the end of the accounting period.

Date	Accounts	Debit	Credit

b. Assume now Rainbow uses the percentage-of-sales method of accounting for uncollectible accounts. If historical data indicate that approximately 3% of net credit sales are uncollectible, what is the amount of uncollectible accounts expense that should be recorded?

What is the balance in the Allowance for Uncollectible Accounts after adjustment?

8-5. Peterson Company, which has a December 31 year-end, completed the following transactions during 2011 and 2012:

2011	
Oct 14	Sold merchandise to Bruce Company, receiving a 60-day, 9% note for $10,000.
Nov 16	Sold merchandise to Marine Company, receiving a 72-day, 8% note for $9100.
Dec 13	Received amount due from Bruce Company.
Dec 31	Accrued interest on the Marine Company note.
2012	
Jan 27	Collected in full from Marine Company.

Requirement

1. Prepare the necessary journal entries to record the preceding transactions.

Date	Accounts	Debit	Credit

Date	Accounts	Debit	Credit

Date	Accounts	Debit	Credit

Date	Accounts	Debit	Credit

Date	Accounts	Debit	Credit

Do It Yourself! Question 1

Uncollectible Accounts Receivable

Now Company's December 31, 2010, balance sheet reported:

Accounts receivable	$1,000
Allowance for uncollectible accounts	(85)
Accounts receivable (net)	$915

Requirements

1. Define and explain common types of receivables

1. How much of the December 31, 2010, balance of accounts receivable did Now expect to collect?

3. Use the allowance method to account for uncollectibles

2. During 2011, Now wrote off accounts receivable totaling $110. Journalize these write-offs as one transaction.

Date	Accounts and Explanation	Debit	Credit

3. During 2011, Now earned $13,000 of service revenues, all on account. Journalize these revenues as one transaction.

Date	Accounts and Explanation	Debit	Credit

4. During 2011, Now collected $12,840 cash from customers. Journalize this transaction and calculate the gross accounts receivable balance at December 31, 2011.

Date	Accounts and Explanation	Debit	Credit

3 Use the allowance method to account for uncollectibles

5. Assume that Now estimates that 10% of accounts receivable will turn out to be uncollectible. Gross accounts receivable at December 31, 2011, were $1,050. Journalize the entry to adjust the allowance at December 31, 2011. What is the December 31, 2011, balance in the allowance?

Date	Accounts and Explanation	Debit	Credit

3 Use the allowance method to account for uncollectibles

6. Ignoring Requirement 5, assume that Now estimates uncollectible account expense to be 0.75% of revenues. Journalize the entry to adjust the allowance at December 31, 2011. What is the December 31, 2011, balance in the allowance?

Date	Accounts and Explanation	Debit	Credit

7. Ignoring Requirements 5 and 6, *assume* that Now has the following information at December 31, 2011:

Age	Gross Accounts Receivable	Percentage Estimated Uncollectible
< 30 days	$ 500	1%
30–60 days	450	10%
> 60 days	100	15%
Total	$1,050	

3 Use the allowance method to account for uncollectibles

5 Report receivables on the balance sheet

Journalize the entry to adjust the allowance at December 31, 2011. What is the December 31, 2011, balance in the allowance? Show how accounts receivable would be reported on the balance sheet at December 31, 2011.

Date	Accounts and Explanation	Debit	Credit

Do It Yourself! Question 1 | Chapter 8

3 Use the allowance method to account for uncollectibles

8. In 2012, Now wrote off $90 of accounts receivable. On September 30, 2012, Now estimated uncollectible accounts expense was $55 for the first nine months of the year, based on the percentage-of-sales method. Journalize these transactions.

Date	Accounts and Explanation	Debit	Credit

Date	Accounts and Explanation	Debit	Credit

3 Use the allowance method to account for uncollectibles

9. At December 31, 2012, based on the percentage-of-receivables method, Now estimated the allowance balance to be $78. Journalize Now's entry to adjust the allowance for the year-end financial statements. (Assume the December 31, 2011, balance in the allowance was $65.) What is total uncollectible accounts expense for 2012?

Date	Accounts and Explanation	Debit	Credit

Do It Yourself! Question 2

Notes Receivable

On June 1 2011, Anderson Company borrowed $6,000 cash from Neo Enterprises. Anderson signed a 10-month, 5% note. Anderson paid the note plus interest in full on the due date. Both Anderson and Neo have December 31 year-ends.

Requirements

[7] Account for notes receivable

1. When is the note due? What is the total interest incurred over the life of the note? What is the maturity value of the note?

[7] Account for notes receivable

2. Prepare all journal entries for this note for *both* companies from June 1, 2011 through the due date. Explanations are not required.

Neo Enterprises:

Date	Accounts and Explanation	Debit	Credit

Anderson Company:

Date	Accounts and Explanation	Debit	Credit

Neo Enterprises:

Date	Accounts and Explanation	Debit	Credit

Anderson Company:

Date	Accounts and Explanation	Debit	Credit

Neo Enterprises:

Date	Accounts and Explanation	Debit	Credit

Anderson Company:

Date	Accounts and Explanation	Debit	Credit

Quick Practice Solutions

True/False

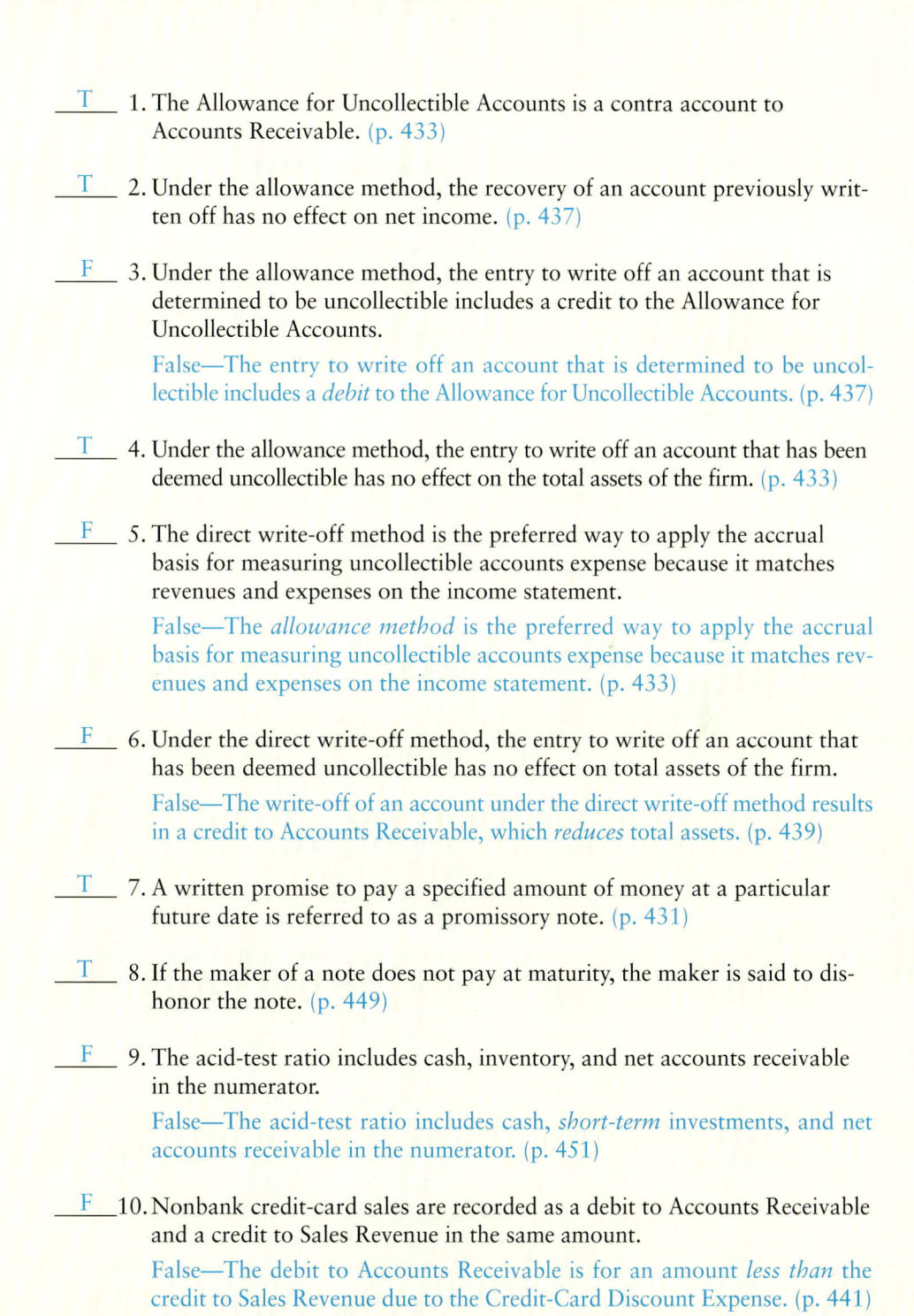

__T__ 1. The Allowance for Uncollectible Accounts is a contra account to Accounts Receivable. (p. 433)

__T__ 2. Under the allowance method, the recovery of an account previously written off has no effect on net income. (p. 437)

__F__ 3. Under the allowance method, the entry to write off an account that is determined to be uncollectible includes a credit to the Allowance for Uncollectible Accounts.

False—The entry to write off an account that is determined to be uncollectible includes a *debit* to the Allowance for Uncollectible Accounts. (p. 437)

__T__ 4. Under the allowance method, the entry to write off an account that has been deemed uncollectible has no effect on the total assets of the firm. (p. 433)

__F__ 5. The direct write-off method is the preferred way to apply the accrual basis for measuring uncollectible accounts expense because it matches revenues and expenses on the income statement.

False—The *allowance method* is the preferred way to apply the accrual basis for measuring uncollectible accounts expense because it matches revenues and expenses on the income statement. (p. 433)

__F__ 6. Under the direct write-off method, the entry to write off an account that has been deemed uncollectible has no effect on total assets of the firm.

False—The write-off of an account under the direct write-off method results in a credit to Accounts Receivable, which *reduces* total assets. (p. 439)

__T__ 7. A written promise to pay a specified amount of money at a particular future date is referred to as a promissory note. (p. 431)

__T__ 8. If the maker of a note does not pay at maturity, the maker is said to dishonor the note. (p. 449)

__F__ 9. The acid-test ratio includes cash, inventory, and net accounts receivable in the numerator.

False—The acid-test ratio includes cash, *short-term* investments, and net accounts receivable in the numerator. (p. 451)

__F__ 10. Nonbank credit-card sales are recorded as a debit to Accounts Receivable and a credit to Sales Revenue in the same amount.

False—The debit to Accounts Receivable is for an amount *less than* the credit to Sales Revenue due to the Credit-Card Discount Expense. (p. 441)

Multiple Choice

1. Chuck Battle's account of $5,000 must be written off. Which of the following would be journalized assuming that the allowance method is used? (p. 437)
   a. A debit to Battle's Accounts Receivable and a credit to Allowance for Uncollectible Accounts
   b. A debit to Allowance for Uncollectible Accounts and a credit to Battle's Accounts Receivable
   c. A debit to Cash and a credit to Uncollectible Account Expense
   d. A debit to Cash and a credit to Battle's Accounts Receivable

2. The current credit balance in Allowance for Uncollectible Accounts before adjustment is $658. An aging schedule reveals $3,700 of uncollectible accounts. What is the ending balance in the Allowance for Uncollectible Accounts? (p. 436)
   a. $3,042
   b. $3,700
   c. $4,029
   d. $4,358

3. The current debit balance in Allowance for Uncollectible Accounts before adjustment is $742. An aging schedule reveals $3,500 of uncollectible accounts. What is the amount of the journal entry for Estimated Uncollectible Accounts? (p. 436)
   a. $742
   b. $2,758
   c. $3,500
   d. $4,242

4. What is the type of account and normal balance of Allowance for Uncollectible Accounts? (p. 433)
   a. Asset, debit
   b. Contra asset, credit
   c. Liability, credit
   d. Contra liability, debit

5. If the direct write-off method is used for uncollectible receivables, what account is debited when writing off a customer's account? (p. 439)
   a. Accounts Receivable
   b. Allowance for Uncollectible Accounts
   c. Uncollectible Account Expense
   d. Sales Returns and Allowances

6. What is the effect on the financial statements of writing off an uncollectible account under the direct write-off method? (p. 439)
   a. Increases expenses and decreases liabilities
   b. Decreases net income and decreases assets
   c. Decreases assets and increases owners' equity
   d. Increases expenses and increases assets

7. Which of the following is *not* avoided when a company uses national credit cards? (p. 441)
   a. Checking a customer's credit rating
   b. Keeping an accounts receivable subsidiary ledger for each customer
   c. Having to collect cash from customers
   d. Paying a credit-card discount expense

8. A 90-day, 12% note for $20,000, dated July 10, is received from a customer. What is the maturity value of the note? (p. 445)
   a. $20,000
   b. $20,600
   c. $21,200
   d. $22,400

9. Carolina Supply accepted an 8-month, $16,000 note receivable, with 8% interest, from Reading Company on August 1, 2011. Carolina Supply's year-end is December 31. What is the amount of interest to be accrued on December 31, 2011? (p. 446)
   a. $320
   b. $853
   c. $533
   d. $1,280

10. Which of the following is recorded on the payee's books when a debtor dishonors a note receivable? (p. 449)
    a. Debit Uncollectible Accounts Expense
    b. Debit Accounts Receivable
    c. No entry required
    d. Debit Notes Receivable

Quick Exercises

8-1. Prepare the adjusting journal entry on December 31, 2011 for the following independent situations: (p. 437)

   a. The Allowance for Uncollectible Accounts has a $700 credit balance prior to adjustment. Net credit sales during the year are $216,000 and 4% are estimated to be uncollectible.
   b. The Allowance for Uncollectible Accounts has a $500 credit balance prior to adjustment. An aging schedule prepared on December 31 reveals an estimated uncollectible accounts amount of $7,300.
   c. The Allowance for Uncollectible Accounts has a $525 debit balance prior to adjustment. An aging schedule prepared on December 31 reveals an estimated uncollectible accounts amount of $5,100.
   d. The Allowance for Uncollectible Accounts has an $800 credit balance prior to adjustment. Net credit sales during the year are $229,000 and 3.5% are estimated to be uncollectible.

Journal				Page 1
	Date	Accounts	Debit	Credit
a.	Dec 31	Uncollectible accounts expense	8,640	
		Allowance for uncollectible accounts		8,640
		($216,000 × .04) = $8,640		

Journal				Page 1
	Date	Accounts	Debit	Credit
b.	Dec 31	Uncollectible accounts expense	6,800	
		Allowance for uncollectible accounts		6,800
		($7,300 − $500) = $6,800		

Journal				Page 1
	Date	Accounts	Debit	Credit
c.	Dec 31	Uncollectible accounts expense	5,625	
		Allowance for uncollectible accounts		5,625
		($5,100 + $525) = $5,625		

Journal				Page 1
	Date	Accounts	Debit	Credit
d.	Dec 31	Uncollectible accounts expense	8,015	
		Allowance for uncollectible accounts		8,015
		($229,000 × 0.35) = $8,015		

8-2. Compute the ending balance in the Allowance for Uncollectible Accounts after the adjusting entries in 8-1 have been prepared for the four independent situations, a–d. (p. 437)

a. $9,340 ($700 + $8,640)

b. $7,300 ($500 + $6,800)

c. $5,100 ($5,625 − $525)

d. $8,815 ($800 + $8,015)

8-3. Record the following independent transactions assuming the allowance method is used. (pp. 433–438)

   a. August 5, 2011—Wrote off Jones Corp. account receivable for $2,200 as uncollectible.
   b. August 17, 2011—Collected the $2,200 from Jones Corp. in full.
   c. August 31, 2011—Recorded uncollectible accounts expense of $16,500.

	Date	Accounts	Debit	Credit
a.	Aug 5	Allowance for uncollectible accounts	2,200	
		Accounts receivable—Jones Corp.		2,200
		To write off Jones Corp. account receivable.		

	Date	Accounts	Debit	Credit
b.	Aug 17	Accounts receivable—Jones Corp.	2,200	
		Allowance for uncollectible accounts		2,200
		To reinstate Jones Corp. account receivable.		

	Date	Accounts	Debit	Credit
	Aug 17	Cash	2,200	
		Accounts receivable—Jones Corp.		2,200
		To record cash collected from Jones Corp.		

	Date	Accounts	Debit	Credit
c.	Aug 31	Uncollectible accounts expense	16,500	
		Allowance for uncollectible accounts.		16,500
		To record estimated uncollectible accounts.		

8-4. On December 31, 2011, Rainbow Appliances has $275,000 in accounts receivable and an Allowance account with a credit balance of $240. Current period net credit sales are $771,000, and cash sales are $68,000. Rainbow Appliances performs an aging schedule; the results follow along with the appropriate percentages that Rainbow applies to the categories shown. (p. 435)

Age	Gross Accounts Receivable	Percentage Estimated Uncollectible
Not yet due	$150,000	1%
31–60 days past due	50,000	5%
61–90 days past due	40,000	10%
91–120 days past due	25,000	25%
Over 120 days past due	10,000	50%
Total	$275,000	

a. Assuming Rainbow uses the aging approach of accounting for uncollectible accounts, prepare the adjusting entry required at the end of the accounting period.

Date	Accounts	Debit	Credit
Dec 31	Uncollectible accounts expense	19,010	
	Allowance for doubtful accounts		19,010
	($150,000 × 0.01) + ($50,000 × 0.05) + ($40,000 × 0.10) + ($25,000 × 0.25) + ($10,000 × 0.5) = $19,250 − $240		

b. Assume now Rainbow uses the percentage-of-sales method of accounting for uncollectible accounts. If historical data indicate that approximately 3% of net credit sales are uncollectible, what is the amount of uncollectible accounts expense that should be recorded? $23,130

What is the balance in the Allowance for Uncollectible Accounts after adjustment?

$23,370 ($240 + $23,130)

8-5. Peterson Company, which has a December 31 year-end, completed the following transactions during 2011 and 2012: (p. 447)

2011	
Oct 14	Sold merchandise to Bruce Company, receiving a 60-day, 9% note for $10,000.
Nov 16	Sold merchandise to Marine Company, receiving a 72-day, 8% note for $9100.
Dec 13	Received amount due from Bruce Company.
Dec 31	Accrued interest on the Marine Company note.
2012	
Jan 27	Collected in full from Marine Company.

Requirement

1. Prepare the necessary journal entries to record the preceding transactions.

Date	Accounts	Debit	Credit
Oct 14	Notes receivable	10,000	
	Sales		10,000

Date	Accounts	Debit	Credit
Nov 16	Notes receivable	9,100	
	Sales		9,100

Date	Accounts	Debit	Credit
Dec 13	Cash	10,150	
	Notes receivable		10,000
	Interest revenue		150

Date	Accounts	Debit	Credit
Dec 31	Interest receivable	91	
	Interest revenue		91

Date	Accounts	Debit	Credit
Jan 27	Cash	9,246	
	Notes receivable		9,100
	Interest revenue		55
	Interest receivable		91

Do It Yourself! Question 1 Solutions

Requirements

1. How much of the December 31, 2010, balance of accounts receivable did Now expect to collect?

Now expects to collect $915 of the accounts receivable balance.

2. During 2011, Now wrote off accounts receivable totaling $110. Journalize these write-offs as one transaction.

Allowance for uncollectible accounts	110	
Accounts receivable		110

3. During 2011, Now earned $13,000 of service revenues, all on account. Journalize these revenues as one transaction.

Accounts receivable	13,000	
Service revenue		13,000

4. During 2011, Now collected $12,840 cash from customers. Journalize this transaction and calculate the gross accounts receivable balance at December 31, 2011.

Cash	12,840	
Accounts receivable		12,840

Accounts receivable			
Dec 31, 2010 Bal	1,000		
2011 Revenues	13,000	2011 Write-offs	110
		2011 Cash collections	11,840
Dec 31, 2011 Bal	1,050		

5. Assume that Now estimates that 10% of accounts receivable will turn out to be uncollectible. Gross accounts receivable at December 31, 2011, were $1,050. Journalize the entry to adjust the allowance at December 31, 2011. What is the December 31, 2011, balance in the allowance?

$$10\% \times \$1{,}050 = \$105 = \text{balance in Allowance account}$$

Allowance for uncollectible accounts

2011 Write-offs	110	Dec 31, 2010 Bal	85
		2011 Uncollectible accounts expense	X
		Dec 31, 2011 Bal	105

So 85 − 110 + X = 105
X = 105 + 110 − 85 = 130

Uncollectible accounts expense	130	
Allowance for uncollectible accounts		130

6. Ignoring Requirement 5, assume that Now estimates uncollectible account expense to be 0.75% of revenues. Journalize the entry to adjust the allowance at December 31, 2011. What is the December 31, 2011, balance in the allowance?

$$0.75\% \times \$13{,}000 = \$97.50$$

Uncollectible accounts expense	97.50	
Allowance for uncollectible accounts		97.50

Allowance for uncollectible accounts

2011 Write-offs	110	Dec 31, 2010 Bal	85
		2011 Uncollectible accounts expense	97.50
		Dec 31, 2011 Bal	72.50

7. Ignoring Requirements 5 and 6, Assume that Now has the following information at December 31, 2011:

Age	Gross Accounts Receivable	Percentage Estimated Uncollectible
< 30 days	$ 500	1%
30–60 days	450	10%
> 60 days	$ 100	15%
Total	$1,050	

Journalize the entry to adjust the allowance at December 31, 2011. What is the December 31, 2011 balance in the allowance? Show how accounts receivable would be reported on the balance sheet at December 31, 2011.

Age	Gross Accounts Receivable		Percentage Estimated Uncollectible		Amount Estimated Uncollectible
< 30 days	$ 500	×	1%	=	$ 5
30–60 days	450	×	10%	=	45
> 60 days	100	×	15%	=	15
Total	$1,050	×		=	$65

Allowance for uncollectible accounts

		Dec 31, 2010 Bal	85
2011 Write-offs	110		
		2011 Uncollectible accounts expense	X
		Dec 31, 2011 Bal	65

So 85 − 110 + X = 65
X = 65 − 85 + 110 = 90

Uncollectible accounts expense	90	
Allowance for uncollectible accounts		90

On the balance sheet:

Accounts receivable	$1,050
Less Allowance for uncollectible accounts	(65)
Accounts receivable (net)	$ 985

8. In 2012, Now wrote off $90 of accounts receivable. On September 30, 2012, Now estimated uncollectible accounts expense was $55 for the first nine months of the year, based on the percentage-of-sales method. Journalize these transactions.

	Allowance for uncollectible accounts	90	
	Accounts receivable		90

	Uncollectible accounts expense	55	
	Allowance for uncollectible accounts		55

9. At December 31, 2012, based on the percentage-of-receivables method, Now estimated the allowance balance to be $78. Journalize Now's entry to adjust the allowance for the year-end financial statements. (Assume the December 31, 2011, balance in the allowance was $65.) What is total uncollectible accounts expense for 2012?

Allowance for uncollectible accounts

		Dec 31, 2011 Bal	65
2012 Write-offs	90		
		Sept 2012 Expense	55
		Bal before Adj	30
		Dec 31, 2012 Adj	X
		Dec 31, 2012 Bal	78

So 65 − 90 + 55 + X = 78
X = 78 − 65 + 90 − 55 = 48

	Uncollectible accounts expense	48	
	Allowance for uncollectible accounts		48

Total uncollectible accounts expense for 2012
= Expense recorded in September 2012 + Expense recorded in December 2012
= $55 + $48
= $103

Uncollectible accounts expense

Jan 1, 2012 Bal	0
Sept 2012 Expense Adjustment	58
Dec 2012 Expense Adjustment	45
Dec 31, 2012 Bal	103

Do It Yourself! Question 2 Solutions

Requirements

1. When is the note due? What is the total interest incurred over the life of the note? What is the maturity value of the note?

The note is due 10 months from June 1, 2011, on April 1, 2012.

The amount of interest incurred over the entire life of the note is calculated as:

$$\text{Interest incurred} = \$6{,}000 \times 5\% \times \frac{10 \text{ months}}{12 \text{ months}}$$
$$= \$250$$

$$\text{Maturity value} = \$6{,}000 + \$250$$
$$= \$6{,}250$$

2. Prepare all journal entries for this note for *both* companies from June 1, 2011, through the due date. Explanations are not required.

June 1, 2011: Anderson borrowed $6,000 from Neo.

Neo Enterprises:

| Jun 1 | Notes receivable | 6,000 | |
| | Cash | | 6,000 |

Anderson Company:

| Jun 1 | Cash | 6,000 | |
| | Notes receivable | | 6,000 |

December 31, 2011: accrue 5% interest on note.

Neo Enterprises:

	Dec 31	Interest receivable	175	
		Interest revenue ($6,000 × 5% × 7/12)		175

Anderson Company:

	Dec 31	Interest expense	175	
		Interest payable		175

April 1, 2012: Note and interest are paid in full.

Neo Enterprises:

	Apr 1	Cash (maturity value)	6,250	
		Notes receivable		6,000
		Interest receivable		175
		Interest revenue ($6,000 × 5% × 3/12)		75

Anderson Company:

	Apr 1	Notes payable	6,000	
		Interest payable	175	
		Interest expense	75	
		Cash		6,250

The Power of Practice

For more practice using the skills learned in this chapter, visit MyAccountingLab. There you will find algorithmically generated questions that are based on these Demo Docs and your main textbook's Review and Assess Your Progress sections.

Go to MyAccountingLab and follow these steps:

1. Direct your URL to www.myaccountinglab.com.
2. Log in using your name and password.
3. Click the MyAccountingLab link.
4. Click Study Plan in the left navigation bar.
5. From the table of contents, select Chapter 8, Receivables.
6. Click a link to work tutorial exercises.

9 Plant Assets and Intangibles

What You Probably Already Know

You probably already know that when you decide to get a car, you must decide if you want to purchase or lease it. If you lease a car, you pay a monthly amount for the use of that vehicle, which is a benefit or expense to you. If you purchase a car for cash instead, there is still a monthly benefit to you, although there are no future payments. The benefit or cost incurred is called depreciation expense. The more a car is used, the less remaining future value to be derived from that asset. In business, the asset is reduced for the loss in usefulness or future benefit as the vehicle is used.

Learning Objectives/Success Keys

1 Measure the cost of a plant asset.

The **cost of a plant asset** should include all of the necessary costs to acquire the asset and get it ready for use. In addition to the purchase price of the plant asset, other items that may be necessary and would increase the cost of the asset include:

- Taxes, commissions, shipping costs, and insurance on the asset while in transit
- Installation and testing costs
- Architectural fees, building permits, and costs to repair and renovate the asset for use
- Interest on money borrowed to construct the plant asset
- Brokerage fees, survey, title and legal fees, payment of back property taxes, and the cost of clearing land and razing unneeded structures

If discounts are available and taken advantage of, those amounts would reduce the cost of the plant asset. *Review Exhibit 9-2 (p. 483) for examples of items that are considered in the cost of land. Review the section "A Lump-Sum (Basket) Purchase of Assets" in the main text to see how the cost of individual plant assets is determined when a single price is charged for the group.*

2 Account for depreciation.

Depreciation is the allocation of cost over a plant asset's useful life. The expense of depreciation is matched against the revenue generated, as shown in Exhibit 9-4 (p. 487). The three most popular methods of depreciation are the straight-line, units-of-production, and double-declining-balance methods. The adjusting entry to depreciate any plant asset is to debit Depreciation expense and credit Accumulated depreciation.

Three elements necessary to calculate depreciation are:

a. Asset cost—known amount on the books
b. Estimated useful life—period of asset usefulness
c. Estimated residual value—expected value at the end of the useful life

Review "Depreciation Methods" in the main text for examples of the various depreciation methods.

3 Record the disposal of an asset by sale or by trade.

When a plant asset is sold, it should be depreciated until the date of disposal. Then the following should be accounted for:

- Debit the cash or other proceeds received
- Debit the accumulated depreciation
- Credit the plant asset cost

The difference between the asset cost and accumulated depreciation is book value. If the book value is greater than the proceeds, a debit must also be recorded as a loss on disposal. If the book value is less than the proceeds, a credit must also be recorded as a gain on disposal.

A plant asset may also be exchanged for a new asset. The book value of the old asset is removed as described earlier. The cash paid on exchange is credited and the market value of the new asset is debited. Any difference between the market value of the new asset and the book value of the old plus cash paid is the gain or loss. *Review the related examples in "Disposing of a Plant Asset" in the main text.*

4 Account for natural resources.

Natural resources are long-term assets that include iron ore, natural gas, and timber. As the inventory of the iron, gas, or other natural resource is used up, it is considered to be depleted. The depletion entry is similar to depreciation (debit Depletion expense and credit Accumulated depletion). The depletion amount is determined using the units-of-production formula.

Accumulated depletion is a contra asset account like Accumulated depreciation. *Review "Accounting for Natural Resources" in the main text.*

5 Account for intangible assets.

Intangible assets are rights that provide future value or benefit to the organization. Patents, copyrights, franchises, and trademarks are examples of these assets. Those intangible assets with a defined useful life are amortized by the straight-line method. The entry to amortize the intangible asset is to debit Amortization expense and to credit the intangible asset.

Goodwill represents the excess of the amount paid to purchase a company over the equity of the company. Goodwill is not amortized but may need to be written down due to a loss of value. *Review the description of the types of intangible assets and especially the treatment of goodwill included under the "Specific Intangibles" section of the main text.*

6 Describe ethical issues related to plant assets.

The main ethical issue in accounting for plant assets is whether to capitalize or expense a cost. Companies want to save on taxes, which motivates them to expense all costs and decrease taxable income. On the other hand, they want to look as good as possible to investors, with high net income and huge assets. This creates ethical dilemmas which need to be resolved. *Review the capitalization Decision Guidelines in the text on p. 506.*

Demo Doc 1

Depreciation

Learning Objectives 1–3

Peters Company purchased a truck for $13,800 cash on January 1, 2011. Peters also had to pay taxes of $1,200 cash. The truck had a residual value of $1,000 and a useful life of 7 years or 100,000 miles driven. Peters has a December 31 year-end.

The truck was driven for 15,000 miles in 2011, 12,000 miles in 2012, and 17,000 miles in 2013.

Requirements

1. Calculate the total cost of the truck.

2. Calculate the depreciation expense and accumulated depreciation balance at December 31 for 2011, 2012, and 2013 using the straight-line, units-of-production, and double-declining-balance methods.

3. Using the double-declining-balance method only, show how the Truck account would look on the December 31 balance sheets for 2011, 2012, and 2013.

4. Which of the three methods maximizes income for 2011? Which method minimizes income taxes for 2011?

5. Peters sold the truck on September 1, 2014, for $7,000 cash. Journalize the sale transaction using each method. (The truck was driven for 8,000 miles in 2014.)

Demo Doc 1 Solutions

Requirement 1

1 Measure the cost of a plant asset

Calculate the total cost of the truck.

| Part 1 | Part 2 | Part 3 | Part 4 | Part 5 | Part 6 | Part 7 | Part 8 | Part 9 | Demo Doc Complete |

The total cost of the truck is the total cost to make it ready for use. Any expenditure that *must be paid in order to use the asset* is part of the asset's total cost.

In this case, the truck cannot be used until the taxes are paid on the truck. Therefore, the taxes are added to the total cost of the truck.

Purchase Price	$13,800
Taxes	1,200
Total Cost of Truck	$15,000

Requirement 2

2 Account for depreciation

Calculate the depreciation expense and accumulated depreciation balance at December 31 for 2011, 2012, and 2013 using the straight-line, units-of-production, and double-declining-balance methods.

Straight-Line Method

| Part 1 | Part 2 | Part 3 | Part 4 | Part 5 | Part 6 | Part 7 | Part 8 | Part 9 | Demo Doc Complete |

The straight-line method allocates an equal amount of depreciation over the useful life.

Straight-line depreciation is calculated as

$$\frac{\text{Cost} - \text{Residual value}}{\text{Years of useful life}} = \text{Annual depreciation expense}$$

Or, in this particular question

$$\frac{\$15,000 - \$1,000}{7 \text{ years}} = \$2,000 \text{ Depreciation expense per year}$$

Remember that cost minus residual value is sometimes called <u>depreciable cost</u> because this is the total depreciation that will be recorded over the asset's life. At the end of the asset's life, the book value equals the residual value.

Remember that the depreciation expense will be the same for *each* year. Depreciation expense does not change (unless there is a partial year as demonstrated in Requirement 5 of this question). This is why the method is called "straight-line:" because if the annual depreciation expense is charted on a graph, it is a straight line (see Exhibit 9-9, p. 492, in the main textbook).

> So depreciation expense in 2011
> = depreciation expense in 2012
> = depreciation expense in 2013
> = $2,000.

Accumulated depreciation is the total of *all* the depreciation expense that the company has accumulated up to a certain time. In other words, it is the sum of the depreciation expense in *every* year that has passed.

You can use a T-account to calculate accumulated depreciation each year:

Accumulated Depreciation—Truck

	12/31/11 2,000
	2011 Bal 2,000
	12/31/12 2,000
	2012 Bal 4,000
	12/31/13 2,000
	2013 Bal 6,000

So in 2011, accumulated depreciation is the 2011 depreciation expense (because this is the only year of depreciation so far) = $2,000. In 2012, accumulated depreciation is the sum of the 2011 and 2012 depreciation expense = $2,000 + $2,000 = $4,000. In 2013, accumulated depreciation is the sum of the 2011, 2012, and 2013 depreciation expense = $2,000 + $2,000 + $2,000 = $6,000.

If you want to make things a little easier on yourself, instead of adding up all of the accumulated depreciation from scratch, you can instead add the current year's depreciation expense to the prior balance. In other words:

Accumulated depreciation this year = Accumulated depreciation last year + This year's depreciation expense

2012 accumulated depreciation of $4,000 + $2,000 depreciation expense for 2013
= $6,000 accumulated depreciation for 2013.

The truck's book value is its cost minus its accumulated depreciation. This is the net value shown for the truck on the balance sheet.

Straight-Line Method

Year	Annual Depreciation Expense	Annual Depreciation	Book Value
2011	$2,000	$2,000	$13,000
2012	2,000	4,000	11,000
2013	2,000	6,000	9,000

Demo Doc 1 Solutions | Chapter 9   **273**

2 Account for depreciation

Units-of-Production Method

| Part 1 | Part 2 | **Part 3** | Part 4 | Part 5 | Part 6 | Part 7 | Part 8 | Part 9 | Demo Doc Complete |

The unit method is similar to the straight-line method, but instead of calculating depreciation expense per *year,* we calculate it per *unit.* It allocates an equal amount of depreciation for each unit of production. Notice how the formula is similar to the straight-line method:

$$\frac{\text{Cost} - \text{Residual value}}{\text{Units of production in useful life}} = \text{Depreciation expense per unit}$$

Or, in this particular question:

$$\frac{\$15,000 - \$1,000}{100,000 \text{ miles}} = \$0.14 \text{ Depreciation expense per actual mile driven}$$

Because a different number of miles is driven every year, the *annual* depreciation expense will be different from year to year; however, the depreciation rate per *unit/mile* remains constant.

Units of production is another way of measuring an asset's life or productivity. For example, we could say that a machine will last for 5 years, or we might say that it will have 50,000 hours of operation. Both statements are reasonable ways to express how long the machine will last. The straight-line method focuses on the *years* (for example, 5 years of life) and the unit method focuses on the *production* (such as the 50,000 hours). It is obvious from reading the question whether there are any ways to measure an asset's life other than by years. In this question, the miles driven are highlighted and are the only other measure of asset life we can use.

Under the unit method, we calculate depreciation as

Depreciation expense this year = Units used this year × Depreciation expense per unit

So, in this question, we can calculate depreciation expense on the truck each year as

	Actual	Rate	Annual Expense
2011	15,000 miles × $0.14 per mile	=	$2,100
2012	12,000 miles × $0.14 per mile	=	$1,680
2013	17,000 miles × $0.14 per mile	=	$2,380

We calculate accumulated depreciation the same way we did for the straight-line method (only the depreciation *expense* is calculated differently from method to method).

We can use a T-account to calculate accumulated depreciation each year:

Accumulated Depreciation	
12/31/11	2,100
2011 Bal	2,100
12/31/12	1,680
2012 Bal	3,780
12/31/13	2,380
2013 Bal	6,160

We can also calculate accumulated depreciation directly:

Accumulated depreciation this year = Accumulated depreciation last year + This year's depreciation expense

So, in this question, we can calculate accumulated depreciation each year as

2011	$ 0 + $2,100 = $2,100
2012	$2,100 + $1,680 = $3,780
2013	$3,780 + $2,380 = $6,160

Units-of-Production Method

Year	Depreciation Expense	Accumulated Depreciation	Book Value (Cost − Acc. Depn.)
2011	$2,100	$2,100	$12,900
2012	1,680	3,780	11,220
2013	2,380	6,160	8,840

2 Account for depreciation

Double-Declining-Balance Method

| Part 1 | Part 2 | Part 3 | **Part 4** | Part 5 | Part 6 | Part 7 | Part 8 | Part 9 | Demo Doc Complete |

This method is somewhat more complicated than straight-line or unit depreciation. It allocates more depreciation in the early years than in the later years.

Instead of a set depreciation amount, we use a depreciation *rate*:

Double-declining-balance (DDB) depreciation rate = 2/years of useful life

Or, in this particular question:

DDB rate = 2/7

Demo Doc 1 Solutions | Chapter 9   275

You may notice that the years of useful life is the *same* denominator as we used in the straight-line method. This is why the method is called *double*-declining-balance: it is two times the amount used for straight-line (that is, $2 \times 1/\text{years of useful life}$).

To get the depreciation expense each year, we need to use the following formula:

> This year's depreciation expense = Book value (= cost − last year's accumulated depreciation) × Depreciation rate

Sometimes the cost − last year's accumulated depreciation is called the *net* value of the asset. You will see why in Requirement 3 of this question.

Because the accumulated depreciation is used in the depreciation expense formula, we need to calculate both together every year; however, the methods we can use to calculate accumulated depreciation are the same as before.

$$\begin{aligned}
&2011 \text{ depn expense} = (\$15{,}000 - \$0) \times 2/7 = \$4{,}286 \\
&\quad\text{Accumulated depn} = \$0 + \$4{,}286 = \$4{,}286 \\
\\
&2012 \text{ depn expense} = (\$15{,}000 - \$4{,}286) \times 2/7 = \$3{,}061 \\
&\quad\text{Accumulated depn} = \$4{,}286 + \$3{,}061 = \$7{,}347 \\
\\
&2013 \text{ depn expense} = (\$15{,}000 - \$7{,}347) \times 2/7 = \$2{,}187 \\
&\quad\text{Accumulated depn} = \$7{,}347 + \$2{,}187 = \$9{,}534
\end{aligned}$$

We can also use a T-account to calculate accumulated depreciation each year:

Accumulated Depreciation—Truck

	12/31/11 4,286
	2011 Bal 4,286
	12/31/12 3,061
	2012 Bal 7,347
	12/31/13 2,187
	2013 Bal 9,534

It is important to keep an eye on accumulated depreciation with the double-declining-balance method. Remember, we did *not* use the residual value to calculate depreciation expense.

However, we need to ensure that the *book value* of the asset does not go below the residual value. When the book value of the asset reaches the residual value, we *stop* taking depreciation expense (even if the asset is still being used).

Double-Declining-Balance Method

Year	Depreciation Expense	Accumulated Depreciation	Book Value (Cost − Acc Depn)
2011	$4,286	$4,286	$10,714
2012	3,061	7,347	7,653
2013	2,187	9,534	5,466

Requirement 3

Account for depreciation

Using the double-declining-balance method only, show how the Truck account would look on the December 31 balance sheets for 2011, 2012, and 2013.

| Part 1 | Part 2 | Part 3 | Part 4 | **Part 5** | Part 6 | Part 7 | Part 8 | Part 9 | Demo Doc Complete |

Although the question only requires this to be done for the double-declining-balance method, keep in mind that the balance sheet presentation is the *same* for *all* depreciation methods:

Cost
− Accumulated depreciation
Net value of asset

This *net* value of the asset is the *same* amount that is used in the double-declining-balance calculation for depreciation expense in the *following* year.

So on the balance sheet for each year (under the double-declining-balance method), you would see:

	2011	2012	2013
Truck	$15,000	$15,000	$15,000
− Accumulated Depreciation	(4,286)	(7,347)	(9,534)
Truck (net)	$10,714	$ 7,653	$ 5,466

Requirement 4

Which of the three methods maximizes income for 2011? Which method minimizes income taxes for 2011?

| Part 1 | Part 2 | Part 3 | Part 4 | Part 5 | **Part 6** | Part 7 | Part 8 | Part 9 | Demo Doc Complete |

The depreciation expense for each method in 2011 is

Straight-Line	$2,000
Units of Production	2,100
Double-Declining-Balance	4,286

Demo Doc 1 Solutions | Chapter 9   **277**

Revenues − Expenses = Net income, so higher expense (holding revenue constant) gives a lower net income.

In this example, the straight-line method has the lowest depreciation expense, which means that it has the highest net income.

The double-declining-balance method has the highest depreciation expense, which means that it has the lowest net income and, therefore, the lowest income taxes.

Requirement 5

Peters sold the truck on September 1, 2014, for $7,000 cash. Journalize the sale transaction using each method. (The truck was driven for 8,000 miles in 2014.)

Straight-Line Method

> **2** Account for depreciation
>
> **3** Record the disposal of an asset by sale or trade

| Part 1 | Part 2 | Part 3 | Part 4 | Part 5 | Part 6 | **Part 7** | Part 8 | Part 9 | Demo Doc Complete |

When an asset is sold, we must journalize that sale. However, before we can do this, we must *update the depreciation* on the asset.

Depreciation represents the portion (the *benefit*) of the asset that has been used. The truck was sold on September 1, which means that Peters got to use it for eight months of 2014 before it was sold. We must represent that use as depreciation expense.

The depreciation expense that we record for eight months is *not* the same as the amount we would record for an entire year, because it is a shorter period of time (and, therefore, the asset was used less). Therefore, we must calculate a partial year's depreciation.

Under straight-line depreciation, the *annual* depreciation expense is $2,000 (that is, for 12 months). So for eight months:

$$2014 \text{ depn expense} = \$2,000 \times \frac{8 \text{ months}}{12 \text{ months}}$$
$$= \$1,333$$

This depreciation would then be recorded as

| Sep 1 | Depreciation expense | 1,333 | |
| | Accumulated depreciation—Truck | | 1,333 |

This brings the total accumulated depreciation to $6,000 + $1,333 = $7,333. Now we can record the sale of the truck.

Cash was received, so it increases (a debit) by $7,000.

The truck has been sold, so that account decreases to a zero balance (a credit) by $15,000. The Accumulated depreciation goes along with it (contra accounts *always* go with their associated account), so that account decreases to a zero balance (a debit) as well by $7,333.

Putting these amounts into the journal entry:

Sep 1	Cash	7,000	
	Accumulated depreciation—Truck	7,333	
	???		
	Truck		15,000

Obviously, the entry is not complete because it *does not balance*. In order to get it to balance, we need equal debits and credits, which means that we need a $15,000 − $7,000 − $7,333 = $667 debit for the entry to work.

This $667 is the balancing amount. It is either a gain on sale or a loss on sale. *Because the balancing amount is a debit,* it is a loss (an increase in expenses is a debit, which is like a loss).

So the completed entry is

Sep 1	Cash	7,000	
	Accumulated depreciation—Truck	7,333	
	Loss on sale of truck (to balance)	667	
	Truck		15,000

2 Account for depreciation

3 Record the disposal of an asset by sale or trade

Units-of-Production Method

| Part 1 | Part 2 | Part 3 | Part 4 | Part 5 | Part 6 | Part 7 | **Part 8** | Part 9 | Demo Doc Complete |

We must record the depreciation expense for the first eight months of the year.

$$2014 \text{ depn expense} = 8{,}000 \text{ miles} \times \$0.14$$
$$= \$1{,}120$$

Notice that we did *not* need to multiply by 8/12 like we did in the straight-line method. This is because the short period of use is *already incorporated* into the 8,000 miles. If the truck had been used for a full year, the number of miles would have been bigger, and so depreciation expense would have been higher. With the unit method, all that matters is the *actual* number of miles the truck was driven.

Depreciation is recorded as

Sep 1	Depreciation expense	1,120	
	Accumulated depreciation—Truck		1,120

Accumulated depreciation is now $6,160 + $1,120 = $7,280.

Cash was received, so it increases (a debit) by $7,000.

The truck has been sold, so that account decreases to a zero balance (a credit) by $15,000. Accumulated depreciation decreases to a zero balance (a debit) as well by $7,280.

Putting these amounts into the journal entry:

Sep 1	Cash	7,000	
	Accumulated depreciation—Truck	7,280	
	???		
	Truck		15,000

In order to get it to balance, we need a $15,000 − $7,000 − $7,280 = $720 debit. *Because the balancing amount is a debit,* it is a loss (an increase in expenses is a debit, which is like a loss).

So the completed entry is

Sep 1	Cash	7,000	
	Accumulated depreciation—Truck	7,280	
	Loss on sale of truck (to balance)	720	
	Truck		15,000

2 Account for depreciation

3 Record the disposal of an asset by sale or trade

Double-Declining-Balance Method

| Part 1 | Part 2 | Part 3 | Part 4 | Part 5 | Part 6 | Part 7 | Part 8 | **Part 9** | Demo Doc Complete |

2014 depreciation expense
= ($15,000 − $9,534) × 2/7
= $1,561.71
= 12 months of depreciation

$1,561.71 × 8 months/12 months = $1,041
= 8 months of depreciation

| Sep 1 | Depreciation expense | 1,041 | |
| | Accumulated depreciation—Truck | | 1,041 |

280 Chapter 9 | Demo Doc 1 Solutions

This brings the accumulated depreciation to

$$\$9{,}534 + \$1{,}041 = \$10{,}575$$

Cash was received, so it increases (a debit) by $7,000.

The truck has been sold, so that account decreases to a zero balance (a credit) by $15,000. Accumulated depreciation decreases to a zero balance (a debit) by $10,575.

Putting these amounts into the journal entry:

Sep 1	Cash	7,000	
	Accumulated depreciation—Truck	10,575	
	???		
	Truck		15,000

We need a $7,000 + $10,575 − $15,000 = $2,575 credit for the entry to work.

Because the balancing amount is a credit, it is a gain (an increase in revenues is a credit, which is like a gain).

So the completed entry is

Sep 1	Cash	7,000	
	Accumulated depreciation—Truck	10,575	
	Gain on sale of truck (to balance)		2,575
	Truck		15,000

| Part 1 | Part 2 | Part 3 | Part 4 | Part 5 | Part 6 | Part 7 | Part 8 | Part 9 | Demo Doc Complete |

Demo Doc 2

Natural Resource Assets

Learning Objective 4

Xander Mining purchased a coal mine for $900 million cash on January 1, 2011. After the purchase, an independent analyst determined that the value of the land was $200 million and that the value of the coal was $800 million (based on an estimate that there were 20 million tons of coal below the ground).

In 2011, Xander mined and sold 1 million tons of coal.

Requirements

1. Give Xander's journal entry to record the purchase of the mine.

2. Give Xander's journal entry to record depletion expense for 2011.

Demo Doc 2 Solutions

Requirement 1

4 Account for natural resources

Give Xander's journal entry to record the purchase of the mine.

| Part 1 | Part 2 | Demo Doc Complete |

Xander purchased two assets at one time *for one price*. This is called a <u>lump-sum purchase</u>. We need to determine how much of the purchase price to allocate to each asset.

This is important because it impacts depreciation and depletion calculations in the future (because the cost of the asset is an important number in these calculations).

We use the independent valuations to determine a *proportional* value for the assets. According to the analyst, the total value of the assets purchased = $200 million + $800 million = $1 billion.

This means that the land has a proportion of 200,000,000/1,000,000,000 = 20%.
The coal has a proportion of 800,000,000/1,000,000,000 = 80%.
The cost of each asset is assigned as this proportion of the total cost.
So the cost of the land = 20% × $900 million total cost = $180 million.
The cost of the coal = 80% × $900 million total cost = $720 million.
In the journal entry, Land and Coal reserves are increased (debit) by these amounts and cash is decreased (credit).

Land (20% × $900,000,000)	180,000,000	
Coal reserves (80% × $900,000,000)	720,000,000	
Cash		900,000,000

Requirement 2

4 Account for natural resources

Give Xander's journal entry to record depletion expense for 2011.

| Part 1 | Part 2 | Demo Doc Complete |

Depletion expense is *the same* as depreciation expense, except that this term is *only* used for natural resource assets. Depletion is always calculated using the *unit* method (never the straight-line or declining-balance methods).

The units are the amount of natural resources purchased. In this case, the units are tons of coal.

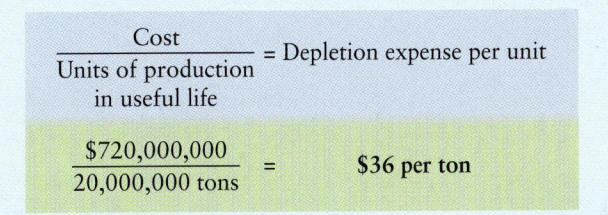

$$\frac{\text{Cost}}{\text{Units of production in useful life}} = \text{Depletion expense per unit}$$

$$\frac{\$720,000,000}{20,000,000 \text{ tons}} = \$36 \text{ per ton}$$

Demo Doc 2 Solutions | Chapter 9   **283**

Under the unit method, we calculate depletion as

Depletion expense this year = Actual units used this year × Depletion expense per unit

Depletion expense for 2011
= 1,000,000 tons × $36 per ton
= $36,000,000

When we record depreciation, we increase (debit) Depreciation expense and increase (credit) Accumulated depreciation. The entry for depletion is *the same* except that we use Depletion expense (debit) and Accumulated depletion (credit).

	Depletion expense ($36 × 1,000,000)	36,000,000	
	Accumulated depletion—Coal reserves		36,000,000

Part 1	Part 2	Demo Doc Complete

Demo Doc 3

Intangible Assets

Learning Objectives 5, 6

On July 1, 2011, Franco Company acquired a patent from Juarez Company for $5,000 cash and by signing a $10,000, 6% note payable. Franco believes that the patent will have a life of 10 years.

On the same date, Franco purchased all outstanding shares of Germano Company for $50,000. The book value of Germano's net assets at this time was $35,000 and the market value was $40,000.

Requirements

1. Journalize Franco's purchase of the patent. What kind of asset is the patent? Why do you think so?

2. Journalize Franco's amortization expense for the patent in 2011.

3. Franco did not make any interest payments on the note in 2011. Journalize Franco's interest expense for the year.

4. Calculate the amount of goodwill that will be recorded for Franco as a result of the Germano purchase.

5. Give any necessary entry to adjust the value of Franco's goodwill if it is determined to be worth $2,500 at the end of the year.

6. What ethical issues did Franco face when attempting to determine the value of its goodwill asset?

Demo Doc 3 Solutions

Requirement 1

5 Account for intangible assets

Journalize Franco's purchase of the patent. What kind of asset is the patent? Why do you think so?

| Part 1 | Part 2 | Part 3 | Part 4 | Part 5 | Part 6 | Demo Doc Complete |

Cash decreases (a credit) by $5,000 and Notes payable increases (a credit) by $10,000.
There is also an increase to Patent (a debit) of $5,000 + $10,000 = $15,000.

Jul 1	Patent		15,000	
	Cash			5,000
	Note payable			10,000

The patent is an <u>intangible asset</u>. This is because the patent is a *right* to produce a certain product or use a certain technology. A right is not a physical asset: It cannot be touched. This means that it is *intangible*.

Requirement 2

5 Account for intangible assets

Journalize Franco's amortization expense for the patent in 2011.

| Part 1 | Part 2 | Part 3 | Part 4 | Part 5 | Part 6 | Demo Doc Complete |

Intangible assets are amortized. This is essentially the same as depreciation for tangible assets (outside of the name). The only difference is that for intangible assets, we usually do not record an "accumulated amortization" account, but instead *directly* reduce the asset account.

Amortization expense is usually calculated using the straight-line method.

$$\text{Amortization expense (annual)} = \frac{\text{Cost of intangible asset}}{\text{Years of useful life}}$$

$$\frac{\$15,000}{10 \text{ years}} = \$1,500 \text{ per year}$$

Because the patent was purchased on July 1, only six months have been used. Therefore, we must calculate a partial year's amortization:

$$\$1,500 \times \frac{6 \text{ months}}{12 \text{ months}} = \$750 \text{ Amortization expense for 6 months}$$

Amortization expense increases (a debit) by $750.

Remember that for intangible assets, we do *not* have an accumulated account. This means that instead we must decrease the Patent account (a credit) *directly* for $750.

| Dec 31 | Amortization expense—Patents | 750 | |
| | Patent | | 750 |

Requirement 3

Franco did not make any interest payments on the note in 2011. Journalize Franco's interest expense for the year.

| Part 1 | Part 2 | **Part 3** | Part 4 | Part 5 | Part 6 | Demo Doc Complete |

Interest expense for the year is

$$\$10,000 \times 6\% \times \frac{6 \text{ months}}{12 \text{ months}} = \$300$$

Interest expense is increased (a debit) and Interest payable is increased (a credit) by $300.

| Dec 31 | Interest expense | 300 | |
| | Interest payable | | 300 |

Requirement 4

5 Account for intangible assets

Calculate the amount of goodwill that will be recorded for Franco as a result of the Germano purchase.

| Part 1 | Part 2 | Part 3 | **Part 4** | Part 5 | Part 6 | Demo Doc Complete |

Goodwill = Purchase price − Market value of net assets
= $50,000 − $40,000
= $10,000

This could also be calculated by preparing the journal entry for Franco to purchase Germano.

Franco increases its Net assets (debit) by the market value of $40,000. Cash is decreased (credit) for the purchase price paid.

The remaining amount in the entry to make it balance is Goodwill:

Jul 1	Net assets	40,000	
	Goodwill (to balance)	10,000	
	Cash		50,000

Requirement 5

5 Account for intangible assets

Give any necessary entry to adjust the value of Franco's goodwill if it is determined to be worth $2,500 at the end of the year.

| Part 1 | Part 2 | Part 3 | Part 4 | **Part 5** | Part 6 | Demo Doc Complete |

Franco recorded the goodwill at $10,000. Because it is now worth only $2,500, it has a loss in value of $10,000 − $2,500 = $7,500. The loss is recorded (a debit) and the value of Goodwill is decreased (a credit).

| | Loss on goodwill | 7,500 | |
| | Goodwill | | 7,500 |

Requirement 6

6 Describe ethical issues related to plant assets

What ethical issues did Franco face when attempting to determine the value of its goodwill asset?

| Part 1 | Part 2 | Part 3 | Part 4 | Part 5 | **Part 6** | Demo Doc Complete |

It is often difficult to properly value intangible assets, which is why accountants are reluctant to record these assets at all, unless they have been purchased. But GAAP requires companies to assess the value of their goodwill each year, and write it down (lower its value) if necessary.

Since this is a very subjective task, Franco has some leeway in determining the current value of their goodwill. The higher the value assigned to goodwill, the lower the company's recorded loss, and therefore the higher the company's recorded net income. Franco's accountants must be careful to remain neutral in their analysis of the goodwill's worth.

| Part 1 | Part 2 | Part 3 | Part 4 | Part 5 | Part 6 | **Demo Doc Complete** |

Quick Practice Questions

True/False

_____ 1. The cost of land improvements includes fencing, paving, sprinkler systems, and lighting.

_____ 2. Land improvements are not subject to annual depreciation.

_____ 3. Book value is equal to the cost of the asset less the expected residual value.

_____ 4. The modified accelerated cost recovery system of depreciation is used for income tax purposes and segments assets into classes by asset life.

_____ 5. A loss on sale of an asset occurs when the book value is less than the cash received.

_____ 6. The depreciable cost of a plant asset is the original cost less the expected residual value.

_____ 7. Depletion expense is computed in the same manner as units-of-production.

_____ 8. Goodwill is recorded only by a company when it purchases another company and is not subject to amortization.

_____ 9. A characteristic of a plant asset is that it is used in the production of income for a business.

_____ 10. Routine repairs and maintenance are capital expenditures.

Multiple Choice

1. Which of the following is *not* a plant asset?
   a. Land
   b. Building
   c. Copyright
   d. Equipment

2. The cost of a building would include all of the following *except:*
   a. Architectural fees
   b. Clearing and grading the land prior to construction of the building
   c. Cost of repairs made to an old building to get it ready for occupancy
   d. Costs of construction

3. Five hundred acres of land are purchased for $130,000. Additional costs include $5,000 brokerage commission, $10,000 for removal of an old building, $6,000 for paving, and an $800 survey fee. What is the cost of the land?
   a. $135,800
   b. $145,800
   c. $155,000
   d. $155,800

4. Westchester Company recently sold some used furniture for $3,800 cash. The furniture cost $19,600 and had accumulated depreciation through the date of sale totaling $17,300. What is the journal entry to record the sale of the furniture?

a.

Cash	3,800	
Accumulated depreciation—Furniture	15,800	
Furniture		19,600

b.

| Cash | 3,800 | |
| Furniture | | 3,800 |

c.

| Cash | 3,800 | |
| Gain on sale of furniture | | 3,800 |

d.

Cash	3,800	
Accumulated depreciation—Furniture	17,300	
Furniture		19,600
Gain on sale of furniture		1,500

5. New equipment with a list price of $100,000, credit terms of 3/10 n/30, and transportation cost of $7,000 is acquired by a company. Insurance while in transit amounts to $200. Insurance on the equipment during its first year of use amounts to $800. Assuming the equipment is paid for within the discount period, what is the amount debited to Equipment?
   a. $97,000
   b. $104,200
   c. $105,000
   d. $107,200

6. Which of the following expenditures would be debited to an expense account?
   a. Cost to replace the company car's engine
   b. Addition of elevator to a building
   c. Replacement of tires
   d. All of the above

7. What is the effect of treating revenue expenditure as a capital expenditure?
   a. Understates expenses and understates owners' equity
   b. Overstates assets and overstates owners' equity
   c. Overstates expenses and understates net income
   d. Understates expenses and understates assets

8. Which of the following is true of Accumulated depreciation?
   a. It is a contra liability account
   b. It is an expense account
   c. It is a contra asset account
   d. It is a contra equity account

9. When the amount of use of a plant asset varies from year to year, which method of determining depreciation best matches revenues and expenses?
   a. Straight-line method
   b. Double-declining-balance method
   c. Units-of-production method
   d. Either the straight-line method or the double-declining-balance method

10. Which depreciation method generally results in the greatest depreciation expense in the first full year of an asset's life?
    a. Double-declining-balance method
    b. Units-of-production method
    c. Straight-line method
    d. Either the straight-line or the double-declining-balance method

Quick Exercises

9-1. Morgan Construction bought land, a building, and equipment for a lump sum of $740,000. Following are the appraised fair market values of the newly acquired assets:

Land, $450,000
Building, $400,000
Equipment, $150,000

Determine the cost of each asset.

a. Land _____

b. Building _____

c. Equipment _____

9-2. Sue Glover purchased a tract of land and contracted with a builder to build an office building on the property. She also engaged other contractors for lighting, fencing, paving, and so forth.

Based on the following transactions, determine the total costs allocated to the Land, Building, and Land improvements accounts.

a. Purchased land for $135,000.
b. Paid a contractor $333,000 to design and build the office building.
c. Paid a demolition company $40,000 to remove an old structure on the property.
d. Paid $14,000 in delinquent taxes on the property.
e. Paid $34,700 for fencing.
f. Paid $39,500 for paving.
g. Paid an electrical contractor $14,900 for outdoor lighting.

Cost of land _____

Cost of building _____

Cost of land improvements _____

9-3. Venus Company acquired equipment on January 1, 2011, for $470,000. The equipment has an estimated useful life of 5 years and an estimated residual value of $30,000. Calculate depreciation expense for 2011 and 2012 under each of the following methods. The equipment is estimated to produce 150,000 units. During 2011 and 2012, the equipment produced 24,000 and 60,000 units, respectively. Round the answer to the nearest dollar where necessary.

	2011	2012
a. Straight-line method	_____	_____
b. Double-declining-balance method	_____	_____
c. Units-of-production method	_____	_____

9-4. On April 1, 2011, Carter Craft & Company purchased a mineral deposit by paying $50,000 in cash and signing a $440,000 promissory note. A geological report estimated the mineral deposit contained 140,000 tons of ore. Carter Craft & Company expects the asset to have a zero residual value when fully depleted. During 2011, 40,000 tons of ore were mined.

Prepare the journal entry for December 31, 2011, to record the depletion of the mineral deposit.

Date	Accounts	Debit	Credit

9-5. On July 31, 2010, Austin Manufacturing acquired an existing patent for $340,000. The remaining legal life of the patent is 13 years; however, management thinks the patent will hold economic benefit for the company for only 7 more years.

Prepare journal entries for July 31, 2010, to acquire the patent and December 31, 2010, to amortize the patent.

Date	Accounts	Debit	Credit

Date	Accounts	Debit	Credit

Do It Yourself! Question 1

Depreciation

Winters Company purchased equipment for $8,000 cash on January 1, 2011. The equipment had a residual value of $500 and a useful life of 6 years or 2,000 hours of operation. Winters has a December 31 year-end.

The equipment was used for 400 hours in 2011, 200 hours in 2012, and 300 hours in 2013.

Requirements

2 Account for depreciation

1. Calculate the depreciation expense and accumulated depreciation balance at December 31 for 2011, 2012, and 2013 using the straight-line method.

Year	Depreciation Expense	Accumulated Depreciation	Book Value (Cost – Acc Depn)
2011			
2012			
2013			

2 Account for depreciation

2. Calculate the depreciation expense and accumulated depreciation balance at December 31 for 2011, 2012, and 2013 using the units-of-production method.

Year	Depreciation Expense	Accumulated Depreciation	Book Value (Cost – Acc Depn)
2011			
2012			
2013			

2 Account for depreciation

3. Calculate the depreciation expense and accumulated depreciation balance at December 31 for 2011, 2012, and 2013 using the double-declining-balance method.

Year	Depreciation Expense	Accumulated Depreciation	Book Value (Cost – Acc Depn)
2011			
2012			
2013			

Account for depreciation

4. Using the units-of-production method only, show how the equipment would look on the December 31 balance sheets for 2011, 2012, and 2013.

Account for depreciation

Record the disposal of an asset by sale or trade

5. Winters sold the machine on March 1, 2014, for $4,000 cash. Show both journal entries to record depreciation and to record the sale transaction using each method. (The equipment was used for 100 hours in 2014.)

Straight-Line Method

Date	Accounts	Debit	Credit

Date	Accounts	Debit	Credit

Units-of-Production Method

Date	Accounts	Debit	Credit

Date	Accounts	Debit	Credit

Double-Declining-Balance Method

Date	Accounts	Debit	Credit

Date	Accounts	Debit	Credit

Do It Yourself! Question 2

Natural Resource Assets

Woody Papers purchased logging rights in a county forest for $800,000 cash. Woody estimates that there are 40,000 tons of lumber that can be harvested from the forest. Because Woody only purchased the right to log, it does not own the land.

Requirement

4 Account for natural resources

1. Show the journal entry to record Woody's depletion expense for the first year, assuming that 15,000 tons of lumber were cut and sold.

Date	Accounts	Debit	Credit

Do It Yourself! Question 3

Intangible Assets

On October 1, 2011, Kevin Company acquired a trademark from Daniel Company for $10,000 cash. Kevin believes that the trademark will have a life of 20 years.

Requirements

[5] Account for intangible assets

1. Journalize Kevin's purchase of the trademark.

Date	Accounts	Debit	Credit

[5] Account for intangible assets

2. Journalize Kevin's amortization expense for the trademark in 2011.

Date	Accounts	Debit	Credit

Quick Practice Solutions

True/False

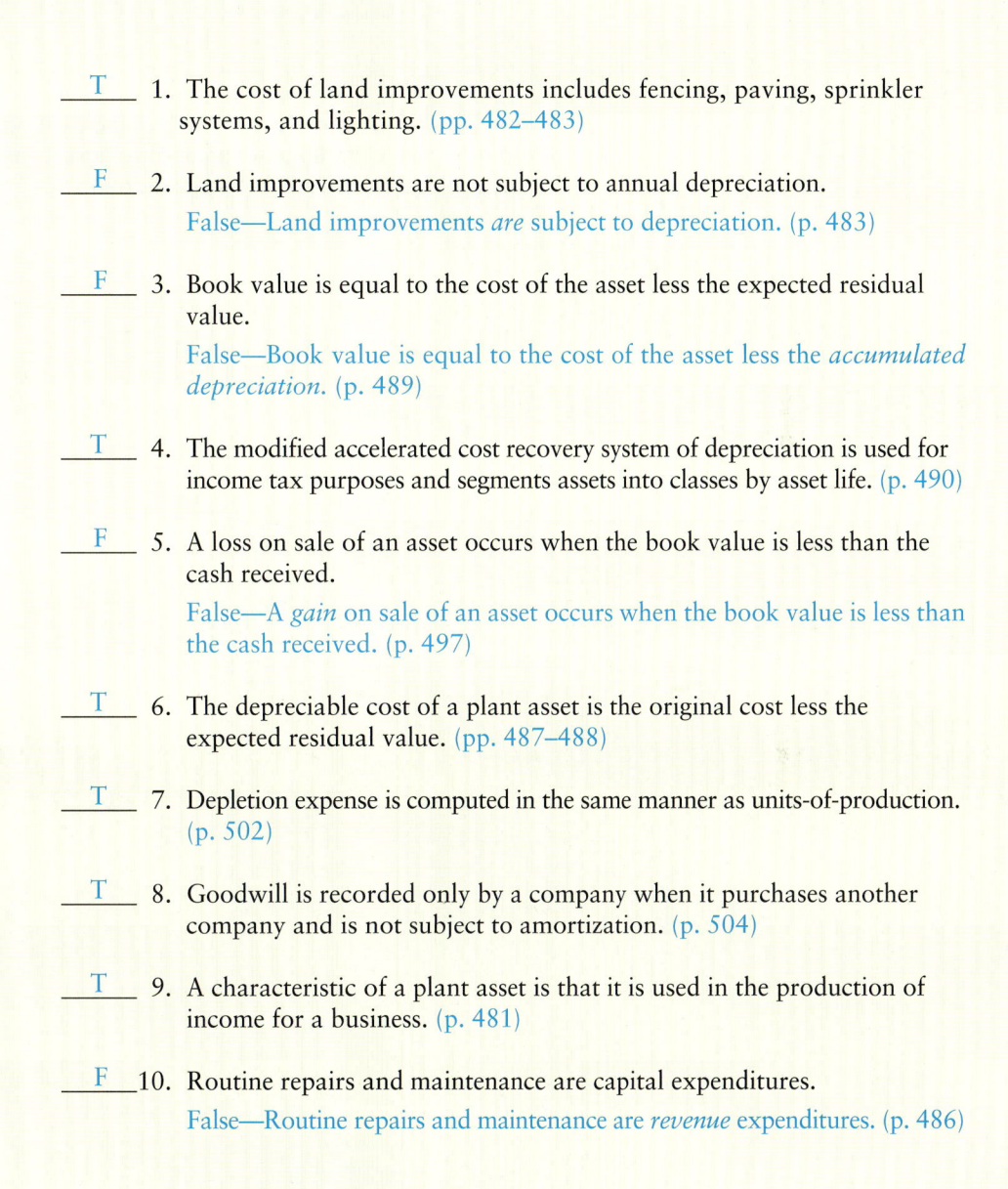

__T__ 1. The cost of land improvements includes fencing, paving, sprinkler systems, and lighting. (pp. 482–483)

__F__ 2. Land improvements are not subject to annual depreciation.
   False—Land improvements *are* subject to depreciation. (p. 483)

__F__ 3. Book value is equal to the cost of the asset less the expected residual value.
   False—Book value is equal to the cost of the asset less the *accumulated depreciation*. (p. 489)

__T__ 4. The modified accelerated cost recovery system of depreciation is used for income tax purposes and segments assets into classes by asset life. (p. 490)

__F__ 5. A loss on sale of an asset occurs when the book value is less than the cash received.
   False—A *gain* on sale of an asset occurs when the book value is less than the cash received. (p. 497)

__T__ 6. The depreciable cost of a plant asset is the original cost less the expected residual value. (pp. 487–488)

__T__ 7. Depletion expense is computed in the same manner as units-of-production. (p. 502)

__T__ 8. Goodwill is recorded only by a company when it purchases another company and is not subject to amortization. (p. 504)

__T__ 9. A characteristic of a plant asset is that it is used in the production of income for a business. (p. 481)

__F__ 10. Routine repairs and maintenance are capital expenditures.
   False—Routine repairs and maintenance are *revenue* expenditures. (p. 486)

Multiple Choice

1. Which of the following is *not* a plant asset? (p. 482)
   a. Land
   b. Building
   c. Copyright
   d. Equipment

2. The cost of a building would include all of the following *except:* (p. 484)
   a. Architectural fees
   b. Clearing and grading the land prior to construction of the building
   c. Cost of repairs made to an old building to get it ready for occupancy
   d. Costs of construction

3. Five hundred acres of land are purchased for $130,000. Additional costs include $5,000 brokerage commission, $10,000 for removal of an old building, $6,000 for paving, and an $800 survey fee. What is the cost of the land? (p. 482)
   a. $135,800
   b. $145,800 (130,000 + 5,000 + 10,000 + 800)
   c. $155,000
   d. $155,800

4. Westchester Company recently sold some used furniture for $3,800 cash. The furniture cost $19,600 and had accumulated depreciation through the date of sale totaling $17,300. What is the journal entry to record the sale of the furniture? (p. 497)

   a.

Cash	3,800	
Accumulated depreciation—Furniture	15,800	
Furniture		19,600

   b.

Cash	3,800	
Furniture		3,800

   c.

Cash	3,800	
Gain on sale of furniture		3,800

   d.

Cash	3,800	
Accumulated depreciation—Furniture	17,300	
Furniture		19,600
Gain on sale of furniture		1,500

5. New equipment with a list price of $100,000, credit terms of 3/10 n/30, and transportation cost of $7,000 is acquired by a company. Insurance while in transit amounts to $200. Insurance on the equipment during its first year of use amounts to $800. Assuming the equipment is paid for within the discount period, what is the amount debited to Equipment? (p. 482)
   a. $97,000
   b. $104,200 (100,000 − 3,000 + 7,000 + 200)
   c. $105,000
   d. $107,200

6. Which of the following expenditures would be debited to an expense account? (p. 486)
   a. Cost to replace the company car's engine
   b. Addition of elevator to a building
   c. Replacement of tires
   d. All of the above

7. What is the effect of treating a revenue expenditure as a capital expenditure? (p. 486)
   a. Understates expenses and understates owners' equity
   b. Overstates assets and overstates owners' equity
   c. Overstates expenses and understates net income
   d. Understates expenses and understates assets

8. What type of account is Accumulated depreciation? (p. 487)
   a. A contra liability account
   b. An expense account
   c. A contra asset account
   d. A contra equity account

9. When the amount of use of a plant asset varies from year to year, which method of determining depreciation best matches revenues and expenses? (p. 489)
   a. Straight-line method
   b. Double-declining-balance method
   c. Units-of-production method
   d. Either the straight-line method or the double-declining-balance method

10. Which depreciation method generally results in the greatest depreciation expense in the first full year of an asset's life? (p. 490)
    a. Double-declining-balance method
    b. Units-of-production method
    c. Straight-line method
    d. Either the straight-line or the double-declining-balance method

Quick Exercises

9-1. Morgan Construction bought land, a building, and equipment for a lump sum of $740,000. Following are the appraised fair market values of the newly acquired assets:

Land, $450,000
Building, $400,000
Equipment, $150,000

Determine the cost of each asset. (pp. 484–485)

a. Land = ($450,000/$1,000,000) × $740,000 = $333,000
b. Building = ($400,000/$1,000,000) × $740,000 = $296,000
c. Equipment = ($150,000/$1,000,000) × $740,000 = $111,000

9-2. Sue Glover purchased a tract of land and contracted with a builder to build an office building on the property. She also engaged other contractors for lighting, fencing, paving, and so forth.

Based on the following transactions, determine the total costs allocated to the Land, Building, and Land improvements accounts. (pp. 482–484)

a. Purchased land for $135,000.
b. Paid a contractor $333,000 to design and build the office building.

c. Paid a demolition company $40,000 to remove an old structure on the property.
d. Paid $14,000 in delinquent taxes on the property.
e. Paid $34,700 for fencing.
f. Paid $39,500 for paving.
g. Paid an electrical contractor $14,900 for outdoor lighting.

Cost of land 189,000 ($135,000 + $40,000 + $14,000 = $189,000; transactions a, c & d)

Cost of building 333,000 (transaction b)

Cost of land improvements 89,100 ($34,700 + $39,500 + $14,900 = $89,100; transactions e–g)

9-3. Venus Company acquired equipment on January 1, 2011, for $470,000. The equipment has an estimated useful life of 5 years and an estimated residual value of $30,000. Calculate depreciation expense for 2011 and 2012 under each of the following methods. The equipment is estimated to produce 150,000 units. During 2011 and 2012, the equipment produced 24,000 and 60,000 units, respectively. Round the answer to the nearest dollar where necessary. (pp. 488–491)

		2011	2012
a.	Straight-line method	88,000	88,000
b.	Double-declining balance method	188,000	112,800
c.	Units-of-production method	70,400	176,000

a.
$$\frac{\$470,000 - 30,000}{5 \text{ years}} = \$88,000/\text{year}$$

b.
DDB rate = 1/5 years × 2 = 40% (0.40)

$470,000 × 0.40 = $188,000
(470,000 − 188,000) × 0.40 = 112,800

c.
$$\frac{\$470,000 - 30,000}{150,000} \times 24,000 \text{ units} = \$70,400$$

$$\frac{\$470,000 - 30,000}{150,000} \times 60,000 \text{ units} = \$176,000$$

9-4. On April 1, 2011, Carter Craft & Company purchased a mineral deposit by paying $50,000 in cash and signing a $440,000 promissory note. A geological report estimated the mineral deposit contained 140,000 tons of ore. Carter Craft & Company expects the asset to have a zero residual value when fully depleted. During 2011, 40,000 tons of ore were mined.

Prepare the journal entry for December 31, 2011, to record the depletion of the mineral deposit. (p. 502)

Date	Accounts	Debit	Credit
Dec 31	Depletion expense	140,000	
	Accumulated depreciation—Ore		140,000
	To record depletion of mineral deposits		
	($50,000 + $440,000)/140,000 tons = $3.50/ton × 40,000 tons		
	= $140,000		

9-5. On July 31, 2010, Austin Manufacturing acquired an existing patent for $340,000. The remaining legal life of the patent is 13 years; however, management thinks the patent will hold economic benefit for the company for only 7 more years.

Prepare journal entries for July 31, 2010, to acquire the patent and December 31, 2010, to amortize the patent. (p. 503)

Date	Accounts	Debit	Credit
Jul 31	Patents	340,000	
	Cash		340,000
	To record purchase of patent		

Date	Accounts	Debit	Credit
Dec 31	Amortization expense—Patents	20,238	
	Patents		20,238
	To amortize patents ($340,000 × 5/84 months = $20,238)		

Quick Practice Solutions | Chapter 9   303

Do It Yourself! Question 1 Solutions

Requirements

1. Calculate the depreciation expense and accumulated depreciation balance at December 31 for 2011, 2012, and 2013 using the straight-line method.

$$\frac{\$8,000 - \$500}{6 \text{ years}} = \$1,250 \text{ depreciation expense per year}$$

2011 accumulated depreciation = $1,250
2012 accumulated depreciation = $2,500
2013 accumulated depreciation = $3,750

Year	Depreciation Expense	Accumulated Depreciation	Book Value (Cost – Acc Depn)
2011	$1,250	$1,250	$6,750
2012	1,250	2,500	5,500
2013	1,250	3,750	4,250

2. Calculate the depreciation expense and accumulated depreciation balance at December 31 for 2011, 2012, and 2013 using the units-of-production method.

$$\frac{\$8,000 - \$500}{2,000 \text{ hours of lifetime operation}} = \$3.75 \text{ depreciation expense per hour of actual operation}$$

Depreciation expense each year is

	Actual		Rate		Expense
2011	400 hours	×	$3.75 per hour	=	$1,500
2012	200 hours	×	$3.75 per hour	=	$ 750
2013	300 hours	×	$3.75 per hour	=	$1,125

Accumulated depreciation each year is

	Accum		Expense		
2011	$ 0	+	$1,500	=	$1,500
2012	$1,500	+	$ 750	=	$2,250
2013	$2,250	+	$1,125	=	$3,375

Year	Depreciation Expense	Accumulated Depreciation	Book Value (Cost − Acc Depn)
2011	$1,500	$1,500	$6,500
2012	750	2,250	5,750
2013	1,125	3,375	4,625

3. Calculate the depreciation expense and accumulated depreciation balance at December 31 for 2011, 2012, and 2013 using the double-declining-balance method.

> DDB Rate = 2/6 = 1/3
> 2011 Depn expense = ($8,000 − $0) × 1/3 = $2,667
> Accumulated depn = $0 + $2,667 = $2,667
>
> 2012 Depn expense = ($8,000 − $2,667) × 1/3 = $1,778
> Accumulated depn = $2,667 + $1,778 = $4,445
>
> 2013 Depn expense = ($8,000 − $4,445) × 1/3 = $1,185
> Accumulated depn = $4,445 + $1,185 = $5,630

Year	Depreciation Expense	Accumulated Depreciation	Book Value (Cost − Acc Depn)
2011	$2,667	$2,667	$5,333
2012	1,778	4,445	3,555
2013	1,185	5,630	2,370

4. Using the units-of-production method only, show how the equipment would look on the December 31 balance sheets for 2011, 2012, and 2013.

	2011	2012	2013
Equipment	$ 8,000	$ 8,000	$ 8,000
− Accumulated Depreciation	(1,500)	(2,250)	(3,375)
Equipment (net)	$ 6,500	$ 5,750	$4,6255

5. Winters sold the machine on March 1, 2014, for $4,000 cash. Show both journal entries to record depreciation and to record the sale transaction using each method. (The equipment was used for 100 hours in 2014.)

Straight-Line Method

$$2014 \text{ depn expense} = \$1,250 \times \frac{2 \text{ months}}{12 \text{ months}}$$
$$= \$208$$

Mar 1	Depreciation expense		208	
	Accumulated depreciation—Equipment			208

Total accumulated depreciation = $3,750 + $208
= $3,958

Mar 1	Cash		4,000	
	Accumulated depreciation—Equipment		3,958	
	Loss on sale of equipment (to balance)		42	
	Equipment			8,000

Units-of-Production Method

$$2014 \text{ depn expense} = 100 \text{ hours} \times \$3.75$$
$$= \$375$$

Mar 1	Depreciation expense		375	
	Accumulated depreciation—Equipment			375

Total accumulated depreciation = $3,375 + $375
= $3,750

Mar 1	Cash		4,000	
	Accumulated depreciation—Equipment		3,750	
	Loss on sale of equipment (to balance)		250	
	Equipment			8,000

Double-Declining-Balance Method

$$2014 \text{ depreciation expense} = (\$8{,}000 - \$5{,}630) \times 1/3$$
$$= \$790 \text{ for 12 months}$$

$$\$790 \times \frac{2 \text{ months}}{12 \text{ months}} = \$132 \text{ for 2 months}$$

| Mar 1 | Depreciation expense | 132 | |
| | Accumulated depreciation—Equipment | | 132 |

$$\text{Total accumulated depreciation} = \$5{,}630 + \$132$$
$$= \$5{,}762$$

Mar 1	Cash	4,000	
	Accumulated depreciation—Equipment	5,762	
	Gain on sale of equipment (to balance)		1,762
	Equipment		8,000

Do It Yourself! Question 2 Solutions

Requirement

1. Show the journal entry to record Woody's depletion expense for the first year, assuming that 15,000 tons of lumber were cut and sold.

$$\text{Depletion per ton} = \frac{\$800,000}{40,000 \text{ tons}}$$

$$= \$20 \text{ per ton}$$

15,000 tons × $20 per ton = $300,000

	Depletion expense	300,000	
	Accumulated depletion—Lumber		300,000

Do It Yourself! Question 3 Solutions

Requirements

1. Journalize Kevin's purchase of the trademark.

Jan 1	Trademark	10,000	
	Cash		10,000

2. Journalize Kevin's amortization expense for the trademark in 2011.

$$\text{Amortization expense} = \frac{\$10,000}{20 \text{ years}}$$
$$= \$500 \text{ per year}$$
$$\$500 \times \frac{3 \text{ months}}{12 \text{ months}} = \$125 \text{ for 3 months}$$

Dec 31	Amortization expense—Trademarks	125	
	Trademark		125

The Power of Practice

For more practice using the skills learned in this chapter, visit MyAccountingLab. There you will find algorithmically generated questions that are based on these Demo Docs and your main textbook's Review and Assess Your Progress sections.

Go to MyAccountingLab and follow these steps:

1. Direct your URL to www.myaccountinglab.com.
2. Log in using your name and password.
3. Click the MyAccountingLab link.
4. Click Study Plan in the left navigation bar.
5. From the table of contents, select Chapter 9, Plant Assets and Intangibles.
6. Click a link to work tutorial exercises.

10 Current Liabilities, Payroll, and Long-Term Liabilities

What You Probably Already Know

You probably already know that, as an employee, you do not receive in your paycheck an amount equal to the number of hours worked times your hourly rate. The total that you have earned is called *gross pay*, which is the amount before withholdings are deducted. You may have noticed that money is withheld for federal income tax, Social Security tax, Medicare tax, and state income tax, if applicable in your state. You did not request that these amounts be deducted; they are required withholdings that your employer must make. Your employer does not keep this money; it must be remitted to the appropriate taxing agencies. When you receive your W-2 form by January 31 of the succeeding year, you can see that you are given credit for the amount of these taxes that your employer withheld on your behalf. In this chapter, we will see how your employer accounts for your paycheck.

You probably already know that when you purchase a home, you will likely need to obtain a mortgage. There are various types of mortgages to choose from, but a popular form is the fixed-rate mortgage. If you obtain a 30-year fixed mortgage, you know that you are locked into the interest rate specified in the mortgage contract for 30 years. Mortgage interest rates may increase or decrease in subsequent years, but it won't affect your fixed monthly payment. If the interest rate decrease is material enough, you may choose to refinance the mortgage to save future interest costs. Refinancing means that the old mortgage is paid off with a new mortgage loan. The characteristics of a bond are similar to a mortgage. The issuer of a bond has incurred a long-term liability and is committed to pay interest at the fixed interest rate included in the bond agreement. Sometimes issuers will refinance their debt if the interest rate decreases by issuing new bonds at the lower interest rate and paying off the higher-rate bonds. In this chapter, we will learn about bonds and how to account for them.

Learning Objectives/Success Keys

1 Account for current liabilities of known amount.

Some current liabilities that are recorded at known amounts include accounts payable, short-term notes payable, sales tax payable, current portion of long-term notes payable, accrued expenses or liabilities, and unearned or deferred revenues. *Review the "Current Liabilities of Known Amount" section of the textbook, and be sure to take note of the presentation of current liabilities in the balance sheet in Exhibit 10-1 (p. 525).*

2 Account for current liabilities that must be estimated.

Sometimes a liability has been incurred but the amount is uncertain. Examples of this may include estimated warranty payable and contingent liabilities. *Review Exhibit 10-2 (p. 530) for contingent liability classifications and treatments.*

3 Calculate payroll and payroll tax amounts.

The **gross pay** is the total amount earned by the employee and includes such items as the salary amount, hourly pay rate multiplied by the hours worked, commissions, bonuses, and overtime. **Net pay** is the amount the employee receives, which is equal to the gross pay less withholdings. Payroll deductions may include income taxes withheld, Social Security (FICA) tax, insurance premiums, retirement savings, and charitable contributions. *Review "Accounting for Payroll" in the main text.*

4 Journalize basic payroll transactions.

To record the periodic payroll, gross pay is debited to Salary Expense. All of the amounts withheld and the net pay due to the employees are credited to current liability accounts. Employers are also liable for payroll taxes. FICA and state and federal unemployment payroll tax expenses are incurred by employers and must be paid.

Most employers offer their employees some benefits such as health insurance or retirement benefits. Similar to the gross payroll and payroll taxes, the benefits are additional expenses to the employer. *Review the payroll costs and payroll accounting in Exhibits 10-5 (p. 537).*

5 Describe bonds payable.

A **bond** is a long-term liability that may be issued by corporations; local, state, or federal governments; and agencies. The **principal amount**, the amount on the bond certificate, is the amount that is to be paid to the investor on the maturity date. It is also the amount that is recorded in the Bond Payable account. Over the life of the bond, interest will be paid at the **stated rate**, the fixed interest rate for the bond. *Review "Issuing Bonds Payable to Borrow Money" in the main text for examples of accounting for bonds payable.*

6 Measure interest expense on bonds using the straight-line amortization method.

A discount occurs when the bond is sold for less than the principal amount. When the stated rate of interest is less than the market rate of interest, a bond is sold at a discount. A premium occurs when the bond is sold for more than the principal amount. When the stated rate of interest is higher than the market rate of interest, a bond is sold at a premium. A Discount on Bonds Payable and a Premium on Bonds Payable need to be amortized into Interest Expense over the life of the bond. Amortization reduces the account balance and Interest Expense is the other account affected. A **d**iscount is a **d**ebit balance; a premium is a credit balance. To reduce a debit balance, a credit entry must be made and then Interest Expense is debited. To reduce a credit balance, a debit entry must be made and then Interest Expense is credited. *Review "Straight-Line Amortization of Bond Discount" and "Straight-Line Amortization of Bond Premium" in the main text for illustrations on the calculation and accounting for amortization.*

7 Report liabilities on the balance sheet.

Similar to the handling of Notes Payable, the portion of the Bond Payable that is due within a year is classified as a current liability. Amounts due beyond one year are listed as long-term liabilities. *Review the illustration under "Reporting Liabilities on the Balance Sheet" in the main text.*

8 Compare issuing bonds to issuing stocks.

Borrowing may result in earning more money than the cost of the interest expense incurred. This concept of **leverage** is favorable because it serves to increase earnings per share. Borrowing has the disadvantage of creating a liability for the repayment of debt. Future interest payments will also be required. This increases the company's risk.

Demo Doc 1

General Current Liabilities

Learning Objectives 1, 2, 7

Freddie Enterprises sells products with warranties included in the selling price. During August 2011, Freddie sold goods for $250,000 cash. These goods cost $180,000 to manufacture. Freddie is required by law to collect 7% sales tax on all sales.

Freddie estimates warranty costs to be 1.5% of the selling price. During August 2011, Freddie made $3,000 of repairs under warranty (paid in cash to a repair service).

On August 31, 2011, Freddie remitted all sales tax collected in August to the state government.

Requirements

1. Journalize all of Freddie's transactions in the month of August 2011.

2. Is sales tax payable a contingent liability? Why or why not?

3. Is warranty payable a contingent liability? Why or why not?

Demo Doc 1 Solutions

Requirement 1

Journalize all of Freddie's transactions in the month of August 2011.

| Part 1 | Part 2 | Part 3 | Demo Doc Complete |

1 Account for current liabilities of known amount

7 Report liabilities on the balance sheet

During August 2011, Freddie sold goods for $250,000 cash. These goods cost $180,000 to manufacture. Freddie is required by law to collect 7% sales tax on all sales.

Freddie sold $250,000 worth of products. This means that Sales Revenue increases (a credit) by $250,000. However, the cash that Freddie collected was *more* than $250,000 because it included the sales tax.

Freddie collected $250,000 × (1 + 7%) = $267,500 cash from the customer.

The $250,000 × 7% = $17,500 Freddie collected in sales tax is *not* revenue because it was *not earned* by Freddie and *does not belong* to Freddie. These taxes belong to the government and are owed/payable by Freddie to the government. Therefore, we must increase (a credit) the Sales Taxes Payable account by $17,500.

Cash ($250,000 × [1 + 7%])	267,500	
Sales revenue		250,000
Sales taxes payable ($250,000 × 7%)		17,500

Freddie has sold these goods and so an adjustment to Inventory is necessary as well. COGS increases (a debit) and Inventory decreases (a credit) by $180,000, Freddie's cost of the products.

COGS	180,000	
Inventory		180,000

2 Account for current liabilities that must be estimated

7 Report liabilities on the balance sheet

Freddie estimates warranty costs to be 1.5% of the selling price.

We must also account for the warranties included in the selling price of the goods. Once the products are sold, the warranty is in effect. This means that Freddie has an *obligation* (that is, a *liability*) to fix the products if they break down. We must record an estimated Warranty Payable liability (a credit) of:

$$1.5\% \times \$250,000 = \$3,750$$

As the liability is recorded, so is the estimated Warranty Expense (a debit) of $3,750. There will be additional expense/cost to Freddie to make the repairs. This is good matching (as required by the matching principle under GAAP) because the expense is recorded *at the same time as the sales revenue, not when the actual cost is incurred (or warranty claim is made)*.

Warranty expense ($250,000 × 1.5%)	3,750	
Warranty payable		3,750

2 Account for current liabilities that must be estimated

7 Report liabilities on the balance sheet

During August 2011, Freddie made $3,000 of repairs under warranty (paid in cash to a repair service).

When Freddie Enterprises makes warranty repairs, it is *meeting its warranty obligation* (that is, it is reducing its warranty liability). This causes a decrease (a debit) to Warranty Payable of $3,000.

Because the repairs were paid for in cash, the Cash account also decreases (a credit) by $3,000.

Notice that the Warranty Expense account is *not* impacted by the repairs! The expense was *already recorded* at the time of sale. To debit it again now would be double-counting the expense.

Warranty payable	3,000	
Cash		3,000

Note that there is $3,750 − $3,000 = $750 left in the Warranty Payable account. This remains to cover any future repairs that might be made under the warranty.

1 Account for current liabilities of known amount

7 Report liabilities on the balance sheet

On August 31, 2011, Freddie remitted all sales tax collected in August to the state government.

The first transaction stated that during August, Freddie sold goods for $250,000 cash and collected 7% sales tax on all sales. At that time, Cash was increased by $267,500, Sales Revenue was increased by $250,000, and Sales Taxes Payable was increased by $250,000 × 7% = $17,500.

Sales taxes payable	17,500	
Cash		17,500

On August 31, Freddie remitted the sales taxes to the government. This means that the sales tax liability was paid in cash.

Cash is decreased (a credit) by $17,500 and Sales Taxes Payable is decreased (a debit) by $17,500.

Requirement 2

1 Account for current liabilities of known amount

Is sales tax payable a contingent liability? Why or why not?

| Part 1 | **Part 2** | Part 3 | Demo Doc Complete |

Sales taxes *must* be collected and remitted to the government by *law*. Ethical companies have no choice but to meet the sales taxes payable obligation. Therefore, this amount *will* be paid and it is *not* a contingent liability, as it is *not* dependent upon any outside event.

Requirement 3

2 Account for current liabilities that must be estimated

Is warranty payable a contingent liability? Why or why not?

| Part 1 | Part 2 | **Part 3** | Demo Doc Complete |

Warranty payable is an *estimate*. It is not known *for sure* whether or not the products will break down or how much it might cost to repair them if they do. For this reason, warranty payable is a contingent liability because it depends upon the performance of the products after they leave Freddie's control.

Because payment for warranty repairs is probable and estimable, warranty expense and warranty payable are recorded in a journal entry, even though they are contingent upon outside events.

| Part 1 | Part 2 | Part 3 | **Demo Doc Complete** |

Demo Doc 2

Current Portion of Long-Term Debt

Learning Objectives 1, 7

On August 1, 2011, Squirrel Co. signed a $400,000 note payable. Squirrel agreed to pay back $25,000 per month, beginning on January 1, 2012, and ending on April 1, 2013. Interest of 12% is paid monthly beginning January 1, 2012.

Requirement

1. Show the presentation of this note on Squirrel's December 31, 2011, balance sheet.

Demo Doc 2 Solutions

Requirement 1

1 Account for current liabilities of known amount

7 Report liabilities on the balance sheet

Show the presentation of this note on Squirrel's December 31, 2011, balance sheet.

Part 1	Demo Doc Complete

Of the $400,000 debt, payments totaling $25,000 × 12 = $300,000 will be repaid within the next year.

This $300,000 is the *current* portion of the debt because it will be repaid within the next year.

The remaining $400,000 − $300,000 = $100,000 will be repaid in more than one year, so it is the *long-term* portion of the debt.

Interest has been incurred on the entire $400,000 liability balance that has been outstanding over the five months since August 1, 2011.

Interest incurred	=	Total debt	×	Interest rate	×	Fraction of year
	=	$400,000	×	12%	×	$\frac{5}{12}$
	=	$20,000				

The amount of $20,000 is recorded as Interest Payable. This interest payable is *current* because it is due in less than one year.

Note that this is *not* the total interest due on the note. It is *only* the amount that has *already* been incurred at December 31, 2011.

Current Liabilities
Current portion of long-term debt $300,000
Interest payable .... $ 20,000

Long-Term Liabilities
Notes payable/long-term debt (net of current portion) $100,000

Part 1	Demo Doc Complete

Demo Doc 2 Solutions | Chapter 10 **319**

Demo Doc 3

Payroll Liabilities

Learning Objectives 3, 4

Gannon Company employees earn a total of $500,000 gross pay per week. All employees have the following items withheld from their pay:

15%	Income taxes
8%	FICA taxes
4%	Pension contributions
2%	Union dues

Gannon pays the following payroll taxes:

8%	FICA taxes
6%	Unemployment taxes

Requirements

1. For a normal week, journalize the following transactions:

   a. Cash payment of employee salaries.

   b. Accrue Gannon's payroll taxes.

   c. Gannon's payment of all payroll taxes.

   d. Gannon's payment of union dues.

   e. Gannon's payment of pension contributions.

2. What is the employees' net pay in a normal week?

3. What is Gannon's total payroll expense in a normal week?

4. The employee at Gannon who hires new employees is also the person who processes the payroll. Is this a good internal control?

Demo Doc 3 Solutions

3 Calculate payroll amounts

4 Journalize basic payroll transactions

Requirement 1

For a normal week, journalize the following transactions:

| Part 1 | Part 2 | Part 3 | Part 4 | Demo Doc Complete |

a. Cash payment of employee salaries.

The entire gross pay of $500,000 is all recorded as Salary Expense (a debit). However, this entire amount is not all paid to the employee in cash.

Employee Income Tax Payable increases (a credit) by:

$$\$500,000 \times 15\% = \$75,000$$

FICA Tax Payable increases (a credit) by:

$$\$500,000 \times 8\% = \$40,000$$

Pension Contributions Payable increases (a credit) by:

$$\$500,000 \times 4\% = \$20,000$$

Union Dues Payable increases (a credit) by:

$$\$500,000 \times 2\% = \$10,000$$

Cash decreases (a credit) by the pay that is *not withheld*:

$$\$500,000 - \$75,000 - \$40,000 - \$20,000 - \$10,000 = \$355,000$$

To summarize:

Employee income tax payable	$500,000 × 15% =	$75,000
FICA tax payable	$500,000 × 8% =	$40,000
Pension contributions payable	$500,000 × 4% =	$20,000
Union dues payable	$500,000 × 2% =	$10,000

Salary expense (gross pay)	500,000	
Employee income tax payable ($500,000 × 15%)		75,000
FICA tax payable ($500,000 × 8%)		40,000
Pension contributions payable ($500,000 × 4%)		20,000
Union dues payable ($500,000 × 2%)		10,000
Cash (net/take home pay)		355,000

The $355,000 Cash amount is often referred to as "take-home pay" because it is the amount the employees actually receive (that is, take home) on their paychecks.

Note that Gannon is *not* paying these taxes out of its own pocket. It is using money that has been held back from *employee paychecks* to make these payments.

The taxes withheld by Gannon are similar to the treatment of sales taxes payable. Gannon has the cash for them (because Gannon never paid this cash to the employees but withheld it instead) and will pass it on to the appropriate agencies in the near future just as sales taxes collected are recorded as a payable and passed on to the state government.

b. Accrue Gannon's payroll taxes.

Gannon must record Payroll Tax Expense (a debit) for all taxes the company must pay.

FICA Tax Payable increases (a credit) by Gannon's portion of the taxes:

$$\$500,000 \times 8\% = \$40,000$$

Unemployment Tax Payable increases (a credit) by:

$$\$500,000 \times 6\% = \$30,000$$

Payroll tax expense (to balance)	70,000	
FICA tax payable ($500,000 × 8%) (matching)		40,000
Unemployment tax payable ($500,000 × 6%)		30,000

Unlike the liabilities recorded in transaction **a** (that are paid by the employees by being taken out of their paychecks), these amounts are being paid directly by Gannon out of its own pocket.

c. Gannon's payment of all payroll taxes.

Cash decreases (a credit) by the total of all taxes paid.
Employee Income Tax Payable decreases (a debit) by its balance of $75,000.
FICA Tax Payable decreases (a debit) by its balance of:

$$\$40,000 + \$40,000 = \$80,000$$

Unemployment Tax Payable decreases (a debit) by its balance of $30,000.

Employee income tax payable	75,000	
FICA tax payable ($40,000 + $40,000) (matching amounts)	80,000	
Unemployment tax payable	30,000	
Cash (to balance)		185,000

d. Gannon's payment of union dues.

Union Dues Payable decreases (a debit) by its balance of $10,000. Cash also decreases (a credit) by $10,000.

	Union dues payable		10,000	
	Cash			10,000

e. Gannon's payment of pension contributions.

Pension Contributions Payable decreases (a debit) by its balance of $20,000. Cash also decreases (a credit) by $20,000.

	Pension contributions payable		20,000	
	Cash			20,000

Requirement 2

Calculate payroll amounts

What is the employees' net pay in a normal week?

| Part 1 | **Part 2** | Part 3 | Part 4 | Demo Doc Complete |

Employees' net pay is the amount of cash they receive each week. This is the $355,000 calculated in Requirement 1a.

Requirement 3

Calculate payroll amounts

What is Gannon's total payroll expense in a normal week?

| Part 1 | Part 2 | **Part 3** | Part 4 | Demo Doc Complete |

Payroll expense is the *total* cost of having an employee. This includes the employee's salary as well as any additional taxes that do not come out of that salary (that is, that are paid out of the employer's pocket).

So payroll expense includes salary expense of $500,000 *and* payroll taxes expense of $70,000.

$$\text{Total payroll expense} = \$500,000 + \$70,000 = \$570,000$$

3 Calculate payroll amounts

Requirement 4

The employee at Gannon who hires new employees is also the person who processes the payroll. Is this a good internal control?

| Part 1 | Part 2 | Part 3 | **Part 4** | Demo Doc Complete |

This is an internal control weakness. It is possible for this person to create fictitious employees and then issue payroll checks to them.

This creates an opportunity for fraud. The person who is responsible for hiring employees should *not* be the person who processes payroll.

| Part 1 | Part 2 | Part 3 | Part 4 | **Demo Doc Complete** |

Demo Doc 4

Bonds Payable (straight-line amortization)

Learning Objectives 5, 6, 7, 8

Blue Co. issued $50,000 maturity value of bonds payable for $51,788 cash on January 1, 2011. The bonds had a stated rate of 12%, but the market rate was 10%. Interest is paid semiannually and the bonds are due in two years.

Blue uses the straight-line method of amortization.

Requirements

1. Are these bonds issued at a discount or premium? How do you know?

2. Journalize Blue's issuance of the bonds on January 1, 2011.

3. Journalize Blue's first two interest payments on June 30, 2011, and December 31, 2011.

4. Show how the bonds would appear on Blue's December 31, 2011, balance sheet.

5. How do interest payments on bonds differ from dividend payments on preferred stock?

Demo Doc 4 Solutions

5 Describe bonds payable

Requirement 1

Are these bonds issued at a discount or premium? How do you know?

| Part 1 | Part 2 | Part 3 | Part 4 | Part 5 | Demo Doc Complete |

These bonds were issued at a **premium**. We know this because the cash received for the bonds is *more* than the maturity value and because the stated rate is *greater* than the market rate.

12% stated rate > 10% market rate

Requirement 2

6 Measure interest expense on bonds using the straight-line amortization method

Journalize Blue's issuance of the bonds on January 1, 2011.

| Part 1 | Part 2 | Part 3 | Part 4 | Part 5 | Demo Doc Complete |

Cash is increased (a debit) by $51,788.
Bonds Payable is increased (a credit) by the bonds' *maturity* value of $50,000.
The difference between these two amounts is balanced to Premium on Bonds Payable. The balancing amount is a credit of:

$51,788 − $50,000 = $1,788

Cash	51,788	
Premium on bonds payable (to balance)		1,788
Bonds payable		50,000

Requirement 3

6 Measure interest expense on bonds using the straight-line amortization method

Journalize Blue's first two interest payments on June 30, 2011, and December 31, 2011.

| Part 1 | Part 2 | Part 3 | Part 4 | Part 5 | Demo Doc Complete |

Under straight-line amortization, the premium will be amortized the *same amount* every interest period.

$$\text{Premium amortization each interest period} = \frac{\text{Discount or Premium}}{\text{Number of interest periods}}$$

326 Chapter 10 | Demo Doc 4 Solutions

The bonds are due in two years and have two interest payments per year. This results in 2 × 2 = 4 interest payment periods.

$$\text{Premium amortization each interest period} = \frac{\$1,788}{4}$$
$$= \$447$$

This means that *every* time interest expense is recorded, the premium will be amortized (that is, *decreased/debited*) by $447.

Cash will be decreased by the cash interest paid.

$$\text{Cash interest paid} = \frac{\text{Maturity value} \times \text{Stated rate}}{\text{Number of interest payments per year}}$$

The question states that the bonds are semiannual; that is, they pay interest twice per year.

$$\text{Cash interest paid} = \frac{\$50,000 \times 12\%}{2}$$
$$= \$3,000$$

Interest Expense is increased (a debit) by the balancing amount of:

$$\$3,000 - \$447 = \$2,553$$

Because the cash interest paid and the premium amortization *do not change* from period to period, the entry to record the interest expense and payment is *always* the same. So the entry for June 30, 2011, *and* December 31, 2011, is:

Interest expense (to balance)	2,553	
Premium on bonds payable ($1,788/4)	447	
Cash (50,000 × 12%/2)		3,000

Requirement 4

7 Report liabilities on the balance sheet

Show how the bonds would appear on Blue's December 31, 2011, balance sheet.

| Part 1 | Part 2 | Part 3 | **Part 4** | Part 5 | Demo Doc Complete |

The bonds are reported in the liabilities section of the balance sheet. The premium is added to the bonds payable to create a net value.

Bonds payable	$50,000
plus Premium	894*
Bonds payable (net)	$50,894

*$1,788 – $1,447 (June amortization) – $1,447 (December amortization)

Requirement 5

8 Compare issuing bonds to issuing stocks

How do interest payments on bonds differ from dividend payments on preferred stock?

Part 1	Part 2	Part 3	Part 4	**Part 5**	Demo Doc Complete

If a company chooses to issue bonds instead of preferred stock, it will have a higher earnings-per-share ratio as a result.

However, large interest payments (and principal payments when the bonds mature) can lead to bankruptcy if the company is unable to pay off the debt.

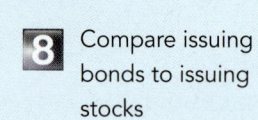

Part 1	Part 2	Part 3	Part 4	Part 5	**Demo Doc Complete**

Quick Practice Questions

True/False

_____ 1. Sales tax payable is shown as a long-term liability on the balance sheet.

_____ 2. An accrued expense is an expense that has not yet been paid.

_____ 3. A contingent liability is not an actual liability.

_____ 4. Optional deductions would include employee income tax, Social Security tax, union dues, and insurance premiums.

_____ 5. State and federal unemployment taxes are two required payroll deductions for employees.

_____ 6. The FICA Social Security tax is withheld from employees and is also paid by the employer in the same amount.

_____ 7. The document that includes every employee's gross pay, deductions, and net pay for the payroll period is called the Wage and Tax Statement.

_____ 8. Two employees who have the same gross pay may have different amounts withheld for income taxes depending on the number of allowances claimed on the W-4 Form.

_____ 9. An example of a contingent liability would be when you cosign a note payable for a friend.

_____ 10. If a company has a note payable at December 31 for $300,000, which will be paid in three equal installments every five months, $100,000 should be classified as a current liability.

_____ 11. The journal entry to record selling $200,000 face value bonds at 98 will involve a credit to Bonds Payable for $196,000.

_____ 12. When a bond is issued at a discount, the discount has the effect of raising the interest expense on the bonds to the market rate of interest.

_____ 13. The carrying value of bonds will decrease each interest period if the bonds were sold at a discount.

_____ 14. When reporting serial bonds on the balance sheet, the portion maturing within one year is shown as a current liability.

_____ 15. Earning more income on borrowed money than the related interest expense increases the earnings for common stockholders and is called using leverage.

_____ 16. Issuing bonds instead of stock generally is less risky to a corporation.

_____ 17. Bondholders are creditors of a corporation.

Multiple Choice

1. Which of the following is true about current liabilities?
   a. Are due within one year or one operating cycle, whichever is longer
   b. Must be of a known amount
   c. Must be of an estimated amount
   d. Are subtracted from long-term liabilities on the balance sheet

2. Which of the following best describes unearned revenue?
   a. Revenue that has been earned and collected
   b. Revenue that has been earned but not yet collected
   c. Revenue that has been collected but not yet earned
   d. Revenue that has not been collected nor earned

3. When is Warranty Expense debited?
   a. In the period the product under warranty is repaired or replaced
   b. In the period after the product is sold
   c. In the period after the product is repaired or replaced
   d. In the period the revenue from selling the product was earned

4. When a product is repaired under warranty, the entry includes which of the following?
   a. A debit to Warranty Expense
   b. A credit to Warranty Expense
   c. A debit to Estimated Warranty Payable
   d. A credit to Estimated Warranty Payable

5. What is meant by a cafeteria plan?
   a. A free lunch program offered by the employer
   b. A choice of insurance coverage
   c. A retirement plan
   d. Employee discounts on company products and services

6. For which of the following taxes is there a ceiling on the amount of annual employee earnings subject to the tax?
   a. Only the FICA tax
   b. Only the FICA tax and the federal unemployment tax
   c. Only the state and federal unemployment taxes
   d. The FICA tax and the state and federal unemployment taxes

7. Sumiko Greer is paid $26 per hour with time and a half her regular hourly pay rate for all hours exceeding 40 per week. During the week ended January 12, Sumiko worked 45 hours. What is the gross payroll?
   a. $1,105
   b. $1,170
   c. $1,235
   d. $1,365

8. Travel America has 24 employees who are paid on a monthly basis. For the most recent month, gross earnings were $78,000, of which $27,000 is subject to unemployment taxes (federal at 0.8% and state at 5.4%). Federal income tax withholdings are 20% of total earnings. All employees have $15 per month withheld for charitable contributions. All earnings are subject to 8% FICA tax.

   What is the total employer's payroll tax expense?
   a. $4,216
   b. $7,114
   c. $7,914
   d. $9,656

9. Referring to the information in the preceding question, what is the amount of salaries payable?
   a. $51,309
   b. $54,471
   c. $55,800
   d. $56,160

10. Under what condition is a contingent liability recorded as an expense and a liability?
    a. Under no condition
    b. When the likelihood of an actual loss is remote
    c. When the likelihood of an actual loss is reasonably possible
    d. When the likelihood of an actual loss is probable and the amount can be estimated

11. On January 2, 2011, Lot Company issues $200,000 face value, 6% bonds for $196,000. What can be concluded about the effective (market) rate of interest?
    a. It is less than 6%.
    b. It is more than 6%.
    c. It is equal to 6%.
    d. It is impossible to determine from the given data.

12. Dalton Company issues 50, $1,000 face value, 10% bonds at 102.5. The journal entry includes which of the following?
    a. A debit to Cash for $50,000
    b. A credit to Premium on Bonds Payable for $1,250
    c. A debit to Discount on Bonds Payable for $1,250
    d. A credit to Bonds Payable for $51,250

13. What are bonds issued on the general credit of the issuing corporation called?
    a. Serial bonds
    b. Term bonds
    c. Debenture bonds
    d. Convertible bonds

14. What are bonds called when the maturities are spread over several dates?
    a. Term bonds
    b. Debenture bonds
    c. Serial bonds
    d. Callable bonds

15. What is the interest rate specified in the bond indenture called?
    a. Stated rate
    b. Discount rate
    c. Yield rate
    d. Effective rate

16. Which of the following statements about the discount on bonds payable is correct?
    a. It is added to bonds payable on the balance sheet.
    b. It is a contra asset.
    c. It is amortized over the life of the bonds.
    d. Both (b) and (c) are correct.

17. All *except* which of the following is an advantage of issuing stock?
    a. It is less risky to the issuing corporation.
    b. It creates no liabilities.
    c. It generally results in higher earnings per share.
    d. It creates no interest expense that must be paid.

Quick Exercises

10-1. Federal United purchased equipment costing $88,000 on October 2, 2011, by paying a 30% cash down payment and signing a 9%, 120-day note payable for the balance. Federal United's year-end is December 31.

Requirement

1. Journalize the following:

a. The purchase of the equipment on October 2, 2011

Date	Accounts	Debit	Credit

General Journal

b. The accrual of interest on December 31, 2011

Date	Accounts	Debit	Credit

General Journal

c. Payment of the note on January 30, 2012

	General Journal		
Date	Accounts	Debit	Credit

10-2. Ideal Food Services had cash sales of $787,000 during the month of August 2011 and collected the 7% sales tax on these sales required by the state in which Ideal Food Services operates.

Requirements

1. Journalize the cash sale and the sales tax on August 31.

	General Journal		
Date	Accounts	Debit	Credit

2. Journalize the September 15 transaction when the sales tax is remitted to the proper agency.

	General Journal		
Date	Accounts	Debit	Credit

10-3. Freedom Vacuums warrants all of its products for one full year against any defect in manufacturing. Sales for 2010 and 2011 were $731,000 and $854,000, respectively. Freedom Vacuums expects warranty claims to run 4.5% of annual sales. Freedom paid $30,150 and $38,290, respectively, in 2010 and 2011 in warranty claims.

   a. Compute Freedom's Warranty Expense for 2010 and 2011.

   b. Compute the balance in Estimated Warranty Payable on December 31, 2011, assuming the January 1, 2010, balance in the account was $2,980.

10-4. Curtis Building Services has one employee, George North, who earns $36 per hour for a 40-hour workweek. He earns time and a half for all overtime hours. George has earned $89,200 in wages prior to the current week. From George's pay, Curtis Building Services deducts 20% for federal income tax and 8% for FICA taxes (up to $90,000 per annum). The company also withholds $100 per week for his health insurance. The federal unemployment tax rate is 0.8% up to $7,000 of employee earnings per annum. The state unemployment tax rate is 5.4% up to $7,000 of employee earnings per annum. Curtis pays $100/week for medical insurance premiums for each employee.

Requirements

1. Compute the gross pay and the net pay for George North for the current week ending December 16, 2011. George worked 48 hours. Round all amounts to the nearest dollar.

Gross Pay:

Net Pay:

2. Journalize the payroll expense.

		General Journal		
Date	Accounts		Debit	Credit

3. Journalize the payroll taxes imposed on Curtis Building Services.

Date	Accounts	Debit	Credit

General Journal

10-5. Use the data in Quick Exercise 10-4 to record the following:

a. Journalize the payment of payroll to the employee on December 16, 2011.

Date	Accounts	Debit	Credit

General Journal

b. Journalize the payment of the income tax withheld and FICA for the employee and employer on December 16, 2011.

Date	Accounts	Debit	Credit

General Journal

c. Journalize the payment of the health insurance premiums withheld.

Date	Accounts	Debit	Credit

General Journal

10-6. For each of the following independent situations, state whether the bonds were issued at a premium, at a discount, or at par.

a. Bonds with a face value of $50,000 were issued for $53,000.
b. Bonds with a contract rate of 8% were issued to yield 7.5%.
c. Bonds with a face value of $75,000 were issued for $75,000.
d. Bonds with a contract rate of 8.25% were issued to yield 8.75%.
e. Bonds with a face value of $110,000 were issued for $106,000.

10-7. Fox Company issued 10-year, 10%, $1,000,000 bonds on January 1, 2011. The bonds pay interest every June 30 and December 31. The bonds were issued for $1,065,000. Fox Company uses straight-line amortization for any discount or premium amortization.

Requirements

1. Journalize the following:

a. Issue the bonds on January 1, 2011.

	General Journal		
Date	Accounts	Debit	Credit

b. Record the interest payment and amortize the premium or discount on June 30, 2011.

	General Journal		
Date	Accounts	Debit	Credit

2. What is the carrying value of the bonds on June 30, 2011?

10-8. On April 1, 2011, Needy Company issued $3,000,000 of 8%, 10-year bonds dated April 1, 2011, with interest payments made each October 1 and April 1. The bonds are issued at 95. Needy Company amortizes any premium or discount using the straight-line method.

Requirement

1. Journalize the following transactions:

a. April 1, 2011, issuance of the bonds.

Date	Accounts	Debit	Credit

General Journal

b. October 1, 2011, payment of interest and the amortization of any discount or premium.

Date	Accounts	Debit	Credit

General Journal

c. December 31, 2011, accrual of interest and the amortization of any premium or discount.

Date	Accounts	Debit	Credit

General Journal

Do It Yourself! Question 1

General Current Liabilities

Nitro Brothers sells products with warranties included in the selling price. During October 2011, Nitro sold goods for $10,000 cash. These goods cost $8,000 to manufacture. Nitro is required by law to collect 8% sales tax on all sales.

Nitro estimates warranty costs to be 1% of selling price. During October 2011, Nitro made $60 of repairs under warranty (paid in cash to a repair service).

On October 31, 2011, Nitro remitted all sales tax collected in October to the state government.

Requirement

1. Journalize all of Nitro's transactions in the month of October, 2011.

Date	Accounts	Debit	Credit

Date	Accounts	Debit	Credit

Date	Accounts	Debit	Credit

Date	Accounts	Debit	Credit

Date	Accounts	Debit	Credit

Do It Yourself! Question 2

Current Portion of Long-Term Debt

On October 1, 2011, Pulter Industries signed a $2,000 note payable. Pulter agreed to pay back $100 per month, beginning on November 1, 2011, and ending on June 1, 2013.

Pulter is also required to pay 10% interest on the note each month.

Requirement

1. Show the presentation of this note on Pulter's December 31, 2011, balance sheet.

Do It Yourself! Question 3

Payroll Liabilities

Oxygen Co. employees earn $200,000 gross pay per week. All employees have the following items withheld from their pay:

20%	Income Taxes
8%	FICA Taxes
3%	401K Plan Contributions
1%	Union Dues

Oxygen pays the following payroll taxes:

8%	FICA Taxes
6%	Unemployment Taxes

Requirement

1. For a normal week, journalize the following transactions:

a. Cash payment of employee salaries.

Date	Accounts	Debit	Credit

b. Oxygen's payroll taxes.

Date	Accounts	Debit	Credit

c. Oxygen's payment of all payroll taxes.

Date	Accounts	Debit	Credit

d. Oxygen's payment of union dues.

Date	Accounts	Debit	Credit

e. Oxygen's payment of 401K plan contributions.

Date	Accounts	Debit	Credit

Do It Yourself! Question 4

Bonds Payable (straight-line amortization)

Circle Company issued $20,000 maturity value of bonds payable for $19,337 cash on January 1, 2011. The bonds had a stated rate of 14%, but the market rate was 16%. Interest is paid semiannually and the bonds are due in two years.
   Circle uses the straight-line method of amortization.

Requirements

1. Are these bonds issued at a discount or premium?

2. Journalize Circle's issuance of the bonds on January 1, 2011.

Date	Accounts	Debit	Credit

3. Journalize Circle's first two interest payments on June 30, 2011, and December 31, 2011.

Date	Accounts	Debit	Credit

General Journal			
Date	Accounts	Debit	Credit

4. Show how the bonds would appear on Circle's December 31, 2011, balance sheet.

Quick Practice Solutions

True/False

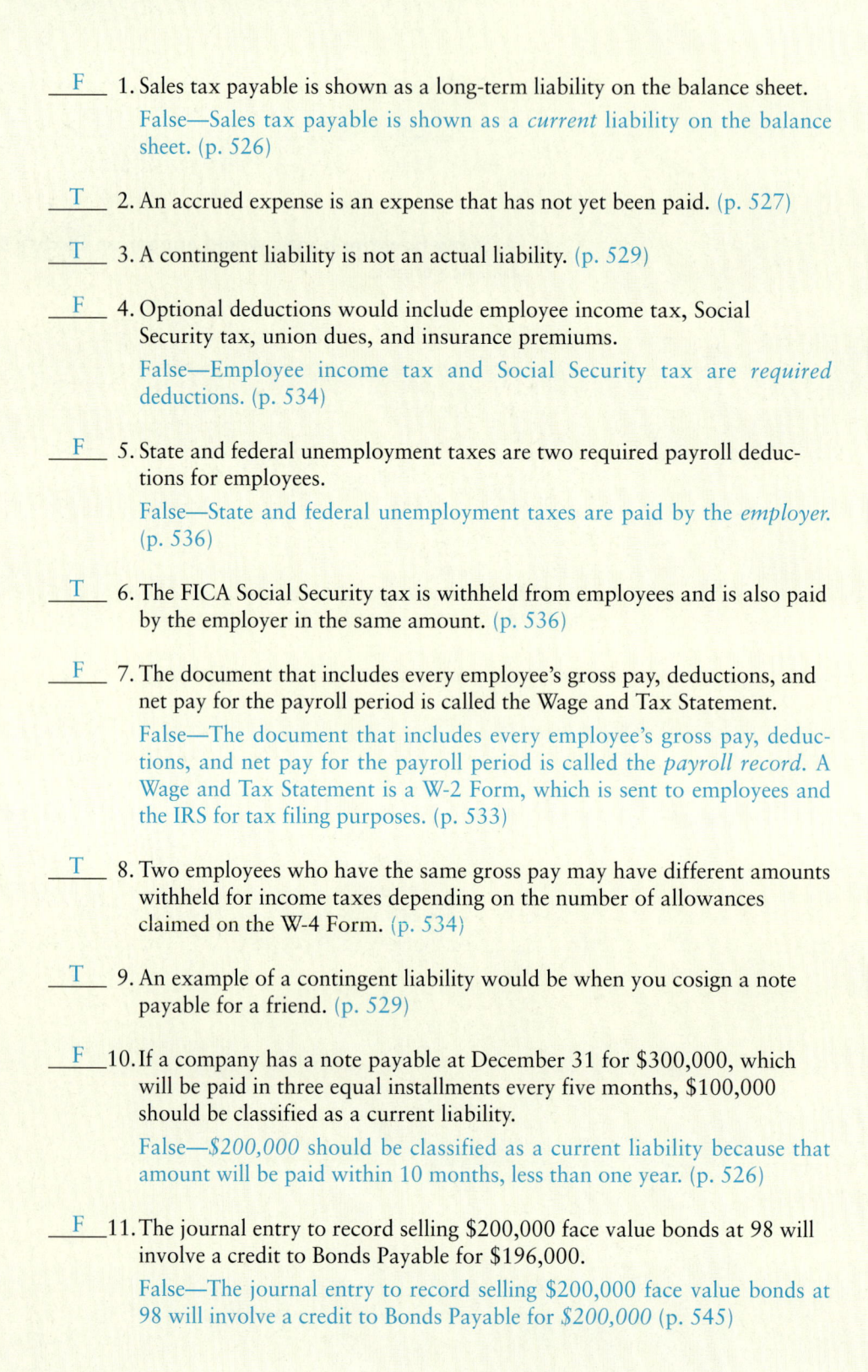

__F__ 1. Sales tax payable is shown as a long-term liability on the balance sheet.

False—Sales tax payable is shown as a *current* liability on the balance sheet. (p. 526)

__T__ 2. An accrued expense is an expense that has not yet been paid. (p. 527)

__T__ 3. A contingent liability is not an actual liability. (p. 529)

__F__ 4. Optional deductions would include employee income tax, Social Security tax, union dues, and insurance premiums.

False—Employee income tax and Social Security tax are *required* deductions. (p. 534)

__F__ 5. State and federal unemployment taxes are two required payroll deductions for employees.

False—State and federal unemployment taxes are paid by the *employer*. (p. 536)

__T__ 6. The FICA Social Security tax is withheld from employees and is also paid by the employer in the same amount. (p. 536)

__F__ 7. The document that includes every employee's gross pay, deductions, and net pay for the payroll period is called the Wage and Tax Statement.

False—The document that includes every employee's gross pay, deductions, and net pay for the payroll period is called the *payroll record*. A Wage and Tax Statement is a W-2 Form, which is sent to employees and the IRS for tax filing purposes. (p. 533)

__T__ 8. Two employees who have the same gross pay may have different amounts withheld for income taxes depending on the number of allowances claimed on the W-4 Form. (p. 534)

__T__ 9. An example of a contingent liability would be when you cosign a note payable for a friend. (p. 529)

__F__ 10. If a company has a note payable at December 31 for $300,000, which will be paid in three equal installments every five months, $100,000 should be classified as a current liability.

False—*$200,000* should be classified as a current liability because that amount will be paid within 10 months, less than one year. (p. 526)

__F__ 11. The journal entry to record selling $200,000 face value bonds at 98 will involve a credit to Bonds Payable for $196,000.

False—The journal entry to record selling $200,000 face value bonds at 98 will involve a credit to Bonds Payable for *$200,000* (p. 545)

__T__ 12. When a bond is issued at a discount, the discount has the effect of raising the interest expense on the bonds to the market rate of interest. (p. 546)

__F__ 13. The carrying value of bonds will decrease each interest period if the bonds were sold at a discount.

False—The carrying value of bonds will *increase* each interest period if the bonds were sold at a discount. (p. 554)

__T__ 14. When reporting serial bonds on the balance sheet, the portion maturing within one year is shown as a current liability. (p. 542)

__T__ 15. Earning more income on borrowed money than the related interest expense increases the earnings for common stockholders and is called using leverage. (p. 553)

__F__ 16. Issuing bonds instead of stock generally is less risky to a corporation.

False—Issuing bonds instead of stock generally is *more* risky to a corporation. (p. 552)

__T__ 17. Bondholders are creditors of a corporation. (p. 542)

Multiple Choice

1. Which of the following is true about current liabilities? (p. 524)
   a. Are due within one year or one operating cycle, whichever is longer
   b. Must be of a known amount
   c. Must be of an estimated amount
   d. Are subtracted from long-term liabilities on the balance sheet

2. Which of the following best describes unearned revenue? (p. 528)
   a. Revenue that has been earned and collected
   b. Revenue that has been earned but not yet collected
   c. Revenue that has been collected but not yet earned
   d. Revenue that has not been collected nor earned

3. When is Warranty Expense debited? (pp. 528–529)
   a. In the period the product under warranty is repaired or replaced
   b. In the period after the product is sold
   c. In the period after the product is repaired or replaced
   d. In the period the revenue from selling the product was earned

4. When a product is repaired under warranty, the entry includes which of the following? (pp. 528–529)
   a. A debit to Warranty Expense
   b. A credit to Warranty Expense
   c. A debit to Estimated Warranty Payable
   d. A credit to Estimated Warranty Payable

5. What is meant by a cafeteria plan? (p. 533)
   a. A free lunch program offered by the employer
   b. A choice of insurance coverage
   c. A retirement plan
   d. Employee discounts on company products and services

6. For which of the following taxes is there a ceiling on the amount of annual employee earnings subject to the tax? (p. 534)
   a. Only the FICA tax
   b. Only the FICA tax and the federal unemployment tax
   c. Only the state and federal unemployment taxes
   d. The FICA tax and the state and federal unemployment taxes

7. Sumiko Greer is paid $26 per hour with time and a half her regular hourly pay rate for all hours exceeding 40 per week. During the week ended January 12, Sumiko worked 45 hours. What is the gross payroll? (p. 533)
   a. $1,105
   b. $1,170
   c. $1,235
   d. $1,365

8. Travel America has 24 employees who are paid on a monthly basis. For the most recent month, gross earnings were $78,000, of which $27,000 is subject to unemployment taxes (federal at 0.8% and state at 5.4%). Federal income tax withholdings are 20% of total earnings. All employees have $15 per month withheld for charitable contributions. All earnings are subject to 8% FICA tax.

   What is the total employer's payroll tax expense? (p. 537)
   a. $4,216
   b. $7,114
   c. $7,914
   d. $9,656

9. Referring to the information in the preceding question, what is the amount of salaries payable? (p. 537)
   a. $51,309
   b. $54,471
   c. $55,800
   d. $56,160

10. Under what condition is a contingent liability recorded as an expense and a liability? (p. 530)
    a. Under no condition
    b. When the likelihood of an actual loss is remote
    c. When the likelihood of an actual loss is reasonably possible
    d. When the likelihood of an actual loss is probable and the amount can be estimated

11. On January 2, 2011, Lot Company issues $200,000 face value, 6% bonds for $196,000. What can be concluded about the effective (market) rate of interest? (p. 545)
    a. It is less than 6%.
    b. It is more than 6%.
    c. It is equal to 6%.
    d. It is impossible to determine from the given data.

12. Dalton Company issues 50, $1,000 face value, 10% bonds at 102.5. The journal entry includes which of the following? (p. 549)
    a. A debit to Cash for $50,000
    b. A credit to Premium on Bonds Payable for $1,250
    c. A debit to Discount on Bonds Payable for $1,250
    d. A credit to Bonds Payable for $51,250

13. What are bonds issued on the general credit of the issuing corporation called? (p. 542)
    a. Serial bonds
    b. Term bonds
    c. Debenture bonds
    d. Convertible bonds

14. What are bonds called when the maturities are spread over several dates? (p. 542)
    a. Under no condition
    b. Debenture bonds
    c. Serial bonds
    d. Callable bonds

15. What is the interest rate specified in the bond indenture called? (p. 544)
    a. Stated rate
    b. Discount rate
    c. Yield rate
    d. Effective rate

16. Which of the following statements about the discount on bonds payable is correct? (p. 546)
    a. It is added to bonds payable on the balance sheet.
    b. It is a contra asset.
    c. It is amortized over the life of the bonds.
    d. Both (b) and (c) are correct.

17. All *except* which of the following is an advantage of issuing stock? (pp. 552–553)
    a. It is less risky to the issuing corporation.
    b. It creates no liabilities.
    c. It generally results in higher earnings per share.
    d. It creates no interest expense that must be paid.

Quick Exercises

10-1. Federal United purchased equipment costing $88,000 on October 2, 2011, by paying a 30% cash down payment and signing a 9%, 120-day note payable for the balance. Federal United's year-end is December 31. (p. 526)

Requirement

1. Journalize the following:

a. The purchase of the equipment on October 2, 2011
b. The accrual of interest on December 31, 2011
c. Payment of the note on January 30, 2012

General Journal

	Date	Accounts	Debit	Credit
a.	Oct 2	Equipment	88,000	
		Cash		26,400
		Notes payable		61,600
		To record purchase of equipment.		

General Journal

	Date	Accounts	Debit	Credit
b.	Dec 31	Interest expense	1,386	
		Interest payable		1,386
		To accrue interest expense 10/2/08–12/31/08 ($61,600 × 9% × 90/360 = 1,386).		

General Journal

	Date	Accounts	Debit	Credit
c.	Jan 30	Notes payable	61,600	
		Interest payable	1,386	
		Interest expense	462	
		Cash		63,448
		To pay off the note payable plus interest ($61,600 × 9% × 30/360 = 462).		

10-2. Ideal Food Services had cash sales of $787,000 during the month of August 2011 and collected the 7% sales tax on these sales required by the state in which Ideal Food Services operates. (pp. 526–527)

Requirements

1. Journalize the cash sale and the sales tax on August 31.

General Journal

Date	Accounts	Debit	Credit
Aug 31	Cash	842,090	
	Sales		787,000
	Sales taxes payable		55,090
	To record cash sales including 7% sales tax.		

2. Journalize the September 15 transaction when the sales tax is remitted to the proper agency.

General Journal

Date	Accounts	Debit	Credit
Sep 15	Sales tax payable	55,090	
	Cash		55,090
	To record sales tax remittance.		

10-3. Freedom Vacuums warrants all of its products for one full year against any defect in manufacturing. Sales for 2010 and 2011 were $731,000 and $854,000, respectively. Freedom Vacuums expects warranty claims to run 4.5% of annual sales. Freedom paid $30,150 and $38,290, respectively, in 2010 and 2011 in warranty claims. (p. 529)

a. Compute Freedom's warranty expense for:

2010: $32,895 ($731,000 × .045)
2011: $38,430 ($854,000 × .045)

b. Compute the balance in Estimated Warranty Payable on December 31, 2011, assuming the January 1, 2010, balance in the account was $2,980.

$5,865 ($2,980 + $32,895 + $38,430 − $30,150 − $38,290)

Quick Practice Solutions | Chapter 10   **349**

10-4. Curtis Building Services has one employee, George North, who earns $36 per hour for a 40-hour workweek. He earns time and a half for all overtime hours. George has earned $89,200 in wages prior to the current week. From George's pay, Curtis Building Services deducts 20% for federal income tax, and 8% for FICA taxes (up to $90,000 per annum). The company also withholds $100 per week for his health insurance. The federal unemployment tax rate is 0.8% up to $7,000 of employee earnings per annum. The state unemployment tax rate is 5.4% up to $7,000 of employee earnings per annum. Curtis pays $100/week for medical insurance premiums for each employee. (p. 537)

Requirements

1. Compute the gross pay and the net pay for George North for the current week ending December 16, 2011. George worked 48 hours. Round all amounts to the nearest dollar.

Gross Pay: $1,872 = (40 × $36) + (8 × $36 × 1.5) = $1,440 + $432 = $1,872

Net Pay: FICA tax withheld = $64 = ($800 × 0.08)
Federal tax withheld = $374 = ($1,872 × .20)
Health insurance withheld = $100
Total deductions = $64 + $374 + $100 = $538
Net pay = $1,872 − $538 = $1,334

2. Journalize the payroll expense.

		General Journal		
Date	Accounts		Debit	Credit
Dec 18	Salary expense		1,872	
	FICA tax payable			64
	Employee income tax payable			374
	Health insurance payable			100
	Salary payable to employees			1,334
	To record payroll expenses.			

3. Journalize the payroll taxes imposed on Curtis Building Services.

		General Journal		
Date	Accounts		Debit	Credit
Dec 18	Payroll tax expense		64	
	FICA tax payable			64
	To record payroll tax expense.*			
	($90,000 − $89,200) × 0.08 = $64			

*Note: Maximum unemployment taxes have been incurred.

10-5. Use the data in Quick Exercise 10-4 to record the following: (p. 537)
   a. Journalize the payment of payroll to the employee on December 16, 2011.
   b. Journalize the payment of the income tax withheld and FICA for the employee and employer on December 16, 2011.
   c. Journalize the payment of the health insurance premiums withheld.

General Journal

	Date	Accounts	Debit	Credit
a.	Dec 18	Salary payable to employees	1,334	
		Cash		1,334
		To record payroll paid to employees.		

General Journal

	Date	Accounts	Debit	Credit
b.	Dec 18	Employee income tax payable	374	
		FICA tax payable	128	
		Cash		502
		To record payment of health insurance premium.		

General Journal

	Date	Accounts	Debit	Credit
c.	Dec 18	Health insurance payable	100	
		Cash		100
		To record payment of health insurance premium.		

10-6. For each of the following independent situations, state whether the bonds were issued at a premium, at a discount, or at par. (p. 542)

   a. Bonds with a face value of $50,000 were issued for $53,000. Premium
   b. Bonds with a contract rate of 8% were issued to yield 7.5%. Premium
   c. Bonds with a face value of $75,000 were issued for $75,000. Par
   d. Bonds with a contract rate of 8.25% were issued to yield 8.75%. Discount
   e. Bonds with a face value of $110,000 were issued for $106,000. Discount

10-7. Fox Company issued 10-year, 10%, $1,000,000 bonds on January 1, 2011. The bonds pay interest every June 30 and December 31. The bonds were issued for $1,065,000. Fox Company uses straight-line amortization for any discount or premium amortization. (pp. 547–550)

Requirement

1. Journalize the following:

    a. Issue the bonds on January 1, 2011.
    b. Record the interest payment and amortize the premium or discount on June 30, 2011.

	Date	Accounts	Debit	Credit
a.	Jan 1	Cash	1,065,000	
		Bonds payable		1,000,000
		Premium on bonds payable		65,000

General Journal

	Date	Accounts	Debit	Credit
b.	Jun 30	Interest expense	46,750	
		Premium on bonds payable	3,250	
		Cash		50,000

2. What is the carrying value of the bonds on June 30, 2011?

Carrying value = $1,000,000 + ($65,000 − $3,250)
= $1,061,750.

10-8. On April 1, 2011, Needy Company issued $3,000,000 of 8%, 10-year bonds dated April 1, 2011, with interest payments made each October 1 and April 1. The bonds are issued at 95. Needy Company amortizes any premium or discount using the straight-line method. (pp. 547–550)

Requirement

1. Journalize the following transactions:

a. April 1, 2011, issuance of the bonds.
b. October 1, 2011, payment of interest and the amortization of any discount or premium.
c. December 31, 2011, accrual of interest and the amortization of any premium or discount.

General Journal

	Date	Accounts	Debit	Credit
a.	Apr 1	Cash	2,850,000	
		Discount on bonds payable	150,000	
		Bonds payable		3,000,000

General Journal

	Date	Accounts	Debit	Credit
b.	Oct 1	Interest expense	127,500	
		Discount on bonds payable		7,500
		Cash		120,000

General Journal

	Date	Accounts	Debit	Credit
c.	Dec 31	Interest expense	63,750	
		Discount on bonds payable		3,750
		Interest payable		60,000

Calculations

a. $3,000,000 × 0.95 = $2,850,000
   $3,000,000 − $2,850,000 = $150,000

b. $3,000,000 × 0.08 × 6/12 = $120,000
   $150,000 × 6/120 months = $7,500

c. $3,000,000 × 0.08 × 3/12 = $60,000
   $150,000 × 3/120 months = $3,750

Do It Yourself! Question 1 Solutions

Requirement

1. **Journalize all of Nitro's transactions in the month of October 2011.**

During October 2011, Nitro sold goods for $10,000 cash. These goods cost $8,000 to manufacture. Nitro is required by law to collect 8% sales tax on all sales.

	Cash ($10,000 × [1 + 8%])	10,800	
	Sales revenue		10,000
	Sales tax payable ($10,000 × 8%)		800
	COGS	8,000	
	Inventory		8,000

Nitro estimates warranty costs to be 1% of the selling price.

	Warranty expense ($10,000 × 1%)	100	
	Warranty payable		100

During October 2011, Nitro made $60 of repairs under warranty (paid in cash to a repair service).

	Warranty Payable	60	
	Cash		60

On October 31, 2011, Nitro remitted all sales tax collected in October to the state government.

	Sales tax payable ($10,000 × 8%)	800	
	Cash		800

Do It Yourself! Question 2 Solutions

Requirement

1. Show the presentation of this note on Pulter's December 31, 2011, balance sheet.

> Payments already made = $100 × 2
> = $200
>
> $2,000 − $200 = $1,800 to be repaid.
>
> 12 × $100 = $1,200 = current portion.
>
> $1,800 − $1,200 = $600 = long-term portion.

Interest payable only relates to the month of December (because November's interest expense was paid on December 1).

> Interest payable = $1,800 × 10% × 1/12
> = $15.

Current Liabilities	
Current portion of long-term debt	$1,200
Interest payable	$ 15
Long-Term Liabilities	
Notes payable/long-term debt (net of current portion)	$ 600

Do It Yourself! Question 3 Solutions

Requirement

1. For a normal week, journalize the following transactions:

a. **Cash payment of employee salari**

Salary expense (gross pay)		200,000	
Employee income tax payable ($200,000 × 20%)			40,000
FICA tax payable ($200,000 × 8%)			16,000
401K plan contributions payable ($200,000 × 3%)			6,000
Union dues payable ($200,000 × 1%)			2,0000
Cash (net/take home pay)			136,000

b. Oxygen's payroll taxes.

Payroll tax expense (to balance)		28,000	
FICA tax payable ($200,000 × 8%) (matching)			16,000
Unemployment tax payable ($200,000 × 6%)			12,000

c. Oxygen's payment of all payroll taxes.

Employee income tax payable		40,000	
FICA tax payable ($16,000 + $16,000) (matching)		32,000	
Unemployment tax payable		12,000	
Cash (to balance)			84,000

d. Oxygen's payment of union dues.

Union dues payable		2,000	
Cash			2,000

e. Oxygen's payment of 401K plan contributions.

Pension contributions payable		6,000	
Cash			6,000

Do It Yourself! Question 4 Solutions

Bonds Payable (straight-line amortization)

Requirements

1. Are these bonds issued at a discount or premium?

These bonds were issued at a **discount**.

2. Journalize Circle's issuance of the bonds on January 1, 2011.

Cash	19,337	
Discount on bonds payable (to balance)	663	
Bonds payable		20,000

3. Journalize Circle's first two interest payments on June 30, 2011, and December 31, 2011.

The entry for both June 30, 2011, and December 31, 2011, would be the same:

Interest expense	1,566	
Discount on bonds payable ($663/4)		166
Cash (20,000 × 14%/2)		1,400

4. Show how the bonds would appear on Circle's December 31, 2011, balance sheet.

Bonds payable	$20,000
– Discount	(331)
Bonds payable (net)	$19,669

The Power of Practice

For more practice using the skills learned in this chapter, visit MyAccountingLab. There you will find algorithmically generated questions that are based on these Demo Docs and your main textbook's Review and Assess Your Progress sections.

Go to MyAccountingLab and follow these steps:

1. Direct your URL to www.myaccountinglab.com.
2. Log in using your name and password.
3. Click the MyAccountingLab link.
4. Click Study Plan in the left navigation bar.
5. From the table of contents, select Chapter 10, Current Liabilities, Payroll, and Long-Term Liabilities.
6. Click a link to work tutorial exercises.

11 Corporations: Paid-In Capital and the Balance Sheet

WHAT YOU PROBABLY ALREADY KNOW

You probably already know that you can purchase shares of a company's stock as an investment. CNBC shows the trading price of various stocks as they take place and the daily prices are reported in your financial newspapers. Much of the trading taking place is between investors rather than from the issuing corporation.

One way that a corporation issues its shares of stock is in an initial public offering (IPO). A recent popular IPO is Google. Google was doing business for six years before its founders took the company public in August 2004. The IPO provided investors an opportunity to purchase Google stock at a stated offer price of $85 a share. The market price of the stock rose quickly in trading and a year and a half after the IPO, the stock traded at over $300 per share. The cash received from the sale of the Google stock and the shareholders' equity interest were recorded on the books of Google Corporation. In this chapter, we will see how to account for the equity transactions of a corporation.

Learning Objectives/Success Keys

1 Identify the distinguishing characteristics of a corporation.

As a **separate legal entity**, a corporation can enter into contracts, own assets in its own name, and be sued. The owners of the corporation are the stockholders. Shares of stock can be transferred to others without affecting the operation of the business. ***No mutual agency*** means that the owners of a corporation (stockholders) cannot commit or obligate the corporation. Stockholders are not personally liable for the obligations of the corporation. The most that a stockholder can lose is the amount invested. This is known as **limited liability**. These are some of the characteristics of a corporation. *Review these and other characteristics in your textbook, and take note of Exhibit 11-1 (p. 596) for a list of advantages and disadvantages of the corporate form of business.*

2 Describe the two sources of stockholders' equity and the classes of stock.

The two basic sources of stockholders' equity are paid-in capital (which represents amounts received from the stockholders) and retained earnings (which is capital earned by profitable operations).

Stock can be classed as common or preferred, which gives the stockholders varying preferences in voting and dividend rights.

Review Exhibit 11-3 (p. 597) in the text to see where the capital and types of stock are placed in the stockholders' equity section of the balance sheet.

3 Journalize the issuance of stock and prepare the stockholders' equity section of a corporation's balance sheet.

When a company incorporates, the **par** or **stated value**, if any, will be indicated in the articles of incorporation. It is usually a nominal amount assigned to a share of stock that represents the minimum legal stated capital and does not indicate the value or worth of the stock. When the stock is sold by the corporation, the Common Stock account is credited for the par or stated value. Usually, the stock is sold above par, which is considered a premium. The excess of the stock sales price over the par or stated value is the amount credited to the **Paid-In Capital in Excess of Par** account. *Review the accounting for stock issuances under "Issuing Common Stock" in the main text.*

The equity accounts are shown in the Stockholders' Equity section in the following order:

- Preferred Stock

- Common Stock

- Paid-In Capital in Excess of Par

- Retained Earnings

Review the Stockholders' Equity section of the balance sheet in Exhibit 11-6 (p. 604).

4 Illustrate Retained earnings transactions.

Companies must close their temporary accounts (revenues, expenses, gains, losses and Dividends) at the end of each accounting period and update retained earnings. *Review the Retained Earnings section in the text (p. 608) to remind yourself of how this process works.*

5 Account for cash dividends.

If the board of directors declares dividends, Retained Earnings is debited and Dividends Payable is credited. On the date of payment, the Liability is debited (reduced); Cash is also credited (reduced). *Read "Account for Cash Dividends" in the main text to review the dividend dates and learn the difference between cumulative and noncumulative preferred stock.*

6 Use different stock values in decision making.

Market value is the current price at which the stock is being offered for sale in the market. This value is of prime importance to investors. **Book value** indicates the amount of net assets that each common shareholder would receive if the assets were sold for the amount reported on the balance sheet. *Review the calculations of book value under "Different Values of Stock" in the main text.*

7 Evaluate return on assets and return on stockholders' equity.

Ratios to assess profitability include the rate of return on total assets and return on stockholders' equity. The rate of return on total assets indicates the amount of profitability per dollar of assets invested (net income + interest expense/average total assets). The rate of return on common stockholders' equity indicates the amount of profitability per dollar of common equity (net income – preferred dividends/average common stockholders' equity). Higher returns for both ratios are more favorable.

8 Account for the income tax of a corporation.

There may be differences between pretax income on the income statement and taxable income on the income tax return for a corporation. The income tax expense on the income statement is based on the pretax income on the income statement. However, the income tax payable liability on the balance sheet is based on the taxable income on the tax return. The difference between these two amounts results in a *deferred tax asset* or *deferred tax liability*.

Demo Doc 1

Common Stock

Learning Objectives 2, 3, 6, 7

Jack Inc. had the following information at December 31, 2011:

Stockholders' Equity	
Common stock, 1,600,000 authorized, 350,000 issued and outstanding shares	$ 437,500
Additional Paid-in capital	787,500
Retained earnings	4,200,000
Total Stockholders' Equity	$5,425,000

Requirements

1. What are Jack's two main sources of corporate capital?

2. What is the par value per share of the common stock?

3. On average, what was the original issue price per share of common stock?

4. On February 12, 2012, Jack issued another 20,000 common shares for $5 cash per share. Journalize this transaction.

5. Jack earned net income of $150,000 and paid no dividends in 2012. There were no other equity transactions in 2012. Prepare the stockholders' equity section of Jack's balance sheet on December 31, 2012.

6. Calculate Jack's return on equity and book value per share for 2012.

Demo Doc 1 Solutions

Requirement 1

What are Jack's two main sources of corporate capital?

[2] Describe the two sources of stockholders' equity and the classes of stock.

| Part 1 | Part 2 | Part 3 | Part 4 | Part 5 | Part 6 | Demo Doc Complete |

Corporate capital is another term for shareholder's equity.

Jack has paid-in capital. This is money that has been received from the stockholders. Jack also has retained earnings. This represents profits earned on the stockholders' behalf (that have not yet been distributed as dividends).

Every corporation has these two sources of capital.

Requirement 2

What is the par value per share of the common stock?

[6] Use different stock values in decision making

| Part 1 | Part 2 | Part 3 | Part 4 | Part 5 | Part 6 | Demo Doc Complete |

Common Stock and Preferred Stock accounts hold *only* the par value of the *issued* shares. So the $437,500 in the Common Stock account represents the par value of *all* the issued shares.

$$\text{Par value per share} = \frac{\text{Common stock balance}}{\text{Number of issued common shares}}$$

$$\text{Par value per share} = \frac{\$437,500}{350,000 \text{ shares}}$$

$$= \$1.25 \text{ per share}$$

Requirement 3

On average, what was the original issue price per share of common stock?

[6] Use different stock values in decision making

| Part 1 | Part 2 | **Part 3** | Part 4 | Part 5 | Part 6 | Demo Doc Complete |

When stock is issued for cash, the Cash account increases (a debit) for cash received. The Common Stock account increases (a credit) for the par value and the excess is Additional Paid-In Capital. Because the selling price per share is almost always more than the par value, this excess balancing amount to Additional Paid-In Capital is usually an increase (a credit).

We know that total debits must equal total credits for any transaction. In this case, the debit is the cash received and the credits are the increases to Common Stock and Additional Paid-In Capital. This means that:

Cash received from share issuance = Common stock + Additional Paid-in capital

So the total cash received from issuance of the common shares is:

$1.25 par × 350,000 shares = $437,500
$437,500 + $787,500 = $1,225,000

This amount represents all 350,000 issued shares.

$1,225,000/350,000 shares = $3.50 cash received per share

The balancing credit to Additional Paid-In Capital is ($3.50 received − $1.25 par) $2.25 × 350,000 shares = $787,500 additional cash paid.

Requirement 4

On February 12, 2012, Jack issued another 20,000 common shares for $5 cash per share. Journalize this transaction.

| Part 1 | Part 2 | Part 3 | **Part 4** | Part 5 | Part 6 | Demo Doc Complete |

Cash increases (a debit) by $5 × 20,000 = $100,000.
Common Stock increases (a credit) by the par value of the new shares:

$1.25 × 20,000 = $25,000

Additional Paid-In Capital is the excess cash paid:

($5 − $1.25) × $3.75
$3.75 × 20,000 shares = $75,000

This is the balancing amount in the journal entry.

Cash ($5 × 20,000)	100,000	
Common stock ($1.25 × 20,000)		25,000
Additional paid-in capital (to balance)		75,000

③ Journalize the issuance of stock and Prepare the stockholders' equity section of a corporation's balance sheet

3 Journalize the issuance of stock and Prepare the stockholders' equity section of a corporate balance sheet

Requirement 5

Jack earned net income of $150,000 and paid no dividends in 2012. There were no other equity transactions in 2012. Prepare the stockholders' equity section of Jack's balance sheet on December 31, 2012.

| Part 1 | Part 2 | Part 3 | Part 4 | **Part 5** | Part 6 | Demo Doc Complete |

Because of the stock issuance in Requirement 4, the number of outstanding common shares has increased to:

$$350{,}000 \text{ shares} + 20{,}000 \text{ shares} = 370{,}000 \text{ shares}$$

This must be shown for Common Stock as part of its descriptive line on the balance sheet.

The dollar amount in the Common Stock account has increased to:

$$\$437{,}500 + \$25{,}000 = \$462{,}500$$

The other impact of this transaction on stockholders' equity was to increase Additional Paid-In Capital to:

$$\$787{,}500 + \$75{,}000 = \$862{,}500$$

The net income earned by Jack will increase Retained Earnings to:

$$\$4{,}200{,}000 + \$150{,}000 = \$4{,}350{,}000$$

These new amounts create a new total stockholders' equity of $5,675,000.

Stockholders' Equity	
Common stock, 1,600,000 authorized, 350,000 issued and outstanding shares	$ 462,500
Additional Paid-in capital	862,500
Retained earnings	4,350,000
Total Stockholders' Equity	$5,675,000

Demo Doc 1 Solutions | Chapter 11 365

7 Evaluate return on assets and return on stockholders' equity

Requirement 6

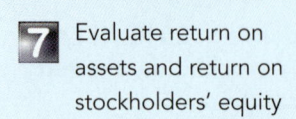

Calculate Jack's return on equity and book value per share for 2012.

| Part 1 | Part 2 | Part 3 | Part 4 | Part 5 | **Part 6** | Demo Doc Complete |

$$\text{Return on Stockholders' Equity} = \frac{\text{Net income} - \text{Preferred dividends}}{\text{Average common Stockholders' Equity}}$$

Common stockholders' equity means the total stockholders' equity less the preferred equity (that is, less any preferred stock or any additional paid-in capital relating to preferred stock).

Average common stockholders' equity is the *mathematical average* of the beginning and ending balances in Common Stockholders' Equity (that is, [beginning balance + ending balance]/2).

So using the data from this question:

$$\text{Return on Stockholders' Equity} = \frac{\$150,000 - \$0}{(\$5,542,000 + \$5,675,000)/2}$$

$$\text{Return on Stockholders' Equity} = 0.027$$

$$= 2.7\%$$

$$\text{Book value per share} = \frac{\text{Common Stockholders's Equity}}{\text{Number of common shares outstanding}}$$

Using the data from this question:

$$\text{Book value per share} = \frac{\$5,675,000}{370,000 \text{ shares}}$$

$$= \$15.34 \text{ per share}$$

| Part 1 | Part 2 | Part 3 | Part 4 | Part 5 | Part 6 | **Demo Doc Complete** |

366 Chapter 11 | Demo Doc 1 Solutions

Demo Doc 2

Preferred Stock

Learning Objectives 2, 4, 5

Jill Co. issued 25,000, 6%, $100 par cumulative preferred shares on January 1, 2011, for $120 cash per share. Jill had never issued preferred shares before this date. Jill paid the following cash dividends (in total, to *all* shares):

2011	$120,000
2012	$160,000
2013	$200,000

Requirements

1. How do preferred shares differ from common shares?

2. Journalize the issuance of the preferred shares on January 1, 2011, and the payment of the preferred share dividends in 2011 (assuming the dividends were declared and paid on the same day).

3. How much in dividends is Jill supposed to pay to the preferred shareholders each year?

4. Did Jill pay all of the required dividends in each year? If not, what happens to the amount not paid? How much in dividends did the preferred and common shareholders receive each year?

5. How does the payment of dividends impact Retained earnings?

Demo Doc 2 Solutions

2 Describe the two sources of stockholders' equity and the classes of stock

Requirement 1

How do preferred shares differ from common shares?

| Part 1 | Part 2 | Part 3 | Part 4 | Part 5 | Demo Doc Complete |

Common shares have ownership in a corporation. This ownership is accompanied by the right to vote at shareholder meetings. Common shares may or may not receive dividends.

Preferred shares usually do not have the right to vote. However, they are supposed to receive regular dividends, and must receive all dividends to which they are entitled before the common stockholders can receive dividends.

Requirement 2

3 Journalize the issuance of stock and Prepare the stockholders' equity section of a corporation's balance sheet

Journalize the issuance of the preferred shares on January 1, 2011, and the payment of the preferred share dividends in 2011 (assuming the dividends were declared and paid on the same day).

| Part 1 | Part 2 | Part 3 | Part 4 | Part 5 | Demo Doc Complete |

5 Account for cash dividends

The issuance of preferred shares is the same as the issuance of common shares, except for the account title.

Cash is increased (a debit) by:

$$\$120 \times 25{,}000 = \$3{,}000{,}000$$

Preferred Stock is increased (a credit) by the par value of the new shares:

$$\$100 \times 25{,}000 = \$2{,}500{,}000$$

Additional Paid-In Capital is the excess cash paid:

$$(\$120 - \$100 \text{ par}) = \$20 \times 25{,}000 \text{ shares}$$
$$= \$500{,}000$$

This is the balancing amount in the journal entry.

	Cash ($120 × 25,000)	3,000,000	
	Additional Paid-in capital (to balance)		500,000
	Preferred stock ($100 × 25,000)		2,500,000

When dividends are paid, Retained Earnings is decreased because the shareholders are removing some of their capital from the company. So Retained Earnings is decreased (a debit) by $120,000.

Cash is also decreased (a credit) by $120,000.

| Retained earnings | 120,000 | |
| Cash | | 120,000 |

It is also acceptable to debit the Dividends account instead of Retained Earnings. Then the Dividends account is closed to Retained Earnings at the end of the accounting period. (See Requirement 5)

Requirement 3

How much in dividends is Jill supposed to pay to the preferred shareholders each year?

| Part 1 | Part 2 | **Part 3** | Part 4 | Part 5 | Demo Doc Complete |

Each year, every preferred share is *supposed* to receive:

"Required" preferred share dividends = Par value per share × Dividend percentage

First, we should calculate the "required" annual dividends per share. In this case, it is:

$$\$100 \times 6\% = \$6 \text{ per share}$$

Because there are 25,000 outstanding preferred shares, this works out to $6 × 25,000 = **$150,000** in dividends per year for all preferred shares.

Requirement 4

Did Jill pay all of the required dividends in each year? If not, what happens to the amount not paid? How much in dividends did the preferred and common shareholders receive each year?

| Part 1 | Part 2 | Part 3 | **Part 4** | Part 5 | Demo Doc Complete |

2011

Because $120,000 is less than the "required" $150,000, we know that Jill did *not* pay all of the required dividends in 2008.

The preferred shares only received:

$$\$120,000/25,000 \text{ shares} = \$4.80 \text{ per share}$$

The difference of $150,000 − $120,000 = $30,000 is <u>dividends in arrears</u>. This amount is *not* recorded in a transaction because it has not yet been declared and, therefore, is not a liability. Dividends in arrears do *not* appear on the balance sheet. However, they are disclosed in a *note* to the financial statements.

Because the full $150,000 was not paid, the entire $120,000 goes to the preferred shareholders as dividends. The common shareholders get no dividends in 2011.

2012

For 2012, Jill must not only pay the $150,000 annual "requirement" but first must also "catch up" on the dividends in arrears of $30,000 from 2011.

So in order to completely fulfill her obligation to the preferred shareholders, Jill must pay $30,000 + $150,000 = $180,000 in dividends to the preferred shareholders.

Because $160,000 is less than $180,000, we know that Jill did *not* pay all of the required dividends in 2012.

The difference of $180,000 − $160,000 = $20,000 is <u>dividends in arrears</u>.

Because the full $180,000 was not paid, the entire $160,000 goes to the preferred shareholders as dividends. The common shareholders get no dividends in 2012.

2013

In 2013, Jill is *supposed* to pay the annual $150,000 of dividends *plus* the $20,000 dividends in arrears from 2012 for a total of $170,000.

Because $200,000 is greater than $170,000, we know that Jill did pay all of the required dividends in 2013.

The $170,000 shown above goes to the preferred shareholders, while the rest ($200,000 − $170,000 = $30,000) goes to the common shareholders.

Requirement 5

How does the payment of dividends impact Retained earnings?

Part 1	Part 2	Part 3	Part 4	**Part 5**	Demo Doc Complete

When dividends are paid, the Retained earnings account is debited. This causes a decrease in Retained earnings, and also in total equity. This is true for all dividends, both common and preferred.

Part 1	Part 2	Part 3	Part 4	Part 5	**Demo Doc Complete**

4 Illustrate Retained earnings transactions

Demo Doc 3

Learning Objectives 1, 8

Joe Danson owns all outstanding common shares of Joseph Corp. The corporation earned net income before tax of $80,000 in 2011 and has an income tax rate of 40%.

Requirements

1. Is Joe Danson personally liable for the income taxes owed by Joseph Corp.?

2. Calculate the amount of income tax expense that will appear on Joseph Corp.'s 2011 income statement.

Demo Doc 3 Solutions

Requirement 1

1 Identify the distinguishing characteristics of a corporation

Is Joe Danson personally liable for the income taxes owed by Joseph Corp.?

| Part 1 | Part 2 | Demo Doc Complete |

Corporations are liable for *their own* taxes. Even as the sole owner, Joe is not liable for the taxes of the corporation.

Requirement 2

8 Account for the income tax of a corporation

Calculate the amount of income tax expense that will appear on Joseph Corp.'s 2011 income statement.

| Part 1 | **Part 2** | Demo Doc Complete |

$$\begin{aligned} \text{Income tax expense} &= \text{Net income before tax} \times \text{Tax rate} \\ &= \$80{,}000 \times 40\% \\ &= \$32{,}000 \end{aligned}$$

| Part 1 | Part 2 | **Demo Doc Complete** |

Quick Practice Questions

True/False

_____ 1. Stockholders in a corporation are personally liable for the debts of the corporation.

_____ 2. Most corporations have continuous lives regardless of changes in the ownership of their stock.

_____ 3. Par value is an arbitrary amount assigned by a company to a share of its stock.

_____ 4. A credit balance in Retained Earnings is referred to as a deficit.

_____ 5. When a corporation sells par value stock at an amount greater than par value, other income is reported on the income statement.

_____ 6. Dividends become a liability of the corporation on the payment date.

_____ 7. The owners of cumulative preferred stock must receive all dividends in arrears plus the current year's dividends before the common stockholders get a dividend.

_____ 8. A stock's market price is the price for which a person could buy or sell a share of the stock.

_____ 9. The book value of a stock is the amount of stockholders' equity on the company's books for each share of its stock.

_____ 10. The rate of return on total assets measures a company's success in using assets to earn income for those financing the business.

Multiple Choice

1. What is the document called that is used by a state to grant permission to form a corporation?
   a. Charter
   b. Proxy
   c. Stock certificate
   d. Bylaw agreement

2. Which of the following statements describing a corporation is true?
   a. Stockholders are the creditors of a corporation.
   b. A corporation is subject to greater governmental regulation than a proprietorship or a partnership.
   c. When ownership of a corporation changes, the corporation terminates.
   d. Stockholders own the business and manage its day-to-day operations.

3. Which of the following best describes paid-in capital?
   a. Investments by the stockholders of a corporation
   b. Investments by the creditors of a corporation
   c. Capital that the corporation has earned through profitable operations
   d. All of the above

4. Which of the following best describes retained earnings?
   a. It is classified as a liability on the corporate balance sheet.
   b. It does not appear on any financial statement.
   c. It represents capital that the corporation has earned through profitable operations.
   d. It represents investments by the stockholders of a corporation.

5. What individual(s) has the authority to obligate the corporation to pay dividends?
   a. Total stockholders
   b. The board of directors
   c. The president of the company
   d. The chief executive officer

6. A corporation issues 1,800 shares of $10 par value common stock in exchange for land with a current market value of $23,000. How would this be recorded in the Land account?
   a. Debited for $23,000
   b. Credited for $18,000
   c. Credited for $20,000
   d. Debited for $18,000

7. Which of the following would be recorded for the issuance of 55,000 shares of no-par common stock at $13.50 per share?
   a. Credit to Paid-In Capital in Excess of No-Par Value—Common for $742,500
   b. Credit to Common Stock for $742,500
   c. Credit to Cash for $742,500
   d. Debit to Paid-In Capital in Excess of No-Par Value—Common for $742,500

8. Which of the following is true for dividends?
   a. Dividends are a distribution of cash to the stockholders.
   b. Dividends decrease both the assets and the total stockholders' equity of the corporation.
   c. Dividends increase retained earnings.
   d. Both (a) and (b) are correct.

9. Dividends on cumulative preferred stock of $2,500 are in arrears for 2011. During 2012, the total dividends declared amount to $10,000. There are 6,000 shares of $10 par, 10% cumulative preferred stock outstanding and 10,000 shares of $5 par common stock outstanding. What is the total amount of dividends payable to each class of stock in 2012?
   a. $5,000 to preferred, $5,000 to common
   b. $6,000 to preferred, $4,000 to common
   c. $8,500 to preferred, $1,500 to common
   d. $10,000 to preferred, $0 to common

10. Which of the following is true about dividends in arrears?
    a. They are a liability on the balance sheet.
    b. They are dividends passed on cumulative preferred stock.
    c. They are dividends passed on noncumulative preferred stock.
    d. They are dividends passed on common stock.

Quick Exercises

11-1. Journalize the following transactions:

a. Firm Body Corporation sells 12,000 shares of $10 par common stock for $13.00 per share.

General Journal				
Date	Accounts		Debit	Credit

b. Firm Body Corporation sells 5,000 shares of $50 par, 10% cumulative preferred stock for $59 per share.

General Journal				
Date	Accounts		Debit	Credit

c. Received a building with a market value of $115,000 and issued 6,400 shares of $10 par common stock in exchange.

General Journal				
Date	Accounts		Debit	Credit

d. Firm Body Corporation reports net income of $66,000 at the end of its first year of operations.

General Journal				
Date	Accounts		Debit	Credit

11-2. The following is a list of stockholders equity accounts appearing on the balance sheet for O'Neil Corporation on December 31, 2011:

Common stock, $10 par value	$300,000
Paid-in capital in excess of par—Common	200,000
Retained earnings	225,000
Preferred stock, $50 par value	125,000
Paid-in capital in excess of par—Preferred	30,000

Determine the following:

a. How many shares of preferred stock have been issued?

b. What was the average issuance price of the preferred stock per share?

c. How many shares of common stock have been issued?

d. What is total paid-in capital?

e. What is total stockholders' equity?

11-3. Bowen Corporation organized on January 1, 2011. Bowen Corporation has authorization for 90,000 shares of $10 par value common stock. As of December 31, 2011, Bowen has issued 50,000 shares of its common stock at an average issuance price of $15. Bowen also has authorization for 50,000 shares of 5%, $50 par value, noncumulative preferred stock. As of December 31, 2011, Bowen has issued 12,000 shares of preferred stock at an average issuance price of $68 per share. Bowen reports net income of $47,000 for its first year of operations ended December 31, 2011.

Requirement

1. Prepare the stockholders' equity section of the balance sheet for Bowen Corporation dated December 31, 2011.

11-4. Following is the stockholders' equity section of the balance sheet for Watson Corporation as of December 1, 2012:

Preferred stock, $100 par, 6% cumulative, 10,000 shares authorized, 7,500 shares issued	$ 750,000
Common stock, $10 par, 200,000 shares authorized, 130,000 shares issued	1,300,000
Paid-in capital in excess of par—Common	520,000
Total paid-in capital	$2,570,000
Retained earnings	450,000
Total Stockholders' Equity	$3,020,000

Watson Corporation reports the following transactions for December 2012:

Dec. 5 Declared the required cash dividend on the preferred stock and a $0.40 dividend on the common stock.

20 Paid the dividends declared on December 5.

Requirements

1. Journalize the transactions.

	General Journal		
Date	Accounts	Debit	Credit

	General Journal		
Date	Accounts	Debit	Credit

2. What is the total stockholders' equity after posting the entries?

11-5. Sparks Corporation has gathered the following data for the current year:

Net income	$40,000
Interest expense	6,000
Income tax expense	12,500
Preferred dividends	3,600

Balance Sheet Data	Beginning of Year	End of Year
Current assets	$ 68,000	$ 81,000
Current liabilities	41,000	39,000
Plant assets	340,000	365,000
Long-term liabilities	100,000	90,000
Common Stockholders' Equity	217,000	267,000
Preferred Stockholders' Equity	50,000	50,000

Requirements

1. Calculate return on assets.

2. Calculate return on equity.

3. Comment on how these measures are used.

Do It Yourself! Question 1

Common Stock

Dinner Co. had the following information at December 31, 2011:

Stockholders' Equity	
Common stock, 500,000 authorized, 50,000 issued and outstanding shares	$100,000
Additional Paid-in capital	50,000
Retained earnings	400,000
Total Stockholders' Equity	$550,000

Requirements

1. What is the par value per share of the common stock?

2. On average, what was the original issue price per share of the common stock?

3. On January 9, 2012, Dinner issued another 10,000 common shares for $4 cash per share. Journalize this transaction.

General Journal			
Date	Accounts	Debit	Credit

Sidebar objectives:
- 6 Use different stock values in decision making
- 6 Use different stock values in decision making
- 3 Journalize the issuance of stock and prepare the stockholders' equity section of a corporation's balance sheet

Do It Yourself! Question 2

Preferred Stock

Lunch Corp. issued 5,000, 8%, $20 par cumulative preferred shares on January 1, 2011, for $25 cash per share. Lunch had never had preferred shares before this date. On December 31, 2011, Lunch paid $5,000 in cash dividends to its shareholders. On December 31, 2012, Lunch paid $15,000 in cash dividends to its shareholders.

Requirements

3 Journalize the issuance of stock and prepare the stockholders' equity section of a corporation's balance sheet

1. Journalize the issuance of the preferred shares on January 1, 2011.

Date	Accounts	Debit	Credit

General Journal

5 Account for cash dividends

2. How much in dividends is Lunch supposed to pay to the preferred shareholders each year?

5 Account for cash dividends

3. How much of the $5,000 paid as dividends in 2011 went to the preferred and common shareholders?

5 Account for cash dividends

4. How much of the $15,000 paid as dividends in 2012 went to the preferred and common shareholders?

Quick Practice Solutions

True/False

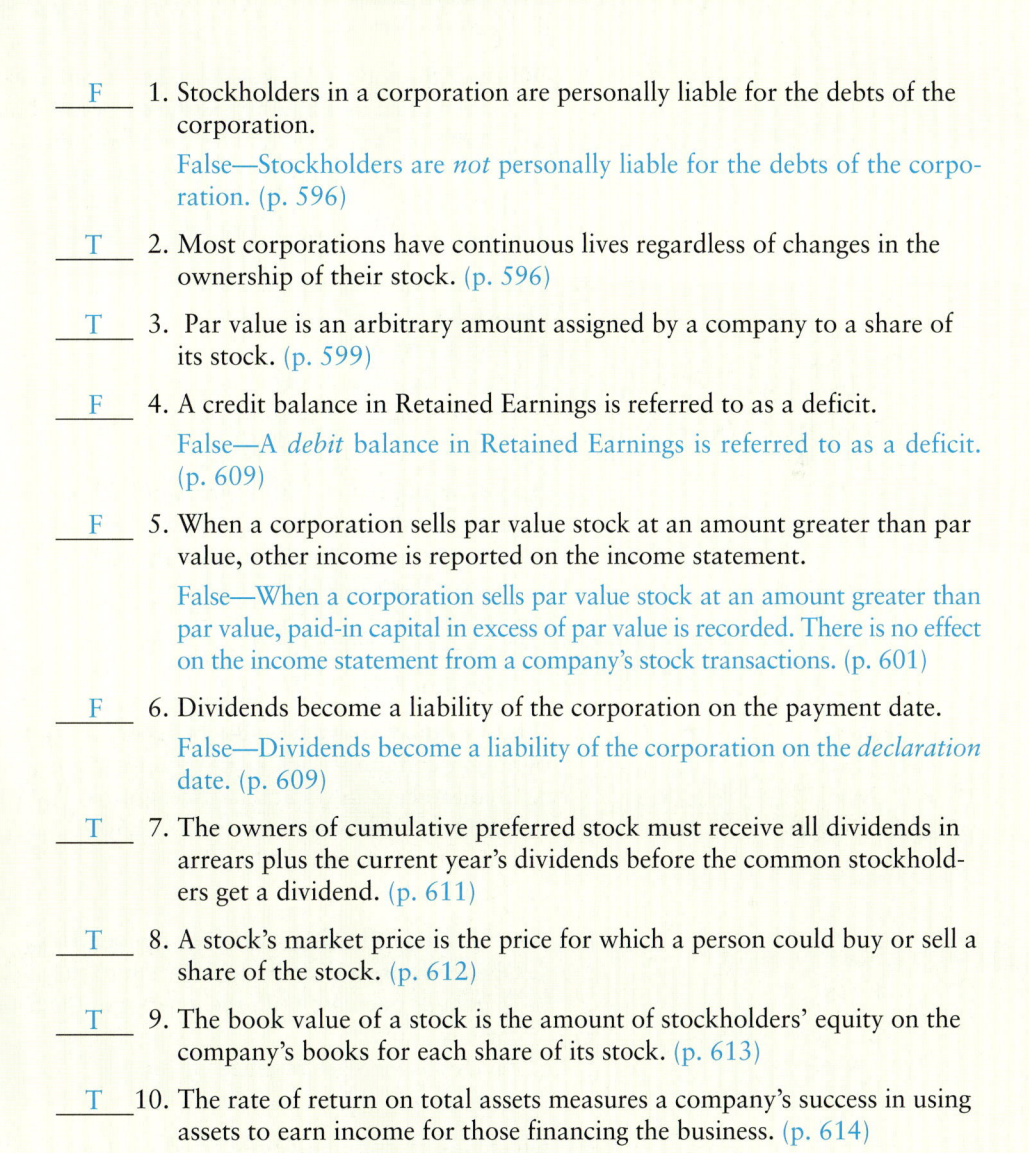

__F__ 1. Stockholders in a corporation are personally liable for the debts of the corporation.

False—Stockholders are *not* personally liable for the debts of the corporation. (p. 596)

__T__ 2. Most corporations have continuous lives regardless of changes in the ownership of their stock. (p. 596)

__T__ 3. Par value is an arbitrary amount assigned by a company to a share of its stock. (p. 599)

__F__ 4. A credit balance in Retained Earnings is referred to as a deficit.

False—A *debit* balance in Retained Earnings is referred to as a deficit. (p. 609)

__F__ 5. When a corporation sells par value stock at an amount greater than par value, other income is reported on the income statement.

False—When a corporation sells par value stock at an amount greater than par value, paid-in capital in excess of par value is recorded. There is no effect on the income statement from a company's stock transactions. (p. 601)

__F__ 6. Dividends become a liability of the corporation on the payment date.

False—Dividends become a liability of the corporation on the *declaration* date. (p. 609)

__T__ 7. The owners of cumulative preferred stock must receive all dividends in arrears plus the current year's dividends before the common stockholders get a dividend. (p. 611)

__T__ 8. A stock's market price is the price for which a person could buy or sell a share of the stock. (p. 612)

__T__ 9. The book value of a stock is the amount of stockholders' equity on the company's books for each share of its stock. (p. 613)

__T__ 10. The rate of return on total assets measures a company's success in using assets to earn income for those financing the business. (p. 614)

Multiple Choice

1. What is the document called that is used by a state to grant permission to form a corporation? (p. 599)
   a. Charter
   b. Proxy
   c. Stock certificate
   d. Bylaw agreement

2. Which of the following statements describing a corporation is true? (p. 596)
   a. Stockholders are the creditors of a corporation.
   b. A corporation is subject to greater governmental regulation than a proprietorship or a partnership.
   c. When ownership of a corporation changes, the corporation terminates.
   d. Stockholders own the business and manage its day-to-day operations.

3. Which of the following best describes paid-in capital? (p. 597)
   a. Investments by the stockholders of a corporation
   b. Investments by the creditors of a corporation
   c. Capital that the corporation has earned through profitable operations
   d. All of the above

4. Which of the following best describes retained earnings? (p. 597)
   a. It is classified as a liability on the corporate balance sheet.
   b. It does not appear on any financial statement.
   c. It represents capital that the corporation has earned through profitable operations.
   d. It represents investments by the stockholders of a corporation.

5. What individual(s) has the authority to obligate the corporation to pay dividends? (p. 609)
   a. Total stockholders
   b. The board of directors
   c. The president of the company
   d. The chief executive officer

6. A corporation issues 1,800 shares of $10 par value common stock in exchange for land with a current market value of $23,000. How would this be recorded in the Land account? (p. 603)
   a. Debited for $23,000
   b. Credited for $18,000
   c. Credited for $20,000
   d. Debited for $18,000

7. Which of the following would be recorded for the issuance of 55,000 shares of no-par common stock at $13.50 per share? (p. 602)
   a. Credit to Paid-In Capital in Excess of No-Par Value—Common for $742,500
   b. Credit to Common Stock for $742,500
   c. Credit to Cash for $742,500
   d. Debit Paid-In Capital in Excess of No-Par Value—Common for $742,500

8. Which of the following is true for dividends? (p. 609)
   a. Dividends are a distribution of cash to the stockholders.
   b. Dividends decrease both the assets and the total stockholders' equity of the corporation.
   c. Dividends increase retained earnings.
   d. Both (a) and (b) are correct.

9. Dividends on cumulative preferred stock of $2,500 are in arrears for 2011. During 2012, the total dividends declared amount to $10,000. There are 6,000 shares of $10 par, 10% cumulative preferred stock outstanding and 10,000 shares of $5 par common stock outstanding. What is the total amount of dividends payable to each class of stock in 2012? (pp. 610–612)
   a. $5,000 to preferred, $5,000 to common
   b. $6,000 to preferred, $4,000 to common
   c. $8,500 to preferred, $1,500 to common
   d. $10,000 to preferred, $0 to common

10. Which of the following is true about dividends in arrears? (p. 611)
    a. They are a liability on the balance sheet.
    b. They are dividends passed on cumulative preferred stock.
    c. They are dividends passed on noncumulative preferred stock.
    d. They are dividends passed on common stock.

Quick Exercise Solutions

11-1. Journalize the following transactions. (pp. 601–608)

a. Firm Body Corporation sells 12,000 shares of $10 par common stock for $13.00 per share.

b. Firm Body Corporation sells 5,000 shares of $50 par, 10% cumulative preferred stock for $59 per share.

c. Received a building with a market value of $115,000 and issued 6,400 shares of $10 par common stock in exchange.

d. Firm Body Corporation reports net income of $66,000 at the end of its first year of operations.

General Journal

	Date	Accounts	Debit	Credit
a.		Cash	136,000	
		Common stock		120,000
		Paid-in capital in excess of par—Common		36,000

General Journal

	Date	Accounts	Debit	Credit
b.		Cash	295,000	
		Preferred stock		250,000
		Paid-in capital in excess of par—Preferred		45,000

General Journal

	Date	Accounts	Debit	Credit
c.		Building	115,000	
		Common stock		64,000
		Paid-in capital in excess of par—Common		51,000

General Journal

	Date	Accounts	Debit	Credit
d.		Income summary	66,000	
		Retained earnings		66,000

11-2. The following is a list of stockholders' equity accounts appearing on the balance sheet for O'Neil Corporation on December 31, 2011:

Common stock, $10 par value	$300,000
Paid-in capital in excess of par—Common	200,000
Retained earnings	225,000
Preferred stock, $50 par value	125,000
Paid-in capital in excess of par—Preferred	30,000

Determine the following: (pp. 601–604)

a. How many shares of preferred stock have been issued?

$$\$125,000/\$50 = 2,500$$

b. What was the average issuance price of the preferred stock per share?

$$(\$125,000 + \$30,000)2,500 = \$62$$

c. How many shares of common stock have been issued?

$$\$300,000/\$10 = 30,000$$

d. What is total paid-in capital?

$$\$300,000 + \$200,000 + \$125,000 + \$30,000 = \$655,000$$

e. What is total stockholders' equity?

$$\$655,000 + \$225,000 = \$880,000$$

11-3. Bowen Corporation organized on January 1, 2011. Bowen Corporation has authorization for 90,000 shares of $10 par value common stock. As of December 31, 2011, Bowen has issued 50,000 shares of its common stock at an average issuance price of $15. Bowen also has authorization for 50,000 shares of 5%, $50 par value, noncumulative preferred stock. As of December 31, 2011, Bowen has issued 12,000 shares of preferred stock at an average issuance price of $68 per share. Bowen reports net income of $47,000 for its first year of operations ended December 31, 2011.

Prepare the stockholders' equity section of the balance sheet for Bowen Corporation dated December 31, 2011. (pp. 601–604)

Bowen Corporation
Stockholders' Equity
December 31, 2011

Paid-in capital:	
Preferred stock, 5%, $50 par, 512,000 shares issued	$ 600,000
Paid-in capital in excess of par—Preferred	216,000
Common stock, $10 par, 90,000 shares authorized, 50,000 shares issued	500,000
Paid-in capital in excess of par—Common	250,000
Total paid-in capital	$1,566,000
Retained earnings	47,000
Total Stockholders' Equity	$1,613,000

11-4. Following is the stockholders' equity section of the balance sheet for Watson Corporation as of December 1, 2012:

Preferred stock, $100 par, 6% cumulative, 10,000 shares authorized, 7,500 shares issued	$ 750,000
Common stock, $10 par, 200,000 shares authorized, 130,000 shares issued	1,300,000
Paid-in capital in excess of par—Common	520,000
Total paid-in capital	$2,570,000
Retained earnings	450,000
Total Stockholders' Equity	$3,020,000

Watson Corporation reports the following transactions for December 2012: (pp. 609–612)

Dec. 5 Declared the required cash dividend on the preferred stock and a $0.40 dividend on the common stock.

20 Paid the dividends declared on December 5.

Requirements

1. Journalize the transactions.

General Journal

Date	Accounts	Debit	Credit
Dec 5	Retained earnings	97,000	
	Dividends payable		97,000

General Journal

Date	Accounts	Debit	Credit
Dec 20	Dividends payable	97,000	
	Cash		97,000

2. What is the total stockholders' equity after posting the entries?

$2,923,000 ($3,020,000 − $97,000)

11-5. Sparks Corporation has gathered the following data for the current year: (p. 615)

Net income	$40,000
Interest expense	6,000
Income tax expense	12,500
Preferred dividends	3,600

Balance Sheet Data	Beginning of Year	End of Year
Current assets	$ 68,000	$ 81,000
Current liabilities	41,000	39,000
Plant assets	340,000	365,000
Long-term liabilities	100,000	90,000
Common Stockholders' Equity	217,000	267,000
Preferred Stockholders' Equity	50,000	50,000

Requirements

1. Calculate return on assets.

> $40,000 + $6,000 = $46,000
> $46,500/$427,000* = 10.8%

> *$68,000 + $340,000 = $408,000
> $81,000 + $365,000 = $446,000
> $408,000 + $446,000 = $854,000
> $854,000/2 = $427,000

2. Calculate return on equity.

> $40,000 − $3,600 = $36,400
> $36,400/$242,000* = 15.0%

> *$217,000 + $267,000 = $484,000
> $484,000/2 = $427,000

3. Comment on how these measures are used.

> The return on assets is used as a standard profitability measure that shows the company's success in using its assets to generate income. It helps investors compare one company to another, especially within the same industry.

> The return on equity is used as a standard profitability measure that shows the relationship between net income and average common stockholders' equity. The higher the rate of return, the more successful the company.

Do It Yourself! Question 1 Solutions

Requirements

1. What is the par value per share of the common stock?

$$\text{Par value per share} = \frac{\$100,000}{50,000 \text{ shares}}$$

$$= \$2 \text{ per share}$$

2. On average, what was the original issue price per share of the common stock?

Total cash received from issuance of the common shares (par + additional paid-in capital):

$$\$100,000 + \$50,000 = \$150,000$$

$$\frac{\$150,000}{50,000 \text{ shares}} = \$3 \text{ cash received per share}$$

3. On January 9, 2012, Dinner issued another 10,000 common shares for $4 cash per share. Journalize this transaction.

Cash ($4 × 10,000)	40,000	
Additional Paid-in capital (to balance)		20,000
Common stock ($2 × 10,000)		20,000

$4 paid − $2 par = $2 excess cash
$2 excess cash × 10,000 shares = Additional Paid-in capital $20,000 balancing amount

Do It Yourself! Question 2 Solutions

Requirements

1. Journalize the issuance of the preferred shares on January 1, 2011.

Cash ($25 × 5,000)	125,000	
Additional Paid-in capital (to balance)		25,000
Common stock ($20 × 5,000)		100,000

2. How much in dividends is Lunch supposed to pay to the preferred shareholders each year?

Preferred shareholders are *supposed* to receive:

$20 par × 8% = $1.60 per share annually
$1.60 × 5,000 dividends per year for all outstanding preferred shares

3. How much of the $5,000 paid as dividends in 2011 went to the preferred and common shareholders?

The full $8,000 was not paid; therefore, the entire $5,000 goes to the preferred shareholders. Common shareholders get nothing.

$8,000 − $5,000 = $3,000 of dividends in arrears

4. How much of the $15,000 paid as dividends in 2012 went to the preferred and common shareholders?

Preferred shareholders received:

$8,000 + $3,000 = $11,000

Common shareholders received:

$15,000 − $11,000 = $4,000

The Power of Practice

For more practice using the skills learned in this chapter, visit MyAccountingLab. There you will find algorithmically generated questions that are based on these Demo Docs and your main textbook's Review and Assess Your Progress sections.

Go to MyAccountingLab and follow these steps:

1. Direct your URL to www.myaccountinglab.com.
2. Log in using your name and password.
3. Click the MyAccountingLab link.
4. Click Study Plan in the left navigation bar.
5. From the table of contents, select Chapter 11, Corporations: Paid-In Capital and the Balance Sheet.
6. Click a link to work tutorial exercises.

12 Corporations: Retained Earnings and the Income Statement

WHAT YOU PROBABLY ALREADY KNOW

You probably already know that it can be helpful to look back at past history to predict the future. Let's assume that you want to join a gym that will cost you $50 a month. You have decided that, although you have savings, you don't want to join if you can't afford to pay for it from your normal monthly earnings. Before you sign the contract, you may calculate your monthly finances. Assume you looked at the previous month's financial activity and found the following:

Revenues:		Expenses:	
Wages earned and received from employer	$ 850	Rent and utilities	$625
Birthday gifts	200	Insurance and gas	75
		College application fee	100
		Food and entertainment	150
Total revenues:	$1,050	Total expenses:	$950

Although there is an excess of revenues over expenses of $100, it cannot be assumed that this is what will occur in the future. The birthday gifts and the college application fee are unusual nonrecurring types of financial events. If those two items are eliminated, the recurring wage revenue of $850 equals the recurring monthly expenses of $850 and your conclusion would be that the gym membership is not affordable. The same concept holds for businesses. Those financial transactions that are nonrecurring and should not be considered when making future projections are identified and segregated from the routine operating results on the income statement.

Learning Objectives/Success Keys

1 Account for stock dividends.

The board of directors may declare a stock dividend instead of a cash dividend. A **stock dividend** gives each shareholder more shares of stock based on the number of shares currently owned. Similar to a cash dividend, Retained earnings is reduced (debited). However, unlike a cash dividend, a liability is not credited because there is no claim on assets; common stock is credited. *Review Exhibit 12-2 (p. 644) for the accounting of a stock dividend.*

2 Account for stock splits.

A **stock split** increases the number of shares issued and outstanding and reduces the par or stated value proportionately. A 3-for-1 split means that each shareholder receives 2 more shares for each 1 currently held and the par or stated value is 1/3 of the amount before the split. There is **no journal entry required** for a stock split because there is no impact on the financial position of the company.

A stock dividend increases (credits) the Common stock and Paid-in capital in excess of par accounts for the additional shares issued. The dividend, a return of equity to the shareholders, also decreases (debits) Retained earnings. *Review Exhibit 12-7 (p. 647) for a comparison of stock dividends and splits.*

3 Account for treasury stock.

Treasury stock is when the company buys back its own shares from existing shareholders. The cost of the shares is debited to a contra equity account, Treasury stock. If the treasury stock is subsequently sold, Cash is debited, Treasury stock is credited for the cost of the shares, and Paid-in capital from Treasury stock transactions is debited or credited for the difference, if any. *Review the impact of treasury stock on stockholders' equity in Exhibit 12-8 (p. 650).*

4 Report restrictions on retained earnings.

A **restriction on retained earnings** means that some of the Retained earnings balance is not available for dividend declaration. The purpose of a restriction is to provide for a minimum amount of equity to remain in Retained earnings. A restriction may be self-imposed or required by creditors or others. *See the required note to the financial statements under "Restrictions on Retained Earnings" in the main text.*

5 Complete a corporate income statement including earnings per share.

The income statement reports **income from continuing operations**, which represents the results of operations that can be expected to proceed in the future. Below continuing operations, there may be special items that do not recur. These items, listed below, are shown individually net of tax on the income statement after continuing operations but before net income.

- **Discontinued operations**—The financial results of a discontinued segment of the business. The segment must be able to be separately identified operationally and for reporting purposes from the remainder of the entity.

- **Extraordinary gains and losses**—The financial effect of events that are **both** unusual (not expected to occur) and infrequent (not expected to recur).

Earnings per share, the net income earned per outstanding share of common stock, must be shown at the bottom of the income statement. This is probably the most important indicator used by analysts and investors for profitability analysis. *Review the multistep income statement containing special items in Exhibit 12-10 (p. 656). Observe the combined income statement and retained earnings statement in Exhibit 12-12 (p. 660) and the presentation of comprehensive income in Exhibit 12-14 (p. 661).*

Demo Doc 1

Stock Splits and Dividends

Learning Objectives 1, 2

On December 31, 2011, Tinker, Corp., had 25,000, $1.20 par common shares outstanding with a market price of $9 per share.
Retained earnings had a balance of $60,000, but there was no balance in Additional paid-in capital.

Requirements

1. On January 1, 2012, Tinker split its common stock 3 for 1. Give the journal entry for the split. What are the par and market values per share after the split? How does this split impact stockholders' equity?

2. On February 1, 2012, Tinker issued a 20% stock dividend. Give the journal entry for this dividend. What is the par value per share after the dividend? How does this dividend impact stockholders' equity?

3. On March 1, 2012, Tinker declared and paid a cash dividend of $0.60 per common share. Give the journal entry for this dividend. How does this dividend impact stockholders' equity?

Demo Doc 1 Solutions

Requirement 1

Account for stock splits

On January 1, 2012, Tinker split its common stock 3 for 1. Give the journal entry for the split. What are the par and market values per share after the split? How does this split impact stockholders' equity?

| Part 1 | Part 2 | Part 3 | Demo Doc Complete |

Before the split, Tinker has 25,000 common shares.
With a 3-for-1 split, there will be **3** new shares **for** every **1** old share.

Number of shares after stock split = Number of shares before stock split × Split ratio

Number of shares after stock split = $25{,}000 \times \dfrac{3}{1}$

= 75,000 shares

Another result of the split is that the par value and the market price are also split.

Par value per share after split = Par value per share before split × $\dfrac{1}{\text{Split ratio}}$

Par value per share after split = $\$1.20 \times \dfrac{1}{3}$

= $0.40 per share

Market price per share after split = Market price per share before split × $\dfrac{1}{\text{Split ratio}}$

Market price per share after split = $\$9 \times \dfrac{1}{3}$

= $3 per share

There has been *no change* to the account balance of Common stock. It remains the same, only it is now spread across more shares (resulting in a lower par value per share, as shown above).

The net impact on common stock is *zero*. Essentially, this means that *there is no journal entry for a stock split*. However, a stock split is described in the notes to the financial statements.

Because there is no journal entry, total equity is *not* impacted by the stock split.

Demo Doc 1 Solutions | Chapter 12   **395**

Requirement 2

1 Account for stock dividends

2 Account for stock splits

On February 1, 2012, Tinker issued a 20% stock dividend. Give the journal entry for this dividend. What is the par value per share after the dividend? How does this dividend impact stockholders' equity?

Part 1	**Part 2**	Part 3	Demo Doc Complete

This is a small stock dividend because the dividend percentage (20%) is less than 25%.

Remember that after the stock split of January 1, Tinker has 75,000 common shares outstanding with a market price of $3 per share and a par value of $0.40 per share.

With a stock dividend, new shares are issued to existing shareholders.

Number of new shares issued for stock dividend = Shares outstanding before dividend × Stock dividend %
Number of new shares issued for stock dividend =   75,000   20%
= 15,000 new shares

Each of these new shares is *identical* to the shares that existed before the stock dividend. They have the same characteristics as the common shares that existed before the stock dividend. The par value of the new shares issued is $0.40 per share, as it is for the other common shares.

So Common stock increases (a credit) by

15,000 new shares × $0.40 par = $6,000

With *any* dividend, there is a decrease (a debit) to Retained earnings because the shareholders are receiving some of their value/equity back from the company.

In the case of a small stock dividend, this value is the *market value* of the new shares issued.

So in this case, Retained earnings decreases (a debit) by

15,000 new shares × $3 market price per share = $45,000

The difference between these two amounts is balanced to Additional paid-in capital—in this case, an increase (a credit) of

$$\$45{,}000 - \$6{,}000 = \$39{,}000$$

Feb 1	Retained earnings (15,000 × $3)	45,000	
	Additional paid-in capital (to balance)		39,000
	Common stock (15,000 × $0.40)		6,000

All of these accounts are part of the equity section. This means that there is an equal debit (decrease) and credit (increase) impact to the equity section. We are simply shifting value from Retained earnings to paid-in capital.

This means that *total* equity *does not change* as a result of this transaction.

	Before Stock Dividend		After Stock Dividend
Common stock	$30,000		$36,000
Additional paid-in capital	0		39,000
Retained earnings	60,000		15,000
Total equity	$90,000	(same)	$90,000

Requirement 3

1 Account for stock dividends

On March 1, 2012, Tinker declared and paid a cash dividend of $0.60 per common share. Give the journal entry for this dividend. How does this dividend impact stockholders' equity?

Part 1	Part 2	**Part 3**	Demo Doc Complete

Cash will decrease (a credit) by the amount of dividends paid. After the stock dividend of February 1, there are 75,000 + 15,000 = 90,000 shares outstanding. Therefore, the cash paid is

$$90{,}000 \text{ shares} \times \$0.60 \text{ per share} = \$54{,}000$$

With *any* dividend, there is a decrease to Retained earnings (a debit). In this case, it is a decrease of the cash paid of $54,000.

Mar 1	Retained earnings	54,000	
	Cash (90,000 × $0.60)		54,000

Part 1	Part 2	Part 3	**Demo Doc Complete**

Demo Doc 2

Treasury Stock

Learning Objectives 3, 4

On January 1, 2011, Unter, Inc., purchased 4,000 shares of treasury stock for $10 each. At this time, Paid-in capital, Treasury stock had a balance of $0.

Unter sold the treasury stock as follows:

April 1, 2011	Sold 1,000 shares for $12 cash each.
July 1, 2011	Sold 2,500 shares for $9.50 cash each.
October 1, 2011	Sold 500 shares for $8.25 cash each.

Requirements

1. Journalize all of Unter's treasury stock transactions.

2. Suppose instead of holding onto the common stock purchased as treasury stock, Unter retired the stock on January 2, 2011. Would it be possible for Unter to later reissue the stock?

Demo Doc 2 Solutions

Requirement 1

3 Account for treasury stock

Journalize all of Unter's treasury stock transactions.

Part 1	Part 2	Demo Doc Complete

On January 1, 2011, Unter, Inc., purchased 4,000 shares of treasury stock for $10 cash each. At this time, Paid-in capital, Treasury stock had a balance of $0.

The Common stock account represents all *issued* common shares. When the company purchases treasury stock, these shares are still issued but are *no longer outstanding*. To represent this decrease in the number of outstanding shares, the Treasury stock account has a debit balance. It is a *contra equity* account.

When treasury stock is purchased, the Treasury stock account increases (a debit) by the cost of the treasury shares:

$$4{,}000 \times \$10 \text{ share} = \$40{,}000$$

Cash decreases (a credit) by $40,000.

| Jan 1 | Treasury stock | 40,000 | |
| | Cash (4,000 × $10) | | 40,000 |

April 1, 2011: Sold 1,000 shares for $12 cash each.

Cash increases (a debit) by

$$1{,}000 \text{ shares} \times \$12 = \$12{,}000$$

Treasury stock decreases (a credit) by the *original cost* of the treasury shares:

$$1{,}000 \text{ shares} \times \$10 = \$10{,}000$$

The difference between these two amounts is a balancing amount to Paid-in capital, treasury stock of ($12,000 – $10,000) = $2,000 credit (increase).

Apr 1	Cash (1,000 × $12)	12,000	
	Paid-in capital, treasury stock (to balance)		2,000
	Treasury stock (1,000 × $10)		10,000

July 1, 2011: Sold 2,500 shares for $9.50 cash each.

Cash increases (a debit) by

$$2{,}500 \text{ shares} \times \$9.50 = \$23{,}750$$

Treasury stock decreases (a credit) by the *original cost* of the treasury shares:

$$2{,}500 \text{ shares} \times \$10 = \$25{,}000$$

The difference between these two amounts is a balancing amount to Paid-in capital, Treasury stock. This is a debit (decrease) of

$$\$25{,}000 - \$23{,}750 = \$1{,}250$$

Note that we *cannot* have a *debit/negative balance* in Paid-in capital, treasury stock. However, from the entry on April 1, we know that there is a balance of $2,000. This is more than enough to cover a $1,250 debit.

Jul 1	Cash (2,500 × $9.50)	23,750	
	Paid-in capital, treasury stock (to balance)	1,250	
	Treasury stock (2,500 × $10)		25,000

After this transaction, Paid-in capital, treasury stock has a balance of $750 credit:

Paid-in capital, treasury stock				Treasury stock			
		Bal	0	Jan 1	40,000		
		Apr 1	2,000			Apr 1	10,000
Jul 1	1,250					Mar 1	25,000
		Bal	750	Bal	5,000		

October 1, 2011: Sold 500 shares for $8.25 cash each.

Cash increases (a debit) by

$$500 \text{ shares} \times \$8.25 = \$4{,}125$$

Treasury stock decreases (a credit) by the *original cost* of the treasury shares:

$$500 \text{ shares} \times \$10 = \$5{,}000$$

The difference between these two amounts would normally be a balancing amount to Paid-in capital, treasury stock, but in this case, the difference is a debit (a decrease) of

$$\$5{,}000 - \$4{,}125 = \$875$$

There is only $750 in the Paid-in capital, treasury stock account. This is not enough to cover the debit that would normally be required.

Instead, we take *as much as possible* from the Paid-in capital, treasury stock account. This means that we debit for the $750 left in the account. The remaining ($875 − $750) = $125 is balanced to Retained earnings (debit/decrease).

Oct 1	Cash (500 × $8.25)	4,125	
	Paid-in capital, treasury stock	750	
	Retained earnings (to balance)	125	
	Treasury stock (500 × $10)		5,000

Requirement 2

4 Report restrictions on retained earnings

Suppose instead of holding onto the common stock purchased as treasury stock, Unter retired the stock on January 2, 2011. Would it be possible for Unter to later reissue the stock?

Part 1	Part 2	Demo Doc Complete

When stock is retired, the stock certificates are *canceled*. This means that the stock ceases to exist.

Retired/canceled stock can no longer be reissued.

Part 1	Part 2	Demo Doc Complete

Demo Doc 3

Income Statement Presentation and Earnings per Share

Learning Objective 5

Vater Industries had the following information for the year ended December 31, 2011:

Common stock, $0.50 par	$ 7,000
Preferred stock, $20 par, 10%	20,000
Treasury stock (2,000 shares at cost)	8,000
Extraordinary items (before tax)	30,000
Tax impact of extraordinary items	(9,000)
Tax impact of income from continuing operations	(65,000)
Income from continuing operations (before tax)	200,000
Tax impact of discontinued operations	11,000
Discontinued operations (before tax)	(40,000)

During 2011, Vater paid all required dividends for the preferred stock and also paid dividends of $1 per share on the common stock.

Requirements

1. Prepare the lower portion of Vater's income statement for the year ended December 31, 2011, beginning with income from continuing operations, including earnings per share calculations.

2. Why are discontinued operations and extraordinary items not included as part of income from continuing operations?

Demo Doc 3 Solutions

5 Complete a corporate income statement including earnings per share

Requirement 1

Prepare the lower portion of Vater's income statement for the year ended December 31, 2011, beginning with income from continuing operations, including earnings per share calculations.

| **Part 1** | Part 2 | Part 3 | Part 4 | Demo Doc Complete |

First, we must get the final numbers to be reported on the income statement for these items. Each of these items is reported *after tax*, so we must combine the pretax numbers with their tax impacts to get the after-tax numbers.

Income from continuing operations (after tax):

$$\$200,000 - \$65,000 = \$135,000$$

Discontinued operations (net of tax):

$$-\$40,000 + \$11,000 = -\$29,000$$

Extraordinary items (net of tax):

$$\$30,000 + \$9,000 = \$21,000$$

Remember that discontinued operations and extraordinary items can be positive *or* negative. In this question, discontinued operations are negative and the extraordinary item is a gain, but either item could also be in the opposite direction. To help recall the order of presentation on this part of the income statement, remember that it is alphabetical: **CDE**.

- **C** Income from **C**ontinuing Operations
- **D** Income from **D**iscontinued Operations
- **E** **E**xtraordinary Items

So the first part of the income statement is

Income from continuing operations	$135,000
− Discontinued operations (net of tax)	(29,000)
+ Extraordinary items (net of tax)	21,000
Net Income	$127,000

Demo Doc 3 Solutions | Chapter 12 **403**

| Part 1 | **Part 2** | Part 3 | Part 4 | Demo Doc Complete |

Next, we must calculate the earnings per share ratios for each of these items.

$$\text{Basic earnings per share} = \frac{\text{Net income} - \text{Preferred share dividends}}{\text{Average number of common shares outstanding}}$$

Notice that there is *no mention* of *common* share dividends because it is *irrelevant* whether or not common share dividends are paid. Net income (after the preferred dividends) goes to the common shareholders. Whether they "receive" this income as an increase to retained earnings or as a cash dividend, it still belongs to the common shareholders.

Therefore, payment of common stock dividends is ignored in the EPS calculation.

It is *only* the preferred dividends (money that does *not* go to the common shareholders) that is subtracted.

So we ignore the common stock dividends in our earnings per share calculation.

We still need the number of common shares outstanding for the earnings per share calculation. The common stock account represents the par value of all issued shares.

So the number of issued common shares is

$$\$7{,}000 / \$0.50 \text{ par per share} = 14{,}000 \text{ shares}$$

To get the number of outstanding common shares, we must take out the treasury stock:

Number of outstanding shares = Number of issued shares − Number of treasury shares

Number of outstanding shares = 14,000 − 2,000

= 12,000 shares of common stock outstanding

The $20,000 in the Preferred stock account represents the par value of *all* preferred stock. Therefore, we can calculate that the preferred share dividends paid in 2008:

$$10\% \times \$20{,}000 = \$2{,}000$$

For income from continuing operations, basic earnings per share is

$$\text{Basic earnings per share} = \frac{\text{Income} - \text{Preferred share dividends}}{\text{Average number of common shares outstanding}}$$

$$= \frac{\$135{,}000 - \$2{,}000}{12{,}000 \text{ common shares}}$$

$$= \$11.08 \text{ per share}$$

The portion of earnings per share relating to discontinued operations is

$$\text{Basic earnings per share} = \frac{\text{Income}}{\text{Average number of common shares outstanding}}$$

$$= \frac{-\$29,000}{12,000 \text{ common shares}}$$

$$= -\$2.42 \text{ per share}$$

The portion of earnings per share relating to extraordinary items is

$$\text{Basic earnings per share} = \frac{\text{Income}}{\text{Average number of common shares outstanding}}$$

$$= \frac{\$21,000}{12,000 \text{ common shares}}$$

$$= \$1.75 \text{ per share}$$

For net income, basic earnings per share is

$$\text{Basic earnings per share} = \frac{\text{Income} - \text{Preferred share dividends}}{\text{Average number of common shares outstanding}}$$

$$= \frac{\$127,000 - \$2,000}{12,000 \text{ common shares}}$$

$$= \$10.41 \text{ per share (rounded down)}$$

As a check, we can add up the portions of earnings per share from the other items:

$$\$11.08 - \$2.42 + \$1.75 = \$10.41$$

Part 1	Part 2	**Part 3**	Part 4	Demo Doc Complete

The full income statement is

Income from continuing operations	$135,000
+ Discontinued operations (net of tax)	(29,000)
− Extraordinary items (net of tax)	21,000
Net income	$127,000

Earnings per share:

Income from continuing operations	$11.08
Discontinued operations (net of tax)	(2.42)
Extraordinary items (net of tax)	1.75
Net income	$10.41

Requirement 2

5 Complete a corporate income statement including earnings per share

Why are discontinued operations and extraordinary items not included as part of income from continuing operations?

Part 1	Part 2	Part 3	**Part 4**	Demo Doc Complete

Accountants must make financial statements helpful to investors (and other people) making decisions. One of the things the users of financial statements want to know is how much profit/income they can expect the business to make in the future. Income from *continuing* operations helps with estimating future profits because it involves income from business activities that will go on (that is, continue) into the future.

Discontinued operations are business activities that are ceasing (such as a subsidiary of the company that is in the process of being sold).

Extraordinary items are supposed to be one-time occurrences (by definition—unusual and infrequent), such as an earthquake.

These numbers are not helpful if you are trying to predict *future* profit levels. The discontinued operations will be gone in the future and the extraordinary events will not happen again. They will have *no* future impact.

These items are legitimately part of net income (and so are included there) but they are separated from income from continuing operations to make it easier for users of financial statements to understand what they can expect to see on future income statements. An analyst who is trying to predict *future* income would *only* use income from continuing operations because this is the only part of net income that will have a future impact (in other words, is *continuing* on into the future).

Part 1	Part 2	Part 3	Part 4	Demo Doc Complete

Quick Practice Questions

True/False

_____ 1. A stock dividend is a distribution by a corporation of its own stock to its stockholders.

_____ 2. Stock dividends increase total stockholders' equity.

_____ 3. A stock split reduces the number of outstanding shares of stock and the par value of the stock.

_____ 4. When treasury stock is purchased, the balance in the Common stock account remains unchanged.

_____ 5. A corporation purchases 200 shares of its $10 par common stock for $12 per share. Subsequently, all 200 shares are resold for $13 per share. The amount of revenue from these transactions is $200.

_____ 6. Only outstanding shares of stock receive cash and stock dividends.

_____ 7. Earnings per share is computed by dividing net income less preferred dividends by the average number of common shares outstanding.

_____ 8. Stock dividends may cause the price of the stock to increase.

_____ 9. Prior-period adjustments adjust retained earnings for discontinued operations.

_____ 10. Comprehensive income is the company's change in total stockholders' equity from all sources other than from its owners.

Multiple Choice

1. What is the effect of a stock dividend distribution on a stockholders' ownership percentage?
   a. It increases.
   b. It decreases.
   c. It can increase or decrease depending on the type of stock dividend.
   d. It will stay the same.

2. What is the ownership percentage used as a cutoff point for distinguishing between a small and a large stock dividend?
   a. 15%
   b. 10%
   c. 25%
   d. 50%

3. What entry is made to record a 2-for-1 stock split?
   a. Credit to Common stock
   b. Credit to Retained earnings
   c. Debit to Retained earnings
   d. There is no journal entry for a stock split.

4. What effect does the purchase of treasury stock have on the number of a corporation's shares?
   a. It causes issued shares to exceed authorized shares.
   b. It causes outstanding shares to exceed issued shares.
   c. It causes outstanding shares to exceed authorized shares.
   d. It causes outstanding shares to be less than issued shares.

5. What type of account is Treasury stock?
   a. Contra asset
   b. Liability
   c. Contra liability
   d. Contra Stockholders' Equity account

6. What is the effect of a common stock retirement?
   a. It decreases the number of shares of common stock outstanding.
   b. It increases the balance in the Common stock account.
   c. It decreases the number of shares of common stock issued.
   d. Both (a) and (c) are correct.

7. Which of the following is true for restrictions on retained earnings?
   a. They are usually reported in the notes to the financial statements.
   b. They happen frequently.
   c. They are disclosed on the income statement.
   d. They reduce total assets on the balance sheet.

8. The Gain on sale of machinery account would appear on the income statement as which of the following?
   a. Extraordinary gain
   b. Component of income from discontinued operations
   c. Component of net sales
   d. Component of income from continuing operations

9. To be considered an extraordinary item on the income statement, the event must be which of the following?
   a. Unusual but not infrequent
   b. Both infrequent and unusual
   c. Neither infrequent nor unusual
   d. Infrequent but not unusual

10. Net income for a corporation for the current year amounts to $200,000. The corporation currently has outstanding 5,000 shares of 5%, cumulative $100 par preferred stock and 20,000 shares of $20 par common stock. What is the numerator to be used in the earnings-per-share calculation?
    a. $175,000
    b. $195,000
    c. $200,000
    d. $225,000

Quick Exercises

12-1. Jonathan Corporation reports the following transactions for 2012:

Jan 10   Sold 6,000 shares of 9%, noncumulative $50 par, preferred stock for $85 per share.

Feb 19   Sold 3,000 shares of $10 par common stock for $15 per share.

Oct 12   The board announced a 15% stock dividend on the common stock. The current market price of the common stock is $22 per share. Jonathan Corporation has 120,000 shares of common stock outstanding on October 12.

Requirement

1. Journalize the above transactions.

Date	Accounts	Debit	Credit

Date	Accounts	Debit	Credit

Date	Accounts	Debit	Credit

12-2. Following is the stockholders' equity section of the balance sheet of Fairfield Corporation as of November 1, 2012:

FAIRFIELD CORPORATION
Stockholders' Equity
November 1, 2012

Paid-in capital:	
Preferred stock, 6%, noncumulative $50 par, 10,000 authorized, 6,500 shares issued	$ 325,000
Common stock, $10 par, 300,000 shares authorized, 120,000 shares issued	1,200,000
Paid-in capital in excess of par—Common	420,000
Total paid-in capital	$1,945,000
Retained earnings	467,200
Total Stockholders' Equity	$2,412,200

Fairfield Corporation reported the following transactions during November 2012:

Nov 1 Declared the required annual cash dividend on the preferred stock and a $0.70 dividend on the common stock.

15 Paid the dividends declared on November 1.

16 Distributed a 10% common stock dividend. The market value of the common stock is $20 per share.

30 The board of directors announced a 2-for-1 stock split.

Requirement

1. Show the dollar amount of the effect of each transaction on both total paid-in capital and total stockholders' equity.

Date	Total Paid-In Capital	Total Stockholders' Equity

12-3. Victory Corporation reported the following stockholders' equity items on December 31, 2011:

Preferred stock, 5%, cumulative $100 par, 7,000 shares authorized, 1,000 shares issued	$100,000
Paid-in-capital in excess of par—Preferred	55,000
Common stock, $50 par, 10,000 shares authorized, 5,000 shares issued	250,000
Paid-in capital in excess of par—Common	235,000
Retained earnings	455,300
Treasury common stock, at cost, 700 shares	96,000

Requirements

1. Compute the

  a. Number of shares of common stock outstanding

  b. Number of shares of preferred stock outstanding

  c. Average issue price of common stock

  d. Average issue price of preferred stock

2. Assume that Victory Corporation declares a 4-for-1 stock split. Compute the

  a. Number of shares of common outstanding

  b. Par value

12-4. Clean Wash Corporation reported the following stockholders' equity on January 1, 2011:

CLEAN WASH CORPORATION
Stockholders' Equity
January 1, 2011

Paid-in capital:	
Preferred stock, 5%, cumulative $50 par, 30,000 authorized,	
7,500 shares issued	$ 375,000
Paid-in capital in excess of par—Preferred	18,750
Common stock, $1 par, 200,000 shares authorized,	
135,000 shares issued	135,000
Paid-in capital in excess of par—Common	472,500
Total paid-in capital	$1,001,250
Retained earnings	218,500
Total Stockholders' Equity	$1,219,750

Requirements

1. On June 15, 2011, the board of directors announced a 10% common stock dividend when the market price of the stock was $6 per share. Journalize the stock dividend.

General Journal

Date	Accounts	Debit	Credit

2. What effect did the distribution of the common stock dividend have on the following?

    a. Total assets

    b. Total liabilities

c. Total paid-in capital

d. Total stockholders' equity

12-5. On June 1, 2011, Hauser Corporation purchased 2,600 shares of its $10 par value common stock for $12.50 per share. The 2,600 shares had originally been issued for $11.25 per share. Hauser Corporation sold 1,700 of its treasury shares on August 4, 2011, for $14.75 per share.

Journalize the transactions on June 1 and August 4, 2011.

Date	Accounts	Debit	Credit

General Journal

Date	Accounts	Debit	Credit

General Journal

Do It Yourself! Question 1

Stock Splits and Dividends

On December 31, 2011, Garbage, Inc., had 12,000 common shares outstanding with a market price of $8 per share and a par value of $2 per share.

Requirements

1 Account for stock dividends

1. On January 1, 2012, Garbage issued a 15% stock dividend. Journalize this dividend.

		General Journal		
Date	Accounts		Debit	Credit

2 Account for stock splits

2. On January 2, 2012, Garbage split its common stock 2 for 1. Journalize the split. What are the par and market values per share after the split?

		General Journal		
Date	Accounts		Debit	Credit

3. On January 3, 2012, Garbage declared and paid a cash dividend of $0.30 per common share. Journalize this dividend.

		General Journal		
Date	Accounts		Debit	Credit

Do It Yourself! Question 2

Treasury Stock

On January 1, 2011, Hartnick, Co., purchased 1,000 shares of treasury stock for $7 cash each. At this time, Paid-In Capital, Treasury Stock had a balance of $0.

Hartnick sold the treasury stock as follows:

February 1, 2011	Sold 200 shares for $10 cash each.
March 1, 2011	Sold 500 shares for $6 cash each.
April 1, 2011	Sold 300 shares for $6.50 cash each.

Requirement

3 Account for treasury stock

1. Journalize all of Hartnick's treasury stock transactions.

General Journal

Date	Accounts	Debit	Credit

General Journal

Date	Accounts	Debit	Credit

Date	Accounts	Debit	Credit

General Journal

Date	Accounts	Debit	Credit

Do It Yourself! Question 3

Income Statement Presentation and Earnings per Share

Gate, Corp., had the following information for the year ended December 31, 2011:

Common stock, $0.50 par	$ 200,000
Preferred stock, $50 par, 8%	500,000
Tax impact of discontinued operations	(80,000)
Discontinued operations (before tax)	400,000
Extraordinary items (before tax)	(100,000)
Tax impact of extraordinary items	30,000
Tax impact of income from continuing operations	(750,000)
Income from continuing operations (before tax)	2,500,000

During the year, Gate paid all required dividends for the preferred stock and also paid dividends of $1 per share on the common stock. Gate has no treasury stock.

Requirement

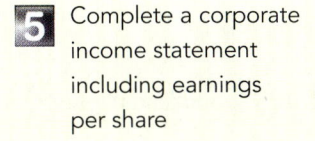

5 Complete a corporate income statement including earnings per share

1. Prepare the lower portion of Gate's income statement for the year ended December 31, 2011, beginning with income from continuing operations, including earnings-per-share calculations.

Quick Practice Solutions

True/False

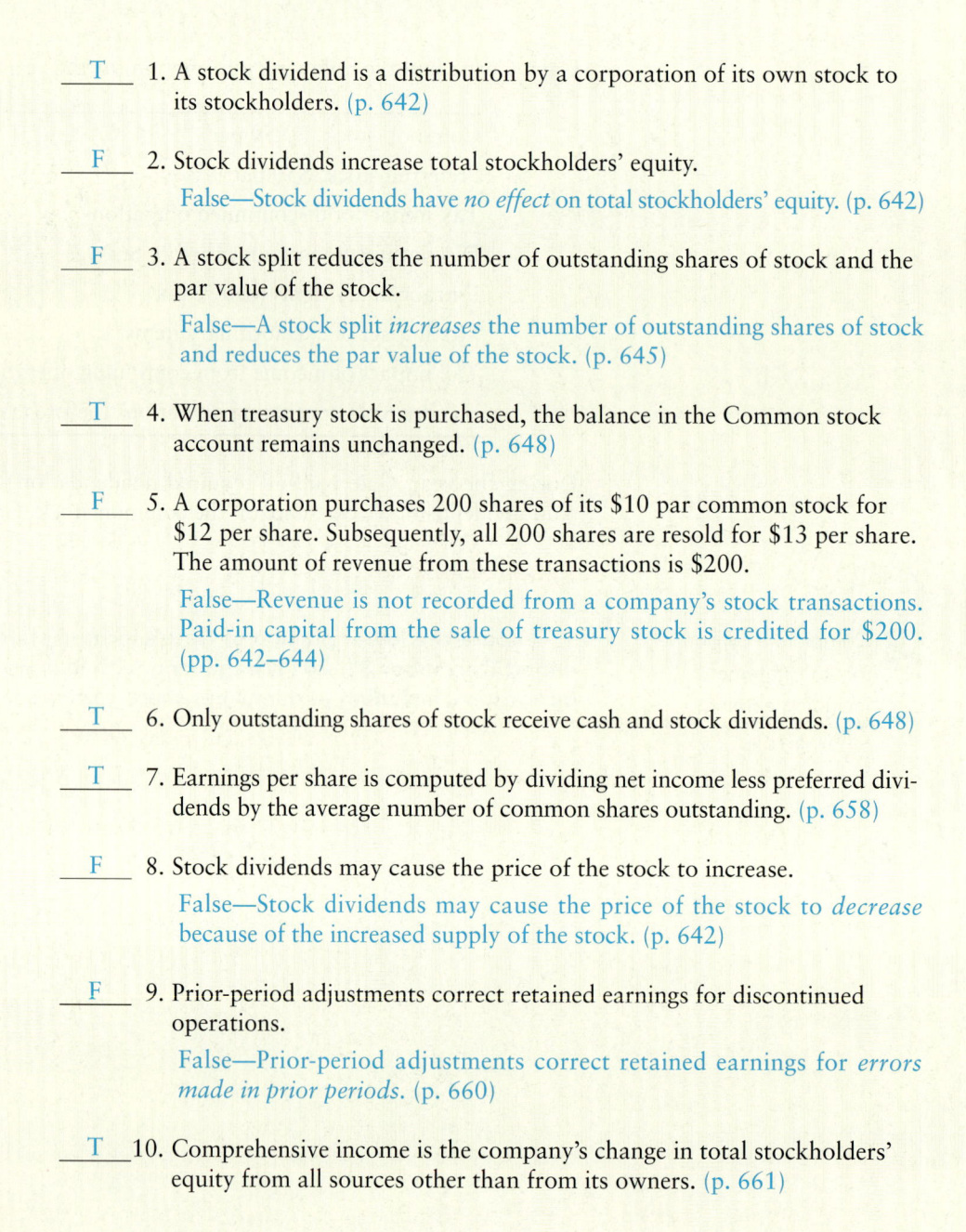

__T__ 1. A stock dividend is a distribution by a corporation of its own stock to its stockholders. (p. 642)

__F__ 2. Stock dividends increase total stockholders' equity.

   False—Stock dividends have *no effect* on total stockholders' equity. (p. 642)

__F__ 3. A stock split reduces the number of outstanding shares of stock and the par value of the stock.

   False—A stock split *increases* the number of outstanding shares of stock and reduces the par value of the stock. (p. 645)

__T__ 4. When treasury stock is purchased, the balance in the Common stock account remains unchanged. (p. 648)

__F__ 5. A corporation purchases 200 shares of its $10 par common stock for $12 per share. Subsequently, all 200 shares are resold for $13 per share. The amount of revenue from these transactions is $200.

   False—Revenue is not recorded from a company's stock transactions. Paid-in capital from the sale of treasury stock is credited for $200. (pp. 642–644)

__T__ 6. Only outstanding shares of stock receive cash and stock dividends. (p. 648)

__T__ 7. Earnings per share is computed by dividing net income less preferred dividends by the average number of common shares outstanding. (p. 658)

__F__ 8. Stock dividends may cause the price of the stock to increase.

   False—Stock dividends may cause the price of the stock to *decrease* because of the increased supply of the stock. (p. 642)

__F__ 9. Prior-period adjustments correct retained earnings for discontinued operations.

   False—Prior-period adjustments correct retained earnings for *errors made in prior periods*. (p. 660)

__T__ 10. Comprehensive income is the company's change in total stockholders' equity from all sources other than from its owners. (p. 661)

Multiple Choice

1. What is the effect of a stock dividend distribution on a stockholders' ownership percentage? (p. 642)
   a. It increases.
   b. It decreases.
   c. It can increase or decrease depending on the type of stock dividend.
   d. It will stay the same.

2. What is the ownership percentage used as a cutoff point for distinguishing between a small and a large stock dividend? (p. 643)
    a. 15%
    b. 10%
    c. 25%
    d. 50%

3. What entry is made to record a 2-for-1 stock split? (p. 646)
    a. Credit to Common stock
    b. Credit to Retained earnings
    c. Debit to Retained earnings
    d. There is no journal entry for a stock split.

4. What effect does the purchase of treasury stock have on the number of a corporation's shares? (p. 648)
    a. It causes issued shares to exceed authorized shares.
    b. It causes outstanding shares to exceed issued shares.
    c. It causes outstanding shares to exceed authorized shares.
    d. It causes outstanding shares to be less than issued shares.

5. What type of account is Treasury stock? (p. 647)
    a. Contra asset
    b. Liability
    c. Contra liability
    d. Contra Stockholders' Equity account

6. What is the effect of a common stock retirement? (p. 650)
    a. It decreases the number of shares of common stock outstanding.
    b. It increases the balance in the Common stock account.
    c. It decreases the number of shares of common stock issued.
    d. Both (a) and (c) are correct.

7. Which of the following is true for restrictions on retained earnings? (p. 650)
    a. They are usually reported in the notes to the financial statements.
    b. They happen frequently.
    c. They are disclosed on the income statement.
    d. They reduce total assets on the balance sheet.

8. The Gain on sale of machinery account would appear on the income statement as which of the following? (p. 657)
    a. Extraordinary gain
    b. Component of income from discontinued operations
    c. Component of net sales
    d. Component of income from continuing operations

9. To be considered an extraordinary item on the income statement, the event must be which of the following? (pp. 657–658)
    a. Unusual but not infrequent
    b. Both infrequent and unusual
    c. Neither infrequent nor unusual
    d. Infrequent but not unusual

10. Net income for a corporation for the current year amounts to $200,000. The corporation currently has outstanding 5,000 shares of 5%, cumulative $100 par preferred stock and 20,000 shares of $20 par common stock. What is the numerator to be used in the earnings-per-share calculation? (p. 658)
   a. $175,000
   b. $195,000
   c. $200,000
   d. $225,000

Quick Exercises

12-1. Jonathan Corporation reports the following transactions for 2012: (p. 643–644)

Jan 10   Sold 6,000 shares of 9%, noncumulative $50 par, preferred stock for $85 per share.

Feb 19   Sold 3,000 shares of $10 par common stock for $15 per share.

Oct 12   The board announced a 15% stock dividend on the common stock. The current market price of the common stock is $22 per share. Jonathan Corporation has 120,000 shares of common stock outstanding on October 12.

Requirement

1. Journalize the above transactions.

General Journal

Date	Accounts	Debit	Credit
Jan 10	Cash	510,000	
	Preferred stock		300,000
	Paid-in capital in excess of par—Preferred		210,000

General Journal

Date	Accounts	Debit	Credit
Feb 19	Cash	45,000	
	Common stock		30,000
	Paid-in capital in excess of par—Common		15,000

General Journal

Date	Accounts	Debit	Credit
Oct 12	Retained earnings	396,000	
	Common stock		180,000
	Paid-in capital in excess of par—Common		216,000

12-2. Following is the stockholders' equity section of the balance sheet of Fairfield Corporation as of November 1, 2012: (pp. 644–646)

FAIRFIELD CORPORATION
Stockholders' Equity
November 1, 2012

Paid-in capital:	
Preferred stock, 6%, noncumulative $50 par, 10,000 authorized, 6,500 shares issued	$ 325,000
Common stock, $10 par, 300,000 shares authorized, 120,000 shares issued	1,200,000
Paid-in capital in excess of par—Common	420,000
Total paid-in capital	$1,945,000
Retained earnings	467,200
Total Stockholders' Equity	$2,412,200

Fairfield Corporation reported the following transactions during November 2012:

Nov 1 Declared the required annual cash dividend on the preferred stock and a $0.70 dividend on the common stock.

15 Paid the dividends declared on November 1.

16 Distributed a 10% common stock dividend. The market value of the common stock is $20 per share.

30 The board of directors announced a 2-for-1 stock split.

Requirements

1. Show the dollar amount of the effect of each transaction on both total paid-in capital and total stockholders' equity.

Date	Total Paid-In Capital	Total Stockholders' Equity
Nov 1	No effect	Decrease of $103,500
Nov 15	No effect	No effect
Nov 16	Increase of $240,000	No effect
Nov 30	No effect	No effect

12-3 Victory Corporation reported the following stockholders' equity items on December 31, 2011: (pp. 643–646)

Preferred stock, 5%, cumulative $100 par, 7,000 shares authorized, 1,000 shares issued	$100,000
Paid-in-capital in excess of par—Preferred	55,000
Common stock, $50 par, 10,000 shares authorized, 5,000 shares issued	250,000
Paid-in capital in excess of par—Common	235,000
Retained earnings	455,300
Treasury common stock, at cost, 700 shares	96,000

Requirements

1. **Compute the**

   a. Number of shares of common stock outstanding

   > $250,00/$50 per share = 5,000 shares
   > 5,000 shares − 700 shares = 4,300 shares

   b. Number of shares of preferred stock outstanding

   > $100,000/$100 per share = 1,000 shares

   c. Average issue price of common stock

   > $250,00 + $235,000 = $485,000
   > $485,000/5,000 shares = $97 per share

   d. Average issue price of preferred stock

   > $100,00 + $55,000 = $155,000
   > $155,000/1,000 shares = $155 per share

2. **Assume that Victory Corporation declares a 4-for-1 stock split. Compute the**

   a. Number of shares of common outstanding

   > 4,300 shares × 4 = 17,200

   b. Par value

   > $50/4 = $12.50

12-4. Clean Wash Corporation reported the following stockholders' equity on January 1, 2011: (pp. 643–647)

CLEAN WASH CORPORATION
Stockholders' Equity
January 1, 2011

Paid-in capital:	
Preferred stock, 5%, cumulative $50 par, 30,000 authorized,	
7,500 shares issued	$ 375,000
Paid-in capital in excess of par—Preferred	18,750
Common stock, $1 par, 200,000 shares authorized,	
135,000 shares issued	135,000
Paid-in capital in excess of par—Common	472,500
Total paid-in capital	$1,001,250
Retained earnings	218,500
Total Stockholders' Equity	$1,219,750

Requirements

1. On June 15, 2011, the board of directors announced a 10% common stock dividend when the market price of the stock was $6 per share. Prepare the necessary journal entry to record the stock dividend.

General Journal

Date	Accounts	Debit	Credit
Jun 15	Retained earnings	81,000	
	Common stock		13,500
	Paid-in capital in excess of par—Common		67,500

2. What effect did the distribution of the common stock dividend have on the following?

    a. Total assets

        No effect

    b. Total liabilities

        No effect

    c. Total paid-in capital

        Increase of $81,000

    d. Total stockholders' equity

        No effect

12-5. On June 1, 2011, Hauser Corporation purchased 2,600 shares of its $10 par value common stock for $12.50 per share. The 2,600 shares had originally been issued for $11.25 per share. Hauser Corporation sold 1,700 of its treasury shares on August 4, 2011, for $14.75 per share. (p. 648)

Journalize the transactions on June 1 and August 4, 2011.

General Journal

Date	Accounts	Debit	Credit
Jun 1	Treasury stock	32,500	
	Cash		32,500

General Journal

Date	Accounts	Debit	Credit
Aug 4	Cash	25,075	
	Treasury stock		21,250
	Paid-in capital from treasury stock transactions		3,825

Do It Yourself! Question 1 Solutions

Stock Splits and Dividends

Requirements

1. On January 1, 2012 Garbage issued a 15% stock dividend. Journalize this dividend.

Number of new shares issued for stock dividend = 12,000 × 15%
= 1,800 new shares

Jan 1	Retained earnings (1,800 × $8)	14,400	
	Additional paid-in capital (to balance)		10,800
	Common stock (1,800 × $2)		3,600

2. On January 2, 2012, Garbage split its common stock 2 for 1. Journalize the split. What are the par and market values per share after the split?

Common shares before split = 12,000 + 1,800
= 13,800

Number of shares after stock split = 13,800 × 2/1
= 27,600 shares

Par value per share after split = $2 × 1/2
= $1

Market price per share after split = $8 × 1/2
= $4

There is no journal entry for a stock split.

3. On January 3, 2012, Garbage declared and paid a cash dividend of $0.30 per common share. Journalize this dividend.

Jan 3	Retained earnings	8,280	
	Cash (27,600 × $0.30)		8,280

Do It Yourself! Question 2 Solutions

Treasury Stock

Requirement

1. Journalize all of Hartnick's treasury stock transactions.

On January 1, 2011, Hartnick, Co., purchased 1,000 shares of treasury stock for $7 cash each. At this time, Paid-in capital, treasury stock had a balance of $0.

| Jan 1 | Treasury stock | 7,000 | |
| | Cash (1,000 × $7) | | 7,000 |

February 1, 2011: Sold 200 shares for $10 cash each.

Feb 1	Cash (200 × $10)	2,000	
	Paid-in capital, treasury stock (to balance)		600
	Treasury stock (200 × $7)		1,400

March 1, 2011: Sold 500 shares for $6 cash each.

Mar 1	Cash (500 × $6)	3,000	
	Paid-in capital, treasury stock (to balance)	500	
	Treasury stock (500 × $7)		3,500

After this transaction:

Paid-In Capital, Treasury Stock				Treasury Stocks			
		Bal	0	Jan 1	7,000		
		Feb 1	600			Feb 1	1,400
Mar 1	500					Mar 1	3,500
		Bal	100	Bal	2,100		

April 1, 2011: Sold 300 shares for $6.50 cash each.

Apr 1	Cash (300 × $6.50)	1,950	
	Paid-in capital, treasury stock	100	
	Retained earnings (to balance)	50	
	Treasury stock (300 × $7)		2,100

Do It Yourself! Question 3 Solutions

Income Statement Presentation and Earnings per Share

Requirement

1. Prepare the lower portion of Gate's income statement for the year ended December 31, 2011, beginning with income from continuing operations, including earnings-per-share calculations.

Income from Continuing Operations (after tax):

$$\$2,500,000 - \$750,000 = \$1,750,000$$

Discontinued Operations (net of tax):

$$\$400,000 - \$80,000 = \$320,000$$

Extraordinary Items (net of tax):

$$-\$100,000 + \$30,000 = -\$70,000$$

Net Income:

$$\$1,750,000 + \$320,000 - \$70,000 = \$2,000,000$$

Number of Common Shares Outstanding:

$$\$200,000/\$0.50 \text{ par per share} = 400,000 \text{ shares}$$

Preferred Share Dividends Paid:

$$8\% \times \$500,000 = \$40,000$$

For income from continuing operations, basic earnings per share is

$$\frac{\$1,750,000 - \$40,000}{400,000 \text{ shares}} = \$4.275 \text{ per share}$$

The portion of earnings per share relating to discontinued operations is

$$\frac{\$320,000}{400,000 \text{ shares}} = \$0.80 \text{ per share}$$

The portion of earnings per share relating to extraordinary items is

$$\frac{-\$70{,}000}{400{,}000 \text{ shares}} = -\$0.175 \text{ per share}$$

For net income, basic earnings per share is

$$\frac{\$2{,}000{,}000 - \$40{,}000}{400{,}000 \text{ shares}} = \$4.90 \text{ per share}$$

Earnings per share:

Income from continuing operations	$1,750,000
+ Discontinued operations (net of tax)	320,000
− Extraordinary items (net of tax)	(29,000)
Net income	$2,000,000

Income from continuing operations	$4.275
Discontinued operations	0.800
Extraordinary items	(0.175)
Net income	$4.900

The Power of Practice

For more practice using the skills learned in this chapter, visit MyAccountingLab. There you will find algorithmically generated questions that are based on these Demo Docs and your main textbook's Review and Assess Your Progress sections.

Go to MyAccountingLab and follow these steps:

1. Direct your URL to www.myaccountinglab.com.
2. Log in using your name and password.
3. Click the MyAccountingLab link.
4. Click Study Plan in the left navigation bar.
5. From the table of contents, select Chapter 12, Corporations: Retained Earnings and the Income Statement.
6. Click a link to work tutorial exercises.

13 Statement of Cash Flows

WHAT YOU PROBABLY ALREADY KNOW

If you find yourself short of cash occasionally, it is not uncommon to wonder where all of the money has gone. You probably already know that you need to keep track of all cash received and spent for a period of time to find out the answer. Not only does that show you the *amount* of money coming in and going out, but you will also identify the *source* of the cash received and the *use* of the cash spent. Identifying the cash activities in your life helps you to predict your future cash flows based on past history, review the decisions you have made in your financial life that result in the creation and disbursement of cash, and assess your ability to meet future financial obligations. The same issues are important to a business. In this chapter, we will see how the statement of cash flows provides this information for an entity.

Learning Objectives/Success Keys

1 Identify the purposes of the statement of cash flows.

The statement of cash flows helps to do the following:

- Predict future cash flows. Recall from Chapter 12 the concept of income from continuing operations and special items. Those results are used to make predictions about the future.

- Evaluate management decisions. The cash-flow result of management's decisions is reflected in the statement of cash flows.

- Predict ability to pay debts and dividends. Investors and creditors will review past cash flows to assess the risk of nonpayment of debt and dividends.

2 Distinguish among operating, investing, and financing cash flows.

The statement of cash flows includes all transactions that increase or decrease Cash. These items are included in one of the following three categories:

- Operating—Activities that affect the income statement and current assets and current liabilities on the balance sheet. These transactions include inflows such as cash receipts from customers, interest, and dividends. Outflows include cash paid to employees and suppliers. *It is most important to have a positive net cash inflow for this activity.*

- Investing—Activities that affect long-term assets. These transactions include cash inflows from the sale of plant, property, and equipment; investments; and the collection from long-term loans. Outflows include the cash payment to purchase plant, property, and equipment; make investments; and make loans.

- Financing—Activities that affect long-term liabilities and stockholders' equity. These transactions include cash inflows from the sale of stock and issuance of long-term debt. Cash outflows include the payment of dividends and the repayment of debt.

Refer to Exhibit 13-2 (p. 684) for the relationship between the activity categories and the balance sheet classifications.

3 Prepare the statement of cash flows by the indirect method.

The **indirect method** reconciles from net income on the income statement to cash from operating activities. The schedule begins with accrual-basis net income and identifies the adjustments or items of difference to convert from the accrual basis of accounting to a cash basis for operating activities. Some of the adjustments include the following:

- eliminating such noncash expenses as depreciation, depletion, and amortization—these expenses need to be added to net income to eliminate the expense from net income.

- eliminating the gains or losses included in net income—gains need to be deducted from net income and losses need to be added to net income to eliminate these from net income. The full proceeds of sales are included as an investing activity.

- changes in the current assets and current liabilities—review the "Changes in the Current Assets and the Current Liabilities" section in the main text for the rules. Review the rationale for the rules.

This can be a challenging concept. Review carefully the "Cash Flows from Operating Activities" section of the main text and Exhibit 13-4 (p. 686).

4 Prepare the statement of cash flows by the direct method (Appendix 13A).

The **direct method** lists the amount of cash receipts and cash payments from operating activities by major category. The FASB recommends the direct method, but most corporations use the indirect method, which requires less work. *Review the direct method of presenting operating activities in Exhibit 13A-4 (p. 723).*

Demo Doc 1

Statement of Cash Flows (Indirect Method)

Learning Objectives 2, 3

Indirect Method

Tanker, Inc., had the following information at December 31, 2011:

TANKER, INC.
Balance Sheet
December 31, 2011

Assets	2011	2010	Change	Liabilities	2011	2010	Change
Current:				Current:			
Cash	$ 700	$1,160	$(460)	Accounts payable	$ 680	$ 530	$150
Accounts receivable	300	420	(120)				
Inventory	800	750	50	Long-term notes payable	660	815	
Prepaid insurance	120	90	30				
				Total liabilities	$1,340	$1,345	
Furniture	1,500	1,400					
Less acc. depn.	(400)	(475)		**Stockholders' Equity**			
Net	1,100	925		Common stock (no par)	$1,800	$1,800	
				Retained earnings	880	200	
Total assets	$3,020	$3,345		Less treasury stock	(1,000)	0	
				Total equity	$1,680	$2,000	
				Total liabilities and equity	$3,020	$3,345	

TANKER, INC.
Income Statement
Year Ended December 31, 2011

Sales revenue	$3,400
Less cost of goods sold	(1,750)
Gross margin	$1,650
Depreciation expense	$ (110)
Insurance expense	(230)
Other operating expenses	(390)
Gain on sale of furniture	80
Net income	$1,000

Other Information

- Every year, Tanker declares and pays cash dividends.
- During 2011, Tanker sold old furniture for $90 cash. Tanker also bought new furniture by making a cash down payment and signing a $200 note payable.
- During 2011, Tanker repaid $500 of notes payable in cash and borrowed new long-term notes payable for cash.
- During 2011, Tanker purchased treasury stock for cash. No treasury stock was sold.

Requirement

1. Prepare Tanker's statement of cash flows for the year ended December 31, 2011, using the indirect method.

Demo Doc 1 Solution

Requirement 1

2 Distinguish among operating, investing, and financing cash flows

3 Prepare the statement of cash flows by the indirect method

Prepare Tanker's statement of cash flows for the year ended December 31, 2011.

Part 1	Part 2	Part 3	Demo Doc Complete

Operating Activities

We first set up the statement of cash flows with the proper title and then start with operating activities.

Net Income

The first item is net income. Because net income is positive, it is added to the Cash balance. Therefore, we add (that is, positive number) $1,000 on our cash-flow statement.

Depreciation Expense

Net income includes depreciation expense, which must be removed because it is a 100% noncash item. Remember, no cash was "spent" for depreciation, yet it was still deducted to arrive at the net income number. Because depreciation expense was *subtracted* to calculate net income, we *add* it back to remove it.

Gain on Sale of Furniture

After depreciation, we must look for gains and losses on disposal of long-term assets. These are treated in a manner similar to the depreciation. No cash was "earned" for the gain, yet it was still added to arrive at the net income number. The gain on sale of furniture was *added* to calculate net income, so we *subtract* it to remove it.

Accounts Receivable

After looking at net income and the depreciation and gain adjustments, we need to incorporate the changes in current assets and current liabilities.

The increases and decreases in these accounts do not tell us whether to add or subtract these items on the cash-flow statement.

The first current asset (other than cash) is Accounts receivable. On the balance sheet we see:

Assets	2011	2010	Change
Current:			
Cash	$700	$1,160	$(460)
Accounts receivable	300	420	(120)

We must add the $120 decrease in Accounts receivable. There are two ways to reason this out:

1. Accounts receivable went down. Why? Tanker is collecting more of the cash that its customers owe. How does this affect Cash? It increases Cash; therefore, we should add the number on the cash-flow statement.

2. Accounts receivable went down. This is a decrease in an asset, which is a credit. If this credit is balanced out by the Cash account, that will be a debit to Cash, which is an increase. If Cash is increased, we should add the number on the cash-flow statement.

Notice that in both of these cases, we are adding or subtracting on the cash-flow statement because of the item's effect on *cash flow*. It doesn't matter if Accounts receivable went up or down; what matters is how that affects cash flow.

Inventory

Let's try the two ways with the next current asset: Inventory. On the balance sheet, we see:

Assets	2011	2010	Change
Current:			
Cash	$700	$1,160	$(460)
Accounts receivable	300	420	(120)
Inventory	800	750	50

During the year, Inventory increased by $50.

1. Why did Inventory increase? Tanker is purchasing inventory with cash. Therefore, this has a negative effect on cash flow.

2. If Inventory is increased, this is an increase in an asset, which is a debit. If this is balanced out by Cash, then Cash is credited, which is a negative effect on cash flow.

Prepaid Insurance

The last current asset is Prepaid insurance. On the balance sheet, we see:

Assets	2011	2010	Change
Current:			
Cash	$700	$1,160	$(460)
Accounts receivable	300	420	(120)
Inventory	800	750	50
Prepaid insurance	120	90	30

During the year, Prepaid insurance increased by $30.

1. Why did Prepaid insurance increase? Tanker paid more insurance costs in advance. This has a negative effect on cash flow.

2. If Prepaid insurance is increased, this is an increase in an asset, which is a debit. If this is balanced out by Cash, then Cash is credited, which is a negative effect on cash flow.

Accounts Payable

The last part of operating activities is to look at the changes in current liabilities. The only current liability in this question is Accounts payable. On the balance sheet, we see:

Liabilities	2011	2010	Change
Current:			
Accounts payable	$680	$530	$150

During the year, Accounts payable increased by $150.

1. Why did Accounts payable increase? Tanker is not paying all of its bills. This means that it is holding onto its cash, which is a positive effect on cash flow.

2. If Accounts payable is increased, this is an increase in a liability, which is a credit. If this is balanced out by Cash, then Cash is debited, which is a positive effect on cash flow.

We total these numbers, and we are finished with operating activities. The completed operating activities section would appear as:

Operating activities	
Net income	$1,000
Depreciation expense	110
Gain on sale of furniture	(80)
Decrease in accounts receivable	120
Increase in inventory	(50)
Increase in prepaid insurance	(30)
Increase in accounts payable	150
Total cash flow provided by operating activities	$1,220

Investing Activities

Part 1	Part 2	Part 3	Demo Doc Complete

Investing activities looks at cash purchases and cash disposals of long-term assets. This means that we need to know how much cash was paid to purchase new furniture and how much cash was received when Tanker sold some of the old furniture. Do we have any of these numbers right away? Yes, we are told in the question that Tanker signed a $200 note payable to purchase new furniture. We also know that the old furniture was sold for $90 cash.

Before we do anything else, we should point out that the $200 note payable is a <u>noncash transaction</u>. Although we will *need* to use it in our analysis, it will *not* appear on the main body of the cash-flow statement. Instead, it will appear in a note for noncash investing and financing activities:

Noncash investing and financing activities	
Purchase of furniture with note payable	$200

We need to calculate the *cash* Tanker paid to purchase new furniture. To do this, we need to analyze the Furniture (net) T-account:

Furniture (net)	
Bal 12/31/10 925	
increases	decreases
Bal 12/31/11 1,100	

We know that the Furniture (net) account increased and decreased. What caused that account to increase? Well, it would increase if Tanker bought new furniture. So obviously the cash paid *and* the note signed for new furniture went into this account.

What would cause the Furniture (net) account to decrease?

If Tanker sold furniture, we would decrease the account, *but* it would be decreased by the *book* value (that is, the *net* amount) of the furniture sold. Remember, the book value is another term for *net* value. We are looking at net value in the T-account, so the Furniture (net) account decreases by its *net/book* value.

We know that some furniture was sold, so obviously this decrease occurred.

We know that this furniture was sold for $90 cash, but this is *not* the net book value (NBV) of the furniture sold. This amount is still unknown.

However, we can calculate this amount using the gain/loss formula:

Gain or loss on sale of fixed assets = Cash received on sale of fixed assets − NBV of fixed assets sold

For this example, this becomes

Gain on sale of furniture = Cash received on sale of furniture − NBV of furniture sold

So: $80 = $90 − NBV of furniture sold.
Therefore, the NBV of furniture sold is $10.

What else would decrease Furniture (net)? Well, when Tanker takes depreciation expense, don't we decrease the net value of its assets? We know from the income statement that depreciation expense is $110. Let's now put all of the numbers in and see what comes out:

Furniture (net)			
Bal 12/31/10	925		
Cash purchases	X		
Noncash purchases	200		
		NBV furniture sold	10
		Depreciation expense	110
Bal 12/31/11	1,100		

So X = Cash paid to purchase furniture = $95.

To summarize, this is how we find missing information for long-term assets:

1. Set up a T-account for the net value of the asset.

2. Fill in as much information as you can in the T-account (such as beginning and ending balances, depreciation expense, and purchases or net book value of disposals).

3. Solve for any missing information.

4. If there is more than one number missing, or if the missing information is not the number you need, use the gain/loss formula to calculate any remaining information.

Now we can put our two numbers, $90 and $95, into the statement of cash flows. *Cash* purchases of equipment were $95. Did this cause Cash to increase or decrease? Obviously, it is a decrease because Tanker *paid* cash, so we will subtract it. Cash received on sale of equipment is $90, which is an increase to Cash, so we will add it.

Remember that for investing activities, we *cannot* combine these two items. They *must* be listed separately because they are two separate transactions.

Totaling these numbers completes investing activities.

The completed investing activities section would appear as

Investing activities	
Cash paid to purchase new furniture	$(95)
Cash proceeds from sale of furniture	90
Total cash flow provided by investing activities	$ (5)

Financing Activities

Part 1	Part 2	**Part 3**	Demo Doc Complete

Financing activities deals with long-term liabilities (debt) and equity accounts. First, we will look at long-term liabilities.

There are new notes payable (for which Tanker received cash) and Tanker repaid some other notes.

Notes Payable

We need the cash numbers involved so that we can put them into the cash-flow statement. Do we have any of them immediately available to us?

Yes, we are told that Tanker repaid $500 of notes payable.

We also know that Tanker took out a noncash note (to purchase furniture) of $200. This noncash transaction has already been recorded in the note to the cash-flow statement (discussed under investing activities).

Knowing this, let us analyze the Notes Payable T-account:

Notes payable			
		Bal 12/31/10	815
decreases		increases	
		Bal 12/31/11	660

What would cause this account to increase? Well, it would increase if Tanker took out new notes payable. What would cause it to decrease? It would decrease if Tanker paid off some of the notes. Let's put in that information:

	Notes payable	
	Bal 12/31/10	815
Note repayments 500		
	New cash notes	X
	New noncash notes	200
	Bal 12/31/11	660

So we can calculate that new cash notes = X = $145.

Now we can put these numbers into the cash-flow statement. *Cash* received from new notes was $145. This increased Cash, so it has a positive effect on cash flow. Cash paid to repay old notes was $500. This decreased Cash, so it has a negative effect on cash flow.

Treasury Stock

Now we must analyze the changes in Tanker's equity. Tanker had some activity with treasury stock during the year. We know that Tanker purchased treasury stock.

Treasury stock	
Bal 12/31/10 0	
increases	decreases
Bal 12/31/11 1,000	

What could cause this account to go up? It would go up if Tanker purchased treasury stock. What could cause it to go down? It would go down if treasury stock were sold. We know that there was no treasury stock sold, so looking at this again

Treasury stock	
Bal 12/31/10 0	
Treasury stock	
Purchased X	
	Treasury stock sold 0
Bal 12/31/11 1,000	

So we can calculate that treasury stock purchased = X = $1,000. This means that cash was paid by Tanker, which is a negative effect on cash flow.

Dividends

The other account in equity is Retained earnings. The two major transactions impacting Retained earnings are net income and dividends.

Net income was already listed in the operating activities section, so all that remains to be included in the financing activities section is dividend activity.

The Retained earnings account looks like this:

	Retained earnings	
	Bal 12/31/10	200
decreases	increases	
	Bal 12/31/11	880

What makes Retained earnings go up? It goes up when Tanker earns net income. What makes it go down? It goes down when Tanker pays dividends. Putting this information in

	Retained earnings	
	Bal 12/31/10	200
Cash dividends paid X		
	Net income	1,000
	Bal 12/31/11	880

So cash dividends paid = X = $320. These were paid in cash so this has a negative effect on Cash.

Totaling these numbers completes financing activities. The completed financing activities section would appear as

Financing activities	
Cash proceeds from new notes	$ 145
Cash repayment of old notes	(500)
Cash purchase of treasury stock	(1,000)
Cash dividends paid	(320)
Total cash flow provided by financing activities	$(1,675)

Now we must combine operating activities, investing activities, and financing activities to get the total cash flow (the change in cash during the year).

Next, we show the Cash balance from the prior year (December 31, 2010) and add it to total cash flow to get this year's Cash balance (December 31, 2011).

TANKER, INC.
Statement of Cash Flows
Year Ended December 31, 2011

Operating activities	
Net income	$ 1,000
+ Depreciation expense	110
– Gain on sale of furniture	(80)
+ Decrease in accounts receivable	120
– Increase in inventory	(50)
– Increase in prepaid insurance	(30)
+ Increase in accounts payable	150
Total cash flow provided by operating activities	$ 1,220
Investing activities	
Cash paid to purchase new furniture	$ (95)
Cash proceeds from sale of furniture	90
Total cash flow provided by investing activities	$ (5)
Financing activities	
Cash proceeds from new notes	$ 145
Cash repayment of old notes	(500)
Cash purchase of treasury stock	(1,000)
Cash dividends paid	(320)
Total cash flow provided by financing activities	$(1,675)
Total cash flow (change in Cash balance)	$ 460
Cash, December 31, 2010	$ 1,160
Cash, December 31, 2011	$ 700
Noncash investing and financing activities	
Purchase of furniture with note payable	$ 200

Part 1   Part 2   Part 3   **Demo Doc Complete**

Demo Doc 2

Statement of Cash Flows (Direct Method)

Learning Objectives 1, 2, 4

Direct Method

Use the information for Tanker, Inc., in the previous question:

TANKER, INC.
Balance Sheet
December 31, 2011

Assets	2011	2010	Change	Liabilities	2011	2010	Change
Current:				Current:			
Cash	$ 700	$1,160	$(460)	Accounts payable	$ 680	$ 530	$150
Accounts receivable	300	420	(120)				
Inventory	800	750	50	Long-term notes payable	660	815	
Prepaid insurance	120	90	30				
				Total liabilities	$1,340	$1,345	
Furniture	1,500	1,400					
Less acc. depn.	(400)	(475)		**Stockholders' Equity**			
Net	1,100	925		Common stock (no par)	$1,800	$1,800	
				Retained earnings	880	200	
Total assets	$3,020	$3,345		Less treasury stock	(1,000)	0	
				Total equity	$1,680	$2,000	
				Total liabilities and equity	$3,020	$3,345	

TANKER, INC.
Income Statement
Year Ended December 31, 2011

Sales revenue		$3,400
Less cost of goods sold		(1,750)
Gross margin		$1,650
Depreciation expense		$ (110)
Insurance expense		(230)
Other operating expenses		(390)
Gain on sale of furniture		80
Net income		$1,000

Requirements

1. Prepare the operating activities section of Tanker's statement of cash flow using the direct method.

2. How is the information a cash-flow statement provides different from the information an income statement provides?

Demo Doc 2 Solutions

Requirement 1

2 Distinguish among operating, investing, and financing cash flows

4 Prepare the statement of cash flows by the direct method (Appendix 13A)

Prepare the operating activities section of Tanker's statement of cash flows using the direct method.

Part 1	Part 2	Demo Doc Complete

We need to list all of the cash transactions involved in Tanker's day-to-day business operations. To do this, we should look at the income statement to get an idea of what these transactions are.

Cash Received from Customers

What is the first item on the income statement? Revenues. How does this translate into a cash transaction? Revenues should result in customers giving Tanker cash, so the appropriate line on the direct method cash-flow statement is "cash received from customers."

For each income statement account that is not 100% cash, there is always a balance sheet account to record the related accrual. In this case, Accounts receivable (on the balance sheet) takes care of revenues when cash has not yet been collected.

Accounts receivable	
Bal 12/31/10	420
increases	decreases
Bal 12/31/11	300

What could cause this account to increase? It would increase if Tanker had more sales. What could cause it to decrease? It would decrease if Tanker collected the cash. We know from the income statement that sales were $3,400, so

Accounts receivable			
Bal 12/31/10	420		
Sales revenue	3,400		
		Cash collected	X
Bal 12/31/11	300		

X = cash collected from customers = $3,520. This is the amount for the direct method cash-flow statement.

Cash Paid to Suppliers

The next line on the income statement is cost of goods sold. How does this relate to a cash transaction? In order to get the goods Tanker sold, it must buy the items from a supplier and pay for them. So the appropriate line on the cash-flow statement is "cash paid to suppliers." Accounts payable is the balance sheet account that takes care of bills to suppliers that have not yet been paid.

Accounts payable			
		Bal 12/31/10	530
decreases	increase		
		Bal 12/31/11	680

What could cause this account to increase? It would increase if Tanker had more bills (that is, if Tanker were to purchase inventory from its suppliers). What could cause it to decrease? It would decrease if Tanker paid the cash it owed to the suppliers. However, we don't know how much inventory was purchased.

We can figure this out using the inventory formula from Chapter 6:

COGS	=	Beginning inventory	+ Purchases –	Ending inventory
$1,750 =		$ 750	+ Purchases –	$800
Purchases =		$1,800		

Putting this into the Accounts Payable T-account

Accounts payable			
		Bal 12/31/10	530
Cash payments	X		
		Inventory purchases	1,800
		Bal 12/31/11	680

X = Cash payments to suppliers = $1,650. This is the amount for the direct method cash-flow statement.

The next item on the income statement is depreciation expense. Because we know that this is 100% noncash, we can ignore it for the direct method.

Cash Paid as Insurance

Next is insurance expense. This would result in "cash paid as insurance." To calculate this number, we need to analyze the Prepaid insurance account.

Prepaid insurance			
Bal 12/31/10	90		
	increases	decreases	
Bal 12/31/11	120		

What could cause this account to increase? It would increase if Tanker paid more insurance in advance. What could cause it to decrease? It would decrease if Tanker incurred that insurance expense. We know from the income statement that insurance expense was $230.

Prepaid insurance			
Bal 12/31/10	90		
Cash payments	X		
		Insurance expense	230
Bal 12/31/11	120		

X = Cash paid as insurance = $260. This is the amount for the direct method statement of cash flows.

Following insurance expense are other expenses. Let's leave this until the end.

After this is the gain on sale of furniture. This is noncash and, therefore, does not impact a direct method cash-flow statement.

Other Cash Expenses

Now we come back to other expenses. Are there any other current asset or current liability accounts with which we have not yet dealt? No, we have analyzed all of them. This means that there is no accrual portion (that is, no *noncash* portion) of these expenses. So we can just assume that they were *all paid in cash*. Therefore, the last line in the operating activities section is "other cash expenses" of $390.

Operating activities	
Cash collected from customers	$ 3,520
Cash paid to suppliers	(1,650)
Cash paid for insurance	(260)
Other cash expenses	(390)
Cash flow provided by operating activities	$ 1,220

Notice that the "cash flow provided by operating activities" of $1,220 is the *same* total we calculated under the indirect method. It is *always* the case that cash flow from operating activities is the same under the direct and indirect methods. This is a good check to confirm that our calculations were correct.

Remember that the investing and financing activities are the same under both methods. So the rest of Tanker's cash-flow statement (investing activities to the end) would be identical to what is shown in Demo Doc 1.

Requirement 2

How is the information a cash-flow statement provides different from the information an income statement provides?

Part 1	**Part 2**	Demo Doc Complete

The income statement shows the determination of net income. Net income is calculated on an accrual basis.

This means that net income not only includes cash transactions *but also* includes noncash transactions. We record revenue earned and expenses incurred *regardless* of whether or not cash has been received or paid.

The cash-flow statement shows the determination of cash flow (that is, the change in the Cash balance during the year). Because the cash-flow statement distills all transactions down to their cash components only, it is missing certain noncash transactions that are included in net income. Cash flow is actually net income *under the cash basis of accounting*.

So the primary difference is that the income statement is prepared under the accrual basis of accounting, whereas the cash-flow statement is prepared under the cash basis of accounting.

Part 1	Part 2	**Demo Doc Complete**

Quick Practice Questions

True/False

_____ 1. The statement of cash flows helps to inform the reader about all of the differences between net income and cash flows from operations.

_____ 2. A company may have net income but still have a net cash outflow.

_____ 3. Cash payments for interest expense would be classified as a financing activity.

_____ 4. Free cash flow is a measure of cash adequacy that focuses on the amount of cash available from operations after paying for planned investments in long-term assets.

_____ 5. Purchases of plant assets for cash would be classified as a financing activity.

_____ 6. Under the indirect method, depreciation expense would be subtracted from net income in the operating activities.

_____ 7. The majority of U.S. corporations use the direct method in preparing the statement of cash flows.

_____ 8. Under the indirect method, the acquisition of land through the issuance of common stock would be an investing activity on the statement of cash flows.

_____ 9. When using the indirect method, a loss on sale of equipment is added to net income under the operating activities.

_____ 10. Interest received on a bond investment would be shown as an investing cash inflow.

Multiple Choice

1. Which of the following statements is *incorrect*?
   a. A statement of cash flows is a basic financial statement required by GAAP.
   b. A statement of cash flows is dated for a period of time as opposed to a point in time.
   c. One purpose of a statement of cash flows is to predict future cash flows.
   d. The statement of cash flows may be combined with the stockholders' equity section of the balance sheet.

2. The operating activities section has a relationship with which part of the balance sheet?
   a. Current assets and current liabilities
   b. Long-term assets
   c. Stockholders' Equity and all liabilities
   d. Stockholders' Equity and long-term liabilities

3. Dividend payments would be included in which section of the statement of cash flows?
   a. Operating activities
   b. Financing activities
   c. Investing activities
   d. Dividend payments are not included on the statement of cash flows.

4. Cash dividends received would be included in which section of the statement of cash flows?
   a. Operating activities
   b. Financing activities
   c. Investing activities
   d. Cash dividends received are not included on the statement of cash flows.

5. The purchase of treasury stock would be included in which section of the statement of cash flows?
   a. Operating activities
   b. Financing activities
   c. Investing activities
   d. The purchase of treasury stock is not included on the statement of cash flows.

6. Activities that create revenues and expenses are included in which section of the statement of cash flows?
   a. Investing activities
   b. Operating activities
   c. Financing activities
   d. Noncash investing and financing activities

7. Where are noncash investing and financing activities reported?
   a. The financing activities section of the statement of cash flows
   b. The investing activities section of the statement of cash flows
   c. Both (a) and (b) are correct
   d. An accompanying schedule to the statement of cash flows

8. Where is the gain resulting from the sale of equipment shown under the indirect method?
   a. In the operating activities section as a deduction
   b. In the operating activities section as an addition
   c. In the investing activities section as an addition
   d. In the financing activities section as a deduction

9. Wilson Companys 2011 income statement reports depreciation expense of $25,000. How would depreciation be shown on the statement of cash flows using the direct method for 2011?
   a. As an addition under financing activities
   b. As a deduction under operating activities
   c. As an addition under operating activities
   d. It would not be reported.

10. Which of the following would be shown as a deduction to net income under the operating activities section using the indirect method?
    a. Depletion expense
    b. Increase in Accounts payable account balance for the period
    c. Increase in Inventory balance for the period
    d. Decrease in Accounts receivable account balance for the period

Quick Practice Questions | Chapter 13   **447**

Quick Exercises

13-1. Your best friend just lost his job because the company he was working for went bankrupt. He was complaining to you that even though the company had been profitable for three years in a row, it still went out of business. He asks you how this can happen.

Requirements

1. Explain the most likely reason for the company's declaring bankruptcy. Could your friend have seen it coming? How?

2. Discuss the four purposes of the statement of cash flows.

13-2. State whether each of the following events should be classified as an operating activity (O), investing activity (I), financing activity (F), shown in a separate schedule of noncash investing and financing activities (N), or not disclosed on the statement of cash flows (NA).

_____ a. Received cash dividends
_____ b. Retired bonds payable by issuing common stock
_____ c. Paid for merchandise purchased on account
_____ d. Paid interest on a short-term note payable
_____ e. Received stock dividends
_____ f. Paid for a three-year insurance policy on property
_____ g. Issued preferred stock in exchange for land
_____ h. Issued common stock for cash
_____ i. Received cash from sale of land
_____ j. Purchased equipment for cash

13-3. Using the following data, prepare the operating activities section of a statement of cash flows for Washington Corporation for the year ended December 31, 2011. Assume the indirect method is used.

Increase in salary payable	$ 1,500
Decrease in accounts payable	2,000
Increase in accounts receivable	3,500
Net income	98,000
Decrease in inventory	5,800
Increase in prepaid expenses	1,200
Depreciation expense—Equipment	5,000
Depreciation expense—Buildings	7,500
Gain on sale of equipment	1,300
Loss on sale of patent	2,500

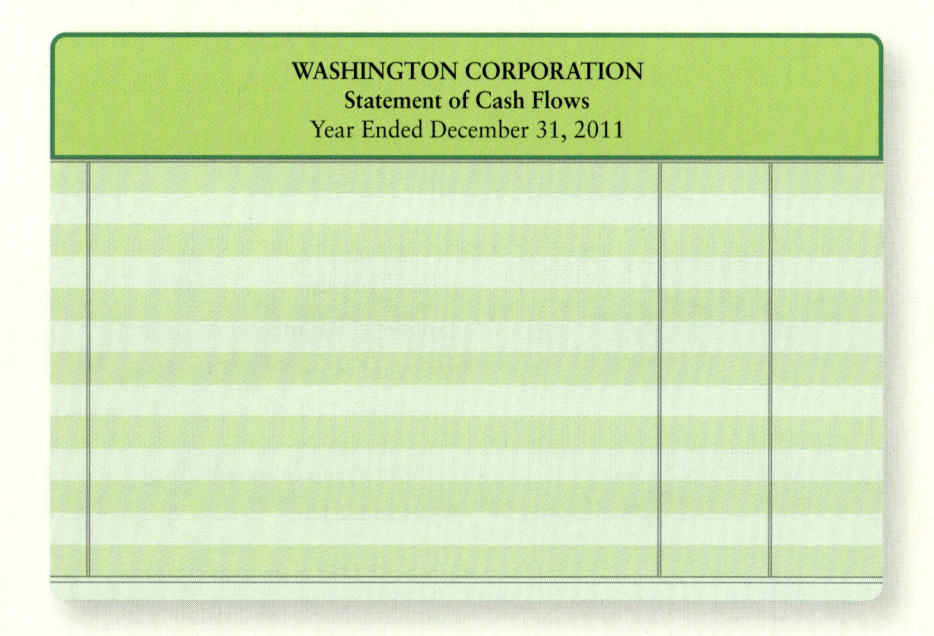

WASHINGTON CORPORATION
Statement of Cash Flows
Year Ended December 31, 2011

13-4. For each of the following events, determine if it should be classified as an operating activity (O), investing activity (I), or financing activity (F). Then determine the increase or decrease to the Cash account using the indirect method.

Transaction description	Type of activity	Cash inflow (outflow)
a. Declared cash dividends of $21,000 during the current period. Dividends payable on January 1 were $1,500; the December 31 balance was $2,300.		
b. Interest income on the income statement for the current period is $22,000. Interest receivable on January 1 was $2,700; the December 31 balance was $2,250.		
c. Issued $1,000,000, 10-year, 10% bonds at 102.		
d. Sales on account for the current period amount to $160,000. The January 1 balance in Accounts receivable was $95,000; the December 31 balance was $106,000.		
e. Purchased equipment for $215,000 cash.		
f. Sold 1,000 shares of $20 par common stock for cash at $29.		
g. Salary expense on the income statement for the current year is $151,500. The Salary payable balance on January 1 was $20,300; the December 31 balance was $17,800.		

13-5A. Aycoth, Inc., gathered the following data from its accounting records for the year ended December 31, 2011:

Depreciation expense	$ 15,900
Payment of income taxes	24,500
Collections of accounts receivable	166,700
Purchase of treasury stock	40,000
Declaration of stock dividend	65,000
Loss on sale of plant assets	8,400
Collection of dividend revenue	13,800
Payments of salaries and wages	83,600
Cash sales	102,900
Net income	61,200
Acquisition of land	73,500
Payment of interest	19,400
Interest received on investments	3,100
Issuance of bonds payable	500,000
Increase in accounts payable	20,300
Payments to suppliers	170,300
Acquisition of equipment by issuing long-term note payable	50,000

Prepare the operating activities section of the statement of cash flows using the direct method.

AYCOTH, INC.
Partial Statement of Cash Flows
Year Ended December 31, 2011

Do It Yourself! Question 1

Indirect Method

Clean, Co., had the following information at December 31, 2011:

CLEAN, CO.
Balance Sheet
December 31, 2011

Assets	2011	2010	Change	Liabilities	2011	2010	Change
Current:				Current:			
Cash	$ 460	$ 320	$140	Accounts payable	$ 800	$ 540	$260
Accounts receivable	510	420	90				
Inventory	710	750	(40)	Long-term notes payable	600	900	
Prepaid rent	170	250	(80)	Total liabilities	$1,400	$1,440	
Equipment	1,350	1,500		**Stockholders' Equity**			
Less acc. depn.	(400)	(650)		Common stock (no par)	$ 200	$ 150	
Net	950	850		Retained earnings	1,200	1,000	
Total assets	$2,800	$2,590		Total equity	$1,400	$1,150	
				Total liabilities and equity	$2,800	$2,590	

CLEAN, CO.
Income Statement
Year Ended December 31, 2011

Sales revenue	$1,800
Less cost of goods sold	(960)
Gross margin	$ 840
Depreciation expense	$ (90)
Rent expense	(140)
Other operating expenses	(195)
Loss on sale of equipment	(55)
Net income	$ 360

Other Information

- Every year, Clean declares and pays cash dividends.
- During 2011, Clean sold old equipment for cash. Clean also bought new equipment for $120 cash and a $140 note payable.
- During 2011, Clean repaid $600 of notes payable in cash and borrowed new long-term notes payable for cash.
- During 2011, new common stock was issued. No stock was retired.

Requirement

2 Distinguish among operating, investing, and financing cash flows

3 Prepare the statement of cash flows by the indirect method

1. Prepare Clean's statement of cash flows for the year ended December 31, 2011, using the indirect method.

Do It Yourself! Question 2

Direct Method

Use the information for Clean, Co., in the previous question.

Requirement

2 Distinguish among operating, investing, and financing cash flows

4 Prepare the statement of cash flows by the direct method (Appendix 13A)

1. Prepare the operating activities section of Clean's statement of cash flows using the direct method.

Quick Practice Solutions

True/False

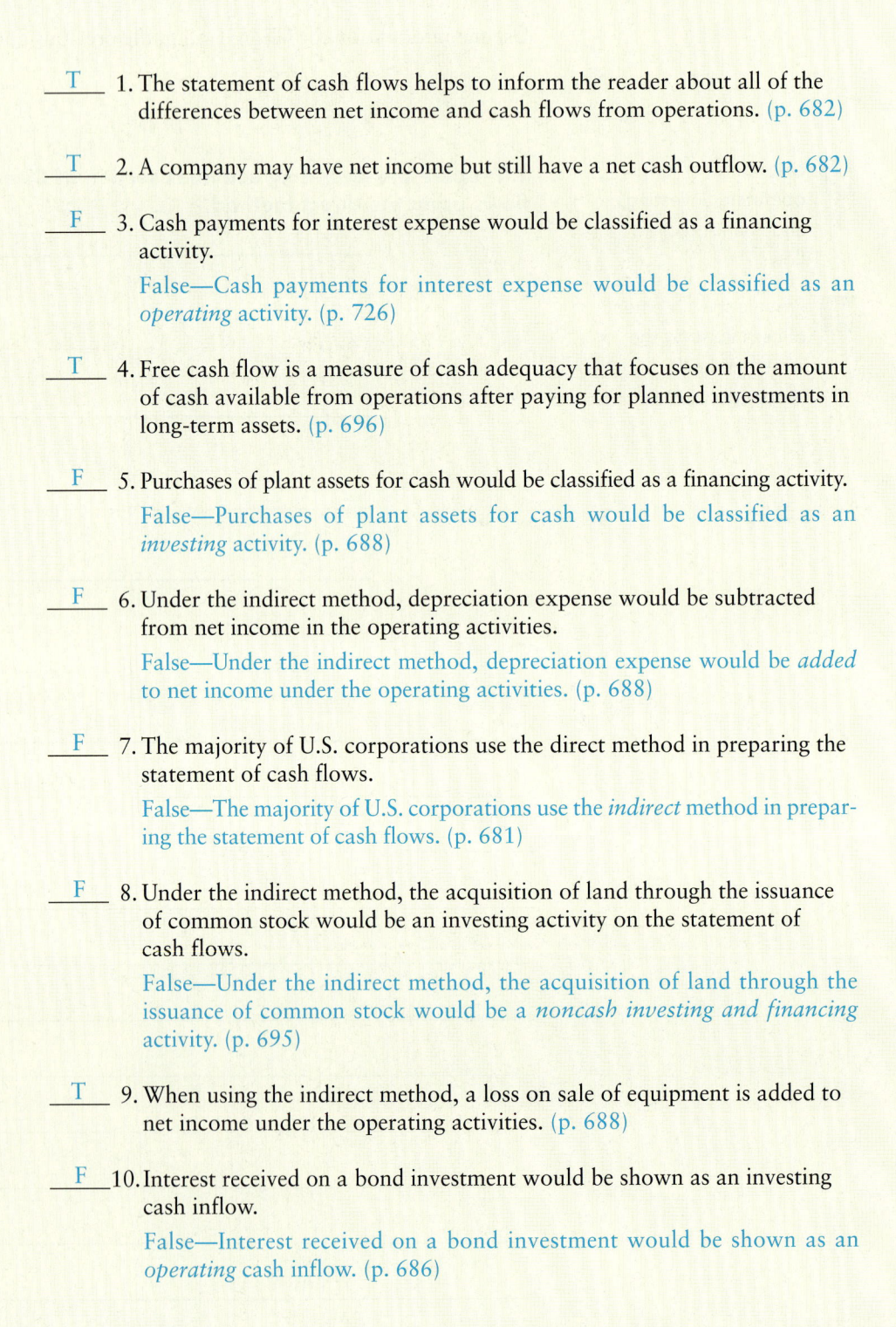

__T__ 1. The statement of cash flows helps to inform the reader about all of the differences between net income and cash flows from operations. (p. 682)

__T__ 2. A company may have net income but still have a net cash outflow. (p. 682)

__F__ 3. Cash payments for interest expense would be classified as a financing activity.

False—Cash payments for interest expense would be classified as an *operating* activity. (p. 726)

__T__ 4. Free cash flow is a measure of cash adequacy that focuses on the amount of cash available from operations after paying for planned investments in long-term assets. (p. 696)

__F__ 5. Purchases of plant assets for cash would be classified as a financing activity.

False—Purchases of plant assets for cash would be classified as an *investing* activity. (p. 688)

__F__ 6. Under the indirect method, depreciation expense would be subtracted from net income in the operating activities.

False—Under the indirect method, depreciation expense would be *added* to net income under the operating activities. (p. 688)

__F__ 7. The majority of U.S. corporations use the direct method in preparing the statement of cash flows.

False—The majority of U.S. corporations use the *indirect* method in preparing the statement of cash flows. (p. 681)

__F__ 8. Under the indirect method, the acquisition of land through the issuance of common stock would be an investing activity on the statement of cash flows.

False—Under the indirect method, the acquisition of land through the issuance of common stock would be a *noncash investing and financing* activity. (p. 695)

__T__ 9. When using the indirect method, a loss on sale of equipment is added to net income under the operating activities. (p. 688)

__F__ 10. Interest received on a bond investment would be shown as an investing cash inflow.

False—Interest received on a bond investment would be shown as an *operating* cash inflow. (p. 686)

Multiple Choice

1. Which of the following statements is incorrect? (p. 683)
   a. A statement of cash flows is a basic financial statement required by GAAP.
   b. A statement of cash flows is dated for a period of time as opposed to a point in time.
   c. One purpose of a statement of cash flows is to predict future cash flows.
   d. The statement of cash flows may be combined with the stockholders' equity section of the balance sheet.

2. The operating activities section has a relationship with which part of the balance sheet? (p. 683)
   a. Current assets and current liabilities
   b. Long-term assets
   c. Stockholders' equity and all liabilities
   d. Stockholders' equity and long-term liabilities

3. Dividend payments would be included in which section of the statement of cash flows? (p. 683)
   a. Operating activities
   b. Financing activities
   c. Investing activities
   d. Dividend payments are not included on the statement of cash flows.

4. Cash dividends received would be included in which section of the statement of cash flows? (p. 683)
   a. Operating activities
   b. Financing activities
   c. Investing activities
   d. Cash dividends received are not included on the statement of cash flows.

5. The purchase of treasury stock would be included in which section of the statement of cash flows? (p. 683)
   a. Operating activities
   b. Financing activities
   c. Investing activities
   d. The purchase of treasury stock is not included on the statement of cash flows.

6. Activities that create revenues and expenses are included in which section of the statement of cash flows? (p. 683)
   a. Investing activities
   b. Operating activities
   c. Financing activities
   d. Noncash investing and financing activities

7. Where are noncash investing and financing activities reported? (p. 694)
   a. The financing activities section of the statement of cash flows
   b. The investing activities section of the statement of cash flows
   c. Both (a) and (b) are correct
   d. An accompanying schedule to the statement of cash flows

8. Where is the gain resulting from the sale of equipment shown under the indirect method? (p. 685)
   a. In the operating activities section as a deduction
   b. In the operating activities section as an addition
   c. In the investing activities section as an addition
   d. In the financing activities section as a deduction

9. Wilson Company's 2011 income statement reports depreciation expense of $25,000. How would depreciation be shown on the statement of cash flows using the direct method for 2011? (p. 726)
   a. As an addition under financing activities
   b. As a deduction under operating activities
   c. As an addition under operating activities
   d. It would not be reported.

10. Which of the following would be shown as a deduction to net income under the operating activities section using the indirect method? (p. 686)
    a. Depletion expense
    b. Increase in Accounts payable account balance for the period
    c. Increase in Inventory balance for the period
    d. Decrease in Accounts receivable account balance for the period

Quick Exercises

13-1. Your best friend just lost his job because the company he was working for went bankrupt. He was complaining to you that even though the company had been profitable for three years in a row, it still went out of business. He asks you how this can happen. (p. 682)

Requirements

1. Explain the most likely reason for the company's declaring bankruptcy. Could your friend have seen it coming? How?

A profitable company is one in which revenues exceed expenses on an accrual basis. This does not necessarily mean that the company is generating enough cash to pay its bills. The most likely reason your friend's company went bankrupt is the lack of cash. If your friend had access to the statement of cash-flows, the cash flow problems would have likely been evident.

2. Discuss the four purposes of the statement of cash flows.

The four purposes of the statement of cash flows are as follows:
1. To help predict future cash flows
2. To evaluate management decisions
3. To determine the company's ability to pay dividends to stockholders and interest and principal to creditors
4. To show the relationship of net income to changes in the business's cash

13-2. State whether each of the following events should be classified as an operating activity (O), investing activity (I), financing activity (F), shown in a separate schedule of noncash investing and financing activities (N), or not disclosed on the statement of cash flows (NA). (pp. 683–684)

O	a.	Received cash dividends
N	b.	Retired bonds payable by issuing common stock
O	c.	Paid for merchandise purchased on account
O	d.	Paid interest on a short-term note payable
NA	e.	Received stock dividends
O	f.	Paid for a three-year insurance policy on property
N	g.	Issued preferred stock in exchange for land
F	h.	Issued common stock for cash
I	i.	Received cash from sale of land
I	j.	Purchased equipment for cash

13-3. Using the following data, prepare the operating activities section of a statement of cash flows for Washington Corporation for the year ended December 31, 2011. Assume the indirect method is used. (pp. 684–696)

Increase in salary payable	$ 1,500
Decrease in accounts payable	2,000
Increase in accounts receivable	3,500
Net income	98,000
Decrease in inventory	5,800
Increase in prepaid expenses	1,200
Depreciation expense—Equipment	5,000
Depreciation expense—Buildings	7,500
Gain on sale of equipment	1,300
Loss on sale of patent	2,500

WASHINGTON CORPORATION
Statement of Cash Flows
Year Ended December 31, 2011

Cash flows from operating activities:		
Net income		$ 98,000
Adjustments to reconcile net income to net cash provided by operating activities:		
Depreciation on equipment	$5,000	
Depreciation on buildings	7,500	
Loss on sale of patent	2,500	
Gain on sale of equipment	(1,300)	
Increase in accounts receivable	(3,500)	
Increase in prepaid expenses	(1,200)	
Decrease in inventory	5,800	
Increase in salary payable	1,500	
Decrease in accounts payable	(2,000)	14,300
Net cash inflow from operating activities		$112,300

13-4. For each of the following events, determine if it should be classified as an operating activity (O), investing activity (I), or financing activity (F). Then determine the cash inflow or (outflow). (pp. 683–684)

Transaction description	Type of activity	Cash inflow (outflow)
a. Declared cash dividends of $21,000 during the current period. Dividends payable on January 1 were $1,500; the December 31 balance was $2,300.	F	$ (20,200)
b. Interest income on the income statement for the current period is $22,000. Interest receivable on January 1 was $2,700; the December 31 balance was $2,250.	O	$ 22,450
c. Issued $1,000,000, 10-year, 10% bonds at 102.	F	$1,020,000
d. Sales on account for the current period amount to $160,000. The January 1 balance in Accounts Receivable was $95,000; the December 31 balance was $106,000.	O	$ 149,000
e. Purchased equipment for $215,000 cash.	I	$ (215,000)
f. Sold 1,000 shares of $20 par common stock for cash at $29.	F	$ 29,000
g. Salary expense on the income statement for the current year is $151,500. The Salary Payable balance on January 1 was $20,300; the December 31 balance was $17,800.	O	$ (154,000)

13-5A. Aycoth, Inc., gathered the following data from its accounting records for the year ended December 31, 2011: (pp. 721–726)

Depreciation expense	$ 15,900
Payment of income taxes	24,500
Collections of accounts receivable	166,700
Purchase of treasury stock	40,000
Declaration of stock dividend	65,000
Loss on sale of plant assets	8,400
Collection of dividend revenue	13,800
Payments of salaries and wages	83,600
Cash sales	102,900
Net income	61,200
Acquisition of land	73,500
Payment of interest	19,400
Interest received on investments	3,100
Issuance of bonds payable	500,000
Increase in accounts payable	20,300
Payments to suppliers	170,300
Acquisition of equipment by issuing long-term note payable	50,000

Prepare the operating activities section of the statement of cash flows using the direct method.

AYCOTH, INC.
Partial Statement of Cash Flows
Year Ended December 31, 2011

Cash flows from operating activities:		
Receipts:		
Collections from customers	$ 269,600*	
Interest received	3,100	
Dividends received	13,800	
Total cash receipts		$286,500
Payments:		
To suppliers	$(170,300)	
To employees	(83,600)	
For interest	(19,400)	
For income tax	(24,500)	
Total cash payments		(297,800)
Net cash outflow from operating activities		$ (11,300)

*($166,700 + $102,900 = $269,600)

Do It Yourself! Question 1 Solutions

Requirements

1. Prepare Clean's statement of cash flows for the year ended December 31, 2011, using the indirect method.

Calculations: Investing Activities

The $140 note payable is a <u>noncash transaction</u>.

Equipment (net)			
Bal 12/31/10	850		
Cash purchases	120		
Noncash purchases	140		
		NBV equipment sold	X
		Depreciation expense	90
Bal 12/31/11	950		

X = NBV of equipment sold = $70
Loss = – $55 = Cash received – $70
Cash received on sale of equipment = $15

Calculations: Financing Activities

Notes payable			
		Bal 12/31/10	900
Note repayments	600		
		New cash notes	X
		New noncash notes	140
		Bal 12/31/11	600

New cash notes = X = $160

Common stock			
		Bal 12/31/10	150
Retirements	0		
		New stock issued	X
		Bal 12/31/11	200

New stock issued = X = $50

Retained earnings			
Cash dividends paid X	Bal 12/31/10	1,000
	Net income	360
	Bal 12/31/11	1,200

Cash dividends paid = X = $160

CLEAN, CO.
Statement of Cash Flows
Year Ended December 31, 2011

Operating activities	
Net income	$ 360
+ Depreciation expense	90
+ Loss on sale of equipment	55
− Increase in accounts receivable	(90)
+ Decrease in inventory	40
+ Decrease in prepaid rent	80
+ Increase in accounts payable	260
Total cash flow provided by operating activities	$ 795
Investing activities	
Cash paid to purchase new equipment	$(120)
Cash proceeds from sale of equipment	15
Total cash flow provided by investing activities	$(105)
Financing activities	
Cash proceeds from new notes	$ 160
Cash repayment of old notes	(600)
Cash proceeds from new stock issue	50
Cash dividends paid	(160)
Total cash flow provided by financing activities	$(550)
Total cash flow (change in Cash during year)	$ 140
Cash, December 31, 2010	$ 320
Cash, December 31, 2011	$ 460
Noncash investing and financing activities	
Purchase of equipment with note payable	$ 140

Do It Yourself! Question 2 Solutions

Requirements

1. **Prepare the operating activities section of Clean's statement of cash flows using the direct method.**

Accounts receivable			
Bal 12/31/10	420		
Sales revenue	1,800		
		Cash collected	X
Bal 12/31/11	510		

X = Cash collected from customers = $1,710
COGS = $960 = $750 + purchases − $710
Purchases = $920

Accounts payable			
		Bal 12/31/10	540
Cash payments	X		
		Inventory purchases	920
		Bal 12/31/11	800

X = Cash payments to suppliers = $660

Prepaid rent			
Bal 12/31/10	250		
Cash payments	X		
		Rent expense	140
Bal 12/31/11	170		

X = Cash paid as rent = $60

Operating activities	
Cash collected from customers	$1,710
Cash paid to suppliers	(660)
Cash paid for rent	(60)
Other cash expenses	(195)
Cash flow from operating activities	$ 795

The Power of Practice

For more practice using the skills learned in this chapter, visit MyAccountingLab. There you will find algorithmically generated questions that are based on these Demo Docs and your main textbook's Review and Assess Your Progress sections.

Go to MyAccountingLab and follow these steps:

1. Direct your URL to www.myaccountinglab.com.
2. Log in using your name and password.
3. Click the MyAccountingLab link.
4. Click Study Plan in the left navigation bar.
5. From the table of contents, select Chapter 13, The Statement of Cash Flows.
6. Click a link to work tutorial exercises.

14 Financial Statement Analysis

WHAT YOU PROBABLY ALREADY KNOW

For years now, you have been a student and have taken many exams. You probably already know that there may be typical responses you have upon receiving your grade. Your first reaction may be the level of satisfaction you have with your grade compared to your previous grades received in that class and the established grading norms for your institution. You may then ask your friends what grade they received so that you can compare your results to them. The instructor may announce the average exam results and you could then determine if you performed better or worse than the average. Students often like to assess their performance by comparing their grade to a standard, their peers, and the average. Businesses often do the same thing. In this chapter, you study various techniques and ratios that a business will use to assess its performance using comparisons to previous results, competitors, and the industry average.

Learning Objectives/Success Keys

1 Perform a horizontal analysis of financial statements.

Horizontal analysis provides comparisons of financial information over time. To analyze a line item in the financial statements, the difference between the current and earlier time period amounts is computed. The dollar amount change of the line item between the periods is useful, but it is more informative to determine the percentage change by dividing the dollar change (current period amount, or this year's balance minus earlier period amount, or last year's balance) by the earlier period amount. *Review the horizontal analysis of the income statement and the balance sheet in Exhibits 14-2 and 14-3 (pp. 747–748).*

2 Perform a vertical analysis of financial statements.

Vertical analysis provides comparisons of individual items on a financial statement to a relative base. The base, which serves as the denominator, is usually net sales for the income statement and total assets for the balance sheet. The vertical analysis percentage is calculated by dividing each financial statement item amount by the relevant base of net sales *or* total assets.

The vertical analysis percentage is shown next to the item amount on the financial statement. *Review the vertical analysis of the income statement and the balance sheet in Exhibits 14-4 and 14-5 (p. 750).*

3. Prepare and use common-size financial statements.

A **common-size statement** is similar to the vertical analysis but shows only the vertical analysis percentages of each item in the financial statement. This presentation permits ready comparisons between companies of various sizes. *Review the common-size comparison of SmartTouch versus Learning Tree in Exhibit 14-6 (p. 751).*

4. Compute the standard financial ratios.

Financial ratios are helpful to assess a company's performance and financial position. Trends can be determined and comparisons to competing companies can be made. Various ratios are presented to measure the following:

- Ability to pay current liabilities

- Ability to sell inventory and collect receivables

- Ability to pay long-term debt

- Profitability

- Return on stock investment

Review "Using Ratios to Make Decisions" in the main text for descriptions and formulas for the financial ratios.

Demo Doc 1

Financial Statement Analysis

Learning Objectives 1–4

MeMe Co. had the following information at December 31, 2011:

MEME CO.
Balance Sheet
December 31, 2011 and 2010

	2011	2010
Assets		
Cash	$150	$130
Accounts receivable	80	145
Inventory	130	190
Total assets	**$360**	**$465**
Liabilities		
Accounts payable	90	140
Loans payable	140	220
Total liabilities	**$230**	**$360**
Stockholders' Equity		
Common stock	20	10
Retained earnings	110	95
Total stockholders' equity	**$130**	**$105**
Total liabilities and equity	**$360**	**$465**

MEME CO.
Income Statement
Years Ended December 31, 2011 and 2010

	2011	2010
Sales revenue	$650	$580
Less cost of goods sold	430	350
Gross profit	**$220**	**$230**
Salary expense	120	140
Rent expense	70	80
Net income	**$ 30**	**$ 10**

At December 31, 2009, MeMe's inventory was $160 and total equity was $95.

Requirements

1. Prepare horizontal and vertical analyses for MeMe's financial statements.

2. Calculate MeMe's inventory turnover and rate of return on stockholders' equity ratios for both years.

Demo Doc 1 Solutions

Requirement 1

1 Perform a horizontal analysis of financial statements

Prepare horizontal and vertical analyses for MeMe's financial statements.

| Part 1 | Part 2 | Part 3 | Demo Doc Complete |

Horizontal Analysis

As its name implies, horizontal analysis goes *across* the rows of the financial statements, looking at *one* account and how it has changed.

For *each* number on the balance sheet and income statement, we calculate the <u>dollar change</u> and the <u>percent change</u>.

> Dollar change = This year's balance − Last year's balance

So in the dollar change of Accounts receivable and Sales revenue:

> Accounts receivable = $80 − $145
> = $(65) change
> Sales revenue = $650 − $580
> = $70 change

Notice that the negative value on the change in Accounts receivable indicates that this account has decreased, whereas the positive value on the change in Sales revenue indicates that this account has increased.

Extra care must be taken when using this calculation on expenses (because they are presented as subtracted/negative numbers on the income statement). The *absolute value* of the expense (that is, ignoring the fact that it is already a negative number) must be used to calculate dollar change. In the dollar change of COGS and Rent expense:

> COGS = $430 − $350
> = $80 change
> Rent expense = $70 − $80
> = $(70) change

Again, the positive value indicates that COGS increased and the negative value indicates that Rent expense decreased.

$$\text{Percent change} = \frac{\text{Dollar change}}{\text{Last year's balance}}$$

So in the percent change of Accounts receivable and Sales revenue:

$$\text{Accounts receivable} = \frac{\$(65)}{\$145} \text{ change}$$
$$= (44.8)\% \text{ change}$$

$$\text{Sales revenue} = \frac{\$70}{\$580}$$
$$= 12.1\% \text{ change}$$

Again, the percent change numbers are negative for Accounts receivable (which decreased in 2011) and positive for Sales Revenue (which increased in 2011).

The percent change is calculated the same way for expenses, again using the *absolute value* of the expenses. In the percent change of COGS and Rent Expense:

$$\text{COGS} = \frac{\$80}{\$350}$$
$$= 22.9\% \text{ change}$$

$$\text{Rent expense} = \frac{-\$10}{\$80}$$
$$= (12.5)\% \text{ change}$$

MEME CO.
Horizontal Analysis of Balance Sheet
Years Ended December 31, 2011 and 2010

	2011	2010	Increase (Decrease) Amount	Percent
Assets				
Cash	$150	$130	$ 20	15.4%
Accounts receivable	80	145	(65)	(44.8)
Inventory	130	190	(60)	(31.6)
Total assets	$360	$465	$(105)	(22.6)
Liabilities				
Accounts payable	90	140	(50)	(35.7)%
Loans payable	140	220	(80)	(36.4)
Total liabilities	$230	$360	$(130)	(36.1)
Stockholders' Equity				
Common stock	20	10	10	100.0%
Retained earnings	110	95	15	15.8
Total stockholders' equity	$130	$105	$ 25	23.8%
Total liabilities and equity	$360	$465	$(105)	(22.6)%

MEME CO.
Horizontal Analysis of Comparative Income Statement
Years Ended December 31, 2011 and 2010

	2011	2010	Increase (Decrease) Amount	Percent
Sales revenue	$650	$580	$70	12.1%
Less cost of goods sold	430	350	80	22.9
Gross profit	$220	$230	(10)	(4.3)
Salary expense	120	140	(20)	(14.3)
Rent expense	70	80	(10)	(12.5)
Net income	$ 30	$ 10	$ 20	200.0%

2 Perform a vertical analysis of financial statements

3 Prepare and use common-size financial statements

Vertical Analysis

Part 1 | **Part 2** | Part 3 | Demo Doc Complete

As its name implies, vertical analysis takes *each* number on the financial statements and compares it to others in the same year (that is, *down* the columns of the financial statements). Vertical analysis is sometimes called common-size analysis because it allows two companies of different sizes to be compared (through the use of percentages).

Balance Sheet Vertical Analysis

On the **balance sheet**, each number, whether it is before an asset, a liability, or an equity account is calculated as a percentage of *total assets*.

$$\text{Vertical analysis percent (balance sheet)} = \frac{\text{Account balance}}{\text{Total assets}}$$

So in the case of Accounts receivable:

$$\text{Vertical analysis percent (2011 Accounts receivable)} = \frac{\$80}{\$360}$$
$$= 22.2\%$$

In other words, about 22% of all the assets in 2011 are in Accounts receivable.

Income Statement Vertical Analysis

On the **income statement**, each number is calculated as a percentage of **net** *sales revenues*.

$$\text{Vertical analysis percent (income statement)} = \frac{\text{Account balance}}{\text{Net sales revenues}}$$

So in the case of Gross Profit:

$$\text{Vertical analysis percent (2011 Gross profit)} = \frac{\$220}{\$650}$$
$$= 33.8\%$$

This means that for every dollar in sales revenues, $0.338 went to Gross Profit. For expenses, the calculation is the same. So in the cases of COGS and Rent Expense:

$$\text{Vertical analysis percent (2011 COGS)} = \frac{\$430}{\$650}$$
$$= 66.2\%$$

$$\text{Vertical analysis percent (2011 Rent expense)} = \frac{\$70}{\$650}$$
$$= 10.8\%$$

MEME CO.
Vertical Analysis of Balance Sheet
December 31, 2011 and 2010

	2011	2011 %	2010	2010 %
Assets				
Cash	$150	41.7%	$130	28.0%
Accounts receivable	80	22.2	145	31.1*
Inventory	130	36.1	190	40.9
Total assets	$360	100.0%	$465	100.0%
Liabilities				
Accounts payable	$ 90	25.0%	$140	30.1%
Loans payable	140	38.9	220	47.3
Total liabilities	$230	63.9%	$360	77.4%
Stockholders' Equity				
Common stock	$ 20	5.5*%	$ 10	2.2%
Retained earnings	110	30.6	95	20.4
Total stockholders' equity	$130	36.1%	$105	22.6%
Total liabilities and equity	$360	100.0%	$465	100.0%

*Rounded down to balance.

MEME CO.
Vertical Analysis of Comparative Income Statement
Years Ended December 31, 2011 and 2010

	2011	2011 %	2010	2010 %
Net sales revenue	$650	100.0%	$580	100.0%
Less cost of goods sold	430	66.2	350	60.3
Gross profit	$220	33.8%	$230	39.7%
Salary expense	120	18.4*	140	24.1
Rent expense	70	10.8	80	13.8
Net income	$ 30	4.6%	$ 10	1.7%

*Rounded to balance.

Requirement 2

4 Compute the standard financial ratios

Calculate MeMe's inventory turnover and rate of return on stockholders' equity ratios for both years.

| Part 1 | Part 2 | **Part 3** | Demo Doc Complete |

$$\text{Inventory turnover} = \frac{\text{COGS}}{\text{Average inventory}}$$

Remember that "average" (when used in a financial ratio) generally means the beginning balance plus the ending balance divided by two.

$$2011 \text{ Inventory turnover} = \frac{\$430}{[½(190+130)]}$$

$$= 2.7 \text{ times}$$

$$2010 \text{ Inventory turnover} = \frac{\$350}{[½(160+190)]}$$

$$= 2 \text{ times}$$

$$\text{Rate of return on stockholders' equity} = \frac{\text{Net income} - \text{Preferred dividends}}{\text{Average common stockholders' equity}}$$

$$2011 \text{ Rate of return on stockholders' equity} = \frac{[\$30 - \$0]}{½(\$105 + \$130)}$$

$$= 25.5\%$$

$$2010 \text{ Rate of return on stockholders' equity} = \frac{[\$10 - \$0]}{½(\$95 + \$105)}$$

$$= 10\%$$

| Part 1 | Part 2 | Part 3 | **Demo Doc Complete** |

Quick Practice Questions

True/False

_____ 1. It is generally considered more useful to know the percentage change in financial statement amounts from year to year than to know the absolute dollar amount of their change.

_____ 2. Benchmarking may be done against an industry average or against a key competitor.

_____ 3. Vertical analysis of financial statements reveals changes in items on the financial statements over time.

_____ 4. Inventory turnover is the ratio of average inventory to cost of goods sold.

_____ 5. Book value per share of common stock has no relationship to market value.

_____ 6. A high current ratio means that a company's current assets represent a relatively large portion (or ratio) of total liabilities.

_____ 7. The debt ratio measures the ability to pay current liabilities.

_____ 8. The acid-test (quick) ratio includes the sum of Cash, Net accounts receivable, and Inventory in the numerator

_____ 9. Earnings per share indicates the net income earned for each share of common and preferred stock.

_____ 10. A signal of financial trouble may include cash flow from operations being lower than net income from period to period.

Multiple Choice

1. Horizontal analysis can be described as which of the following?
   a. Percentage changes in various financial statement amounts from year to year
   b. The changes in individual financial statement amounts as a percentage of some related total
   c. The change in key financial statement ratios over a certain time frame or horizon
   d. None of the above

2. Trend percentages can be considered a form of which of the following?
   a. Ratio analysis
   b. Vertical analysis
   c. Profitability analysis
   d. Horizontal analysis

3. In 2011, net sales were $1,600,000 and in 2012, net sales were $1,750,000. How is the percent change calculated?
   a. Divide $1,600,000 by $1,750,000
   b. Divide $1,750,000 by $1,600,000
   c. Divide $150,000 by $1,750,000
   d. Divide $150,000 by $1,600,000

4. Vertical analysis can be described as which of the following?
   a. Percentage changes in the balances shown in comparative financial statements
   b. The change in key financial statement ratios over a specified period of time
   c. The dollar amount of the change in various financial statement amounts from year to year
   d. Individual financial statement items expressed as a percentage of a base (which represents 100%)

5. What is the base that is used when performing vertical analysis on an income statement?
   a. Net sales
   b. Gross sales
   c. Gross profit
   d. Total expenses

6. What is the base that is used when performing vertical analysis on a balance sheet?
   a. Total assets
   b. Stockholders' equity
   c. Total liabilities
   d. Net assets

7. Which ratio measures the ability to pay long-term debt?
   a. Rate of return on net sales
   b. Earnings per share
   c. Times-interest-earned ratio
   d. Acid-test (quick) ratio

8. Which of the following would be most helpful in the comparison of different-sized companies?
   a. Performing horizontal analysis
   b. Looking at the amount of income earned by each company
   c. Comparing working capital balances
   d. Preparing common-size financial statements

9. Which ratio(s) help(s) in the analysis of working capital?
   a. Current ratio
   b. Acid-test ratio
   c. Debt ratio
   d. Both a and b are correct

10. Assume that collections from customers on account are being received faster. Which of the following would be true?
    a. The accounts receivable turnover would be higher.
    b. The days' sales in receivables would be higher.
    c. The current ratio would be higher.
    d. None of the above.

Quick Exercises

14-1. Selected items from the balance sheet and income statement follow for the Brothers Company for 2010 and 2011.

Requirement

1. Calculate the amount of the change and the percentage of change for each item.

	2011	2010	$ Change	% Change
Cash	$121,000	$100,000		
Accounts receivable	117,000	125,000		
Merchandise inventory	70,000	85,000		
Accounts payable	63,500	50,000		
Sales	144,000	135,000		
Cost of goods sold	74,000	67,500		

14-2. The income statement for Commerce Corporation for the year ended December 31, 2010, follows:

COMMERCE CORPORATION
Income Statement
Year Ended December 31, 2010

Net sales		$661,000
Expenses:		
Cost of goods sold	$268,500	
Selling expenses	45,000	
General expenses	49,300	
Interest expense	35,000	
Income tax expense	30,000	
Total expenses		427,800
Net income		$233,200

Requirements

1. Prepare a vertical analysis of the income statement showing appropriate percentages for each item listed.

COMMERCE CORPORATION
Vertical Analysis of Income Statement
Year Ended December 31, 2010

2. What additional information would you need to determine whether these percentages are good or bad?

14-3. Match the function with the appropriate ratio.

Functions:

a. Gives the amount of net income earned for each share of the company's common stock
b. Measures the number of times operating income can cover interest expense
c. Shows ability to pay all current liabilities if they come due immediately
d. Shows the percentage of a stock's market value returned to stockholders as dividends each period
e. Measures ability to collect cash from credit customers
f. Measures ability to pay current liabilities with current assets
g. Indicates the market price of $1 of earnings
h. Measures the difference between current assets and current liabilities
i. Indicates percentage of assets financed with debt
j. Shows the percentage of each sales dollar earned as net income

Ratios:

1. ____ Dividend yield
2. ____ Rate of return on net sales
3. ____ Accounts receivable turnover
4. ____ Working capital
5. ____ Debt ratio

6. ____ Current ratio
7. ____ Price/earnings ratio
8. ____ Times-interest-earned ratio
9. ____ Acid-test ratio
10. ____ Earnings per share of common stock

14-4. Using the following data for Dream Corporation for 2011, calculate the ratios that follow:

Market price per share of common stock at 12/31/11	$ 9.00
Net income	50,000.00
Number of common shares outstanding	25,000.00
Dividend per share of common stock	$ 0.71

a. earnings per share of common stock

b. price/earnings ratio

c. dividend yield

14-5. Following are selected data from the comparative income statement and balance sheet for Deerfield Corporation for the years ended December 31, 2011 and 2010:

	2011	2010
Net sales (all on credit)	$97,600	$93,000
Cost of goods sold	53,500	52,500
Gross profit	44,700	40,500
Income from operations	16,300	15,000
Interest expense	3,100	3,500
Net income	9,800	9,000
Cash	7,700	7,500
Accounts receivable, net	10,700	12,500
Inventory	20,000	26,000
Prepaid expenses	1,000	900
Total current assets	39,400	46,900
Total long-term assets	50,000	67,000
Total current liabilities	32,000	44,500
Total long-term liabilities	11,000	39,800
Common stock, no par*	10,000	10,000
Retained earnings	25,400	19,600

*NOTE: Two thousand shares of common stock have been issued and outstanding since the company started operations. During the entire fiscal year ended December 31, 2011, the stock was selling for $45 per share.

Requirement

1. Calculate the following ratios at December 31, 2011:

   a. Acid-test ratio

   b. Inventory turnover

   c. Days' sales in receivables

   d. Book value per share of common stock

   e. Price/earnings ratio

   f. Rate of return on total assets

   g. Times-interest-earned ratio

   h. Current ratio

   i. Debt ratio

Do It Yourself! Question 1

Tykes, Inc., had the following information at December 31, 2011:

TYKES, INC.
Balance Sheet
December 31, 2011 and 2010

	2011	2010
Assets		
Cash	$400	$300
Accounts receivable	290	350
Inventory	150	220
Total assets	$840	$870
Liabilities		
Accounts payable	140	75
Loans payable	450	600
Total liabilities	590	675
Stockholders' Equity		
Common stock	40	40
Retained earnings	210	155
Total stockholders' equity	250	195
Total liabilities and equity	$840	$870

TYKES, INC.
Income Statement
Years Ended December 31, 2011 and 2010

	2011	2010
Sales revenue	$1,200	$1,000
Less cost of goods sold	800	600
Gross profit	400	400
Insurance expense	200	190
Interest expense	60	80
Net income	$ 140	$ 130

At December 31, 2009, Tykes's inventory was $200 million and total equity was $165 million.

Requirements

1. Prepare a horizontal analysis of Tykes's financial statements.

1 Perform a horizontal analysis of financial statements

TYKES, INC.
Horizontal Analysis of Balance Sheet
December 31, 2011 and 2010

	2011	2010	Increase (Decrease) Amount	Percent
Assets				
Cash	$400	$300		
Accounts receivable	290	350		
Inventory	150	220		
Total assets	$840	$870		
Liabilities				
Accounts payable	140	75		
Loans payable	450	600		
Total liabilities	590	675		
Stockholders' Equity				
Common stock	40	40		
Retained earnings	210	155		
Total stockholders' equity	250	195		
Total liabilities and equity	$840	$870		

TYKES, INC.
Horizontal Analysis of Comparative Income Statement
Years Ended December 31, 2011 and 2010

	2011	2010	Increase (Decrease) Amount	Percent
Sales revenue	$1,200	$1,000		
Less cost of goods sold	800	600		
Gross profit	400	400		
Insurance expense	200	190		
Interest expense	60	80		
Net income	$ 140	$ 130		

2 Perform a vertical analysis of financial statements

3 Prepare and use common-size financial statements

2. Prepare a vertical analysis of Tykes's financial statements.

TYKES, INC.
Vertical Analysis of Balance Sheet
December 31, 2011 and 2010

	2011	2011 %	2010	2010 %
Assets				
Cash	$400		$300	
Accounts receivable	290		350	
Inventory	150		220	
Total assets	$840		$870	
Liabilities				
Accounts payable	140		75	
Loans payable	450		600	
Total liabilities	590		675	
Stockholders' Equity				
Common stock	40		40	
Retained earnings	210		155	
Total stockholders' equity	250		195	
Total liabilities and equity	$840		$870	

TYKES, INC.
Vertical Analysis of Comparative Income Statement
Years Ended December 31, 2011 and 2010

	2011	2011 %	2010	2010 %
Net sales revenue	$1,200		$1,000	
Less cost of goods sold	800		600	
Gross profit	400		400	
Insurance expense	200		190	
Interest expense	60		80	
Net income	$ 140		$ 130	

4 Compute the standard financial ratios

3. Calculate Tykes's inventory turnover and rate of return on stockholders' equity ratios for both years.

Do It Yourself! Question 1 | Chapter 14   **485**

Quick Practice Solutions

True/False

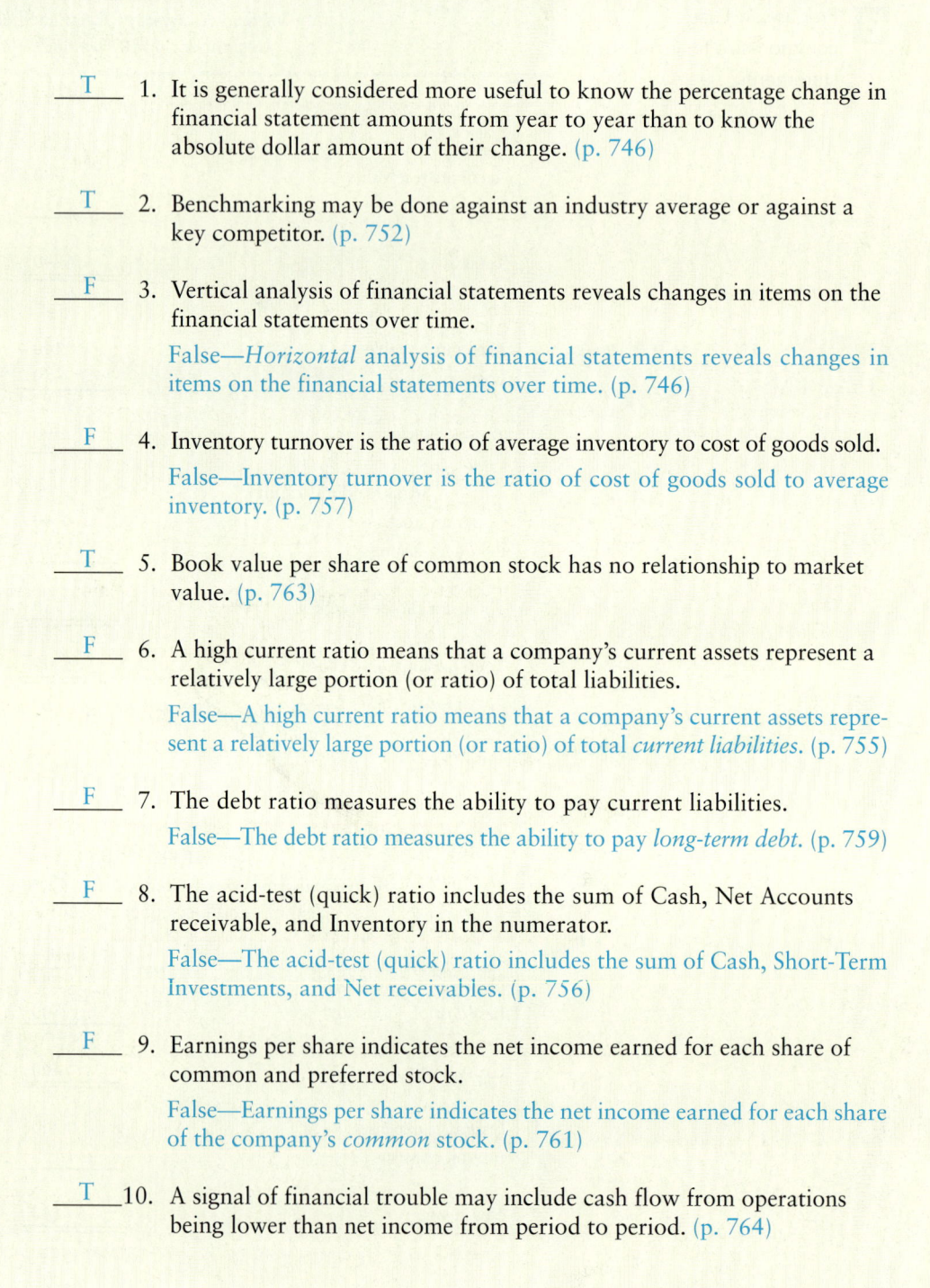

__T__ 1. It is generally considered more useful to know the percentage change in financial statement amounts from year to year than to know the absolute dollar amount of their change. (p. 746)

__T__ 2. Benchmarking may be done against an industry average or against a key competitor. (p. 752)

__F__ 3. Vertical analysis of financial statements reveals changes in items on the financial statements over time.

False—*Horizontal* analysis of financial statements reveals changes in items on the financial statements over time. (p. 746)

__F__ 4. Inventory turnover is the ratio of average inventory to cost of goods sold.

False—Inventory turnover is the ratio of cost of goods sold to average inventory. (p. 757)

__T__ 5. Book value per share of common stock has no relationship to market value. (p. 763)

__F__ 6. A high current ratio means that a company's current assets represent a relatively large portion (or ratio) of total liabilities.

False—A high current ratio means that a company's current assets represent a relatively large portion (or ratio) of total *current liabilities*. (p. 755)

__F__ 7. The debt ratio measures the ability to pay current liabilities.

False—The debt ratio measures the ability to pay *long-term debt*. (p. 759)

__F__ 8. The acid-test (quick) ratio includes the sum of Cash, Net Accounts receivable, and Inventory in the numerator.

False—The acid-test (quick) ratio includes the sum of Cash, Short-Term Investments, and Net receivables. (p. 756)

__F__ 9. Earnings per share indicates the net income earned for each share of common and preferred stock.

False—Earnings per share indicates the net income earned for each share of the company's *common* stock. (p. 761)

__T__ 10. A signal of financial trouble may include cash flow from operations being lower than net income from period to period. (p. 764)

Multiple Choice

1. Horizontal analysis can be described as which of the following? (p. 746)
   a. Percentage changes in various financial statement amounts from year to year
   b. The changes in individual financial statement amounts as a percentage of some related total
   c. The change in key financial statement ratios over a certain time frame or horizon
   d. None of the above

2. Trend percentages can be considered a form of which of the following? (p. 748)
   a. Ratio analysis
   b. Vertical analysis
   c. Profitability analysis
   d. Horizontal analysis

3. In 2011, net sales were $1,600,000 and in 2012, net sales were $1,750,000. How is the percent change calculated? (p. 747)
   a. Divide $1,600,000 by $1,750,000
   b. Divide $1,750,000 by $1,600,000
   c. Divide $150,000 by $1,750,000
   d. Divide $150,000 by $1,600,000

4. Vertical analysis can be described as which of the following? (p. 749)
   a. Percentage changes in the balances shown in comparative financial statements
   b. The change in key financial statement ratios over a specified period of time
   c. The dollar amount of the change in various financial statement amounts from year to year
   d. Individual financial statement items expressed as a percentage of a base (which represents 100%)

5. What is the base that is used when performing vertical analysis on an income statement? (p. 749)
   a. Net sales
   b. Gross sales
   c. Gross profit
   d. Total expenses

6. What is the base that is used when performing vertical analysis on a balance sheet? (p. 750)
   a. Total assets
   b. Stockholders' equity
   c. Total liabilities
   d. Net assets

7. Which ratio measures the ability to pay long-term debt? (p. 759)
   a. Rate of return on net sales
   b. Earnings per share
   c. Times-interest-earned ratio
   d. Acid-test (quick) ratio

8. Which of the following would be most helpful in the comparison of different-sized companies? (p. 751)
   a. Performing horizontal analysis
   b. Looking at the amount of income earned by each company
   c. Comparing working capital balances
   d. Preparing common-size financial statements

9. Which ratio(s) help(s) in the analysis of working capital? (p. 755)
   a. Current ratio
   b. Acid-test ratio
   c. Debt ratio
   d. Both a and b are correct

10. Assume that collections from customers on account are being received faster. Which of the following would be true? (p. 758)
    a. The accounts receivable turnover would be higher.
    b. The days' sales in receivables would be higher.
    c. The current ratio would be higher.
    d. None of the above.

Quick Exercises

14-1. Selected items from the balance sheet and income statement follow for the Brothers Company for 2010 and 2011. (p. 747)

Requirement

1. Calculate the amount of the change and the percentage of change for each item.

	2011	2010	$ Change	% Change
Cash	$121,000	$100,000	$21,000	21.0%
Accounts receivable	117,000	125,000	(8,000)	(6.4)
Merchandise inventory	70,000	85,000	(15,000)	(17.6)
Accounts payable	63,500	50,000	13,500	27.0
Sales	144,000	135,000	9,000	6.7
Cost of goods sold	74,000	67,500	6,500	9.6

14-2. The income statement for Commerce Corporation for the year ended December 31, 2010, follows: (p. 749)

COMMERCE CORPORATION
Income Statement
Year Ended December 31, 2010

Net sales		$661,000
Expenses:		
Cost of goods sold	$268,500	
Selling expenses	45,000	
General expenses	49,300	
Interest expense	35,000	
Income tax expense	30,000	
Total expenses		427,800
Net income		$233,200

Requirements

1. Prepare a vertical analysis of the income statement showing appropriate percentages for each item listed.

COMMERCE CORPORATION
Vertical Analysis of Income Statement
Year Ended December 31, 2010

	Amount	Percentage
Net sales	$661,000	100.0%
Expenses		
Cost of goods sold	268,500	40.6
Selling expenses	45,000	6.8
General expenses	49,300	7.5
Interest expense	35,000	5.3
Income tax expense	30,000	4.5
Total expenses	427,800	64.7
Net income	$233,200	35.3%

2. What additional information would you need to determine whether these percentages are good or bad?

Additional information to determine whether these percentages are good or bad might include:
- industry averages to compare to Commerce Corporation
- the change in each line item percentage over a relevant period of time

14-3. Match the function with the appropriate ratio. (pp. 765–766)

Functions:

a. Gives the amount of net income earned for each share of the company's common stock
b. Measures the number of times operating income can cover interest expense
c. Shows ability to pay all current liabilities if they come due immediately
d. Shows the percentage of a stock's market value returned to stockholders as dividends for each period
e. Measures ability to collect cash from credit customers
f. Measures ability to pay current liabilities with current assets
g. Indicates the market price of $1 of earnings
h. Measures the difference between current assets and current liabilities
i. Indicates percentage of assets financed with debt
j. Shows the percentage of each sales dollar earned as net income

Ratios:

1. __d__ Dividend yield
2. __j__ Rate of return on net sales
3. __e__ Accounts receivable turnover
4. __h__ Working capital
5. __i__ Debt ratio
6. __f__ Current ratio
7. __g__ Price/earnings ratio
8. __b__ Times-interest-earned ratio
9. __c__ Acid-test ratio
10. __a__ Earnings per share of common stock

14-4. Using the following data for Dream Corporation for 2011, calculate the ratios that follow: (pp. 761–763)

Market price per share of common stock at 12/31/11	$ 9.00
Net income	50,000
Number of common shares outstanding	25,000
Dividend per share of common stock	0.71

a. earnings per share of common stock

$50,000/25,000 = $2.00

b. price/earnings ratio

$$\$9.00/\$2.00 = 4.5$$

c. dividend yield

$$\$0.71/\$9.00 = 0.08$$

14-5. Following are selected data from the comparative income statement and balance sheet for Deerfield Corporation for the years ended December 31, 2011 and 2010: (pp. 765–766)

	2011	2010
Net sales (all on credit)	$97,600	$93,000
Cost of goods sold	53,500	52,500
Gross profit	44,700	40,500
Income from operations	16,300	15,000
Interest expense	3,100	3,500
Net income	9,800	9,000
Cash	7,700	7,500
Accounts receivable, net	10,700	12,500
Inventory	20,000	26,000
Prepaid expenses	1,000	900
Total current assets	39,400	46,900
Total long-term assets	50,000	67,000
Total current liabilities	32,000	44,500
Total long-term liabilities	11,000	39,800
Common stock, no par*	10,000	10,000
Retained earnings	25,400	19,600

*NOTE: Two thousand shares of common stock have been issued and outstanding since the company started operations. During the entire fiscal year ended December 31, 2011, the stock was selling for $45 per share.

Requirement

1. Calculate the following ratios at December 31, 2011:

a. Acid-test ratio

$$(\$7,700 + \$10,700)/\$32,000 = 0.58$$

b. Inventory turnover

$$\frac{\$53,500}{(\$20,000 + \$26,000)/2} = 2.33$$

c. Days' sales in receivables

$$\frac{(\$10,700 + \$12,500)/2}{\$97,600/365} = 43.4 \text{ days}$$

d. Book value per share of common stock

$$\frac{\$10,000 + \$25,400}{2,000} = \$17.70$$

e. Price/earnings ratio

$$\frac{\$45}{\$9,800/2,000} = 9.18$$

f. Rate of return on total assets

$$\frac{\$9,800 + \$3,100}{(\$39,400 + \$50,000 + \$46,900 + \$67,000)/2} = 0.13$$

g. Times-interest-earned ratio

$$\frac{\$16,300}{\$3,100} = 5.26 \text{ times}$$

h. Current ratio

$$\frac{\$39,400}{\$32,000} = 1.23$$

i. Debt ratio

$$\frac{\$32,000 + \$11,000}{\$39,400 + \$50,000} = 0.48$$

Do It Yourself! Question 1 Solutions

Requirements

1. Prepare a horizontal analysis for Tykes's financial statements.

TYKES, INC.
Horizontal Analysis of Balance Sheet
December 31, 2011 and 2010

	2011	2010	Increase Amount	(Decrease) Percent
Assets				
Cash	$400	$300	$100	33.3%
Accounts receivable	290	350	(60)	(17.1)
Inventory	150	220	(70)	(31.8)
Total assets	$840	$870	$ (30)	(3.4)
Liabilities				
Accounts payable	140	75	65	86.7
Loans payable	450	600	(150)	(25.0)
Total liabilities	$590	$675	(85)	(12.6)
Stockholders' Equity				
Common stock	40	40	0	0.0
Retained earnings	210	155	55	35.5
Total stockholders' equity	$250	$195	55	28.2
Total liabilities and equity	$840	$870	$ (30)	(3.4)%

TYKES, INC.
Horizontal Analysis of Comparative Income Statement
Years Ended December 31, 2011 and 2010

	2011	2010	Increase Amount	(Decrease) Percent
Sales revenue	$1,200	$1,000	$200	20.0%
Less cost of goods sold	800	600	$200	33.3
Gross profit	400	400	0	0.0
Insurance expense	200	190	(10)	5.3
Interest expense	60	80	(20)	(25.0)
Net income	$ 140	$ 130	$ 10	7.7%

2. Prepare a vertical analysis for Tykes's financial statements.

TYKES, INC.
Vertical Analysis of Balance Sheet
December 31, 2011 and 2010

	2011	2011 %	2010	2010 %
Assets				
Cash	$400	47.6%	$300	34.5%
Accounts receivable	290	34.5	350	40.2
Inventory	150	17.9	220	25.3
Total assets	$840	100.0%	$870	100.0%
Liabilities				
Accounts payable	140	16.7%	75	8.6%
Loans payable	450	53.5	600	69.0
Total liabilities	590	70.2	675	77.6
Stockholders' Equity				
Common stock	40	4.8	40	4.6
Retained earnings	210	25.0	155	17.8
Total stockholders' equity	250	29.8	195	22.4
Total liabilities and equity	$840	100.0%	$870	100.0%

TYKES, INC.
Vertical Analysis of Comparative Income Statement
Years Ended December 31, 2011 and 2010

	2011	2011 %	2010	2010 %
Net sales revenue	$1,200	100.0%	$1,000	100.0%
Less cost of goods sold	800	66.7	600	60.0
Gross profit	400	33.3	400	40.0
Insurance expense	200	16.6	190	19.0
Interest expense	60	5.0	80	8.0
Net income	$ 140	11.7%	$ 130	13.0%

3. Calculate Tykes's inventory turnover and rate of return on stockholders' equity ratios for both years.

$$2011 \text{ Inventory turnover} = \frac{\$800}{\frac{1}{2}(220 + 150)}$$

$$= 4.3 \text{ times}$$

$$2010 \text{ Inventory turnover} = \frac{\$600}{\frac{1}{2}(200 + 220)}$$

$$= 2.9 \text{ times}$$

$$2011 \text{ Rate of return on stockholders' equity} = \frac{\$140 - \$0}{\frac{1}{2}(\$195 + \$250)}$$

$$= 62.9\%$$

$$2010 \text{ Rate of return on stockholders' equity} = \frac{\$130 - \$0}{\frac{1}{2}(\$165 + \$195)}$$

$$= 72.2\%$$

The Power of Practice

For more practice using the skills learned in this chapter, visit MyAccountingLab. There you will find algorithmically generated questions that are based on these Demo Docs and your main textbook's Review and Assess Your Progress sections.

Go to MyAccountingLab and follow these steps:

1. Direct your URL to www.myaccountinglab.com.
2. Log in using your name and password.
3. Click the MyAccountingLab link.
4. Click Study Plan in the left navigation bar.
5. From the table of contents, select Chapter 14, Financial Statement Analysis.
6. Click a link to work tutorial exercises.

Glindex
A Combined Glossary/Subject Index

A

Account The detailed record of the changes in a particular asset, liability, or owner's equity during a period. The basic summary device of accounting, 29, 32

Accountants, 2

Accounting The information system that measures business activities, processes that information into reports, and communicates the results to decision makers, 1

Accounting and the business environment
 basic transactions (demo doc), 4–11
 concepts and principles, applying, 2
 learning objectives, 1–3
 practice questions, 12–19
   solutions to, 20–26
 vocabulary, 1

Accounting cycle Process by which companies produce their financial statements for a specific period, 99

Accounting cycle, completing
 closing entries (demo doc), 101–109
 learning objectives, 99–100
 practice questions, 110–117
   solutions to, 118–125

Accounting equation The basic tool of accounting, measuring the resources of the business and the claims to those resources: Assets = Liabilities + Stockholders' Equity, 2–3, 5
 components of, 2
 using, 5, 8
 Accounting period concept, 64, 68, 69

Account payable A liability backed by the general reputation and credit standing of the debtor, 109, 435

Account receivable A promise to receive cash from customers to whom the business has sold goods or for whom the business has performed services, 7, 108, 223, 224, 433–434

Accrual-basis accounting Accounting that records the impact of a business event as it occurs regardless of whether the transaction affected cash, 63, 73
 adjusting entries for, 65–73

Accrued expense An expense that the business has incurred but not yet paid, 68

Accrued revenue A revenue that has been earned but not yet collected in cash, 68

Accumulated depletion, 270, 283–284

Accumulated depreciation The sum of all depreciation expense recorded to date for an asset, 67, 273, 275, 276

Acid-test ratio Ratio of the sum of cash plus short-term investments plus net current receivables, to total current liabilities. Tells whether the entity could pay all its current liabilities if they came due immediately. Also called the quick ratio, 225, 235

Adjusted trial balance A list of all the accounts with their adjusted balances, 64, 71

Adjusting entries Entries made at the end of the period to assign revenues to the period in which they are earned and expenses to the period in which they are incurred. Adjusting entries help measure the period's income and bring the related asset and liability accounts to correct balances for the financial statements, 63
 for accrual accounting (demo doc), 65–73
 learning objectives, 63–64
 practice questions, 74–85
   solutions to, 86–96
 process of, 64
 types of, 67–68

Aging-of-accounts method A way to estimate bad debts by analyzing individual accounts receivable according to the length of time they have been receivable from the customer. Also called the balance-sheet approach, 235

Allowance for doubtful accounts A contra account, related to accounts receivable, that holds the estimated amount of collection losses. Also called allowance for uncollectible accounts, 224

Allowance for uncollectible accounts A contra account, related to accounts receivable, that holds the estimated amount of collection losses. Also called allowance for doubtful accounts, 224

Allowance method A method of recording collection losses on the basis of estimates instead of waiting to see which customers the company will not collect from, 224, 228, 230–234

Amortization expense, 270, 286–287

Amortization method, straight-line, 313, 325–328

Asset An economic resource that is expected to be of benefit in the future, 5, 29, 30
 classifying, 100
 current, 100, 108
 estimated residual value, 270
 estimated useful life, 270
 intangible, 270
 long-term, 100, 108
 return on, 361
 See also Plant assets
 Asset cost, 270

Audit An examination of a company's financial situation, 188

Average, 136

Average cost, 156

Average-cost method Inventory costing method based on the average cost of inventory during the period. Average cost is determined by dividing the cost of goods available for sale by the number of units available, 156, 163–165, 166

B

Bad-debt expense Cost to the seller of extending credit. Arises from the failure to collect from credit customers. Also called doubtful-account expense or uncollectible-account expense, 224

Balance sheet An entity's assets, liabilities, and stockholders' equity as of a specific date. Also called the statement of financial position, 3, 8, 9, 10, 11
 classified, 100, 108–109
 preparing, 73
 reporting liabilities on, 313, 315, 316, 319, 326–328
 reporting receivables on, 224, 228, 233
 stockholders' equity section of, 360, 364–365
 vertical analysis, 473–474
 See also Paid-in capital and the balance sheet

Balance sheet approach A way to estimate bad debts by analyzing individual accounts receivable according to the length of time they have been receivable from the customer. Also called the aging-of-accounts method, 235

Bank account Helps control cash because banks have established practices for safeguarding customers' money, 188, 192

Bankcards Issued by banks, with an operation much like a credit card. VISA and MasterCard are the two main bankcards, 224, 241–242

Bank errors Posting errors made by the bank that either incorrectly increase or decrease the bank balance, 193

Bank reconciliation Document explaining the reasons for the difference between a depositor's cash records and the depositor's cash balance in its bank account, 188, 190–197

Bank statement Document the bank uses to report what it did with the depositor's cash. Shows the bank account beginning and ending balance and lists the month's cash transactions conducted through the bank, 188

Benefits, 312

Bond discount Excess of a bond's maturity value over its issue price. Also called a discount (on a bond), 313, 326

Bond premium Excess of a bond's issue price over its maturity value. Also called a premium, 313, 326

Bonds, 311, 312
 compared with stocks, 313, 328
 discount on, 313, 326
 interest expense on, 313
 practice questions, 342–343
 premium on, 313, 326
 principle amount, 312
 state rate, 312
 straight-line amortization, 313, 325–328
 See also Long-term liabilities

Bonds payable Groups of notes payable issued to multiple lenders called bondholders, 312

Book value, of asset, 270

Book value per share of stock Amount of owners' equity in the company's books for each share of its stock, 361, 366

Business decisions, ethics in, 189, 200

Business organizations, types of, 2, 5

G-1

C

Capital account, 103, 106–107
Capitalization decisions, 270
Cash, 108
  petty, 189, 198–200
  See also Internal control and cash;
    Statement of cash flows
Cash-basis accounting Accounting that records transactions only when cash is received or paid, 63, 73
Cash dividends, 361, 368–370
Cash flows Cash receipts and cash payments
  predicting future, 429
  See also Statement of cash flows
  Cash payments, 188, 199–200
  Cash receipts, 188, 197
  Certified public accountants (CPAs), 2
Chart of accounts A list of all the accounts with their account numbers, 29, 32
Check Document that instructs a bank to pay the designated person or business a specified amount of money, 188
  NSF, 193, 196
  outstanding, 193
Classified balance sheet A balance sheet that classifies each asset and each liability as either current or long-term, 100, 108–109
Closing entries Entries that transfer the revenue, expense, and dividend balances to the retained earnings account, 100
  demo doc, 101–109
Closing the accounts Step in the accounting cycle at the end of the period. Closing the accounts consists of journalizing and posting the closing entries to set the balances of the revenue, expense, and dividend accounts to zero for the next period, 100, 103–107
Code of ethics, 189
Common-size financial statement A financial statement that reports only percentages (no dollar amounts), 468
Common stock Represents the basic ownership of every corporation, 360, 362–366, 368, 379
Computer virus A malicious program that (a) reproduces itself, (b) enters program code without consent, and (c) performs destructive actions, 188
Conservatism Reporting the least favorable figures in the financial statements, 155
Consistency principle A business should use the same accounting methods and procedures from period to period, 155
Contingent liability, 317
Continuing operations, 392, 404–406
Contra account An account that always has a companion account and whose normal balance is opposite that of the companion account, 135, 399
Copyright Exclusive right to reproduce and sell a book, musical composition, film, other work of art, or computer program. Issued by the federal government, copyrights extend 70 years beyond the author's life, 270
Corporate capital. *See* Stockholders' equity
Corporation A business owned by stockholders. A corporation begins when the state approves its articles of incorporation and the first share of stock is issued. It is a legal entity, an "artificial person," in the eyes of the law, 2
  characteristics of, 2, 5, 359, 372
  income tax, accounting for, 361, 372
  See also Paid-in capital and the balance sheet; Retained earnings and the income statement
Cost of goods available for sale The total cost spent on inventory that was available to be sold during a period, 156, 157
Cost of goods sold (COGS) The cost of the inventory that the business has sold to customers. Also called cost of sales, 127, 128, 157
  calculating, 159–160
Cost of plant asset, 269
Cost principle A principle that states that acquired assets and services should be recorded at their actual cost, 2
Credit The right side of an account, 30, 32
Credit-card sales, 224, 240–242
Current assets Assets that are expected to be converted to cash, sold, or consumed during the next 12 months, or within the business's normal operating cycle if the cycle is longer than a year, 100, 108
Current liabilities Debts due to be paid with cash or with goods and services within one year, or within the entity's operating cycle if the cycle is longer than a year, 100, 108–109
Current liabilities and payroll
  balance sheet, reporting on, 326–328
  current portion of long-term debt (demo doc), 318–319
  general current liabilities (demo doc), 314–317
  learning objectives, 312–313
  payroll liabilities (demo doc), 320–324
  practice questions, 329–343
    solutions to, 344–357
  See also Liabilities
Current ratio Current assets divided by current liabilities. This ratio measures the company's ability to pay current liabilities from current assets, 100, 109
Custodian of the petty cash fund The individual assigned responsibility for the petty cash fund, 189

D

Days' sales in receivables Ratio of average net accounts receivable to one day's sales. Tells how many days' sales it takes to collect the average level of receivables. Also called the collection period, 225, 235
Debit Total liabilities divided by total assets. This ratio reveals the proportion of a company's assets that it has financed with debt, 10, 32
Debit-card sales, 224, 241–242
Debt, ability to pay, 429
Debt ratio Total liabilities divided by total assets. This ratio reveals the proportion of a company's assets that it has financed with debt, 100, 109
Decision makers, 2
Deferred tax asset, 361
Deferred tax liability, 361
Depletion expense Portion of a natural resource's cost used up in a particular period. Computed in the same way as units-of-production depreciation, 270, 283–284

Depreciable cost The cost of a plant asset minus its estimated residual value, 272
Depreciation The allocation of a plant asset's cost to expense over its useful life, 67
  accounting for, 269–270
  accumulated, 269, 270, 273, 275, 276
  calculating, 270
  demo doc, 271–281
  double-declining-balance, 269, 275–278, 280–281
  methods, 269, 272–281
  practice questions, 294–296
  straight-line method, 272–283, 277–278
  units-of-production, 269, 274–275, 279–280
Depreciation expense, 272–273, 274, 276, 433
Direct method Format of the operating activities section of the Statement of Cash Flows; lists the major categories of operating cash receipts and cash payments, 430, 441–445, 455
Direct write-off method A method of accounting for uncollectible receivables, in which the company waits until the credit department decides that a customer's account receivable is uncollectible and then debits Uncollectible account expense and credits the customer's Account receivable, 224, 228–229
Disclosure principle A business's financial statements must report enough information for outsiders to make knowledgeable decisions about the company, 155
Discontinued operations, 393, 405–406
Discount (on bond) Excess of a bond's maturity value over its issue price. Also called a bond discount, 313, 326
Dividend payments, 328
Dividends Distributions by a corporation to its stockholders
  ability to pay, 429
  cash, 361, 368–370
  on statement of cash flows, 438–439
  stock, 392, 394–397, 414
Double-declining-balance (DDB) method An accelerated depreciation method that computes annual depreciation by multiplying the asset's decreasing book value by a constant percent that is two times the straight-line rate, 269, 275–278, 280–281
Doubtful-account expense Cost to the seller of extending credit. Arises from the failure to collect from credit customers. Also called uncollectible account expense or bad-debt expense, 224

E

Earnings per share Amount of a company's net income for each share of its outstanding stock, 393, 402–406, 417
E-commerce, control procedures for, 188
Employee compensation. *See* Payroll
Entity concept, 2
Equity, 9
Equity accounts, 360
Estimated residual value Expected cash value of an asset at the end of its useful life. Also called salvage value, 270
Estimated useful life Length of the service period expected from an asset. May be expressed in years, units of output, miles, or another measure, 270

Ethics Analyzing right from wrong, 189, 200, 270
Expense account, closing, 100, 103–107
Expenses Decrease in equity that occurs from using assets or increasing liabilities in the course of delivering goods or services to customer
    accrued, 68
    depletion, 270, 283–284
    depreciation, 272–273, 274, 276, 433
    prepaid, 67
Extraordinary gains and losses A gain or loss that is both unusual for the company and infrequent. Also called extraordinary items, 393, 406

F

Federal Insurance Contributions Act (FICA) tax Federal Insurance Contributions Act (FICA) tax, which is withheld from employees' pay and matched by the employer. Also called Social Security tax, 312, 322
Financial Accounting Standards Board (FASB) The private organization that determines how accounting is practiced in the United States, 2
Financial information, users of, 2, 11
Financial ratios, 468, 476
Financial statement analysis
    common-size financial statements, 468
    demo doc, 469–476
    financial ratios, 468, 476
    horizontal analysis, 467, 471–473
    learning objectives, 467–468
    practice questions, 477–485
        solutions to, 486–495
    vertical analysis, 467–468, 473–475
Financial statements Documents that report on a business in monetary amounts, providing information to help people make informed business decisions, 3, 8–10
    evaluating business performance using, 3, 11
    merchandiser's, 128, 135
    preparing, from adjusted trial balance, 64, 72–73
Financing activities Activities that obtain the cash needed to launch and sustain the business; a section of the Statement of Cash Flows, 430, 437–438
First-in, First-out (FIFO) inventory costing method Inventory costing method: The first costs into inventory are the first costs out to cost of goods sold. Ending inventory is based on the costs of the most recent purchases, 156, 160–161, 166
Fixed interest rate, 311
Fixed-rate mortgage, 311
Franchises Privileges granted by a private business or a government to sell a product or service under specified conditions, 270
Furniture, 108, 433

G

Gain on sale of furniture, 433
Generally accepted accounting principles (GAAP) Accounting guidelines, formulated by the Financial Accounting Standards Board, that govern how accountants measure, process, and communicate financial information, 288
Going-concern concept This concept assumes that the entity will remain in operation for the foreseeable future, 2

Goodwill Excess of the cost of an acquired company over the sum of the market values of its net assets (assets minus liabilities), 270, 287–288
Gross pay Total amount of salary, wages, commissions, or any other employee compensation before taxes and other deductions, 311, 312
Gross profit Excess of net sales revenue over cost of goods sold. Also called gross margin, 128
Gross profit method A way to estimate inventory on the basis of the cost-of-goods-sold model: Beginning inventory + Net purchases = Cost of goods available for sale. Cost of goods available for sale – Cost of goods sold = Ending inventory, 157, 167–168
Gross profit percentage Gross profit divided by net sales revenue. A measure of profitability. Also called gross margin percentage, 128, 136

H

Horizontal analysis Study of percentage changes in comparative financial statements, 467, 471–473

I

Income
    net, 8–10, 103–105, 157, 430, 433
    pretax, 361
    taxable, 361
Income from continuing operations, 392, 404–406
Income statement Summary of an entity's revenues, expenses, and net income or net loss for a specific period. Also called the statement of earnings or the statement of operations, 3, 8, 11
    corporate, 392–393
    merchandiser's, 128, 135
    multi-step, 128
    preparing, 9, 72
    single-step, 128
    versus statement of cash flows, 445
    vertical analysis, 474–475
    See also Retained earnings and the income statement
Income summary A temporary "holding tank" account into which revenues and expenses are transferred prior to their final transfer to the retained earnings account, 100, 105–106
Income taxes, 312
    corporations, accounting for, 361, 372
Indirect method Format of the operating activities section of the Statement of Cash Flows; starts with net income and reconciles to net cash provided by operating activities, 430, 431–440, 452
Initial public offering (IPO), 359
Installment payments, 194, 196
Intangible assets Assets with no physical form. Valuable because of the special rights they carry. Examples are patents and copyrights, 270
    accounting for, 270, 285–288
    practice questions, 298
    See also Plant assets and intangibles
Interest The revenue to the payee for loaning money; the expense to the debtor, 225
Interest earned, 194, 196
Interest expense, 287, 313, 327

Interest rate The percentage rate of interest specified by the note. Interest rates are almost always stated for a period of one year, 311, 312
Internal control Organizational plan and all the related measures adopted by an entity to safeguard assets, encourage employees to follow company policy, promote operational efficiency, and ensure accurate and reliable accounting records, 187, 197
Internal control and cash
    bank reconciliations (demo doc), 190–197
    cash receipts, applying to, 197
    e-commerce, 188, 197
    learning objectives, 187–189
    petty cash (demo doc), 198–200
    practice questions, 201–210
        solutions to, 211–220
    procedures, good, 187–188, 198, 200
    for receivables, 223, 235
    separation of duties, 188, 197, 223, 235
Inventory All the goods that the company owns and expects to sell to customers in the normal course of operations
    adjusting and closing accounts, 128, 134–135
    calculating costs of, 127
    estimating ending, 157, 159–160, 168
    purchase of, accounting for, 128, 130, 132–133
    sale of, accounting for, 128, 131, 133
    on statement of cash flows, 434
    See also Merchandise inventory
Inventory accounting systems, 127, 130
Inventory costing methods, 156, 158–166
Inventory errors, 157, 167–168
Inventory transaction analysis, 129–136
Inventory turnover Ratio of cost of goods sold divided by average inventory. Measures the number of times a company sells its average level of inventory during a year, 128, 136, 476
Investing activities Activities that increase or decrease long-term assets; a section of the Statement of Cash Flows, 430, 435–437

J

Journal The chronological accounting record of an entity's transactions, 29, 33
    adjusting entries, 64, 67–68
    recording transactions in, 30, 33–35

L

Last-in, Last-out (LIFO) inventory costing method Inventory costing method: The last costs into inventory are the first costs out to cost of goods sold. The method leaves the oldest costs—those of beginning inventory and the earliest purchases of the period—in ending inventory, 156, 161–163, 166
Ledger The record holding all the accounts, 29
    posting transactions to, 30, 36–37
Leverage Earning more income on borrowed money than the related interest expense, thereby increasing the earnings for the owners of the business, 313
Liabilities Economic obligations (debts) payable to an individual or an organization outside the business, 5, 29, 30
    balance sheet, reporting on, 313, 315, 316, 319, 326–328
    classifying, 100
    contingent, 317

G-4 Glindex

current, 100, 108–109
  demo doc, 314–317
  estimated, 312, 315–317
  of known amount, 312, 315–317
  reporting on balance sheet, 326–328
long-term, 100, 108–109
  See also Current liabilities and payroll; Long-term liabilities
Limited liability, 359
Limited-Liability Company (LLC) Company in which each member is only liable for his or her own actions or those under his or her control, 2
Limited-Liability Partnership (LLP) Company in which each partner is only liable for his or her own actions or those under his or her control, 2
Liquidity Measure of how quickly an item can be converted to cash, 100, 225
Long-term assets Any assets that will NOT be converted to cash or used up within the business's operating cycle, or one year, whichever is greater, 100, 108
Long-term liabilities Liabilities that are not current, 100, 108–109
  bonds payable, 312–313
  bonds payable, straight-line amortization (demo doc), 325–328
  current portion of long-term debt (demo doc), 318–319
  learning objectives, 312–313
  practice questions, 342–343
Lower-of-cost-or-market (LCM) rule Rule that an asset should be reported in the financial statements at whichever is lower—its historical cost or its market value, 156, 166

M

Management decisions, evaluating, 429
Market value Price for which a person could buy or sell a share of stock, 270, 361, 395, 396
Matching principle Guide to accounting for expenses. Identify all expenses incurred during the period, measure the expenses, and match them against the revenues earned during that same time period, 64, 68, 69, 315–316
Materiality concept A company must perform strictly proper accounting only for items that are significant to the business's financial situations, 155
Merchandise inventory
  costing methods and lower of cost or market (demo doc), 158–166
  gross profit method and inventory errors (demo doc), 167–168
  learning objectives, 155–157
  practice questions, 169–174
    solutions to, 175–184
  See also Inventory
Merchandiser Businesses that sell merchandise or goods to customers, 127
Merchandising Consists of buying and selling products rather than services, 127
Merchandising operations
  financial statements for, 128, 135
  inventory transaction analysis (demo doc), 129–136
  learning objectives, 127–128
  practice questions, 137–144
    solutions to, 145–152

Mortgage Borrower's promise to transfer the legal title to certain assets to the lender if the debt is not paid on schedule, 311
Multi-step income statement Format that contains subtotals to highlight significant relationships. In addition to net income, it reports gross profit and operating income, 128
Mutual agency The ability of partners in a partnership to commit other partners and the business to a contract, 2

N

Natural resources Plant assets that come from the earth. Natural resources are like inventories in the ground (oil) or on top of the ground (timber), 270
  accounting for (demo doc), 282–284
  practice questions, 297
Net income Excess of total revenues over total expenses. Also called net earnings or net profit, 8, 433
  adjustments to, 430
  calculating, 9–10, 103–105
  inventory errors and, 157
  overstatement of, 187
Net loss Excess of total expenses over total revenues, 8
Net pay, 312
Net value, 135
No mutual agency, 359
Noncash transaction, 435
Nonrecurring transactions, 391, 392
Nonsufficient funds (NSF) check A "hot" check; one for which the maker's bank account has insufficient money to pay the check, 193, 196
Notes payable Represents debts the business owes because it signed promissory notes to borrow money or to purchase something, 437–438
Notes receivable A written promise for future collection of cash, 223, 225, 236–239
  practice questions, 253–254

O

Objectivity principle Principle that asserts that data are verifiable and objective. Also called the reliability principle, 2
Operating activities Activities that create revenue or expense in the entity's major line of business; a section of the Statement of Cash Flows. Operating activities affect the Income Statement, 430, 433
Operating income Gross profit minus operating expenses plus any other operating revenues. Also called income from operations, 128
Outstanding check A check issued by the company and recorded on its books but not yet paid by its bank, 193
Owner's equity The claim of a corporation's owners to the assets of the business. Also called shareholders' or stockholders' equity, 5, 9, 10, 29, 30
  See also Stockholders' equity

P

Paid-in capital The amount invested in the corporation by its owners, the stockholders. Also called contributed capital, 360
Paid-in capital and the balance sheet
  common stock (demo doc), 362–366
  demo doc, 371–372

  learning objectives, 359–361
  practice questions, 373–380
    solutions to, 381–388
  preferred stock (demo doc), 367–370
Paid-in capital in excess of par account, 360
Partnership A business with two or more owners and not organized as a corporation, 2
Par value The amount a borrower must pay back to the bondholders on the maturity date. Also called principal amount or maturity value, 360, 363, 395
Patent An intangible asset that is a federal government grant conveying an exclusive 20-year right to produce and sell a process or formula, 270
Payroll A major expense. Also called employee compensation
  calculating, 312, 321, 323–324
  transactions, recording, 321–322
  See also Current liabilities and payroll
Payroll deductions, 312
Payroll taxes, 311, 312, 321–322
Percent-of-sales method A method of estimating uncollectible receivables that calculates uncollectible account expense. Also called the income statement approach, 224, 230, 231, 232
Performance evaluation, business, 3, 11
  acid-test ratio, 225, 235
  days' sales in receivables, 225, 235
Periodic inventory system A system in which the business does not keep a continuous record of inventory on hand. At the end of the period, the business takes a physical count of on-hand inventory and uses this information to prepare the financial statements, 127
Perpetual average cost, 163–165
Perpetual inventory system The accounting inventory system in which the business keeps a constant/running record of inventory and cost of goods sold, 127, 128
  inventory costing methods, 156
  inventory transaction analysis (demo doc), 129–136
Perpetual LIFO, 161–163
Petty cash Fund containing a small amount of cash that is used to pay for minor expenditures, 189, 198–200
Petty cash ticket Supports all petty cash fund payments. The petty cash ticket serves as an authorization voucher and explanation of the expenditure, 189
Plant assets Long-lived tangible assets—such as land, buildings, and equipment—used in the operation of a business
  cost of, measuring, 269, 272
  disposal of, 270, 278–281
  ethical issues, 270, 288
Plant assets and intangibles
  depreciation (demo doc), 271–281
  intangible assets (demo doc), 285–288
  learning objectives, 269–270
  natural resource assets (demo doc), 282–284
  practice questions, 289–298
    solutions to, 299–309
  See also Depreciation
Postclosing trial balance List of the accounts and their balances at the end of the period after journalizing and posting the closing entries. This last step of the accounting cycle

ensures that the ledger is in balance to start the next accounting period. It should include only balance sheet accounts, 100, 107

Posting Copying amounts from the journal to the ledger, 30

Preferred stock Stock that gives its owners certain advantages over common stockholders, such as the right to receive dividends before the common stockholders and the right to receive assets before the common stockholders if the corporation liquidates, 328, 360, 367–370, 380

Premium Excess of a bond's issue price over its maturity value. Also called bond premium, 313, 326

Prepaid expenses Expenses paid in advance of their use, 67

Prepaid insurance, 63, 434
Prepaid rent, 108
Prepayments, 63
Pretax income, 361
Principle amount, 312
Profitability, 361
Profitability analysis, 393

Proprietorship A business with a single owner, 2, 5

R

Rate of return on stockholders' equity Net income minus preferred dividends, divided by average common stockholders' equity. A measure of profitability. Also called return on equity, 476

Rate of return on total assets The sum of net income plus interest expense divided by average total assets. Measures the success a company has in using its assets to earn income for those financing the business. Also called return on assets, 361

Receivables Monetary claims against a business or an individual
  aging of, 224, 232
  allowance method, 224, 228, 230–234
  balance sheet, reporting on, 224, 228, 233
  credit-card (demo doc), 240–242
  days' sales in, 225, 235
  demo doc, 226–235
  direct write-off method, 224, 228
  internal controls for, 223, 235
  learning objectives, 223–225
  notes receivable (demo doc), 236–239
  practice questions, 243–254
    solutions to, 255–267
  types of, 223, 228, 237

Refinancing, 311

Reliability (objectivity) principle Principle that asserts that data are verifiable and objective. Also called the objectivity principle, 2

Rent expense, 194
Rent payment, 196
Restrictions on retained earnings, 392, 401

Retained earnings The amount earned over the life of a business by income-producing activities and kept (retained) for use in the business, 360, 370
  restrictions on, 392, 401

Retained earnings and the income statement
  income statement presentation and earnings per share (demo doc), 402–406
  learning objectives, 392–393

practice questions, 407–417
  solutions to, 418–427
stock splits and dividends (demo doc), 394–397
Treasury stock (demo doc), 398–401
See also Income statement; Stock

Return on assets The sum of net income plus interest expense divided by average total assets. Measures the success a company has in using its assets to earn income for those financing the business. Also called rate of return on total assets, 361

Return on stockholders' equity Net income minus preferred dividends, divided by average common stockholders' equity. A measure of profitability. Also called rate of return on common stockholders' equity, 361, 366

Revenue Amounts earned by delivering goods or services to customers. Revenues increase retained earnings
  accrued, 68
  unearned, 68
Revenue account, closing, 100, 103–107

Revenue principle The basis for recording revenues; tells accountants when to record revenue and the amount of revenue to record, 64, 68, 69

Revenue recognition timing, 64

S

Salary payable, 109

Sales The amount that a merchandiser earns from selling its inventory. Short name for Sales revenue, 128

Sales discounts Reduction in the amount of cash received from a customer for early payment. Offered by the seller as an incentive for the customer to pay early. A contra account to Sales revenue, 128

Sales returns and allowances Decreases in the seller's receivable from a customer's return of merchandise or from granting the customer an allowance from the amount owed to the seller. A contra account to Sales revenue, 128

Sales revenue The amount that a merchandiser earns from selling its inventory. Also called Sales, 128

Sales tax, 315, 316–317, 322

Sarbanes-Oxley Act An act passed by Congress, abbreviated as SOX. SOX revamped corporate governance in the United States and affected the accounting profession, 187, 197

Separate legal entity, 359

Separation of duties Dividing responsibility between two or more people, 188, 197, 223, 235

Service charge A cash payment that is the bank's fee for processing your transactions, 194–195, 196

Share. See Stock

Shareholder A person who owns stock in a corporation, 359

Shareholders' equity. See Stockholders' equity

Single-step income statement Format that groups all revenues together and then lists and deducts all expenses together without drawing any subtotals, 128

Social Security (FICA) tax Federal Insurance Contributions Act (FICA) tax, which is withheld from employees' pay and matched by the employer. Also called FICA tax, 312, 322

Sole proprietorship, 2, 5

Stable monetary unit concept The concept that says that accountants assume that the dollar's purchasing power is stable, 2

Stated rate, 312

Stated value An arbitrary amount that accountants treat as though it were par value, 360

Statement of cash flows Report of cash receipts and cash payments during a period, 3, 9, 11, 429
  accounts payable, 435
  accounts receivable, 433–434
  cash
    other expenses, 445
    paid as insurance, 444
    paid to suppliers, 443–444
    received from customers, 443
  depreciation expense, 433
  dividends, 438–439
  financing activities, 430, 437–438
  gain on sale of furniture, 433
  versus income statement, 445
  inventory, 434
  investing activities, 430, 435–437
  learning objectives, 429–430
  net income, 433
  notes payable, 437–438
  operating activities, 430, 433
  practice questions, 446–455
    solutions to, 456–464
  prepaid insurance, 434
  preparing, 430
    direct method (demo doc), 441–445
    indirect method (demo doc), 431–440
  purposes of, 429
  Treasury stock, 438

Statement of owner's equity, 3, 8, 9, 10, 11, 72

Stock A document indicating ownership of a corporation. The holders of stock are called stockholders or shareholders
  book value of, 361, 366
  classes of, 360, 362, 368
  common, 360, 362–366, 368, 380
  compared with bonds, 313, 328
  dividends, 361, 368–370
  earnings per share, 393, 402–406
  issuance of, recording, 360, 364–365, 368–369
  market value of, 361, 395, 396
  par value, 360, 363, 395
  preferred, 328, 360, 367–370, 380
  stated value, 360
  Treasury, 392, 398–401, 415, 438
  values of, in decision making, 361, 363–364

Stock dividend A distribution by a corporation of its own stock to its shareholders, 392, 394–397, 414

Stockholder A person who owns stock in a corporation. Also called a shareholder, 359

Stockholders' equity The claim of a corporation's owners to the assets of the business. Also called owners' equity or shareholders' equity
  on balance sheet, 360, 364–365
  return on, 361, 366, 476
  sources of, 360, 362, 368

Stock split An increase in the number of outstanding shares of stock coupled with a proportionate reduction in the value of the stock, 392, 394–397, 414

Straight-line amortization method, 270, 313, 325–328

Straight-line depreciation method Depreciation method in which an equal amount of depreciation expense is assigned to each year of asset use, 269, 272–283, 277–278

Supplies, 108

T

T-account Summary device that is shaped like a capital "T" with debits posted on the left side of the vertical line and credits on the right side of the vertical line, 30
 computing balance of, 36–37
 opening, 32–33, 67
 preparing trial balance from, 38

Take-home pay, 322

Taxable income, 361

Temporary accounts The revenue and expense accounts that relate to a particular accounting period and are closed at the end of that period. For a corporation, the dividend account is also temporary, 100, 360

Time-period concept Ensures that information is reported at regular intervals, 64, 68, 69

Transaction An event that affects the financial position of a particular entity and can be measured and recorded reliably, 3

Transaction analysis
 basic (demo doc), 4–11
 debit/credit, 30
  demo doc, 31–38
  practice questions, 46–50
  solutions to, 58–60
 inventory (demo doc), 129–136
 steps in, 30, 33
 See also Transactions, recording

Transactions, recording, 4–11
 journalizing, 30, 33–35
 learning objectives, 29–30
 posting to ledger, 36–37
 practice questions, 39–50
  solutions to, 51–60
 steps in, 30, 33
 See also Transaction analysis

Treasury stock A corporation's own stock that it has issued and later reacquired, 392, 398–401, 415, 438

Trial balance A list of all the accounts with their balances, 29, 30
 adjusted, 64, 71
 postclosing, 100, 107
 preparing, 38
 unadjusted, 64

Trojan A malicious computer program that hides inside a legitimate program and works like a virus, 188

U

Uncollectible account expense Cost to the seller of extending credit. Arises from the failure to collect from credit customers. Also called doubtful-account expense or bad-debt expense, 224

Uncollectibles, accounting for
 allowance method, 224, 228, 230–234
 direct write-off method, 224, 228–229
 practice questions, 249–252

Unearned revenue A liability created when a business collects cash from customers in advance of doing work. Also called deferred revenue, 68

Unemployment compensation tax Payroll tax paid by employers to the government, which uses the money to pay unemployment benefits to people who are out of work, 322

Units-of-production depreciation method Depreciation method by which a fixed amount of depreciation is assigned to each unit of output produced by an asset, 269, 274–275, 279–280

Units-of-production formula, 270

V

Vertical analysis Analysis of a financial statement that reveals the relationship of each statement item to a specified base, which is the 100% figure, 467–468, 473–475
 balance sheet, 473–474
 income statement, 474–475

W

Warranty expense, 315–316, 317

Withdrawal account, closing, 100, 103–107

Withheld income tax Income tax deducted from employees' gross pay, 322

Work sheet A columnar document designed to help move data from the trial balance to their financial statements, 99
 preparing, 102
 using, 99, 102

SINGLE PC LICENSE AGREEMENT AND LIMITED WARRANTY

READ THIS LICENSE CAREFULLY BEFORE OPENING THIS PACKAGE. BY OPENING THIS PACKAGE, YOU ARE AGREEING TO THE TERMS AND CONDITIONS OF THIS LICENSE. IF YOU DO NOT AGREE, DO NOT OPEN THE PACKAGE. PROMPTLY RETURN THE UNOPENED PACKAGE AND ALL ACCOMPANYING ITEMS TO THE PLACE YOU OBTAINED THEM FOR A FULL REFUND OF ANY SUMS YOU HAVE PAID FOR THE SOFTWARE. *THESE TERMS APPLY TO ALL LICENSED SOFTWARE ON THE DISK EXCEPT THAT THE TERMS FOR USE OF ANY SHAREWARE OR FREEWARE ON THE DISKETTES ARE AS SET FORTH IN THE ELECTRONIC LICENSE LOCATED ON THE DISK:*

1. GRANT OF LICENSE and OWNERSHIP: The enclosed computer programs and data ("Software") are licensed, not sold, to you by Pearson Education, Inc. publishing as Prentice Hall ("We" or the "Company") and in consideration of your payment of the license fee, which is part of the price you paid and your agreement to these terms. We reserve any rights not granted to you. You own only the disk(s) but we and/or our licensors own the Software itself. This license allows you to use and display your copy of the Software on a single computer (i.e., with a single CPU) at a single location for academic use only, so long as you comply with the terms of this Agreement. You may make one copy for backup, or transfer your copy to another CPU, provided that the Software is usable on only one computer.

2. RESTRICTIONS: You may not transfer or distribute the Software or documentation to anyone else. Except for backup, you may not copy the documentation or the Software. You may not network the Software or otherwise use it on more than one computer or computer terminal at the same time. You may not reverse engineer, disassemble, decompile, modify, adapt, translate, or create derivative works based on the Software or the Documentation. You may be held legally responsible for any copying or copyright infringement that is caused by your failure to abide by the terms of these restrictions.

3. TERMINATION: This license is effective until terminated. This license will terminate automatically without notice from the Company if you fail to comply with any provisions or limitations of this license. Upon termination, you shall destroy the Documentation and all copies of the Software. All provisions of this Agreement as to limitation and disclaimer of warranties, limitation of liability, remedies or damages, and our ownership rights shall survive termination.

4. LIMITED WARRANTY AND DISCLAIMER OF WARRANTY: Company warrants that for a period of 60 days from the date you purchase this SOFTWARE (or purchase or adopt the accompanying textbook), the Software, when properly installed and used in accordance with the Documentation, will operate in substantial conformity with the description of the Software set forth in the Documentation, and that for a period of 30 days the disk(s) on which the Software is delivered shall be free from defects in materials and workmanship under normal use. The Company does not warrant that the Software will meet your requirements or that the operation of the Software will be uninterrupted or error-free. Your only remedy and the Company's only obligation under these limited warranties is, at the Company's option, return of the disk for a refund of any amounts paid for it by you or replacement of the disk. THIS LIMITED WARRANTY IS THE ONLY WARRANTY PROVIDED BY THE COMPANY AND ITS LICENSORS, AND THE COMPANY AND ITS LICENSORS DISCLAIM ALL OTHER WARRANTIES, EXPRESS OR IMPLIED, INCLUDING WITHOUT LIMITATION, THE IMPLIED WARRANTIES OF MERCHANTABILITY AND FITNESS FOR A PARTICULAR PURPOSE. THE COMPANY DOES NOT WARRANT, GUARANTEE OR MAKE ANY REPRESENTATION REGARDING THE ACCURACY, RELIABILITY, CURRENTNESS, USE, OR RESULTS OF USE, OF THE SOFTWARE.

5. LIMITATION OF REMEDIES AND DAMAGES: IN NO EVENT, SHALL THE COMPANY OR ITS EMPLOYEES, AGENTS, LICENSORS, OR CONTRACTORS BE LIABLE FOR ANY INCIDENTAL, INDIRECT, SPECIAL, OR CONSEQUENTIAL DAMAGES ARISING OUT OF OR IN CONNECTION WITH THIS LICENSE OR THE SOFTWARE, INCLUDING FOR LOSS OF USE, LOSS OF DATA, LOSS OF INCOME OR PROFIT, OR OTHER LOSSES, SUSTAINED AS A RESULT OF INJURY TO ANY PERSON, OR LOSS OF OR DAMAGE TO PROPERTY, OR CLAIMS OF THIRD PARTIES, EVEN IF THE COMPANY OR AN AUTHORIZED REPRESENTATIVE OF THE COMPANY HAS BEEN ADVISED OF THE POSSIBILITY OF SUCH DAMAGES. IN NO EVENT SHALL THE LIABILITY OF THE COMPANY FOR DAMAGES WITH RESPECT TO THE SOFTWARE EXCEED THE AMOUNTS ACTUALLY PAID BY YOU, IF ANY, FOR THE SOFTWARE OR THE ACCOMPANYING TEXTBOOK. BECAUSE SOME JURISDICTIONS DO NOT ALLOW THE LIMITATION OF LIABILITY IN CERTAIN CIRCUMSTANCES, THE ABOVE LIMITATIONS MAY NOT ALWAYS APPLY TO YOU.

6. GENERAL: THIS AGREEMENT SHALL BE CONSTRUED IN ACCORDANCE WITH THE LAWS OF THE UNITED STATES OF AMERICA AND THE STATE OF NEW YORK, APPLICABLE TO CONTRACTS MADE IN NEW YORK, AND SHALL BENEFIT THE COMPANY, ITS AFFILIATES AND ASSIGNEES. HIS AGREEMENT IS THE COMPLETE AND EXCLUSIVE STATEMENT OF THE AGREEMENT BETWEEN YOU AND THE COMPANY AND SUPERSEDES ALL PROPOSALS OR PRIOR AGREEMENTS, ORAL, OR WRITTEN, AND ANY OTHER COMMUNICATIONS BETWEEN YOU AND THE COMPANY OR ANY REPRESENTATIVE OF THE COMPANY RELATING TO THE SUBJECT MATTER OF THIS AGREEMENT. If you are a U.S. Government user, this Software is licensed with "restricted rights" as set forth in subparagraphs (a)-(d) of the Commercial Computer-Restricted Rights clause at FAR 52.227-19 or in subparagraphs (c)(1)(ii) of the Rights in Technical Data and Computer Software clause at DFARS 252.227-7013, and similar clauses, as applicable.

Should you have any questions concerning this agreement or if you wish to contact the Company for any reason, please contact in writing at the following address or online at http//247.prenhall.com:
Pearson Education
Director, Media Production
1 Lake Street
Upper Saddle River, New Jersey 07458